# 𝔑arrative 𝔒f 𝔗he 𝔗exan 𝔖ante 𝔉é 𝔈xpedition

Comprising A Description Of A Tour Through Texas, And Across The Great Southwestern Prairies, The Camanche And Caygüa Hunting-Grounds, With An Account Of The Sufferings From Want Of Food, Losses From Hostile Indians, And Final Capture Of The Texans, And Their March, As Prisoners, To The City Of Mexico ; With Illustrations And A Map (Volume II)

Geo. Wilkins Kendall

Alpha Editions

This Edition Published in 2021

ISBN: 9789354505423

Design and Setting By
**Alpha Editions**
www.alphaedis.com
Email – info@alphaedis.com

As per information held with us this book is in Public Domain. This book is a reproduction of an important historical work. Alpha Editions uses the best technology to reproduce historical work in the same manner it was first published to preserve its original nature. Any marks or number seen are left intentionally to preserve its true form.

# CONTENTS

OF

## THE SECOND VOLUME.

### CHAPTER I.

Departure from Fray Cristobal.—A broken Gourd.—Cold and dreary night March.—Encounter with a Regiment of Dragoons.—Wild and picturesque night Scenes.—Southern Women in a Northern Climate.—News of Colonel Cooke's Party.—Sufferings upon the "Dead Man's Journey," or "Journey of Death."—A morning Halt.—The "Lake of Death."—Startling Reports.—Murder of Golpin.—A short night Halt.—Farther Sufferings.—Sleep impossible.—Another gloomy night March.—Salezar and his comfortable Quarters.—Wild roadside Scenes.—Sufferings on the increase.—Another cruel Murder.—Death of Griffith.—Our Feelings on the Occasion.—Once more on the Rio Grande.—The "Journey of Death" passed.—Appearance of the Prisoners.—Food and Sleep.—A singular Incident.—Easier learning to Swear than Pray in a Language.—Farther Inhumanities.—Threat of Salezar to search the Prisoners.—Trick to outwit him.—A Batch of valuable Bread.—More of Salezar's Rascality.—A sunset Scene. Death of Gates.—Gross Inhumanity of a Mexican.—Dreary Passage of the Rio Grande.—Salezar's last Command.—Arrival at El Paso.—Old Friends seen.—Find ourselves in more humane Hands.—General Elias.—Our hospitable Treatment by him.—Captain Ochoa.—Sumptuous Living.—Salezar in Disgrace . . . . . . . . . . Page 11

### CHAPTER II.

Ramon Ortiz, the young Cura of El Paso.—His Benevolence.—A pleasant Ride with the Cura.—Description of El Paso.—Its irrigating Canals, Streets, and Rivers.—Residence of Ortiz.—Farther Acts of his Kindness.—A comfortable Change of Linen.—An Opportunity to vex Salezar improved.—Last Encounter with that Miscreant.—Arrival of a Courier from Mexico.—Departure from El Paso.—Hospitality of the Inhabitants.—Parting with Ortiz.—Inquiries respecting General Pike.—A Camp without Water.—Ochoa's Attention to our Wants.—Description of our Escort and Procession.—Mexican Carts and Mexican Character.—Opposition of the Inhabitants to Improvements.—Another dry Camp.—Arrival at the "Diamond of the Desert," a noted Spring.—A Rest.—Difficult Passage of the Sand Mountains.—Appearance of the Country.—A travelling Stone :

its strange History.—Superstitions of the Mexicans.—The "Well of the Star."—Poor and sandy Country.—Appearance of the Texan Prisoners.—Strange Variety of Costume.—Laughing at Misery . . Page 34

## CHAPTER III.

A singular Hot Spring.—Medicinal Properties of the Waters.—"Doing" our Washing.—Carazal.—Appearance of the Town.—Dr. Whittaker in Business.—Charley Tirrell, the Delaware.—A strange Contract.—Kirker, and the Stories told of him. — Captain Spybuck killed by Apaches. — More of Kirker.—Arrival of the Señora Ochoa, and her Style of Travelling.—Opportunity to Escape unimproved.—A Mountain Spring.—Laguna Encinillos.—Desolate Appearance of the Country.—Inroads of the Apaches.—Their Prowess and Daring.—Increase of the Tribe.—Visiters from Chihuahua.—Hospitality and the Jesuits' Hospital.—Situation of Chihuahua.—Mines in the Vicinity. — Governor Condé. — Excitement of the Inhabitants. — The Military of Chihuahua.—Entrance to the City.—Carcel de Ciudad.—The Women of Chihuahua.—The Plaza.—Description of the Cathedral.—The Presidio.—Jesuits' Hospital.—Salon los Distinguidos. — Names upon the Walls.—Description of the Hospital.—Apache Prisoners.—Hidalgo, with a short Account of the first Mexican Revolution, and the Death of that celebrated Leader . . . . . . . . . . 54

## CHAPTER IV.

The old Jesuits' Hospital of Chihuahua.—American Visiters.—Asked for the Particulars of my own Death. — A stealthy Interview.—Dr. Jennison.—Clean Beds.—A sumptuous English Breakfast.—Prisoner in the adjoining Dungeon.—A Meeting.—The Mystery unveiled.—Singular Trial.—Testimony of General McLeod and Messrs. Van Ness and Navarro.—A Release from Chains.—An excellent Dinner from the Señora Magoffin.—Visiters at our Room.—Letters to my Friends.—"La Luna."—Armijo's Letter to Garcia Condé.—Implicated with the Leaders of the Expedition.—Lewis's probable Agency in the Affair.—A Gasconading Editor.—Poetic Address to a Horse.—Movements of Lewis.—A lively little French Woman.—Our Treatment by the Foreigners in Mexico.—Departure from Chihuahua.—Collection of the Inhabitants.—Furnished a Horse by a Friend.—Difficulty of mounting the Pony.—His Feats and Antics.—The Mexican Saddle, and its Advantages.—El Ojito.—Encounter with American Wagoners.—Arrival at San Pablo.—A Chihuahua Major.—Our Accommodations at San Pablo.—Practical Knowledge of Entomological Science.—Mexican Horse Jockeys.—Mr. Falconer mounted again.—Sancillo.—An Escape agitated.—Death of Larrabee.—A young Mexican Musician.—Santa Rosalia.—The Alcalde and his Daughter.—A stolen Horse claimed.—Military *versus* Civil Law.—Roadside Graves and Crosses.—Stories in relation to them . 74

## CHAPTER V.

Arrival at Guajuaquilla.—An Invitation.—Inhospitable Hospitality.—A little Mexican Lawyer.—His Self-importance.—A disagreeable Night.—Our Companions fare better.—Again on the Road.—Rejoicing at Guajuaquilla. —Tricks of a Wag.—Amusing Anecdote.—Montezuma's Brother.—Arrival at El Rio Florido.—General Pike.—The Hacienda of La Noria.—Its former Wealth and present Condition.—Inroads of the Apaches and Camanches. —A young Irishman.—Visited by pretty Girls.—A well-informed Mexican Lady.—Musical Soirée and Dancing.—Change of Scene.—Arrival at Cerro Gordo, in the State of Durango.—Our new Commander, Colonel Velasco, pointed out to us.—His sinister Appearance.—Visited by a French Woman. —A Fandango and Cock-fight.—Departure from Cerro Gordo.—A general Turn-out of the Inhabitants.—Suspicions in relation to Ochoa's Integrity. —Our new Guard of Dragoons.—Their Treatment of the Prisoners.—Honourable Conduct of Ochoa.—A roadside Camp.—Colonel Velasco's Character begins to develope itself.—Excellent Provisions provided.—Large Droves of Horses passed.—An immense Hacienda.—Former Wealth of the Proprietress.—Condition of the Peons, or Working Classes of Mexico.—Farther Insight into the Character of Velasco.—The Texan Officers allowed their Parole . . . . . . . . . . Page 96

## CHAPTER VI.

Arrival at El Gallo, or The Cock.—Singular Names for Towns.—A rich Silver Mine.—Scenes at a Fandango.—The Well of El Gallo.—Arrival at Dolores.—Guadalupe.—The Prisoners reach Cuencamé.—A small Party of us quartered at the House of a Castilian.—Hospitable Treatment.—Strange Superstition in relation to a Statue.—Gullibility of the Poorer Classes.—We are turned over to a new Guard.—Selling a Watch.—La Señorita Juana.—Colonel Velasco takes leave of the Prisoners.—Captain Roblado.—Story in relation to him.—Superiority of the Bread of Cuencamé. —Our Departure.—Hacienda of Juan Perez.—Roblado, and his Treatment of an Alcalde.—A tedious March.—Arrival at San Sebastian.—Frightened Girls and wounded Dogs.—Freaks and Endurance of the genus Donkey. —Arrival at Saenea.—Picturesque Situation of the Town.—The Maguey Plant; its Uses and Abuses.—One Drink of Pulque sufficient.—A Gang of "Involuntary Volunteers."—Mode of Recruiting for the Mexican Army.—Rancho Grande.—Decay in Mexico.—An American Traveller.—Arrival at Fresnillo.—The Mines in the Vicinity.—Meeting with an Englishman.—The *Tienda del Gato*.—Stories and Egg-nog.—More "Involuntary Volunteers."—A Stage-coach, and Thoughts of Home.—La Caleta.—First Appearance of Small-pox among the Texans . . . . . . 115

## CHAPTER VII.

Approach to Zacatecas.—Tedious mountain March.—Picturesque View.—First Sight of Zacatecas.—Its singular Situation.—Specimen of Roblado's

vi                       CONTENTS.

Vanity.—Entrance into Zacatecas.—Character of the Inhabitants.—Passage through the City.—Arrival at a deserted Mining House.—Miserable Quarters.—Permission obtained to visit the City.—Inquisitive Urchins.—Arrival at an Irish Restaurat.—A sumptuous Breakfast.—Visit to a New-York Gentleman.—A Stroll through Zacatecas.—Dinner at the Restaurat.—Invitation to another Dinner.—A goodly Company.—Painting of Washington.—A pleasant Evening in Perspective.—Unrealized Hopes.—Again at our old Quarters at the Mining House.—Mr. Falconer in Trouble.—Mexican Justice.—Dr. Whittaker's Mode of getting rid of a troublesome Sentinel.—Subscription raised for the Prisoners.—Liberality of a Mexican Lawyer.—Departure from Zacatecas.—Convent of Guadalupe. — Santa Anna, and his Fight with the Zacatecans.—Sack of the City.—Refugio.—Arrival at Ojo Caliente.—A Bathing Scene.—Customs of the Mexican Women, and their Fondness for Swimming.—El Carro.—Arrival at Salina.—A Kentucky Circus Proprietor.—His Adventure with Roblado.—The Mexican House of Entertainment, or Meson.—The Foreigner meets with but poor Fare.—Modes of living, and Customs of the Lower Orders of Mexico        .        .        .        .        .        .        .        .        . Page 133

## CHAPTER VIII.

Departure from Salina.—Last Speech of the Kentucky Circus Proprietor.—His Wishes in relation to Roblado. — Arrival at Espiritu Santo. — Pass a pleasant Evening.—A Contrast.—La Parada.—Wild mountain Scenery.—The Organo.—A picturesque View.—First Sight of San Luis Potosi.—A beautiful Valley.—Innumerable Wells.—Large Prickly Pears.—The Peruvian Tree.—Our Approach to San Luis heralded.—Arrival within the City.—Beauty of the Women.—Description of San Luis.—Its Churches, Convents, and public Buildings.—Convent of the Augustine Friars.—Benevolence of the Brotherhood.—Wants of the Sick provided for.—An evening Stroll through the City.—Market Scenes.—Encounter with a Company of Equestrians. — A droll Specimen of the Yankee Genus. — " Old Hundred" in San Luis.—Return to the Convent.—Visited by the Foreigners.—Our Yankee Wag and his Stories. — Subscription for the Prisoners raised.—Allowed our Parole.—An interesting Scotch Lady.—Visit to the Circus.—Appearance of the Audience.—An Invitation to Supper.—Find ourselves in the wrong House.—Apologies unnecessary.—Supper at last.—An Opportunity to write to my Friends improved.—Departure from San Luis.—A new Guard and new Commander.—An interesting Incident.—Las Pilas.—Arrival at El Jaral.—Anecdote of General Mina.—Wealth of the Proprietor.—A singular Funeral Procession.—A " Hog on Horseback."—Description of the Arrieros of Mexico .        .        .        .        .        .        .        .        . 154

## CHAPTER IX.

A Night at San Felipe.—Meeting with one of Mina's Soldiers.—Santa Anna, and the Estimation in which he is held by his Countrymen.—San Juan de

CONTENTS. vii

los Llanos.—Sickness and Suffering.—Tedious Mountain March.—Picturesque Scenery.—Arparos; its romantic Situation.—Arrival at Silao.—An American Physician.—Kindness of an English Gentleman and his Lady.—Approach to Guanajuato.—Singular Entry.—Laughable Scenes.—Arrival within the City.—Visits from the Foreigners.—Fitzgerald and others taken to the Hospital.—Liberal Contributions.—Opportunity to escape.—Departure from Guanajuato.—Singular Location of the City.—La Puerta.—Arrival at Salamanca.—System of Recruiting Volunteers.—Celaya.—Generous Conduct of Cortazar.—Sunday at Celaya.—The Cathedral.—Singular Customs of the Indians.—Cock-fighting at the Theatre.—"El Campanero de San Pablo."—A Spanish Play.—Lady Smokers.—Departure from Celaya.—Fertility of the Baxio.—Calera.—An early Morning March.—Distant View of Queretaro.—Arrival within the City.—Singular Currency and amusing Anecdote.—Soap a legal Tender.—A Stroll through Queretaro.—American Prisoners.—Spanish System of Shaving.—Texans Stoned in the Market-place.—A Mexican Restaurant.—Adventure with a Friar.—Return to our Quarters . . . . Page 173

## CHAPTER X.

Departure from Queretaro.—A stupendous Aqueduct.—View of Queretaro from a Mountain Summit.—Number and Magnificence of its Churches.—Meeting with Englishmen.—News that Colonel Cooke's Party were in Chains.—The Diligence.—Letter from Mr. Lumsden.—Liberation of Frank Combs.—Arrival at San Juan del Rio.—Escape of two of our Companions.—They are retaken and punished.—The Indian Village of Tula.—Strange Celebration.—Queer Characters.—Crackers and Sky-rockets.—Approach to the City of Mexico.—Speculations as to our future Lot.—Mr. Navarro separated from his Companions. — Route altered. — "Quien Sabe?"—Kindness of the Indian Women.—Arrival at the old Palace of San Cristobal.—The Texans locked within its gloomy Walls.—Visited by Mr. Lumsden and other Americans.—A joyful Meeting.—Prospects of Release.—Description of San Cristobal.—Release of Falconer and Van Ness.—Visited by Members of the United States Legation.—Difference in the Policy of the United States and English Governments.—Cause of Mr. Falconer's Release.—Another Visit from the Americans.—File of American Papers.—A Letter from Chihuahua, and its Effects.—Gloomy Presentiments.—Our Men supplied with Clothing and Blankets.—Celebration in Honour of Santa Anna's Leg.—Supplies cut off.—Sufferings on the Increase.—Nothing to Eat.—Resorts of the Texans to obtain Food.—Singular Tribunals, with the Results.—A Humorous Witness.—Wild Revel in San Cristobal . . . . . . . . . . . 191

## CHAPTER XI.

Supply of Money received.—Our Sick examined.—Visited by a large Party of Americans from the City.—Hopes of Liberation still offered.—Reflections as to the Nature of my Case.—Departure from San Cristobal.—Start for the City of Mexico upon Asses.—The easy Gait of the genus Donkey.—Arrival at the Shrine of "Our Lady of Guadalupe."—Flimsy Imposture which caused its Erection.—Anecdote from Latrobe.—Nuestra Señora de los Remedios.—Mexican Beggars.—Tiresome Travel across the Plains.—The Garita.—Mexico, as seen in the Distance.—Arrival within the City.—Forlorn appearance of the Texans.—Commiseration of the Women.—Anecdote of Major Bennett.—Arrival at the Hospital of San Lazaro.—Hideous appearance of the Inmates.—A dreary Night.—Visited by the Hospital Physician.—His Prescriptions.—Description of San Lazaro and the unfortunate Lazarinos.—Speculations as regards the Leprosy.—Happiness among the Lepers.—New Sports and Dances.—We are visited by Mr. Mayer and other Americans.—Our Food at San Lazaro.—Kindness of the Mexicans in their Hospitals.—Smuggled Food.—Visits of the Physician.—Removed to other Quarters.—Worse and Worse.—Find our Room overrun with Chinches.—Our Friends gain Access by Bribery.—Departure of Mr. Lumsden and Friends for the United States.—Thoughts of an Escape . . . . . . . . . . . Page 209

## CHAPTER XII.

Taken ill with the Small-pox.—Washington's Birthday.—A Patriotic American.—An excellent Dinner.—More of the Small-pox.—Ordered to move our Quarters.—Once more among the Lepers of San Lazaro.—Eight of our Companions marched to Santiago.—Philosophy in Chains.—The Irons nothing *after* one gets used to them.—Fresh Air and Exercise.—Determination to forego them.—System of Anointing in San Lazaro.—Anecdote of Lieutenant Burgess.—Visit from Mr. Lawrence.—His Departure for the United States.—Death of an unfortunate Leper.—A midnight Funeral in San Lazaro.—Its imposing yet gloomy Character.—Mass in the Church of San Lazaro.—Decorations of the Establishment.—Disgusting Figure of St. Lazarus.—A Procession and a Present.—Don Antonio.—The Fruits of Mexico.—A File of American Newspapers.—Present from Mr. Ellis.—Visited by Mr. Falconer.—Beauties of the "Vicar of Wakefield."—Death of another Leper.—Five of our Companions marched to Santiago.—Preparations for a Celebration.—The 11th of March in San Lazaro.—The Hospital visited by Throngs.—Compelled to receive Alms.—Dinner provided for us by a Party of Ladies.—Take an Account of Stock.—Strange Present from a Mexican Lady.—"Charles O'Malley" in San Lazaro.—Another Celebration among the Lepers.—Fondness of the Mexicans for Flowers and Ornaments. — A dolorous Chant.—The Celebration closes with a Dance.—Wild Revels of the Lepers . . . . . . . 231

## CHAPTER XIII.

Another Dance in San Lazaro.—Mexican Improvisatores.—Accident to a couple of Dancers. — Fondness of the Mexicans for Music. — American Visiters. — An agreeable Afternoon passed. — Good Friday, and a better Dinner.—Fasts preferable to Feasts.—A drunken Lazarino. — Touching

Incident.—Visits of our Friends prohibited.—Speculations as to the different Modes of escaping from San Lazaro.—Several Plans agitated.—The Foreigners once more permitted to visit us.—News of the Appearance of an American Fleet upon the Mexican Coast.—Advised not to attempt an Escape.—A severe Epidemic in San Lazaro.—Horrible Colds and worse Coughs.—Death of another Leper.—A second midnight Funeral.—Rarity of the Atmosphere of Mexico.—A regular Uproar in San Lazaro.—José Maria and his inhuman and vicious Conduct.—Mexican Gamblers.—Farther Annoyances from José Maria.—An early morning Visit.—Prospects of Release.—Santa Anna's Reasons for not liberating us immediately.—General Thompson at Vera Cruz.—Santa Anna anxious to shuffle out of a Dilemma.—Bright Anticipations of being once more at Liberty.—More American Visiters.— Arrival of General Thompson in Mexico.—The Annoyance of Suspense.— A File of American Papers.— Visit of General Thompson to San Lazaro.—Letters from Friends.—A Visit from Mr. Perrin.—Prospects of Liberation again clouded.—An Opportunity of Escape thrown in my Way.—Determination to improve it.—Anxiously await the arrival of Assistance from without . . . . . . Page 250

## CHAPTER XIV.

Hours of Expectation.—One of the Santiago Prisoners brought to San Lazaro, sick with the Small-pox.—Disappointed Hopes.—Arrival of a Guard of Soldiers at San Lazaro.—Mysterious Conduct of the Commander.—Ordered to prepare for Departure.—A vile Litter produced.—Refusal to enter it.—Leave San Lazaro.—"Farewells" of the Texans and "Adios" of the Lepers.—Gloomy and mysterious night March.—Interior of the City of Mexico.—Stared at by the Populace.—A Coach ordered.—Misery likes Company.—Dogs in the Outskirts of Mexico.—Arrive at our Destination.—Farther Uncertainty. — Ushered into the Presence of Women.— The Mystery unravelled.—Find myself in Santiago, and among Friends.—Ordered to make Choice of a Partner in Chains.—Select Major Bennett.—First Appearance in Fetters.—Congratulations of my Friends on the Occasion.—Major Bennett quotes Scripture again.—Determination to escape.—Santa Anna's Motives in the Removal to San Lazaro.—Action of the Mexican and United States Governments in relation to the American Prisoners.—Consider the Chances of Liberation as hopeless as ever.—Strange Conduct of Santa Anna.—No Difficulty in shaking off the Irons.—The "Secrets of our Prison-house."—Character of the old Commandante of Santiago.—Texan Tricks upon a Mexican Blacksmith.—The Blacksmith and Santa Anna in Converse.—Description of Santiago, and Chances of an Escape.—The Texans going out to labour in the Streets.—More Play than Work . . . . . . . . . . . . . 270

## CHAPTER XV.

Fare of the Texans in Santiago.—Their Companions at Puebla not as well treated.—The Latter compelled to work and associate with Mexican Malefactors.—Anecdote of the Old Commandante of Santiago.—The Texan achieve a decided Victory over their Oppressor.—The Puebla Prisoners at their Tricks.—Attending Mass in Chains.—Mad Pranks of the Texans in Church.—Additional Ceremonies ingrafted upon the Catholic Ritual.—The Reader taken back to Santiago.—Foreign Visiters.—Farther Thoughts of escaping.—Action of General Thompson in my Behalf.—The Foreign Policy of the United States — Its Weakness and Inefficiency.—Santa Anna "Laughing in his Sleeve."—Plan to bribe our Guard at Santiago.—Evening Amusements of the Prisoners.—Major Bennett and his Bible.—Agreeable Soirées.—Character of the Anglo-Saxon Race under Misfortune.—Anticipation worse than Reality.—The Texans taken to their Morning Work.—Reasons for Slighting the Author.—More Visiters at Santiago.—Advised to defer an Escape.—Preparations for celebrating the Anniversary of the Battle of San Jacinto.—The Texans at their Work.—Experiments as to the smallest possible Amount of Labour a Man can perform when he exerts himself.—The Mexicans Outwitted.—Decorations of our Room.—San Jacinto and Patriotism.—The Texans at their Celebration.—Close of the Anniversary . . . . . . . . . . Page 291

## CHAPTER XVI.

Intelligence of immediate Release.—Its Effect.—Close of the Celebration.—Night Visiters at Santiago.—Arrival of Mr. Ellis with an Order for our Release.—The old Blacksmith again. — His Services dispensed with.—Once more free from Chains.—Leave Santiago and Imprisonment.—Cheers of the Texans at our Departure.—Congratulations of the young Mexican Officers.—Another night Ride through Mexico.—Encounter with a religious Procession.—Arrival at the United States Legation.—The Gran Sociedad.—Comfortable Quarters. — Sleep impossible. — Change of Circumstances.—The Watchwords of Mexico.—Encounter with a Sentinel.—Early Morn in Mexico.—Strange Cries.—"Carbon."—Appearance of the Streets.—Picture of morning Life in Mexico.—Change of Wardrobe.—Visit to a French Barber.—A Shearing and Shaving Operation.—Improvement in personal Appearance.—Beggars in front of a Church.—Description of the wretched Throng. — Return to the Gran Sociedad.—A sumptuous Breakfast.—Visit to the British Minister, Mr. Pakenham.—Once more in Santiago.—Mexican Girls.—Visit to our old Quarters at San Lazaro.—Bribing a Sentinel.—Meeting with the Texans and Lepers.—Call at the Dwelling of a Mexican Lady, an old Friend.—Her musical Attainments.—Anecdote of her Spirit and Patriotism . . . . 310

## CHAPTER XVII.

An early Morning Walk.—Beggars at their Work.—The Plaza Mayor.—The Cathedral and Stone of the Calendar.—Strange Belief.—Interior of the Cathedral.—Its Appearance.—Filthy State of the Establishment.—Agency of a Pair of new Boots in preventing an Examination of the Cathedral.—Shops of the Portales.—The Streets of Mexico.—Another Visit to Santiago.—The "True Blue."—More of Lieutenant Hull.—Encounter with Major Howard.—His Disguise.—Particulars of the daring Escape of Captain Hudson and Major Howard.—The Italian Opera.—Castellan.—Another Encounter with Major Howard.—Farther Particulars of his Escape.—Temerity of Captain Hudson.—Mexican Pickpockets.—Their Dexterity.—Mexican Modes of Salutation.—Cordiality of Greeting.—Anecdote of a Meeting with a fair Mexican.—The Mystery solved.—An excellent Trait in Mexican Character.—Hospitality of the Lower and Middle Classes.—Their Benevolence towards the Sick.—The present Priesthood in Mexico.—Domestic Relations of the Padres.—Influence of the Priests.—Their Reluctance in resigning Power . . . . . . . Page 327

## CHAPTER XVIII.

Mode of passing our Time.—Herr Cline.—Mexico by Moonlight.—Note from Madame Calderon.—Rambles over Mexico.—A Dance.—The Jarabe.—Change of Scene.—A murdered Soldier.—Touching Instance of Grief.—More Moonlight.—"Quien Vive?"—A staggering Padre.—Release of Americans through the Exertions of General Thompson.—Visit to Tacubaya.—Cruel and mysterious Murder of Egerton and his Mistress.—Visit to the Acordada.—A Show-case of Murder.—Gloomy Entrance to the Acordada.—Some Description of the Interior.—Release of a Female Prisoner.—Mr. Navarro.—Story of his Wrongs.—Robbery and Crime in the Acordada.—Texan Prisoners within its dreary Walls.—Take Leave of Mr. Navarro.—Farther Description of the Prison.—Encounter with Dutch Broom Girls.—An old Acquaintance in the Broom Line.—The Balladmongers badly patronised.—Evangelistas, or Letter-writers of Mexico.—Their singular Calling.—Stock in Trade of the Evangelista.—Mexican Coaches and Mexican Coachmen.—Another Visit to Santiago.—More of the Mexican Coachmen . . . . . . . . 345

## CHAPTER XIX.

The Alameda.—Visit to that noted Pleasure-ground.—A Yankee Livery-stable-keeper in Mexico.—A Shower.—Paseo Nuevo.—Family Parties in their Carriages.—Mexican Cavaliers on Horseback.—Singular Gait of their Steeds.—Manner of training them.—Race with a Shower.—Santa Anna.—His Courtesy, Policy, Power, and ambitious Projects.—Reasons for the Decline of the Mexican Republic.—Our last Night in Mexico.—More of Captain Hudson.—Santa Anna's Benevolence!—Take leave of our

II.—A

xii                       CONTENTS.

Friends.—San Lazaro again.—Mexican Escort.—Mexico from the Mountain Sides.—Arrival at a Breakfast-House.—Arms and Equipments of our Party.—A Yankee Driver.—Roadside Crosses and Graves.—Stories of Robbers.—Robbing the Stages reduced to a System.—Señor Garcia and the Ladrones.—Rio Frio.—Mexican Dogs.—Cholula in the Distance. —Arrival at Puebla.—Visit to the Texan Prisoners at the Presidio.—Their unfortunate Condition.—The Cathedral of Puebla.—Its great Riches.— Anecdote of the Angels.—Superstition from which Puebla received its Name.—In Bed and Asleep . . . . . . . Page 361

## CHAPTER XX.

Preparations for Departure.—High Words with a Mexican Stage-agent.— A Victory.—A Scotch Traveller.—No Room for another Passenger.— Leave the "City of the Angels."—Approach of an Escort.—Appearance of the Dragoons.—Arrival at El Pinal.—Roadside Graves.—Change of Horses.—A wild Mexican Steed and his Antics.—A rapid Start.—A noted Stand for Robbers.—Another doughty Escort.—The Mal Pais and Cerro de Pizarro.—Arrival at Peroté.—Visit to the Texan Prisoners.— Their Condition.—A vile Supper.—A French Lady.—Another early Start. —Coldness of the Mountain Air.—A false Alarm.—Colder and Colder.— Tierras Frias.—Arrival at Las Vigas.—In want of Refreshments.—" No hai" and "Quien sabe" again.—Wild Mountain Scenery.—Volcanic Formations.—El Cofre de Peroté.—Strange Indian Legend.—Leave the Region of Lava.—Remarkable Change of Scene and Climate.—Sudden Transition.—Halt at the House of a Mexican Lady.—Singularity of her Conduct.—La Guerra Rodriguez.—Examination of our Passports at the Garita —Arrival at Jalapa . . . . . . . . . . . 378

## CHAPTER XXI.

The Cracovienne.—Large Body of Mexican Troops.—Their Inefficiency.— Speculations as to the Result of an Invasion of Mexico.—The *Vomito* at Vera Cruz.—Determination to remain at Jalapa.—The Scotchman we had left at Puebla arrives.—Work of the Robbers.—Indian Girls from the Tierra Caliente.—Picturesque and neat Style of Dressing their Hair.—A pleasant Ride.—Departure from Jalapa.—Description of the Litera.— Changing Teams.—Mexican Drivers.—Puente Nacional.—Night Ride through the Hot Country.—Residence of Santa Anna.—Fireflies.—Santa Fé.—Number of Dogs in the Vicinity.—Singular District.—The Gulf of Mexico in Sight.—Arrival at Vera Cruz.—A Conducta.—Sopilotes.—The Black Vomit again.—Arrival on board the Woodbury.—Commodore Marin.—Salutes.—Under Way.—Pleasant Passage.—The Balize in Sight.— Author's Leave of his Reader . . . . . . . . . 394

# NARRATIVE

OF THE

# FIRST TEXAN SANTA FÉ EXPEDITION.

## CHAPTER I.

Departure from Fray Cristobal.—A broken Gourd.—Cold and dreary night March.—Encounter with a Regiment of Dragoons.—Wild and picturesque night Scenes.—Southern Women in a Northern Climate.—News of Colonel Cooke's Party.—Sufferings upon the "Dead Man's Journey," or "Journey of Death."—A morning Halt.—The "Lake of Death."—Startling Reports.—Murder of Golpin.—A short night Halt.—Farther Sufferings.—Sleep impossible.—Another gloomy night March.—Salezar and his comfortable Quarters.—Wild roadside Scenes.—Sufferings on the increase.—Another cruel Murder.—Death of Griffith.—Our Feelings on the Occasion.—Once more on the Rio Grande.—The "Journey of Death" passed.—Appearance of the Prisoners.—Food and Sleep.—A singular Incident.—Easier learning to Swear than Pray in a Language.—Farther Inhumanities.—Threat of Salezar to search the Prisoners.—Trick to outwit him.—A Batch of valuable Bread.—More of Salezar's Rascality.—A sunset Scene. Death of Gates.—Gross Inhumanity of a Mexican.—Dreary Passage of the Rio Grande.—Salezar's last Command.—Arrival at El Paso.—Old Friends seen.—Find ourselves in more humane Hands.—General Elias.—Our hospitable Treatment by him.—Captain Ochoa.—Sumptuous Living.—Salezar in Disgrace.

WE remained at Fray Cristobal until near night, the snow, in the mean time, thawing away entirely under the influence of the sun. Salezar said aloud, on starting, that we were to be driven through the entire ninety miles without sleep or a morsel of food, and as there was no water on the route, he advised such of us as had gourds or canteens to fill them before setting out: an exhibition of humanity truly considerate and unlooked for in him.

At a steady pace we journeyed onward till dark, the weather mild and pleasant for walking; but now a raw night wind sprang up, fresh and piercing, from the snow-clad mountains, and chilling our weak frames so thoroughly that the most violent exercise could not keep us warm. A water-gourd, holding some two quarts, which I had filled on starting, after taking a hearty draught at the river, slipped from my benumbed fingers, and was dashed to pieces on the frozen ground. The animals of our guard went begging for riders, for even their hardy owners were obliged to dismount and run on foot to prevent their limbs from freezing.

About nine o'clock at night we met a regiment of dragoons, under Colonel Muñoz, on their way from Durango to Santa Fé: troops that had been despatched by the Central Government to take part in any hostilities that might occur with the Texans. Being from a more southern and temperate climate, they suffered excessively from the cold, so much so that many of them were leading their horses and setting fire to every little tuft of palm or dry grass on either side of the road. Around these blazing tufts, and scattered along the road for miles, were to be seen knots of half-frozen dragoons, mingled with a large number of women, who always follow the Mexican soldiery on a march. How the latter, who were but half clad even in the warmest climate, could withstand the bitter cold of that dreary night, is to me incomprehensible.

Wild and picturesque was the scene presented by the train of roadside fires, each with a little bevy huddling and shivering around the red-glaring and fitful lights, the lengthened and flitting shadows coming and going, and losing themselves in the sombre obscuration of night. There would be seen the officer, cloaked and blanketed, standing side by side with one of his men, the head of the latter covered with a clumsy, bearskin dragoon cap, while he would share his sky-blue military cloak with some woman who had followed him, mayhap, from the *tierra caliente*, or sunny south, and was now, for the first time, visiting the region of snow. As tuft after tuft would fall away at the touch of fire, the wild group would hurry on to others, soon kindle them, and as they in turn would suddenly flash up, blaze for a few moments, and then as suddenly expire, away they would hie to the next. Eldrich and spectre faces came and vanished on that barren moor, that did strongly remind me of the witch scenes in Macbeth. While standing around these fires some of the dragoons informed our men that they had met Colonel Cooke's party near Chihuahua, and that they were well treated on the road. There was consolation in this, for we had heard many rumours of the bad treatment we might expect on the other side of the Paso del Norte.

The sufferings, the horrors of that dreadful night upon the Dead Man's Journey cannot soon be effaced from the memory of those who endured them. Although my sore and blistered feet, and still lame ankle, pained me excessively, it was nothing to the biting cold and the helpless drowsiness which cold begets. No halt was called—had any of us fallen asleep by the roadside after midnight, it would have been the sleep of death. Towards daylight many of the prisoners were fairly walking in their sleep and staggering about, from one side of the road to the other, like so many drunken men. Completely chilled through, even their senses were benumbed, and they would sink by the roadside and beg to be left behind, to sleep and to perish. A stupor, a perfect indifference for life, came over many of us, and the stronger found employment in rousing and assisting the weaker. Anxiously did we wait the coming of the sun, for that would at least bring warmth and animation to our paralyzed limbs and faculties.

Daylight came at last, and with it came a halt of an hour, to bring up the stragglers and count the prisoners. By the time the last of us were up the trumpet again sounded the advance, and once more we were upon the road. Towards noon we passed the Dead Man's Lake, or Lake of Death, its bed perfectly dry. The coolness of the weather, however, and the fact that we had nothing to eat, prevented that thirst which in a warmer temperature would have caused sufferings of a nature that cannot be described.

As the sun was about setting, those of us who were in front were startled by the report of two guns, following each other in quick succession. We turned to ascertain the cause, and soon found that a poor, unfortunate man, named Golpin, a merchant, who had joined the expedition with a small amount of goods, had been shot by the rear-guard for no other reason than that *he was too sick and weak to keep up!* He had made a bargain with one of the guard to ride his mule a short distance, for which he was to give him his only shirt! While in the act of taking it off, Salezar ordered a soldier to shoot him. The first ball only wounded the wretched man, but the second killed him instantly, and he fell, with his shirt still about his face. Golpin was a citizen of the United States, and reached Texas a short time before the departure of the expedition. He appeared to be a harmless, inoffensive man, of delicate constitution, and during a greater part of the time we were upon the road, before the capture of the expedition, was obliged to ride in one of the wagons. The brutal Salezar, rather than be troubled with him any longer, took this method of ridding himself of an encumbrance! It may be difficult, for many of my readers, to believe that such an act of wanton barbarity could be perpetrated by a people pretending to be civilized—to be Christians! I should certainly be loath to hazard my reputation by telling the story were there not nearly two hundred witnesses of the scene.

In half an hour after the murder of Golpin, and before it was yet dark, we were ordered to halt for a short time, the horses and mules of our guard absolutely requiring a little rest after being constantly in motion for more than twenty-four hours. Had Salezar consulted only the feelings of the prisoners, no halt would have been called.

During the short rest now allowed us we were permitted to lie down, but sleep was impossible. Had we been granted rest during the day, when the warm sun was shining over us, we might have slept, and soundly, too: now, it was so cold we could but curl up close, one to another, in a state of discomfort that forbade sleep. At ten o'clock at night, or near that hour, we were again roused and ordered to resume the march. The short rest which had been granted was far from restoring us to strength, far from removing the soreness and stiffness from our bones: on the contrary, we were now more unfitted for the gloomy march than ever. We had travelled but a short half mile before we passed the two wagons in which the baggage and camp equipage of the Mexicans were carried. In one of these, stowed snugly under the cotton cover, were Salezar and his lieutenant, the redoubtable Don Jesus. They, at least, had made themselves comfortable, and were snoring away, utterly regardless of the sufferings around them.

About midnight we reached a part of the desert where the high branches of palm had not been burned, the dragoons probably passing this section in the daytime. These dry tufts were at once set on fire by the Mexicans to warm their benumbed and half-frozen hands and feet. We, too, crowded around them, and as one would burn down to a level with the ground we rushed hurriedly to the next. Our line now extended nearly a mile along the road, and the blazing clumps, which flashed up like powder on being ignited, gave a wild and romantic appearance to the scene, more especially when the dark and swarthy faces of the Mexicans and the wild and haggard features of our men were seen congregated round the same fire.

The early hours of the morning were colder than any which had preceded them, as the biting winds from the mountains appeared to have a more open sweep across the desert plain. The sufferings, too, of the previous night were increased in proportion as we had less strength to endure them; and here it should be remembered that we had had no food given us from our commencement of the Dead Man's Journey, now thirty-six hours, and that we had been in active exercise nearly the whole time. How this dreary road across the waste ever obtained its congenial name is more than I could learn. It certainly deserves it, more especially since the murders committed along its line by Salezar.

That faint streak of lightish gray which heralds daylight had but just appeared in the eastern horizon when a man named Griffith, who had been wounded by the Indians before we were taken prisoners and had no entirely recovered, gave out, and declared his inability to proceed any farther. He had ridden a mule until his faculties were nearly paralyzed by the cold, when he jumped off and again undertook to walk. Too weak, however, and too lame to travel, he sank to the ground. A soldier told him to rise, or he would obey the orders, given by Salezar, to put all to death who could not keep up. Griffith made one feeble but ineffectual attempt. The effort was too much: he cast an imploring look at the soldier, and while doing so the brutal miscreant *knocked his brains out with a musket!* His blanket was then stripped from him, as the reward of his murderer, his ears were cut off, and he was thrown by the roadside, another feast for the buzzards and prairie wolves!

And how, it will be asked, did we feel while acts like these—acts that leave barbarian deeds of cruelty and blood far behind—were enacted in our midst? The reader must understand that not one of us knew but that he might be called upon as the next victim; that we were completely worn and broken down, sick and dispirited. Callous, too, we had become; and although we could not look upon the horrible butchery of our comrades with indifference, we still knew that any interference on our part would bring certain death, without in any way aiding our unfortunate friends. Inly we prayed that a time might come when their death could be avenged—that the damnable crimes hourly enacted around us might be atoned for. There was the breast of many a hero in that sorry band; and in its pent-up chamber were recorded deep vows of vengeance *yet to be executed* upon Armijo and his congenial satellites.

It was not until about eight o'clock in the morning

that the waters of the Rio Grande, which in its course had swept around the bend, a distance of more than one hundred and sixty miles, were seen by those in the advance. With hurried and eager steps we all pressed forward, for we knew that now, at least, we were to have food, water, and sleep. To attempt a delineation of our men as they appeared at that time were a bootless task. We had now been forty hours on the road, without food or water; in this time, although we had travelled ninety miles, we had had scarcely four hours' rest; the scanty wardrobe which each man carried upon his back, and which was all he possessed, had not been changed since we were made prisoners, and was now filled with every species of vermin known in Mexico. Add to this the sunken, hollow cheeks, pale and haggard countenances of men who had been unshaved for a month, and the reader will have a faint idea of our miserable aspect.

Salezar here ordered another ox killed—one that had made the entire journey with us from Austin, that had escaped the stampedes and Indian perils, and had borne a due share of the labour of dragging our wagons across the immense prairies of the West. With his former masters he had suffered and been captured, and now that he, too, was lame and broken down, weak and unable to travel, like them he was ordered to the sacrifice. It did not seem right to make a meal of an old and tried companion; yet necessity knows no law, neither has it feelings, and in three quarters of an hour after the poor animal was killed he was cooked and devoured, and his quondam masters were lying about on the grass fast asleep. In the afternoon we were awakened and ordered to march some miles farther—to a place where the animals of the guard could obtain better picking than at the camp where we were now lying. As we were about starting, a little incident occurred in which were strangely mixed the painful and the ludicrous. For some trifling cause Salezar drew his sword, and with the flat of it struck one of the prisoners a violent blow across the shoulders. The poor fellow had only learned one Spanish expression, *muchas gracias*—the common phrase employed in New Mexico to thank a person for any favour received. Thinking he must say something, and not knowing anything else to say, the unfortunate Texan ejaculated, "*Muchas gracias, Señor!*" Another terrible whack from the sword of Salezar was followed by a shrug of the shoulders and another "Many thanks, sir." The captain was now more infuriate than ever. To be thus publicly and openly thanked by a person upon whom he was inflicting a painful punishment, he looked upon as a defiance, and he accordingly redoubled his blows. How long this might have continued I am unable to say; had not some of the friends of the man told him to hold his tongue, Salezar might have continued his blows until exhausted by the very labour. It is astonishing with what facility many of our men picked up enough Spanish to hold conversation with our guard, however little advance the punished individual just spoken of had made. The oaths, in particular, they soon learned, and in return they gave the Mexicans an insight into the many imprecatory idioms with which the English abounds. It is singular how much more easily men learn to swear and blaspheme in any language than to pray in it.

Our march, on the day after we had finished the Dead Man's Journey, was one of unusual length and severity; numbers of the men giving out miles before we reached our camping-ground. Salezar, as fortune ordained it, rode in advance this day, and although the rear-guard beat and mercilessly abused some of the more unfortunate stragglers, they did not go so far as to take their lives. One brute in particular, our more lame and unfortunate companions can never forget. His name, if I ever knew it, has now slipped from my memory, but to recall him to the recollections of all who made the gloomy journey from San Miguel to the Pass, I have only to refer to the fellow who was continually annoying us by his harsh and most discordant efforts at singing. As a general thing, the lower classes of Mexico have voices of rare sweetness and touching melody, and often, while at San Miguel, did we listen to the lays of a party of soldiers with pleasure, as, with tones harmoniously blending, they sang a rude but cheerful catch in praise of Santa Anna; but the notes of this scoundrel were of the most grating nature. Continually was he trotting his mule up and down the line, uttering sounds which were almost demoniacal, and, as though he thought it a fit accompaniment, he sought every occasion to insult, ride over, and strike the sick and the lame, the halt and the weary. Not without shuddering did we hear the horrible tones of this fellow's voice, as he would approach us; and I cannot doubt that this simple mention will bring the grating sounds again ringing in the ears of those who heard him, and who may happen to read this chapter.

Some of the poor prisoners parted with their shoes and shirts, and in many cases even with their blankets, in payment for a ride of a few miles—the unfeeling owners of the animals ever ready to take advantage of such as were unable to walk. In some few instances men were found among the Mexicans who had humanity enough to take up some unfortunate Texan and carry him a few miles; but those instances were extremely rare.

It was pitchy dark when we reached our halting-place this night, a grove of cotton-woods within thirty miles of El Paso del Norte, and so tired were the men that a majority of them sank supperless upon the ground, too weak to cook the scanty ration of meal which was distributed among them.

We had been but a few moments in this camp before Van Ness, with whom Salezar intrusted many of his secrets, informed Falconer and myself that the miscreant intended to search us all the next day: he suspected, from many little circumstances, that there was still no inconsiderable sum of money among the wretched prisoners, and if his suspicions were true, he determined to gain possession of it.

Knowing, full well, that his search would extend to every portion of our tattered vestments, making it impossible to hide our valuables about our persons, we now tasked our wits to devise some scheme wherewith to cheat Salezar of his anticipated plunder. Various plans were revolved in our minds, but dismissed as not feasible, until finally I bethought me of one which promised success even though the search should prove ever so rigorous. It was to make a small batch of cakes with a quantity of meal we had in a bag, the cakes to be seasoned with our doubloons and such other gold pieces as we had in our possession. This plan was adopted at once, and in an hour, one kneading the dough and forming the cakes, while the other watched the sentinel on duty to see that he did not discover our trick, we had our money all carefully baked with the exception of a few dollars. The latter we carried openly in our pockets to avoid suspicion, and for its loss we cared but little so that the main amount was saved. My gold watch and chain I gave to Van Ness, who carefully folded them in his cravat and tied them about his neck. As the prisoners had frequently made their meal into cakes of similar size and appearance, we had full confidence of outwitting the avaricious scoundrel should he make his threatened search.

On resuming our march the next morning, Salezar left the oxen which had been furnished for our sustenance on the road, and of which sixteen were still left, behind him: with the oxen he also left some thirty horses and mules, animals then in possession of his guard, but which, it was afterward ascertained, had been either stolen from the inhabitants of El Paso by their present owners themselves, or purchased from the Apaches with the full knowledge that they had been stolen. This bit of rascality arranged satisfactorily by Salezar, and a small guard being left behind to herd the animals out of sight of the main road, we were again on the move.* About sunset we arrived at an encampment directly in the mouth of the gorge through which the Rio Grande has forced a passage—the well-known gap in the mountains called by the Mexicans El Paso del Norte, or the Pass of the North, and within eight miles of the large town of El Paso.

* The pack mule which Salezar took from me, at the time of our arrest, he frequently rode upon the journey between San Miguel and El Paso. She was a strong, powerful animal, but an extremely hard one to ride, having, in addition to a trick of throwing people over her head, a jolting and most uneasy and unsteady trot. To show the cool effrontery of Dimasio, he complained, on several occasions, of the gait of the animal, and said that he was disappointed in her! It is generally considered indelicate to "look a gift horse in the mouth," or allude to any little faults he may possess; I do not see why the same rule should not apply to a stolen mule. That she might take the whim to throw Salezar over her head, as had frequently been her wont when her riders were Americans, was a result I am frank enough to say I hoped for; but I could never learn that she indulged in any of her old tricks while in the hands of her new master.

I have said that the sun was about setting when we arrived at our camping-ground: that luminary lacked some half hour yet of his going down, and never have I seen him sink below the western horizon with such a glow of splendour and magnificence around him as on that occasion. Immediately in front of us, running nearly north and south, rose a chain of frowning mountains, through which, although at the time we could not tell how or where, the Rio Grande has forced its way. The table-land on which we stood reached far as the eye could see to the west. Those who have watched the sun in his setting, may have fancied that on approaching near his apparent resting-place he drops, as it were, several feet at a time, then lingers stationary for a moment, then drops towards his nightly retreat again, as if hurrying to finish his day's work and reach his evening couch of rest. So it was on this occasion, and from some peculiarity in the atmosphere the broad face of the god of day appeared of deeper yet more subdued red, and of four times its ordinary size. The evening air was of a most wooing temperature—mild and bland. The eastern sky received a reflection of softened yet golden lustre, while the mountain sides were clothed with a gorgeous but mellow atmosphere, and the shadows sent among the frowning clefts by the last rays of the setting sun were softened and suffused by the universal glow. While contemplating the lovely scene, and lost to all around me in admiration of its rare and almost holy beauty, I was suddenly aroused by the report that a poor fellow named Gates was dying in one of the wagons. He had taken a severe cold the night we were all penned in the two small rooms, and inflammation of the lungs had ensued; and now, without medicine, without the kind offices of relations, without the thousand charities and home-comforts that are not to be found in such a wo-worn band as ours, he was dying, and among those who would deny him even the last sad rites of sepulture!

On looking towards the wagon in which the unfortunate man was lying, it was evident he had but a few moments to live: there was a glassy wildness in his eye, a slight rattle and convulsive throe about his neck, which too plainly denoted that his sufferings were soon to terminate. At such a time as this it would hardly seem credible that one could be found, clothed in the outward semblance of humanity, fiendish enough to inflict farther pain and anguish upon his fellow-being: yet such was the fact, and a case of more heartless cruelty up to this time probably stands not on record.

Gates retained his senses, and had just asked one of his comrades, in weak and broken accents, for a cup of water. He had scarcely swallowed it ere a young Mexican, who went by the name of Ramon, took up an empty musket standing by the wagon, and after wantonly pointing it directly in the face of the dying man, snapped it! The latter, unconscious whether the musket was loaded or not, raised his hands convulsively to his face and shrunk instinctively back. The wretch, apparently enjoying the torture he was thus inflicting, again pointed and snapped the gun. This was too much for one who was already wrestling with death. He gave one shudder, his limbs relaxed, and all was over! He was instantly dragged from the wagon by our merciless guard, his ears were cut off by order of Salezar, and the body was thrown by the roadside

"a stiffen'd corse,
Stretch'd out and bleaching in the northern blast!"

On the morning succeeding this revolting act of

cruelty, which was the 5th of November, we started upon our last march under the detestable Salezar. Two or three miles above El Paso, and immediately on the eastern base of the ridge of mountains, we were obliged to ford the Rio Grande at a fall. The river was waist, and in some places even chin deep, the bottom uneven and rocky, while the cold current of water ran with such force that we were obliged to hold each other by the hand in strings to prevent being washed down the stream and drowned. Chilled completely through, and with feet cut and bruised by the sharp and jagged rocks, we were finally fortunate in making the passage, the rear-guard upon their mules and horses whipping and swearing at the lame and weak stragglers of our party who scarcely had strength to buffet with the swift-running stream.

Once safely across, we were ordered to form in sections of four, while the guard paraded in regular order on either side. The last command of Salezar, before galloping forward to give notice of our arrival, was to shoot the Texans who should leave the position in the ranks assigned them! In this order, and with this last threat hanging over us, we were marched into the beautiful and romantic town or city of El Paso.

Our feelings, on entering this town, it is almost impossible to describe. On the route from San Miguel we had been regaled, by our guard, with innumerable tales of the ill-treatment we might expect on reaching the Pass, and also with speculations as to our ultimate fate. Some said that we should be marched by the nearest road to Matamoros, and thence shipped to the United States or Texas; others, again, gave it as their decided opinion that we should be shot, so soon as orders could be received from Santa Anna. As to the two latter opinions, we gave no credit to either of them; as to our being treated worse by the inhabitants of the lower country than we had been by the New Mexicans, that we knew could not be, as Salezar had taxed his ingenuity to the utmost in devising means to harass and torture us. Still, our feelings were sensitively alive as the time rapidly approached when we were to be placed under new masters, and our minds unusually active in speculations upon our future lot.

As we turned the corner of a street leading into the principal plaza, we saw one of our companions, who had left San Miguel the morning before us, standing upon a distant housetop. Another turn, and Doctor Whittaker, with two or three Texan officers, was seen standing by a small bridge thrown across one of the irrigating canals which traverse this pleasant town in every direction. They appeared to have the liberty of parole, if nothing more, were clean shaved and neatly enough dressed, and bore every appearance of having fallen into kinder hands, and to have received infinitely better treatment than had fallen to our lot.

In a few minutes more, in presence of the alcalde and other officers, we were marched into a large yard, having rooms on every side, and then, after being counted, consigned to the keeping of a new guard. Shrewd and close observers of physiognomy had we all become by this time—we looked at the countenances of those who were now over us, and a single glance sufficed to assure us that we might expect better treatment; nor were we disappointed.

In two hours after our arrival, and without the most remote expectation of any such good fortune, the Texan prisoners found themselves, in squads of six or eight, billeted about at the different houses of the inhabitants, and feasting upon the best the place afforded. Well-cooked meats, eggs, the finest bread, and in many cases even the wines of the place were served out to them, and in an abundance to which for months they had been strangers. From the different doors and windows they could see small knots of their late guard passing and repassing; and with the recollection of their recent brutal treatment fresh within them, they did, in the fulness of their hearts, heap upon their former insolent and overbearing, but now craven and powerless enemies, all the Spanish terms of indignity and reproach they had learned while in their company, mixed with good hearty curses in the vernacular whenever they ran out of foreign objurgations.

In the mean time, Falconer, Van Ness, and myself were taken to the house of the commandant of this military department, Don J. M. Elias Gonzàlez, or, as he was generally termed, General Elias, a well-bred, liberal, and gentlemanly officer. No sooner had he been made acquainted with the conduct of Salezar, than he expressed great indignation; and as our men had suffered so much from want of food and excessive fatigue, he at once said they should be allowed three days' rest to recruit and strengthen.

The family of General Elias consisted of his *prima*, or first cousin, a portly, handsome, and good-hearted lady, some forty years of age, who attended to his household affairs, and a well-educated young nephew, on a visit from Sonora. His name was Don Jesus,* and to him we were all under obligations for repeated acts of kindness and attention. Captain Francisco Ochoa, said to have been an aid-de-camp of the Em-

* No relation to our old acquaintance of New Mexican memory, but a different personage altogether.

peror Iturbide, was also a guest at the house—a good-humoured, laughing, and dashing officer of some forty years of age, although at first view he seemed much younger. Ochoa was frank and soldierlike in his bearing, expressed the greatest abhorrence of Salezar and his herd of *ladrones* and *picaros** as he called them, and in travelling with us some five or six hundred miles, ever proved himself a friend and a gentleman.

About five o'clock in the afternoon a servant brought us in cakes and chocolate, the latter of the richest quality and most delicious flavour. At eight o'clock General McLeod and Mr. Navarro, who took all their meals with our generous host, arrived, when we immediately sat down to a well-arranged and sumptuous supper. It was the first table we had seen for five months—so with the chairs. What a contrast! On that very morning, and within twenty yards of the spot where the body of the unfortunate Gates was lying, Falconer, Van Ness, and myself had hastily swallowed a meal of badly-made mush, upon the ground, our minds full of misgivings as to the treatment we might receive on getting out of the hands of Salezar—now we were seated at a table covered with luxuries, the guests of a gentleman attentive to our every want. Even the fact that we were still prisoners was forgotten.

As the mind of the reader wanders back through the gloomy vista of the preceding five months, it will find but few bright spots for the memory to linger upon. During that time we had been living "out of doors"— the ground, whether wet or dry, warm or cold, our only bed—the sky, whether blue or black, clear or cloudy, our only canopy. For weeks, I might almost say

---

* Loafers, scoundrels, thieves—the terms mean anything and everything opprobrious.

months, previous to our capture, we had lived upon an allowance which barely saved us from starvation, and even this small pittance of food was more fitting the mouths of prairie wolves than human beings. After our capture, in addition to the cruel insults and indignities that were heaped upon us, we were fed and driven along our involuntary pilgrimage under treatment that would have claimed the intervention of civil laws if inflicted upon droves of cattle, sheep, or hogs in a civilized land. Let the reader recollect these facts, and he will not marvel that our hearts were now rejoiced within us, prisoners though we were, on once more finding ourselves in the midst of plenty and treated as men. But our supper is getting cold, and as it is the first we have had for nearly half a year, we must commence upon it.

It consisted of a variety of dishes, all well cooked, and, but that some of them may have been seasoned rather too highly with red pepper, garlic, or onions for Anglo-Saxon tastes, all extremely palatable. And here were veritable chairs, knives and forks, plates, tumblers, and the many appurtenances of a supper-table—we had not entirely forgotten their uses, as the cook of our kind host could testify. The *vino del pais*, or wine of the country, too, was placed before us, of a quality far from inferior, and in the greatest profusion. The inhabitants of El Paso, or many of them, drink it from tumblers of the largest size, and in quantities which would startle a Frenchman over his claret, or a New-England farmer over his cider—I have reference, in speaking of the latter, to times before the establishment of temperance societies and root beer associations. Supper over, some two hours were spent in smoking and conversation, when we retired to bed.

Here was another comfort which for months we had not enjoyed—had almost forgotten—and for a long time we could not close our eyes in sleep, so novel was the luxury. We were under a roof. Our beds were of the very best—sheets as white as the driven snow, and pillow-cases neatly fringed and of the finest linen. We kicked, tossed, and rolled about for hours; and our various antics, some of them ludicrous enough, might be likened to the feats of tumblers in a ring. Sleep finally overtook us, nor was it broken until a little before sunrise, when a neat and pretty girl brought us in cakes and chocolate. Without his chocolate in the morning, the Mexican gentleman would be miserable all day.

After partaking of our chocolate, we arose refreshed and invigorated, and with feelings very different from those of the previous morning. At nine o'clock we had breakfast, consisting of some five or six courses, with wine, but no coffee. At two dinner was served, late in the afternoon we again had chocolate and cakes, and at eight o'clock supper. I have been thus particular in giving the number and order of our meals to show the difference between the customs there and in this country.

Although meats may be seen in profusion, at both breakfast and supper, on the table of the Mexican gentleman in the northern and middle departments of the Republic, the principal and most substantial meal, as with us, is the dinner. The meal generally commences with mutton soup or broth—then comes a dish of boiled mutton, frequently followed by a stew of the same meat. A favourite dish with the Mexicans in the State of Chihuahua is made of the blood of sheep, fried and seasoned, which is very palatable. Chickens and eggs, cooked in different ways, but the former never roasted as with us, make their appearance during the meal. A standing article is the *chile guisado*, mention of which I have already made in a former chapter. *Frijoles*,* a species of dark beans of large size, stewed or fried in mutton fat and not too highly seasoned, wind up the substantial part of a dinner, breakfast, or supper, and seldom is this favourite and national dish omitted. In fact, *frijoles*, especially to the lower order of Mexicans, are what *potatoes* are to the Irish—they can live very well so long as they have them in abundance, and are lost without them. A failure of the bean crop in Mexico would be looked upon as a national calamity.

Among the higher order of Mexicans the dinner finishes with fruits, *dulces* or sweetmeats, and the never-failing paper or shuck cigar. In the southern department these cigars are manufactured of tobacco, neatly rolled in paper, put up in bunches, and then sold at a low price; but in the States of Chihuahua, Sonora, and New Mexico, and more particularly the latter, every man is provided with a small pouch of *punche*, a species of plant somewhat resembling tobacco, for the cultivation of the latter is specially prohibited except in some of the southern departments. In another pouch or case he carries a parcel of corn husks, and a flint and steel. With these materials he makes his *cigarrito*, strikes a fire, and smokes almost incessantly. Women and men are alike addicted to the practice, and the prettiest *señora* in the land can be seen at almost any time with a *cigarrito* in her mouth, the smoke puffing from her nose in two straight volumes, somewhat resembling the escape pipes of a double-engine steamer on a small scale. It may be thought singular, however, that the

---

* Pronounced *freeholeys* by the Mexicans. From the similarity in the pronunciation, our men always called them *freeholders*.

children of either sex are not addicted to smoking. It appears to be a habit taken up after the person has attained full growth, and when once contracted is never abandoned.

On the afternoon after our arrival at El Paso, and while we were drinking wine and partaking of a truly sumptuous dinner at the table of the commandante, the notorious Salezar entered the room, the object of his visit being to render an account of his stewardship in relation to the Texan prisoners. He appeared struck with mute astonishment, as his eye glanced in the direction of our table, at seeing those whom he had so recently treated like brutes now in such excellent quarters and associating with an officer infinitely above him; and there was an air of sneaking and cowardly inquietude about the monster as he opened his business with General Elias.

He began by saying that Governor Armijo had intrusted him with the charge of guarding a certain number of men from San Miguel to El Paso; that he had turned over the whole number with the exception of five, who had unfortunately died upon the road; and to prove that they had really died, and had not escaped, he *had brought their ears*, at the same time throwing upon the table five pairs of them which he had strung upon a strip of buckskin! General Elias at once told him that he had murdered, basely murdered, three of these men. The miscreant denied this charge, at the same time turning a black look in the direction where we were quietly smoking. He said that he was a brave man, and that when he was in the advance his master, Armijo, could always sleep in quiet and security. The commandante coolly told him that the business before them had nothing to do with his personal prowess and bravery, or with the estimation in which Armijo held him; they were talking of three men whom he had cruelly put to death for no crime. Salezar, finding that his superior officer had abundant proof of the facts, made no farther denial; but he turned upon Van Ness a look of bitter hatred, for he had treated him with so much kindness and consideration upon the road that he supposed in him, at least, he would find a defender. Van Ness had very properly informed General Elias of every circumstance that had occurred upon the road, and the cunning Salezar, now seeing that he had no one to defend him, made no farther denials.

The commandante next told Salezar that there were sixteen head of cattle, honestly belonging to the Texan prisoners, which had been left some thirty or forty miles back upon the road. This was a thunderbolt to the scoundrel, for he had fondly hoped to secure these cattle as his own plunder. With a twitch of the shoulders he began to stammer forth some excuse or denial; but he was cut short by General Elias, who all the while preserved his temper, with the remark that there were also a number of horses and mules left at the same camp, which he had strong reasons to believe were the property of some of the citizens of El Paso. At all events they must be immediately sent for—cattle, horses, and all—and until they were all brought in, and their brands and marks examined, Captain Dimasio Salezar must consider himself under arrest. The scoundrel gave us another scowl of mingled hatred and revenge at the conclusion of this interview, and then skulked from the room, an abject, pitiful wretch.

## CHAPTER II.

Ramon Ortiz, the young Cura of El Paso.—His Benevolence.—A pleasant Ride with the Cura.—Description of El Paso.—Its irrigating Canals, Streets, and Fruits.—Residence of Ortiz.—Farther Acts of his Kindness. —A comfortable Change of Linen.—An Opportunity to vex Salezar improved.—Last Encounter with that Miscreant.—Arrival of a Courier from Mexico.—Departure from El Paso.—Hospitality of the Inhabitants.— Parting with Ortiz.—Inquiries respecting General Pike.—A Camp without Water.—Ochoa's Attention to our Wants.—Description of our Escort and Procession.—Mexican Carts and Mexican Character.—Opposition of the Inhabitants to Improvements.—Another dry Camp.—Arrival at the "Diamond of the Desert," a noted Spring.—A Rest.—Difficult Passage of the Sand Mountains.—Appearance of the Country.—A travelling Stone: its strange History.—Superstitions of the Mexicans.—The "Well of the Star."—Poor and sandy Country.—Appearance of the Texan Prisoners. —Strange Variety of Costume.—Laughing at Misery.

AMONG the daily visiters at the house of General Elias was the young and generous *cura* of El Paso, Ramon Ortiz, to whom I was particularly indebted for many attentions, and whose acts of disinterested kindness to all the prisoners it is impossible to forget. The young priest could not be more than twenty-five years of age, and was of a mild and benevolent countenance —in short, there was an open and ingenuous expression in his really handsome face that at once endeared him to every one. For some cause or other he was unremitting in his attentions to me, continually seeking opportunities to do some delicate act of kindness, which, by the manner of its bestowal, showed that he possessed all the more refined feelings of our nature.

On one occasion he asked me if I would not be pleased to see the town and visit him at his residence, some mile or two distant from the house of General Elias. On my accepting his invitation, he sent a servant for one of his horses for my use. The servant soon returned with a noble animal, richly caparisoned, and the young cura mounting his mule, we rode over the beautiful town.

The situation of El Paso is delightful. Seated in a beautiful and fertile valley, a circle of mountains on its northern and western sides break off and neutralize the cold winds which sweep from the snowy summits in the region of Santa Fé. The thoroughfares of the town are for the most part wide and airy, and on either side runs a cool and rippling stream of transparent water, brought from the Rio Grande by means of irrigating canals, so that it can at any time be turned upon the vineyards or grain-fields when the land requires it. These delicious streams are shaded by rows of large, overarching trees, planted with great regularity, while the plain but neat dwellings of the inhabitants are, many of them, built among clusters of apple and other fruit-trees. The cultivation of the vine, with the manufacture of wine and raisins, appears to be a source of no inconsiderable profit to the inhabitants, who, take them as a body, are more honest, industrious, cleanly, and better disposed towards foreigners than those of any town of equal size I passed through in my long journey.

Arrived at the residence of my kind friend, a neat dwelling surrounded by fruit-trees and vines, he called a servant to take charge of the animals, and at once led the way to the interior. Here I found Captain Caldwell and a number of our officers, comfortably enjoying the hospitalities of the young priest, and loud in their praises of his kind attentions and exceeding liberality: for they had all been provided with neat and clean clothing by their charitable entertainer.

To myself he was even more unremitting in his offices of attention and kindness. He asked me to write my name, and then give the correct pronunciation of it, after which he gave me his own on a strip of paper. Fortunately for me, when first captured I had been able to secrete a valuable gold pen, neatly encased in silver, which also served as a handle, and this I at once presented to the cura. He at first was reluctant to accept the pen, fearing that I might be in want of it, but on being assured that it was of no real service to me, he received it with new protestations of friendship.

During a visit of some two hours, young Ortiz appeared to be studying my every want. In addition to an excellent dinner, with wine of his own making, which he gave me, he invited me into his private study, where a bath was provided. Hardly had I partaken of this luxury, before a girl brought me clean flannel and linen throughout—and when I say that for the previous seven weeks I had had no change of clothing, and that the vermin which infest the lower orders of Mexico had taken forcible possession of all my ragged and dirty vestments, the luxury of once more arraying myself in clean linen will be appreciated. But the liberality of Ortiz did not stop here, for, notwithstanding I told him I had a sufficiency, and obstinately refused taking it until farther resistance would have been rude and almost insulting, he still pressed a sum of money into my hands. It was carefully wrapped in paper, and the amount I did not at the time know. From its weight I knew, however, that it was specie, and hence my extreme reluctance to receive it at his hands. He may have thought it an imperative duty thus to press it upon my acceptance, in order to cancel the obligation he evidently considered himself under for the pen I had presented him.

Towards sunset, the cura having ordered the same horse to be again saddled for me, we left his quiet and hospitable mansion for the residence of General Elias; and if I before had reason to thank Ortiz for his kindness, I soon had still greater cause of gratitude for the opportunity he gave me, although unintentional on his part, of repaying, with interest, the many instalments of indignity and abuse I had received at the hands of Salezar—in short, of making this latter person completely and perfectly unhappy.

Prominent among the vicious traits of Salezar was his insatiable avarice. In the leather panniers which contained my clothing, when we were taken prisoners, he found three or four pairs of heavily-gilt spurs, articles which I had purchased in New-Orleans as presents to such Mexicans as might show me attentions on my journey through that country. These spurs he had sold for a mere song, as they were of a pattern different from those used in New Mexico, and as he suppposed their real value trifling. A telescope which he had taken from Mr. Falconer, and which was an instrument of great value, he had parted with for a few dollars—not one tenth, perhaps, of its first cost.

On the road from San Miguel he had spoken of these articles to one of my comrades, and mentioned the prices he had received for them. Out of pure hatred to the wretch, and from a desire to vex and goad him, my friend expressed great surprise that Salezar had parted with them, and more especially the spurs, at such a sacrifice—said they were of pure gold and extremely rich workmanship, and that they would have been worth twenty times the sum he received for them, to melt down.

This story fretted and chafed the avaricious wretch

excessively. He ground his teeth for being such a fool, and with an oath promised that should a similar opportunity to plunder offer itself, he would make more money out of it than he had done in the present instance. In fact, nothing could exceed his rage, and he vented deep imprecations upon himself for allowing such golden opportunities to escape with comparatively so little gain. So much by way of episode—I will now relate the manner in which Ortiz helped me to punish Salezar.

While at the cura's house he had told me that whatever jewelry I had saved I might now wear or expose openly, as there was no farther danger of my being robbed—I was now out of the hands of the *picaros* of New Mexico, and would find officers on the route to the capital who were gentlemen, and who would not take my private or personal property. With these assurances, and to show that I had implicit confidence in his words, I immediately displayed about my person, rather ostentatiously, perhaps, a valuable breastpin, together with the gold watch and chain which I had kept hid from the searching eyes of the greedy Salezar.

After leaving the house of the cura we rode leisurely along until we reached the principal plaza, taking a different route from that which we had travelled in the morning. Almost the first person I saw, on entering the plaza, was the detestable Salezar, standing in front of a small *tienda*, or store, and conversing with some of his officers. Here was an opportunity to show the fellow that I had outwitted him, and I determined that it should not slip by unimproved. Telling Ortiz that I wished to purchase a handkerchief, or some trifling article, he kindly held my horse while I dismounted. As I walked directly towards the little knot of our former oppressors I placed a hand in each pocket of my pantaloons, which were now tolerably well filled with the doubloons and other gold pieces I had taken from the cakes after reaching El Paso. Grasping as many of them as I could in either hand, I let them drop jingling to the bottom of my pockets when within five yards of Salezar, and so that he could plainly hear them. The sound, I am confident, entered his soul. When immediately in front of the avaricious wretch I gave as loud and as important a "*hem*" as I was able, and then, with a consequential swagger, and as much ostentation as I could assume, drew forth my gold watch, as if to ascertain the time. I gave the fellow one glance and was satisfied. His face was a perfect index to the workings of his selfish mind, and with a pleasure, malicious perhaps, I watched it. That he would not close his eyes in sleep that night I felt confident, so well I knew his nature. No punishment I could inflict would have been so severe. That black scowl, so full of hatred, avarice, and all the worst feelings of the human heart!—to me it was "a receipt in full" for all the indignities and injuries I had received at his hands—that look, so full of rage, baffled desire, and unsated avarice, more than paid for the property of which he had stripped me, and the many cruelties he had inflicted upon myself and friends.

After this last and most gratifying interview with Salezar, for I have never seen him since, I remounted my horse, and with Ortiz rode to my quarters at the house of General Elias. I more than half suspected that my young friend was aware of my object in thus "showing off" before Salezar; but not a word did he say.

During my visit to the house of the cura, a courier had arrived from Mexico. The only news that in the least interested us was a mention made of the departure of Colonel Cooke and Dr. Brenham, with the first party, from Chihuahua, and a report that they had been well treated on the road.

About noon, the next day, we took our departure from El Paso. As we were on the point of leaving the house of General Elias, to join the main party, the servant of young Ortiz arrived with a horse, saddle, and bridle for my use as far as Chihuahua, a distance of nearly three hundred miles. Of this most unexpected charity I had not before received the least intimation; nor did the liberality of the incomparable cura end here. He ordered his domestics to bake two or three cart-loads of excellent bread for the use of the prisoners on the road, and sent his own teams of oxen to transport it. To those who were most in need he gave articles of comfortable clothing, and imitating the charitable example of their pastor, the citizens were very liberal in their gifts. Mrs. Stevenson, the wife of an American merchant who was absent at the time, was unceasing in her acts of kindness. Although a Mexican by birth, and not understanding a word of our language, she was indefatigable in her exertions to procure clothing, provisions, and necessaries for our comfort and subsistence on the road.

The entire population of El Paso—men, women, and children—turned out to see us off; General Elias sent his nephew, the young Don Jesus, with his own private carriage for the accommodation of General McLeod, and Messrs. Navarro, Falconer, and Van Ness, as far as Chihuahua. A very gentlemanly man, Colonel Morales, provided several of our officers with mules to the same city, and his example was followed by others whose names I have now forgotten. General Elias himself, accompanied by the cura and several of the wealthier and more respectable inhabitants, rode some distance with us, and after expressing the hope that we might arrive safely at the city of Mexico and be speedily liberated, bade us an affectionate farewell. Seldom have I parted from a friend with more real regret than with Ortiz, and as I shook him by the hand for the last time, and bade him, perhaps, an eternal adieu, I thought if ever a noble heart beat in man it was in the breast of this young, generous, and liberal priest. Professing a different religion from mine, and one, too, that I had been taught to believe, at least in Mexico, inculcated a jealous intolerance towards those of any other faith, I could expect from him neither favour nor regard. How surprised was I, then, to find him liberal to a fault, constant in his attentions, and striving to make my situation as agreeable as the circumstances would admit. I can never hope for an opportunity to repay all his kindness to me, and must content myself with this simple tribute to his worth. His charity and his manly virtues adorn the faith which he professes and illustrates by his life; and should this page ever meet his eye, let it assure him of the deep respect and reverence with which the moral excellence of the pious cura of El Paso inspired more than one Protestant American.

Almost the only place in Mexico I turned my back upon with anything like regret was the lovely town or city of El Paso. Its delightful situation in a quiet and secluded valley, its rippling artificial brooks, its shady streets, its teeming and luxurious vineyards, its dry, pure air and mild climate, and, above all, its kind and hospitable inhabitants, all held me to the spot by their endearing ties. What its population may be I have not the means of ascertaining, neither can I give the extent of the fertile valley in which it is situated; but if I may be allowed to make a rough estimate, I should put down the number of inhabitants at from five to seven thousand, and the settled portions of the valley at some eight or ten miles in length by from one to three in width.* With the single exception of the little walled town of Carazal, which is rapidly depopulating, there is scarcely even a rancho, or small farm, within hundreds of miles of El Paso—Socorro being the nearest town north, while the city of Chihuahua is the first settlement as the traveller journeys southward. Far removed from neighbours, the rural inhabitants of Paso have made a garden, an oasis, as it were, in the midst of a desert, and appear to have been in a great measure uncontaminated by association with the world beyond. We here found several families of Castilian blood, unmixed with even a shade of the Indian—and we found them liberal, gentlemanly, and of most courteous address, although born on the spot, and having had the advantages neither of travel nor association. Even the very lowest of the population—and here we saw little of that squalid poverty which characterizes almost every town in Mexico—even the poorest of the inhabitants treated us with respect and kindness, insulting neither our religion, our country, nor our unfortunate position. Surely, not one of the Texan prisoners can ever think of El Paso, or the dwellers therein, without lively gratitude.

Our first day's march, on leaving this place, was short, bringing us to the last well or spring of sweet water we were to find before reaching a dry and sandy desert—in fact, we were obliged to travel nearly the

---

* I have never seen any account of this isolated town except a mere notice from the pen of General Pike, who was marched through it, a prisoner, almost forty years since. Some of the older inhabitants asked us several questions in relation to this gallant officer, for they well remembered his passage through their town, but had never heard of his death.

whole of the two succeeding days before we reached water. The road from El Paso to Chihuahua runs, for the greater part of the way, through a dry and barren region, although there are some fertile valleys as the traveller approaches the latter city; and as there are no settlements or houses on the way, we were again compelled to make our lodging upon the ground. But as I now had procured an extra blanket, the cold did not prevent me from sleeping, as was the case in New Mexico.

Taking advantage of the large escort which accompanied the prisoners, the inhabitants of El Paso sent their fall crop of fruits and other products under its convoy. These commodities consisted, for the most part, of apples, raisins, pears, onions, and no inconsiderable quantity of wine and Paso brandy, all of which find a ready market at Chihuahua: in return, the owners take back sugar, chocolate, paper cigars, and also their English and fancy goods. Their reason for accompanying us was the protection they supposed our guard afforded against the much-dreaded Apaches, who are ever on the look-out from the mountains, ready to pounce upon any travellers seen upon this route. So numerous was the company that now availed itself of our escort, that the road, for a long distance, was filled with pack mules and Mexican carts. A more miscellaneous procession, take it altogether, has probably never been seen since the days of Peter the Hermit. The exact number I did not take the trouble to ascertain; but including prisoners, guards, traders, muleteers, drivers, servants, and camp-followers in the shape of women and children, there could not be much less than a thousand, and in the order in which we marched, the motley crowd must have extended more than a mile. The dress of our guard, which was for the most part composed of the militia of El Paso, differed but little from that of the same class in New Mexico—ragged and motley, and having no pretensions to uniformity. They were better armed, perhaps, than their neighbours under Salezar, having a greater number of carbines, or old Spanish muskets: yet they were all on foot, and were weak and inefficient in every way. Many of them had no shoes, but in their stead they wore sandals of their own make—rudely manufactured, and affording little protection save to the soles of their feet. The leading traits in the characters of these men appeared to be much good-nature, and a disposition to treat the prisoners with the utmost leniency—points in which they differed materially from the savage brutes who dwell north of them.

I have several times spoken of Mexican carts—a more rude contrivance, take it all in all, can scarcely be conceived. If in this country of locomotives, railroad cars, and well-built stage-coaches, the searcher after antiquarian relics and curiosities should, by any chance, meet with a Mexican cart, he would look upon it as the first, the original attempt of man to construct a kind of wheel-carriage. Neither iron nor steel, paint nor polish, spoke-shave nor plane, is used in its fabrication—but give a Mexican a sufficiency of brittle cotton-wood and raw-hide, and he has the materials; give him but one of his own clumsy and ill-contrived axes and an auger, and he has all the tools he wants wherewith to furnish a cart. Out of the first cutting of a cotton-wood he hews an oblong block, through the centre of which he bores and burns a hole for the axletree; he next digs, you cannot say cuts, two pieces from the same tree, forming them into segments of a circle, which he pins to the sides of the aforesaid oblong mass by means of long, wooden pegs. The wheel is now finished. Should it not happen to be round, it is of little consequence—it is near enough that shape for all Mexican purposes. From the same wood he next cuts his axletree and the body of his cart, the latter fastened together by raw-hide. Then comes the tongue, also dug from the same source whence came the wheels, and the vehicle is finished. When in motion, the wheels stagger, wabble and wander about, apparently in every direction but the right one, and as they slowly revolve upon their axletrees, the want of friendly grease is made painfully manifest by the most distressing groans and screeches—excruciating noises which can be heard for miles. Should his journey be of but one or two days' duration, the driver only carries one or two extra axletrees to guard against breakages; if he is to be absent a week, one half of his load consists of those indispensables, else he never gets to his journey's end. With all his precautions, however, he frequently meets with break-downs for which there is no remedy; and were not the wrecks instantly seized by the next passer for firewood, the principal roads in the northern departments of Mexico, on either side, would long since have been fenced with broken-down carts.

And then it would fairly drive the substantial American farmer distracted, to see the manner in which the Mexican oxen are compelled to draw these carts. They are not yoked and allowed the full use and strength of their shoulders and chests, but a straight piece of timber is placed directly on their heads behind the horns, and this is tied to the latter with raw-hide. Another piece of raw-hide is next made fast around the centre of the stick, and this, in turn, is tied to the tongue of the cart or to the next pair of unfortunate oxen. In this way, four, five, and even six pairs of cattle are frequently seen pushing, as it were, not drawing, a cart along, while a single yoke of oxen in the United States could do the same work with all ease. Yet nothing could convince the Mexicans that their mode is not the best. Their forefathers, five generations back, adopted this system, and their rule is never to alter. So with their long, heavy, clumsy ploughs; three times the space of ground might be ploughed with one of the modern improvement, yet they will suffer no innovation. Their axes, with long, straight handles, would be small hoes were the blades turned round after the manner of those implements: while the Mexican is pecking away at a tree, in process of felling it, the American would cut down, chop, and split one of the same size into cord-wood, and very likely have time to pile it— yet the patient Mexican pecks away, regardless of labour and time so that his object is eventually attained. Strange, that with a country as fair as any upon the face of the earth, abounding in every species of soil, climate, fruit, and mineral, the Mexicans will not profit by the lessons, and adopt the systems of their Saxon neighbours. They pertinaciously cling to the customs of their forefathers, and are becoming every year more and more impoverished—in short, they are morally, physically, and intellectually distanced in the great race of improvement which is run in almost every other quarter of the earth. Give them but tortillas, frijoles, and chile colorado to supply their animal wants for the day, and seven tenths of the Mexicans are satisfied; and so they will continue to be until the race becomes extinct or amalgamated with Anglo-Saxon stock; for no political change, no revolution, can uproot that inherent indolence and antipathy to change which in this age of improvement and advancement must sooner or later work their ruin and downfall. In these wonder-working days of steam, to stand still is to retrograde. But I will leave speculation and return to matter of fact.

The second night after our departure from El Paso we encamped in the midst of an arid and sandy plain, without water and with but scanty picking for the large *cavallada* of horses, mules, and cattle. To remedy any want on the part of the former, however, the officer who now had charge of us, Captain Ochoa, had provided and filled several large casks at the springs and wells we left in the morning. A sufficiency of beef, bread, and salt was provided for the men, our marches were neither so long nor so tiresome as while under Salezar, and as carts had been provided at El Paso especially for such as might be sick or unable to travel, our sufferings were now comparatively light.

Towards noon, on the third day, we arrived at a celebrated water-hole, called the *Diamond of the Desert*.\* Immediately beyond were large mountains of loose sand, and as for a distance of some ten miles it was impossible to drag the carts over without doubling the teams, we were ordered to remain behind until all had made the passage. These sand mountains were plainly visible from our camp, their yellow tops entirely destitute of vegetation of any kind, and presenting an appearance of dreary sterility.

The 10th of November we spent in lying, sleeping, or walking about camp, mending our tattered clothing

---

\* The Mexican name for this spring is "Ojo de San Malayuque." How it came by the title of the Diamond of the Desert is more than I can say, but so it was called by our men.

and washing such articles as most needed an introduction to the turbid spring near us. This Diamond of the Desert was by no means of the first water, the dark and sluggish element being brackish and extremely unpalatable; but as it is the only spring, if it can be dignified with that title, in any direction for miles, it is a general stopping-place for all travellers between El Paso and Chihuahua. There are two things about it which render it invaluable—it quenches thirst and never fails. A thousand men with horses might encamp around it for a week, so we were told, and it would bear the heavy demand upon it without exhaustion. The soil is exceedingly poor in the vicinity, having nothing in the way of vegetation except a few scattering thorns and dwarfish prickly pears. From El Paso the Rio Grande bears off to the southeast, while our course was nearly south, leaving the river some distance to the left.

On the 11th of November our march was resumed, our route leading directly through the sand mountains. Nearly as far as the eye could reach, after we were fairly among them, nothing could be seen but immense piles of light, yellow sand, not a solitary blade of grass relieving the prospect in any direction. The horses sank below their fetlocks at every step, and both men and animals were completely worn out with fatigue before the passage was made across the dreary Saharra. At times our course—for the continual changes made by the winds forbid the existence of any permanent road—lay along the sides of huge piles of sand; then we were groping our way through dreary ravines at their base, and the next half hour we were climbing steep pyramids which raised their heads high in air. A more desolate scene cannot be imagined; and although the general features of this dreary waste will ever remain the same, the topography will be ever varying. The traveller who passed this desert a month after us found, instead of the mountains over which we toiled, nothing but gullies. Like an immense panorama, the scene is ever changing, and as the desert is shut in on every side by high mountains of stone and vegetation, these shifting sand-hills will remain there until the end of time. The unchanging mountains I have just mentioned in the far distance were clothed with stunted cedars, prickly pears, and a variety of dwarfish shrubs and plants, and were the abodes of the daring Apaches, the fierce grizzly bear, and the black-tailed deer so common in the mountainous region of Northern Mexico.

We had made an early start in the morning, and the distance across the sandy waste was only ten miles; yet it was near night before we had made the tedious passage. Again we encamped, with no other water than that we had brought from the Diamond of the Desert, and it was with the greatest difficulty we could find brush and sticks enough to cook our beef; but we had now safely crossed the last desert on our route, were promised an abundance of good water farther onward, and were satisfied.

Near our encampment was a celebrated stone, weighing some two hundred pounds, the history of which is singular enough. Many years ago this stone was found near the Diamond of the Desert, and was the only one within miles of the pool. A band of muleteers commenced lifting it, and finally one or two of them were found strong enough to raise it to a level with, and then to throw it over their heads. By accident the stone first fell towards the city of Mexico; and singularly enough, in the course of time it has come to be superstitiously regarded as a duty among the muleteers who travel this road to facilitate the progress of the stone towards the capital, a distance of some fourteen or fifteen hundred miles! Every muleteer who passes along gives the stone a trial, although scarcely one in fifty is able to throw it over his head, and in no other way is it allowed to be moved. By this strange system of journeying the stone has advanced some twelve or fourteen miles on its travel, and this within the last century and a half. The number of travellers upon this road is very great, all the trade between New Mexico and the States of Chihuahua and Sonora being forced to take this route; yet the stone makes remarkably slow progress, the same person not being allowed to throw it over his head more than once. After it gets farther down the country, some ages hence, its transit may be more rapid; but centuries upon centuries will pass away before the wayfarer arrives at its journey's end.

Such was the history of this singular stone as we learned it from Captain Ochoa. It is called *la puerta de piedra*,* but why it has received this name I know not. Throughout the country, the inhabitants have many strange customs, superstitions, and observances, borrowed from the Indians, and all taking their rise from some circumstance of trifling import; but this idea of starting a stone which few can lift, upon so long a journey and by such ludicrous, not to say preposterous means, is the most singular of all.

By making an early start on the morning of the 12th of November, we were enabled to reach the *Ojo del Lucero*, or *Fountain of the Star*, as it is called, a spring near the roadside, and distant some twenty miles from our encampment of the night before. Our route still led

---

* Stone door, or door of stone.

us through a poor and sandy country, the walking extremely tiresome and slow.

Could a correct Daguerréotype view have been taken of us, at any point on the march between El Paso and Chihuahua, I know not whether it would excite more pity or mirth—in fact, I am inclined to believe it would occasion a little of both. The haggard and sickly appearance of the men when first captured, as well as while in the hands of the detestable Salezar, had now given place to fuller cheeks and a more healthy colour—the consequence of a bountiful supply of nutritious food at El Paso, and the comparatively light marches since we had left that place. Still, such a motley collection surely never was seen before—such variety of costume, and such a picturesque, not to say grotesque, appearance as we made would put to the blush and break up a *mardi gras*, rag-fair, fantastical militia, or any other *fancy-dress* procession ever invented. No two were costumed with any attempt at uniformity, and each individual stood forth a distinct and decided character. But few of us had shaved for weeks, and, as a consequence, there was a large and general assortment of unbrushed black, gray, red, and sandy beards, as well as ferocious mustaches and whiskers—enough to rig out an army of Fra Diavolos, Rinaldo Rinaldinis, or West India bucaniers. A more brigandish set of Anglo-Saxon faces has never been collected. Then, as to costume, it is utterly impossible to paint the variety our little crowd of one hundred and eighty-one men presented.* A few shabby-genteel, Jeremy Diddlerish men

---

* The reader may recollect that we set out from San Miguel, one hundred and eighty-seven persons in all. Five were either killed or died before reaching El Paso. At that place a gunsmith, named Neal, was left, under pretence of being too ill to travel. It *may* be that his services were much

there were in the party—men who had neither sold nor "swapped" off the clothes they had on when taken—but nine out of ten were, to use a common expression, rigged out almost any and every way. Here would be a fellow trudging along with a pair of ragged, Mexican-made trousers, open from the knee downward, and the sides studded with a profusion of tarnished brass bell buttons. On his head might be stuck the remnant of a straw hat, while a faded Texan dragoon jacket would perhaps complete his outfit. His neighbour, very likely, was arrayed in short buckskin breeches, without stockings, a coarse, Mexican woollen shirt, and no hat at all. Then would come a man with a dragoon cap worn jauntily upon his head, while part of a shirt and occasional fragments only of what had once been a pair of military pantaloons, made up the rest of his attire. Hardly one in the crowd had anything like a complete suit even of rags; almost every one was either hatless, coatless, pantaloonless, or shirtless. Neither St. Giles's nor the Five Points at New-York could furnish such a set of rough, ragged, and I may add rowdyish characters in appearance.

Falstaff's ragged regiment was well uniformed in comparison with ours; but, singular as it may seem, there could hardly be found a merrier—I might be going too far in saying a happier—set of fellows in Christendom. Our very looks bred good-humour, for there was something irresistibly ludicrous in the appearance of each man—a quaint solemnity and droll gravity of countenance which would elicit some facetious and good-natured remark from his neighbour. The comic

wanted by some of the inhabitants, and that his sickness "was got up expressly for the occasion." At all events, I will venture the assertion that the expense of medicine in his case was trifling.

and eccentric were strangely mingled with the tragic and melo-dramatic; but the former preponderated to a degree that completely stifled any pathetic feelings which might otherwise have arisen, and fairly induced us to laugh rather than cry at the forlorn but fantastic figure each one presented in the moving panorama. So completely disguised were we all, that I doubt whether our anxious mothers, even had the liberty of their unfortunate sons depended on the recognition, could have picked us out by the most rigid scrutiny. And even could they, by some well-remembered mark, have detected an errant son, methinks they would have been slow to acknowledge one who had wandered so far from their hearth-stone as to have lost his very identity.

The free lines of Hogarth might have done justice to a scene that was before me for months, but which words are wholly inadequate to describe. Forty times a day I could not resist laughing heartily at forty different persons, and nine times out of ten these same persons would turn the laugh upon myself, and remark that there was nothing particularly prepossessing in my own appearance. And they were right; for almost the heartiest laugh I had was while surveying my own face in a bit of looking-glass. It was the first time I had the pleasure of seeing myself for a month. A luxuriant growth of whiskers and mustaches—I am speaking of quantity, not quality—had sprung up, disguising me thoroughly. I could only see my face in spots, but I could still see enough fully to appreciate the ludicrous, serio-comico figure I presented, and inly I determined to take no offence at any laugh raised, or any remarks made upon my visage or equipment.

## CHAPTER III.

A singular Hot Spring.—Medicinal Properties of the Waters.—" Doing" our Washing.—Carazal.—Appearance of the Town.—Dr. Whittaker in Business.—Charley Tirrell, the Delaware.—A strange Contract.—Kirker, and the Stories told of him. — Captain Spybuck killed by Apaches. — More of Kirker.—Arrival of the Señora Ochoa, and her Style of Travelling.—Opportunity to Escape unimproved.—A Mountain Spring.—Laguna Encinillos, —Desolate Appearance of the Country.—Inroads of the Apaches.—Their Prowess and Daring.—Increase of the Tribe.—Visiters from Chihuahua.—Hospitality and the Jesuits' Hospital.—Situation of Chihuahua.—Mines in the Vicinity. — Governor Condé. — Excitement of the Inhabitants. — The Military of Chihuahua.—Entrance to the City.—Carcel de Ciudad.—The Women of Chihuahua.—The Plaza.—Description of the Cathedral.—The Presidio. —Jesuits' Hospital.—Salon los Distinguidos. — Names upon the Walls.—Description of the Hospital.—Apache Prisoners.—Hidalgo, with a short Account of the first Mexican Revolution, and the Death of that celebrated Leader.

WE passed a singular hot spring on the 13th of November, our road leading us directly by it. The water boils up from the top of a square mound, some twenty feet high, which, at a short distance, has the appearance of a fortification. That the mound is a natural formation there can be little doubt; but it is in shape square, and has as much precision of angle and regularity of outline as though the hand of man had fashioned it. The top of this mound forms an area of twenty or twenty-five square yards, and is perfectly level, the spring boiling up in the very centre. It is situated in the midst of a desert, bare of all vegetation save a few bushes of the thorn species, and may certainly be considered a great natural curiosity. The water is clear, but warm, and slightly brackish.

A few miles farther on, we encamped by a large and beautiful spring, of warm but excellent water. Like the one I have just mentioned, it boils up out of the sand, and in such quantities as to form a brook of no inconsiderable size from the fountain-head. After running some three or four miles this brook empties into, or rather forms, a large pond or lake. Within a league is another spring of water, which was visited by a small party of our officers, accompanied by Captain Ochoa. The Mexicans say that it possesses medicinal qualities, which are highly efficacious in rheumatism and many chronic diseases. We reached the first-named spring about meridian, and remained all the afternoon, our men employing their time in bathing, and washing such articles of their scanty wardrobe as might legitimately be termed washable.

The next morning we passed the town of Carazal, leaving it about a mile and a half or two miles on our right. It is situated in a fertile valley at the foot of a mountain, once contained over a thousand inhabitants, and was a place of considerable trade; but the Apaches have completely broken it up by stealing the cattle and crops of the farmers in the vicinity, and destroying any small parties of citizens that unfortunately might be caught too far from its walls. From a point in the road we could plainly see these walls, and also the domes and spires of two or three churches within. We travelled some two miles beyond the town, encamping for the afternoon and night in an old field, and by the side of a swift-running irrigating canal, now rendered comparatively valueless by the inroads of the daring and ever-active Apaches.

While passing Carazal, three or four Mexicans came dashing from the place on horseback, rode up to our party, and inquired if there was a physician among us. Dr. Whittaker, our surgeon, was pointed out, and in company with Van Ness to interpret he was taken to the house of a woman in the town who was confined to her bed by illness. After he had prescribed some medicines, an excellent dinner was provided for the doctor and Van Ness, and shortly after their return to camp in the afternoon a fine fat sheep was sent out to the former, as the fee for his professional services. There are few Mexican physicians except in the large cities of the country, and so far as I could learn they have very little need of the services of any, especially on the high tablelands or *tierras templadas*. Still, American and foreign physicians may be found scattered all over Mexico, and frequently they accumulate ample fortunes by their practice.

We had been but a short time encamped by the irrigating canal when we were visited by a half-breed Delaware Indian, a tall, well-made fellow, named Charley Tirrell, who spoke very fair English, although strangely mixed with Spanish and Indian idioms. He had been regularly educated in Indiana, with one or two sisters, so he said; had visited Washington city once or twice, and was well acquainted with General Dodge and several United States officers. It required but a very short time for us to ascertain that Charley was extremely fond of dealing in gasconade, and that in his own estimation he was a very important personage; whether this failing was inherent, or he had contracted it by commerce with the Mexicans, who are heavy dealers in that line, I am unable to say. He was accompanied by a quiet-seeming, badly pock-marked Shawnee, and a pert little Mexican officer, who said he had visited the United States, and was incessantly pouring forth a stream of rascally bad English to prove his assertion. Charley informed us that himself and some twelve

Shawnees and Delawares, the party under command of a noted chief named Captain Spybuck, had come to this part of Mexico, from the great Western Prairies of the United States, under contract with the government of Chihuahua to kill the Apaches at so much a head—five dollars, I think, was the price. Some of the Mexicans also told us that a well-known American, named Kirker, had been engaged in the same business, and with a party of his countrymen had been very successful; but it being soon suspected that he was in the practice of bringing in counterfeit scalps—or in other words, that he did not scruple to kill any of the lower order of Mexicans he might meet with, where there was slight chance of being discovered, and pass off their top-knots for those of true Apaches—a stop was put to the game, and afterward, instead of paying him a certain sum for each scalp, he was allowed only one dollar a day for his services. This was the story I heard from the Mexicans, who added that Kirker immediately gave up the business and retired to Sonora, or the western part of Chihuahua, setting all attempts to arrest him at defiance.

Captain Spybuck and his party, at all events, remained in the service of the government of Chihuahua, receiving for their pay one dollar per diem. He was a brave and noted chief, well known on the Western frontiers of the United States to many of our officers and soldiers. His Mexican expedition had cost him his life; for, but a week previous to our reaching the vicinity of Carazal, he had been killed upon a side of the mountain, near that town, in a desperate encounter with the Apaches. Charley related the particulars of his captain's death with not a little feeling, and said that, now he was gone, both himself and companions were extremely anxious to return to the United States. He attributed the death of Spybuck to the cowardice of the little Mexican I have spoken of. The latter commanded a party of his countrymen at the time of the engagement, but retreated precipitately with his men when he ascertained that the Apaches were nearly equal in number, and left his Indian friends to fight it out as best they could. This was not told us in the hearing of the little Mexican, who was a talking, blustering fellow, extremely fond of relating his exploits. I could not but be amused at a remark of Charley—one that plainly showed he had had much intercourse with the Americans and well understood their cant phrases. The little Mexican had just finished a recital of some dangerous exploit, of which he had been the hero, when the Delaware remarked, aside, that he was "all talk and no cider."

I was extremely loath, at the time, to credit the Mexican accounts of Kirker and his doings, and have since been informed, by Americans who know him well, that they are destitute of foundation. For many years Kirker led a wild, border life, engaged in continual strife with the hostile Indians of the prairies and of Mexico, and in all his encounters with them came off victorious. He is now, or was a year since, quietly occupied in overlooking a hacienda not many days' travel from Chihuahua, ready to repel any attack his old enemies, the Apaches, may make upon him. His superior prowess and great daring may have first imbittered the Mexicans against him, for no sooner has any foreigner signalized himself by deeds of noble daring in their cause, than he is looked upon with jealousy and distrust, and the first opportunity is embraced to oust him from the high estate his talents have destined him to fill. This spirit, in all probability, first engendered hostility against Kirker on the part of the Mexicans, and induced them to fabricate numerous stories of his cruelty and dishonesty.

At Carazal resided, for the time, the Señora Ochoa, wife of our friend, the captain. Just before we left our camp, on the morning of the 15th of November, she arrived with the intention of accompanying her husband to Chihuahua. Although on the cloudy side of thirty, she was still a pretty woman, with large, sparkling black eyes, and the winning, easy, and sociable manners which belong to Mexican females of whatever degree. On her arrival she was dressed in a neatly-worked linen chemise and bluish woollen petticoat, a rosary with a small cross around her neck, and wore her reboso with that grace which is peculiar to the females of her land.

My readers may be a little astonished at the style in which she made her first appearance among us. Her travelling-carriage was nothing more or less than a huge Pennsylvania or Conestoga wagon, drawn by four yokes of oxen. This vehicle had found its way from Pittsburgh to St. Louis; there had been purchased by traders who had sent it to Santa Fé, and by some strange mutation it had finally reached Carazal and been promoted to the high office of transporting a Mexican officer's lady. Everything was comfortable, however, under the white cotton canopy which served as a top; and I doubt whether the Lord-mayor of London ever felt happier, while showing himself in his richly-caparisoned coach of state, than did Señora Ochoa while riding in her Conestoga wagon drawn by eight oxen. On her arrival in camp her husband politely invited General McLeod and myself to mess with him and *la señora* as far as Chihuahua, an invitation which we accepted.

Although we did not leave our camp until a late hour on the morning after Charley Tirrell, the Delaware, had visited us, we saw no more of him. After our departure from Carazal I felt annoyed that I had not made an attempt to escape through his agency and by his assistance. I did not place much faith either in his valour or his honesty, although in this I may have wronged him; but I could easily gather, from his conversation, that he was anxious once more to visit his native land, and that nothing but the want of money prevented him. With a small sum in hand, and the promise of a larger on reaching the United States, I have little doubt he would not only have started off on the night he visited our camp, but would have provided horses for the journey. Our march would have been tedious and dangerous, leading directly through a part of the Apache and Camanche country; we should also have been compelled to travel by night, and endure great hardships and sufferings; still, I would have run all risks for the sake of once more gaining that liberty of which I was most unjustly deprived. The opportunity to escape was lost, however, when we left the neighbourhood of Carazal, and unpleasant as was the prospect before me—that of a march of some fifteen hundred miles, and an uncertainty as to what disposition would be made of me on reaching the city of Mexico—I was obliged to submit.

The night we left Carazal we encamped at another hot well, and on the next afternoon we arrived at a cool spring upon the side of a mountain, at the base of which we halted. On the 18th of November we journeyed along the margin of *Laguna Encinillos*, a lake some twenty miles in length by three or four in width. The country in the vicinity affords most excellent pasturage for cattle and sheep, and several years since there were immense herds of both kept in this vicinity; but the dreaded Apaches have extended their ravages even to the very walls of Chihuahua, and laid the whole country waste. At one time a revenue of several hundred thousand dollars was produced from a single hacienda on the borders of the lake—now the place is desolate, and the owner dare not even visit it without a strong guard. Some of the best land in Mexico lies on the borders of Laguna Encinillos, but at present it is entirely useless from the depredations of the Apaches. A few cattle and horses are still pastured in the vicinity; yet where there is one at present, there were one hundred twenty years since.

The Apaches live, for the most part, in the neighbourhood of the chain of mountains lying between New Mexico and the States of Sonora and Chihuahua. They are extremely expert as horsemen, keeping immense droves of those animals, and in using the lance and bow and arrow are said to be surpassingly adroit. It is within a few years only that fire-arms have been introduced among them, and those of so inferior a quality that their former weapons are far more effective. They are a proud, independent, and hardy tribe, but little contaminated by intercourse with the whites, and are said to present the singular anomaly of a tribe of aborigines increasing in numbers and in such wealth as the Indian most covets—horses and arms, trinkets and finery. In their attacks upon the Mexicans they are said to be very daring, coming upon them with the speed of the whirlwind, and making off to their fastnesses and retreats in the mountains before organized pursuit can be commenced. The Spaniards, when they first subjugated the country, drove this tribe to the mountains and confined them there; but of late years, as I have said, they have increased in numbers, are very systematic in their attacks, and are gradually wresting their lands back from the Mexicans.

On the night of the 19th of November we arrived at a camp within some five or six miles of Chihuahua. Here we were visited by several gentlemen of the town who had heard of our approach. They spoke to Mr. Navarro very kindly, and said that himself and friends need expect nothing but *hospitality* while in the city. The next night we found ourselves closely confined in the old Jesuits' *Hospital!*

The city of Chihuahua is situated near the southern base of a chain of precipitous mountains, which, at this point, form a kind of crescent, in the curve of which the city stands. As it is approached from the north, the traveller is at a loss how a passage over the rough and steep hills to the south can be made; and even after he has entered the city he is still in doubt. But a ride of an hour brings him to an open defile turning abruptly off, unseen almost until the traveller enters it, and through this passage an excellent road has been cut.

As we approached the city, the mines on the mountain sides could be plainly seen, excavations and smoke marking the points at which the work of digging for silver was then in progress. When within a couple of miles, the inhabitants commenced flocking out—some on foot, others on horseback—while a number of heavy, clumsy-looking, but costly and elaborately-carved coaches, drawn by five or seven mules, with postillions after the old Spanish custom, were on the spot, filled with the ladies of the place. I noticed that two or three of

them wore gowns, after the fashion of my own land—
the first I had seen in a journey of six hundred miles
through the country.

When within one mile of the city a halt was called,
and immediately after the governor, Garcia Condé,
made his appearance, attended by his suite. He is a
portly, handsome man, gentlemanly in his manners, and
from his complexion appears to be of pure Castilian
blood. Dismounting from his horse, he was introduced
to and shook hands with General McLeod, Mr. Navarro, and several of the officers, after which the march
was resumed.

As we drew closer to the city, it was evident enough
that our coming had created an unusual excitement and
commotion. The top of the large and magnificent cathedral, the domes of the churches, convents, and other
public buildings, as well as the housetops, were covered with the inhabitants, all anxious to obtain a sight of
the much-talked-of *Tejanos*. Immediately outside the
city the entire military strength of the place, comprising some hundreds of regular and raw troops, was
drawn up in lines upon either side of the road. When
we were between these lines, another short halt was
called, for what purpose I know not, unless it was to allow the miserable burlesques upon soldiers time to
wheel with their faces towards the city. This evolution performed in a bungling manner, amid the suppressed jeers of our own men, we were commanded to
advance in regular order, the Chihuahua troops marching in single file on either side of us to the blowing of
trumpets and the beating of drums. In this order we
entered the northern or eastern part of the city; but
why they marched us in with so much state and ceremony I am utterly at a loss to imagine, unless it was in

ambitious emulation of a Roman triumph, which we poor devils were thought worthy to adorn.

While riding along, and wondering at all I saw, I was accosted by a person in the crowd, outside the city, whose face plainly told that he was other than a Mexican. Stealthily, for we were allowed no converse with any but our guard, he asked information of a young man who had started upon the expedition full of health and hope. I told him that the person was dead—had been killed by Indians on the prairie. Farther than this I was not allowed to communicate, the soldier by my side commanding me to silence. Afterward I learned that the individual who addressed me was an American; that the young man of whom he spoke was a nephew; and the startled and desolate look of the man, the feeling with which he ejaculated "dead!" plainly denoted that he was far from anticipating such ill-tidings.

Once inside the city, we found every window, balcony, door, and housetop crowded with men, women, and children. The sides of the streets, too, were lined with a dense throng of half-dressed men and women, the lower orders of the place, and all gazing at us with an intentness as earnest as if we had been so many wild beasts. All was hurry, bustle, and confusion. Children were running about and struggling through the crowd to obtain a look at us, and "Mira! mira! Los Tejanos! los Tejanos!"* was on every lip.

A few steps brought us to the *Carcel de Ciudad*, or city prison, from the close-grated windows of which desperate and villanous faces were peering at us with much apparent satisfaction. Little did I then think

---

* "Look! look! The Texans! the Texans!"

that I was yet to be furnished with lodgings in a place even more revolting than this most dreary and dismal prison.

Our march led us on through streets in the direction of the *plaza*, and at every step the crowd seemed to increase and become more dense. The balconies and windows of the better classes were filled with women, their full, black eyes beaming upon us with looks of mingled pity and astonishment. They had never before seen a people whom they had been taught to believe worse than the savages themselves—they gazed upon a crowd of unfortunate men, in whose faces they could discover no trace of those evil passions, of that cruelty of disposition and purpose they had supposed us to possess. The commonest observer must have noticed that instinct in children which teaches them, even before they can talk, to read unerringly the countenance of a man or an animal, and to shrink with intuitive fear from an expression sinister or unkind, while they will approach and soon become familiar with any one whose countenance indicates good-nature. That same instinct appeared to govern the females of Mexico in their conduct towards us—the same pure, gentle, and childlike spirit within them was touched by our distresses, and inspired their soft exclamation of pity —*pobrecitos*—which was murmured in sweet accents from the lips of many a kind-hearted girl of Chihuahua. They saw that we were not the monsters we had been represented to them, that we were at least human, and that we were unfortunate—and had they possessed the power to bid us be free and happy, not a man in the ragged crowd of Texans would have remained an hour in bondage.

We passed through the principal plaza, which was

also thronged with gazers. In the centre of the square is a fountain—the celebrated Cathedral of Chihuahua occupying one of the sides, while the shops of the principal foreign and native merchants fill up the other three. The cathedral is a magnificent edifice, as regards both its architecture and adornments. The front is decorated with numerous statues of apostles and saints, nearly or quite as large as life, standing in niches expressly built for their reception, while the doors and windows are richly ornamented with elaborate sculpture, done in the most costly style. The interior is also said to be very expensively decorated with gold and silver ornaments, paintings, and statuary. The entire cost of all was between a million and a half and two millions of dollars, a monument of the immense sums which the Spaniards, even in their more remote provinces, were willing to expend in order to give full effect to their religion.

On the top of a *fonda*, or hotel, which was kept by an Englishman, we noticed a number of Anglo-Saxons, whose light hair and fair complexions formed a striking contrast to the dark and swarthy faces around them. On arriving at the *Presidio*,* which was set apart as our prison, we were halted and counted. A short time after, an officer took me to an old establishment of the Jesuits, commenced a great many years since by that ambitious, bold, and enlightened order, but which had never been finished. Here, in a small, badly-lighted room, having the words " *Salon los Distinguidos*"* painted over the entrance, I found General McLeod, and Messrs. Navarro, Van Ness, and Falconer, from whom I had been accidentally separated on entering the city,

\* The garrison or barracks for soldiers.
† Room or apartment for distinguished persons.

all close prisoners. On the walls of this room were the names of Colonel Cooke and Dr. Brenham, and also that of a Mr. Thurston. The latter had been confined a few days in consequence of a letter of introduction, directed to him, having been found among the papers of the Santa Fé Expedition. It being ascertained, however, upon investigation, that he had no connexion with the Texans, he was released.

The apartment immediately adjoining ours was a dark dungeon, and occasionally we imagined we could hear the clanking of chains which probably confined an unfortunate inmate. The guard who paced up and down in front of our room informed us that an American was the only occupant—his name, or the crime for which he was incarcerated, the sentinel would not disclose.

The building in which we were confined was one of those old Jesuit establishments to be found in every part of America where that order first obtained a footing. That part of it intended for a hospital, prison, and offices, was finished ; but the work was stopped before the church was completed. Had the original plan of the Jesuits been carried out, the church would have been a magnificent edifice, and the building generally would have served as a fortress, impregnable, at least, against the attacks of Indians; but from some cause the work was suspended before its completion, although immense arches, columns, and a part of the dome of the church are still standing.

The room in which we were confined looked out upon a large *corral*, or yard, in the interior. The rear wall of the church formed one side of this yard, the kitchen and other apartments for servants another side, while the other two were appropriated to quarters for soldiers, rooms for the sick, offices, a place for punishment, and a dungeon. In the yard an Apache woman, with her child, was confined. She was allowed such liberty as she might find in roaming about the building, but was not permitted to go into the streets. She was extremely fat, and appeared to bear her confinement, such as it was, without a murmur.

During the first struggle of the Mexicans for independence, the Spaniards confined no less than thirty-one of their most important revolutionary prisoners in the very room in which we were now placed, among them the celebrated *Hidalgo*, the prime mover and principal leader in the earlier outbreak.

At the commencement of the year 1810, Hidalgo was but the poor and unimportant cura of Dolores, a little town some thirty miles northeast of Guanajuato. From all accounts he was a man of strong mind, and of no inconsiderable reading and information, possessing great powers of endurance combined with resolution and activity, and, in common with the natives of the country at that day, entertained a most cordial hatred for the Spanish-born taskmasters under whose tyrannical yoke they groaned.

The circumstance that every office of honour and emolument in Mexico was filled by a native of Old Spain was enough, of itself, even were the offices held by honourable men, to drive the natives to revolt; how easy, then, to kindle the flames of revolution, when the band of office-holders were, for the most part, mere mercenary and broken-down adventurers, unprincipled men, who cheated and defrauded those whom they governed, and whose many acts of insolence and overbearing tyranny tended to render the natives infuriate, against not only the agents themselves, but the parent country that had sent them over! I do not intend to say that the poorer classes of Mexico are in a much better situation now than when under the domination of Spain—it appears to be the destiny of the ignorant and moneyless of this unfortunate race to be the prey of the more wealthy and crafty; but the lesson they had received from their neighbours of the United States, co-operating with the excessive and increasing burdens and indignities their mother-country was heaping upon them, prepared the minds of all to echo a *grito*, or cry of revolution, whenever any one was found bold enough to raise it. This man appeared in the person of Don Miguel Hidalgo y Costilla, the humble but discontented cura of Dolores.

He is said to have received some private insults from the king's officers, which rankled in his bosom; and when to these were joined the common wrongs that were felt by all his countrymen alike, it is not to be wondered at that a man of his characteristic boldness and ambition raised the standard of revolt. His first attempt proved remarkably successful. With but a dozen assistants he seized upon the few Spaniards in Dolores, threw them into prison, and, after dividing their effects equally among his followers, proclaimed war against the common enemies of all, the *Gachupines*, or natives of Old Spain. This was on the 16th of September, 1810.

No sooner had his first success become known than the entire population of the vicinity flocked to his banner. With a motley, ill-armed crowd, he marched immediately upon San Felipe, a town containing some fifteen thousand inhabitants. Here he was again successful, imprisoning and pillaging all the Spaniards, and dividing the plunder thus obtained among his ragged but enthusiastic adherents. San Miguel el Grande, a town as large as San Felipe, next fell into his hands; the property of all the foreigners was confiscated and divided, after which Hidalgo marched forthwith upon Guanajuato, then containing a population of more than seventy thousand, and immense riches.

In front of this city, and with twenty thousand ragged, undisciplined, and almost unarmed adherents around him, he publicly proclaimed the independence of Mexico, and caused himself to be elected commander-in-chief of the army, with the title of *Captain-general of America.* I cannot dwell long upon particulars: Guanajuato, with all its immense treasures, soon fell into the hands of Hidalgo, the Gachupines were indiscriminately slaughtered by his Indian allies, and all their houses razed to the ground. With this additional success, and with the immense amount of gold and silver the plunder of Guanajuato gave him, the little breeze of rebellion was now fanned into a perfect hurricane of revolution.

Thousands and tens of thousands now hurried to the standard of the victorious Hidalgo. All had wrongs to redress: the native priest, who under the Spanish rule could never rise above a petty curacy, now had a chance for advancement; the native officers of the army, who were never allowed to fill other than subordinate stations, now saw a bright opening for advancing and signalizing themselves; the ladrones, or common thieves, could now reap a rich harvest of plunder; while the poor Indians, who for centuries had groaned silently and patiently under the iron yoke of their conquerors, saw an opportunity for revenge and a chance to regain their long-lost liberty, and with holy zeal joined the common cause against the common tyrants.

Hidalgo remained but ten days at Guanajuato, his

motley crowd of adherents, in the mean time, committing the most outrageous excesses. His next move was towards Valladolid, a place which he found evacuated by all the government officers and foreigners. By this time the rabble army he had drawn around him numbered more than fifty thousand men; yet a more undisciplined, ineffective, and ungovernable band were never collected. A large portion of them were drawn from the Indian population, and were armed only with clubs, stones, slings, bows and arrows, lances, axes, and machetes, or heavy swords. It was not until the celebrated patriot general, Morales, then a poor cura like Hidalgo, joined the disorderly throng, that anything like system, either in marching or fighting, was established. Hidalgo had depended only upon numbers, and the blind enthusiasm of his Indians, in encountering the systematic but feeble opposition he had met with only at Guanajuato. From Valladolid, his next movement was towards the city of Mexico, then in the hands of the Spanish viceroy, Venegas.

On the 30th of October Hidalgo defeated the force sent out from the city at the pass of Las Cruces, his ignorant Indians even rushing up to the mouths of the cannon planted to intercept their onward march, and endeavouring to stop the death-dealing muzzles with their straw hats! Hundreds of them were mowed down by the cannon, which were well directed by the regular troops under Truxillo and Augustin Iturbide. The latter was at that time a lieutenant in the Spanish service—afterward Emperor of Mexico. These officers were defeated, but defeated only by the number and phrensy of Hidalgo's rabble. The latter immediately advanced within sight of Mexico, and then suddenly retreated with all his host. He well knew that another such victory as that of Las Cruces would ruin him, for his undisciplined Indians had suffered terribly, and had learned the full power of cannon when advantageously posted and well directed.

On the 7th of November following, Hidalgo was defeated, with immense loss, on the plains of Aculco, by General Calleja. We next hear of his entering Valladolid a second time, putting to death many Spaniards. He then marched to Guadalaxara, the second city in Mexico, which was at that time in possession of one of his generals, Allende. While there, Hidalgo secretly assassinated no less than seven hundred of the principal Gachupines, and committed many acts that illustrate the bloody manner in which the early revolution was conducted. Nor were the Spaniards guiltless of the most horrible atrocities; for they gave no quarter to such of the unfortunate patriots as fell into their hands.

On the 17th of January, although he now had cannon and had brought a part of his force into something like discipline, Hidalgo was once more defeated by Calleja. This battle was fought at the bridge of Calderon. Hidalgo, with his principal officers and about four thousand men, made good his retreat to Saltillo, in the State of Nueva Leon. Leaving his principal force under Rayon, one of his best generals, Hidalgo hastened towards the United States, in company with Allende and other principal officers, for the purpose of purchasing arms and military stores, and raising efficient recruits to carry on the war against the well-disciplined Spaniards. He got as far as the borders of Texas, with a large sum of money, but was betrayed and captured by Elisondo, one of his former friends and compatriots, marched a prisoner to Chihuahua, and confined in the room where we were now guarded. This was in

March, 1811, only six months after he had first raised the *grito* of revolution.

After undergoing a long trial, Hidalgo, with thirty of his officers, was sentenced to death, and is said to have met his fate with great coolness and bravery. Such is a broken and hurried account, gleaned from Ward and other English writers, of the first revolution in Mexico, and of the short but eventful career of the celebrated Hidalgo, who began it. Some of the sentinels on guard over our little party told a strange tale in relation to the death of Hidalgo and his officers, thirty-one in all—a story undoubtedly destitute of foundation, but which I give to show the passion of the lower orders in Mexico for the marvellous. As the tale ran, Hidalgo and his officers were ordered to be shot in the yard of the hospital, one each day until they were all executed; but as the month in which the sentence was first passed had but thirty days in it, the Spaniards waited until the ensuing month, which numbered a day for each prisoner. When it came to Hidalgo's turn, the soldiers, in such high respect and reverence was the old cura held by them, could hardly be induced to aim their muskets at him, and many volleys were fired before he received his death-wound. The very spot where he fell was pointed out to us.

## CHAPTER IV.

The old Jesuits' Hospital of Chihuahua.—American Visiters.—Asked for the Particulars of my own Death.— A stealthy Interview.—Dr. Jennison.—Clean Beds.—A sumptuous English Breakfast.—Prisoner in the adjoining Dungeon.—A Meeting.—The Mystery unveiled.—Singular Trial.—Testimony of General McLeod and Messrs. Van Ness and Navarro.—A Release from Chains.—An excellent Dinner from the Señora Magoffin.—Visiters at our Room.—Letters to my Friends.—"La Luna."—Armijo's Letter to Garcia Condé.—Implicated with the Leaders of the Expedition.—Lewis's probable Agency in the Affair.—A Gasconading Editor.—Poetic Address to a Horse.—Movements of Lewis.—A lively little French Woman.—Our Treatment by the Foreigners in Mexico.—Departure from Chihuahua.—Collection of the Inhabitants.—Furnished a Horse by a Friend.—Difficulty of mounting the Pony.—His Feats and Antics.—The Mexican Saddle, and its Advantages.—El Ojito.—Encounter with American Wagoners.—Arrival at San Pablo.—A Chihuahua Major.—Our Accommodations at San Pablo.—Practical Knowledge of Entomological Science.—Mexican Horse Jockeys.—Mr. Falconer mounted again.—Saucillo.—An Escape agitated.—Death of Larrabee.—A young Mexican Musician.—Santa Rosalia.—The Alcalde and his Daughter.—A stolen Horse claimed.—Military *versus* Civil Law.—Roadside Graves and Crosses.—Stories in relation to them.

It was about two o'clock on the afternoon of the 21st of November when we were introduced to the Salon los Distinguidos of the Jesuits' Hospital at Chihuahua. At dusk, two American gentlemen made their way, by some means, through the ponderous gate which leads from the street to the interior of the hospital, and came to our door, but were denied admittance by the sentinel. One of the gentlemen, however, while walking up and down in front of our open door, stealthily, and in low and hurried tones, asked me if I could give him the particulars of the death of Fitzgerald, Van Ness, Howard, and Kendall. To be asked the particulars of one's own death! I gave the American my name, pointed to Van Ness, who was sitting on a hospital-cot close by, in such ruddy health that he seemed likely to live seventy years to come, and then told the gentleman that the other victims mentioned as among the killed were both in Chihuahua, at the Presidio, enjoying the full measure of life and strength, and ready to corroborate my statement. I hardly know which were the most astonished—we to hear of our own deaths, or the gentleman to learn, from our own lips, that we were still in the land of the living. There was no opportunity, however, for an outward expression of surprise, as the sentinel at the door showed great uneasiness even at our few hurried questions and answers, not one word of which could he understand. I simply told the American that we had been fortunate enough to escape with our lives thus far, although nothing but a miracle had saved us. Our visiters then left, but not until they had promised to use every endeavour, with Governor Condé, for permission to visit us in our room, and do all in their power to soften the rigours of our confinement.

It is so seldom that a man is called upon to relate the particulars of his own death, that few of my readers can know what feelings the inquiry will excite. Our own were of a nature exceedingly mixed. There was something pleasant, to be sure, in the fact that we were able to answer all anxious inquiries in person; but it was not without a slight misgiving as to our chances in perspective that we hastily recounted the particulars of our recent fortunate escape from a death that seemed almost inevitable.

On the following day we learned the name of the gentleman who had questioned us, and the reasons which had induced him to suppose us dead. It seems that Colonel Cooke and Dr. Brenham had reported that we were shot at San Miguel, with Howland and his unfortunate companions, believing such to be the case from the statements made to them while in New Mexico, and from the fact that we were not seen by any of them nor marched in their company towards the capital. The name of the gentleman who first visited us at the hospital was Dr. Jennison, a native of New-England, but at that time the principal conductor of the mint at Chihuahua. He has since paid the debt of nature; but the memory of his courteous and gentlemanly manners, and of his kindness and exceeding liberality in furnishing the prisoners with shoes and other articles of which they stood in utmost need, still lives in the hearts of those he befriended.

Our visiters had scarcely left us before clean mattresses and sheets were brought to our room, and comfortable beds made, after which we passed a quiet night in sleep. The next morning an English gentleman sent us in a sumptuous breakfast—the first really substantial meal I had seen since I left the United States. It consisted of plain beefsteak, tender and of delicious flavour, baked Irish potatoes and most excellent bread, with a generous supply of coffee. The Mexican servant who brought it informed us that the gentlemen who had called upon us the previous evening would endeavour to see and converse with us during the day; and one of them, passing our door in the course of the morning, said that so soon as our depositions were taken in relation to the prisoner confined next door, the foreigners would all be permitted to visit us. We were still left in profound ignorance as to the name of the unfortunate man, or the nature of the charge against him; but the whole story was soon to be told.

Although there was no entrance to the interior of the square, on one side of which we were confined, save through a large archway from the street, we were not allowed even to cross this yard unaccompanied by one of the sentinels. While passing a gateway near the entrance to the kitchen, a dragoon trailing close at my heels, I encountered, face to face, the prisoner confined in the dungeon adjoining our apartment. He was dressed in a green blanket coat, with black collar and cuffs, had large, black whiskers, and wore his hair extremely long, and although his complexion at the time appeared dark, his face was extremely pale. I was about to accost him, when he gave me a look that appeared to be so full of mingled scorn, hatred, and enmity, that I was for a moment chilled into silence. I may have mistaken its expression, or he might deem it prudent to act thus coldly and strangely in the presence of Mexican witnesses; but at the time I felt confident that he considered himself indebted to us for his sufferings and the loss of his liberty—I thought there was no mistaking that black scowl he gave me as I passed him.

Ignorant alike of his name, business, and the circumstances of his arrest, and conscious of my own innocence in the matter, I had no sooner passed him than I was extremely anxious to come to some explanation; but my watchful guard would allow no communication, and I was forced onward without a chance to justify myself from the erroneous impressions under which I thought he must be labouring. Two soldiers accompanied the prisoner, and he was shortly locked up in his gloomy cell.

This accidental meeting, which troubled me not a little, was early in the morning. Towards noon, the mystery which veiled our neighbour was dispelled.

The secretary of Governor Condé, accompanied by another officer of state and a Mexican lawyer who understood a little English, arrived at our quarters to take depositions in relation to the case of Captain Dryden, which turned out to be the name of the prisoner. It seems that he had been mentioned in some of the papers of the Texan Commissioners as a man whom they might consult on reaching New Mexico. When the expedition arrived in the neighbourhood of Santa Fé, Captain D. was residing in Chihuahua. On receiving the intelligence of his name being found among the Texan papers, the authorities caused him to be arrested and confined in chains in the strongest dungeon of the place.

On the arrival of the persons appointed to take our depositions, General McLeod, Messrs. Van Ness, Falconer, and myself were called from the room, and Mr. Navarro was examined alone. Afterward General McLeod was taken into the room and questioned in private, the Mexican officers taking every precaution to prevent anything like collusion. Mr. Van Ness was next examined, and the testimony of all taken down in writing—as Mr. Falconer and myself knew nothing of the prisoner, we were not examined. The testimony of all went to show that they knew nothing of Mr. Dryden—that his name might have appeared among the papers, but that it was probably without his consent—at all events, he was in no way identified with the Santa Fé Expedition, so far as they were concerned. The effect of this testimony was to procure the release of the prisoner from chains, to give him a greater degree of personal liberty, and his American friends were afterward allowed to converse with him. Some twelve months afterward, as I have been pleased to learn, Captain Dryden was released from confinement through the intervention of our minister at Mexico, General Waddy Thompson.

Scarcely had the officers of state left our room before an excellent dinner, comprising a great variety of Mexican dishes, with two bottles of Champagne, was sent to us by the Señora Magoffin, wife of the merchant who had furnished us with the coffee and other luxuries at San Miguel, and whom we had afterward passed on the road to El Paso. We had not the pleasure of seeing the señora, but she was represented to us as a kind-hearted, affable, and exceedingly well-informed woman, a Mexican by birth. Mr. Navarro was acquainted with her, she having lived at San Antonio de Bexar prior to the Texan Revolution, and I believe he received permission to call upon her while we were in Chihuahua. Two or three of her children, fine, intelligent boys, called upon us daily at meal-times, for their mother furnished us regularly with three meals a day, having obtained permission from the governor to that effect.

After dinner, we were visited by nearly all the Americans and foreigners in the place, the governor having no objection to their calling upon us after the testimony in relation to Captain Dryden had been taken. They offered us every attention and kindness, and supplied us with books and writing materials, as well as clean clothing. From this place I wrote letters to Mr. Ellis, then our minister at Mexico, and to my friends in the United States. A part of these letters only reached their destinations; but as the larger portion of them were written with the belief that they might possibly fall into the hands of the Mexicans, I was guarded in my language, and cared but little whether they ever got safe through or not.

Among other papers, brought to our room by the

foreigners, was a copy of *La Luna*, a small weekly sheet published at Chihuahua. It contained a letter from Armijo to Governor Condé, giving him the number and rank of the prisoners. The last sentence of this letter was in substance as follows: "You will please guard with especial care Señors Navarro, McLeod, Cooke, Brenham, and Kendall, on account of their superior intelligence, standing, and influence." Here I was expressly implicated as one of the leaders of the expedition, and for this I at once supposed that I was indebted to the traitor Lewis. Armijo, as I well knew, contemplated giving me my liberty at San Miguel—the reasons for his not doing so were obvious. Lewis was probably fearful that I should be in his way at Santa Fé, and accordingly made such statements to Armijo as induced him to send me to Mexico as a prisoner of importance. It had the effect of ensuring me better treatment upon the road, if nothing else; for the Mexicans invariably treat their more important prisoners with the greater deference.

The same paper contained several stirring appeals, both in prose and verse, to the known patriotism and valour of the citizens of Chihuahua! An immediate invasion of Texas was urged, with all the force that can be infused through the Spanish language into a war proclamation. To drive the usurping Texans from a soil which did not belong to them, to sweep them from the face of the earth as with a whirlwind, was set down as the easiest thing imaginable, especially when the oft-tried and impetuous bravery of the Chihuahua soldiers was brought to bear upon them. When it is considered that the inhabitants of that city are really prisoners within their own walls, hardly daring to venture outside on account of the hordes of Apache and Camanche warriors continually prowling in their vicinity, the idea of an invasion of Texas from that quarter is somewhat ludicrous. But the editor had seen evidences that the Texans were not absolutely invincible; he had seen some three hundred half-starved prisoners from that country marched by his doors, and his long-pent-up and furious wrath found vent, on paper, in a laughable tissue of bombast and gasconade. The same paper, too, contained a stirring appeal from some poetical correspondent to a favourite gray horse, imploring said horse to start immediately with him to the bloodstained prairies of Texas, and when there to ride down, run over, and trample under foot the Texan heretics until not even one was left. Of the two, I am strongly inclined to believe that the animal was much more ready to undertake the perilous journey than the man.

From conversations I have had with several American merchants, who are engaged in the Santa Fé and Chihuahua trade, and who visited the United States during the summer of 1843, I have learned the movements of Lewis since the capture of the expedition. On his arrival at Santa Fé the foreigners treated him with much coolness and distrust, convinced that he had acted badly, although not aware of the extent of his treachery. No positive insults were offered him, but Lewis was soon led to imagine that his countrymen suspected him of some agency in inducing Colonel Cooke to surrender, and with this belief he quietly and secretly started for Chihuahua. This city, in which he had lived several years, he entered in the night, and at once presented himself to one of his former intimate friends and associates. The meeting, so far as the latter was concerned, was far from cordial—the whilom friend of the traitor had heard of his perfidy, and at once advised him to leave Chihuahua if he would escape the just indignation of the foreign population.

But Lewis could not or would not believe that a mark had thus been set upon him, and accordingly, on the following morning, openly walked the streets, apparently resolved to retreat no farther, but brave public opinion on the spot. While a clerk in the place, he had gained the good-will and esteem of the residents, many of whom were still there, and when, in company with the brave but unfortunate Howland, he had left to join the revolutionists in Texas, somewhere about the year 1835, no one bore a better name or reputation; now, the tables were turned. His former associates treated him coldly and with suspicion, either cutting him directly, or plainly manifesting that all their former confidence and friendship were lost. Lewis saw and felt this, and that very evening was on the road to the Pacific.

His bad name, however, had travelled faster than himself, for, arrived at Guaymas, he found the same coldness and distrust on the part of the foreign residents—the mark, even here, was upon him. His advances were repulsed, his society avoided, and as if to flee from himself, he embarked for the Sandwich Islands. From thence, under an assumed name, he is known to have sailed for Valparaiso, or some other port on the South American coast, and since then nothing farther has been heard from him.

Judging from his previous conduct, I cannot believe that Lewis was aware of the enormity of his offence until he saw the disposition made of Colonel Cooke and his former friends and associates by Armijo. He did not lack good sense, but he lacked resolution—a fact which the quick eye of Armijo at once saw, and which he immediately turned to his own advantage. In Lewis he found an instrument upon whose fears he could play, and by threats probably converted him into a tool wherewith to work his treacherous and cowardly schemes. On awaking to a full realization of the extent of his crime, the same lack of resolution prevented Lewis from seeking to undo the black web of treachery in which he was entangled, but rather induced him to the commission of farther acts of a like nature and of almost equal atrocity. How often does the heedless first offence lead to the commission of well-matured and more heinous crimes—crimes at the bare thought of which the perpetrator would at first revolt with horror, but which he soon deems necessary to cover the original sin and fortify his present precarious position. So it is in nine cases out of ten, so it was with Lewis: but I must leave this dark subject, and return to the *Salon los Distinguidos*.

On the evening of the 26th of November, we were visited by a lively, chattering little French woman, who came accompanied by a pretty and intelligent Mexican girl, a native of the place, and belonging to one of the first families. The former was some twenty-eight or thirty years of age, not handsome, but extremely *naïve* and entertaining, and speaking four or five languages with much fluency.

Her visit lasted nearly an hour, during which she ran on with the greatest volubility—evincing no little emotion at the recital of our sufferings, and then laughing merrily as some ludicrous circumstance would be related. She gave us a short history of herself—a history which showed that her life had been eventful. She had travelled the world over, and finally had settled down at that most out-of-the-way place, Chihuahua. There she was assisting her husband, a German druggist, in his shop, and teaching music and the languages to the rising generation of her own sex. She talked to us and appeared to look upon us as her countrymen, and this is the light in which we were held by all the foreigners whom we encountered in Mexico. The kindest feelings were manifested towards us by the English, Irish, and Scotch, and also by the French and Germans we met on our sorrowful journey. They manifested the liveliest emotions of pity at our unfortunate situation, and extended to us a sympathy that appeared to spring from genuine fraternal feelings.

Our departure from Chihuahua was fixed for the next day after the interview with the little French woman, a fact we had no sooner learned than we set about making preparations for the long journey. A young merchant from Massachusetts offered me every assistance in the way of money, clothing, or necessaries. Of the former I had a sufficiency; but not wishing to expend it, I accepted his kind offer so far as to purchase some clothing, chocolate, *piloncillos*,* and other little luxuries for the road, for which I gave him drafts. Doctor Jennison gave each of the Texans a pair of shoes and a tin cup, and in addition to this a large supply of clothing and blankets was purchased of an American merchant for the use of the Texan soldiers, besides several mules for the officers to ride. For these, drafts on the Texan government were given by General McLeod and Mr. Navarro. The situation of all the prisoners was materially improved by this seasonable supply, and the long journey to Mexico still before us was robbed of many of its terrors by the fact

---

* The *piloncillo* is a small loaf of coarse brown sugar, manufactured in the middle districts of Mexico, weighing some pound and a half. I think I have given the word the correct spelling.

that we were now in a condition better to encounter its hardships.

After partaking of an excellent dinner on the 27th of November, provided as usual by Mrs. Magoffin, we took our leave of Chihuahua and our kind friends. I cannot depart from this city, however, without relating one little circumstance which did not help me forward much in the estimation of the more ignorant among the native inhabitants. Some old meddling busybody of a Mexican, whose name I have now forgotten, got up a small breeze of excitement by saying that in the paper I published at New-Orleans I had called the great Mexican people a nation of brutes—quadrupeds was the term he used. I had no recollection, at the time, of ever having applied any such term to the people of Mexico, but thought that if ever the opportunity occurred, I most certainly should, at least to a portion of them. I should be loath to insult the larger part of the brute creation by comparing them with the inhabitants of New Mexico, always making a few honourable exceptions. The hyenas, wolves, and jackals can find innumerable kindred spirits on two legs north of El Paso del Norte, and many of them even south of that place. But to return to our departure from Chihuahua.

Mr. Navarro had a brother-in-law, a colonel in the Mexican service, who had sent an order to a friend in Chihuahua to furnish him with a carriage and pair of mules. A Mexican officer had informed our little party that we were to be furnished with transportation as far as Cerro Gordo, a small town some two hundred miles distant; but on starting we found that he had disappointed us, and that we were again to proceed on foot. The horse furnished me by the kind-hearted cura of El

Paso was completely worn down and unable to travel, and I determined to purchase another if possible.

The entire population of the place turned out to see us off, the streets on both sides being lined, as usual, with the lower orders of men, women, and children. The foreigners, too, rode out some little distance, and I had an opportunity of seeing nearly every one of them, with the exception of the gentleman who had furnished me with clothing. We were to proceed but a few miles the first evening; I therefore asked one of the Americans to inform my friend in the city that I was in want of a horse, saddle, and bridle, and at the same time desire him to send them out early the next morning. This he promised to do, and then bade us farewell.

At dark we encamped by the roadside, and at a place where there was neither wood nor water. The night was extremely raw and cold, and we were again compelled to take lodgings upon the ground; but as we were now well provided with clothing and blankets, our situation was far more comfortable than even between El Paso and Chihuahua.

Early the next morning a servant arrived from my friend in town, bringing me a strong and very serviceable Mexican pony. He was wild and frisky as a mustang at my first approach, performed a variety of unseemly antics, and for some time manifested a set determination not to allow me the innocent little familiarity of bestriding him. A ragged, grim-visaged Mexican, with an expression of countenance sinister enough to frighten any well-bred animal from his propriety, would walk directly up to and mount him without the least trouble; but the moment I undertook such a liberty he would sheer off, jump and kick about "like mad," and keep such distance between us as a twenty-foot rope would admit. At one time he wound me up in the rope, threw me down, and came near injuring me seriously; and it was not until I had made repeated efforts that I succeeded in reaching the saddle. Once there, I permitted him to show off his eccentricities *ad libitum;* but after snorting, shying, rearing, pitching, dancing, and capering about for some five minutes, and whirling in circles, much to the amusement of a score of half-clad Mexicans, he finally cooled down into an easy, mincing pace, and I ever after found him a very well-behaved and extremely serviceable animal. I have just remarked that the Mexicans were amused on my first effecting a lodgment upon the back of the horse. In truth, it was my first appearance in one of their saddles, and my horsemanship probably partook more of the awkward than the graceful on the occasion. At all events, I did not feel that perfect security which is agreeable as I mounted upon a saddle of a shape I was entirely unused to, with a horse under it displaying a variety of anything but gentle antics and curvettings. I attempted to act with perfect indifference, but I am far from denying that I had serious misgivings all the while, lest by some extra feat of the horse I should be compelled to leave him in that unceremonious manner which is generally styled, among jockeys, "being thrown."

To one unaccustomed to the Mexican saddle it is extremely awkward, and far from being easy at first; but when once habituated to its use, it is almost invariably preferred to those of English or American manufacture. The rider has more command over himself, sits easier and steadier, and is far less liable to be thrown. The one I purchased with the horse, at Chihuahua, I rode to within twelve miles of the city of Mexico, and on afterward mounting an English saddle I felt unsteady, and like being thrown from it every moment. For the horse and saddle I gave a draft, written upon a piece of paper resting on my hat, and oddly enough, this draft, with others I gave the same person while in Chihuahua, reached the city of New-Orleans on the very day I myself arrived: while I travelled by way of the city of Mexico, subject to slight detention upon the road, the draft came by way of Santa Fé, the immense Western Prairies, and St. Louis—in all a distance of nearly four thousand miles.

On the night of the 28th of November, and an extremely cold night it was, we reached El Ojito, a poor hacienda where we could obtain no accommodations in-doors. We passed three or four wagons during the day, loaded with piloncillos and dry goods, on the way from Parras to Chihuahua. The drivers of these wagons were Americans, stalwart and robust men, who had strayed thus far by way of Santa Fé. They informed us that Colonel Cooke's party were some three weeks in advance of us, and taking the road towards Durango; well treated on the road, and generally in good health. They manifested no little astonishment that so large a party of Americans had been taken prisoners by a population so contemptible as that of New Mexico; but when we informed them of the treachery of Lewis, and our previous starvation and sufferings, they appeared better to understand the matter. After a conversation of some ten minutes with these men, we were forced to pursue our journey.

The night of the 29th of November we passed at another small and poor rancho, the name of which I have forgotten. On the afternoon of the next day we reached the village of San Pablo. The inhabitants, numbering some ten or twelve hundred, all flocked out to see us on our approach, for the officer who now had charge of us, a dapper little major of the redoubtable Chihuahua militia, had heralded our approach by the clangour of two badly-blown trumpets. He was a proud and ignorant fellow, extremely fond of display, and I have no doubt honestly thought himself a very great man. Our old friend Ochoa was still with us, however, acting as a man-of-all-work, and from him we invariably received every kindness and attention. I have entirely forgotten the little major's name, else I might make farther mention of him, and the many annoyances we were subjected to while under his charge.*

On one side of the principal plaza of San Pablo, which was entered through a large and heavy gate, Ochoa had provided rooms for the principal officers and merchants, while the men were compelled to occupy the centre of the square, with no shelter from the weather. This was the case on nearly the entire march, the men

* This petty little tyrant frequently beat his own men most unmercifully with the flat of his sword, and almost invariably without provocation. The half-clad, sandalled, and ill-fed wretches stood in continual fear of him, while from Ochoa they experienced the kindest treatment and all becoming respect. I never saw the latter strike but one man, a New Mexican horse-thief, who doubtless well deserved the severe castigation he received. While journeying between El Paso and Chihuahua we met a party of New Mexican traders on their way from Sonora to Santa Fé. One of them was mounted upon a miserable hack, raw-boned and rough-coated, and to give the horse an additional forlorn appearance, his mane and tail had been close shaved. The unhealed mark of a fresh brand was also seen upon the animal—a mark which not one of us would have noticed, but which the eagle eye of Ochoa at once detected. The fellow was commanded to halt, half a minute's examination convincing our captain that the fresh brand had been placed over a former mark. Another minute was sufficient to assure Ochoa that the horse had been stolen, and that he was really the property of the government in disguise. The thief was instantly dragged from the animal, and the next moment a shower of blows from Ochoa's sword was falling upon his back. With perfect indifference did we look upon this scene, and I doubt whether a single Texan prisoner would have shed a tear had the New Mexican horse-thief received a blow at every step between El Paso and Santa Fé.

sleeping in the open air except in the large cities, where convents or other spacious buildings could be obtained for their reception. Generally, I am inclined to think, the Texan soldiers had the best of it. They suffered occasionally from the cold; but nine times out of ten the officers found their rooms overrun with fleas and chinches, besides innumerable other vermin, the names of which I do not care to mention. Little did I think, on first leaving the United States, that my vestments were ever to afford harbour and shelter for swarms of insects of the most loathsome description; but imprisonment and misfortune bring strange companionships. They enabled me to get a practical knowledge upon entomological subjects, of which before I did not understand even the theory.

While at San Pablo, Mr. Falconer and others expressed a wish to purchase horses for the journey. But a few minutes elapsed before several nags were paraded in the square, their Mexican riders mounting, spurring, and showing them off in every pace and to every possible advantage. At this game the Mexican jockey is far more expert than his brother of the same calling even in Yorkshire or Yankeeland. Mr. Falconer, after having tried several, finally made choice, as was his wont in the selection of horseflesh, of a discreet and very well-behaved animal, for which, with a saddle and bridle, he paid twenty-four dollars. The nag was considerably advanced in years, set in his ways withal, and notable for taking a jog to suit his own convenience, regardless alike of whip and spur and other incentives to rapid locomotion; but then he was fat and strong, and as his purchaser chose him rather for use and comfort than show or fancy, he made an excellent bargain. Two or three other ponies were purchased at the same time, and at prices varying from ten to fifteen dollars apiece, the purchasers having obtained small loans of money while at Chihuahua.

Leaving San Pablo early on the morning of the 1st of December, we were enabled to reach Saucillo the same night, although the distance was more than ten leagues. The only business carried on at Saucillo is the manufacture of lead, there being a mine of that mineral in the immediate vicinity. There are but few inhabitants, and they are wretchedly poor and ignorant.

At this place the plan of an escape was agitated by a number of the bravest spirits among our officers and men, and although opposed by others, was finally determined upon. The plan was to seize upon the guard the next morning, shortly after starting, disarm them at once, and then make a forced march for the Rio Grande. It failed from a want of unanimity, and from the impossibility of inducing every person to keep the station assigned him. Our guard usually marched on either side of us, and although they were tolerably well armed, we outnumbered them. We could have seized upon and disarmed them with the greatest ease, and probably not a man would have been killed on either side in the scuffle; but it is extremely problematical whether any of the Texans would ever have reached home had the plan been carried out. Between us and the Rio Grande ran a ridge of bold, steep, and in many places impassable mountains; the plains were covered with thick and scraggy thornbushes, rendering the travel extremely slow and painful at every step; the exact route and distance were unknown to any one, and there was no certainty that water or provisions could be found on the route. I have enumerated but few of the difficulties to be encountered, and from what I have since learned of the country between our road and the Rio Grande, by the route we should have taken, I am led to believe that hardly a man would have got through alive.

Mr. Navarro opposed the scheme, and mainly by reason of his opposition it fell through. He was so lame that he could neither walk nor ride on horseback, and it was utterly impossible to go with his carriage across the rough and broken mountains. His own destruction would have been inevitable, and this he told the men. He farther stated that not a man, with the single exception of himself, would be detained six months in Mexico; that we should endanger the safety of Colonel Cooke's party by an escape, and be certain to bring about his own death, as the exasperated Mexicans would shoot him on the spot. Few of our men believed his words; but, as matters have since turned out, the old gentleman spoke with a spirit of prophecy—he alone has been kept in prison at the city of Mexico, while all the others have been liberated.*

During the night we spent at Saucillo a man named Larrabee died in one of the carts. He was the same person whom Major Howard had pursued upon the prairies, mistaking him for an Indian, and it was said that poor L. never got over the fright of that singular chase. When first discovered in the morning, the body of the man was perfectly cold; but Captain Ochoa asked Dr. Whittaker, our surgeon, to examine him, and see

* The attempt since made by the prisoners captured at Mier, in which both Brenham and Fitzgerald were killed, proves, beyond doubt, that we must either have been all retaken or have starved to death. The Mier prisoners were successful in securing all the arms of their guard after a short struggle, and this, too, at a point much nearer and more accessible to the Rio Grande than ours at the time of our contemplated escape. The former were finally retaken, half starved, in the mountains, and what were left after a barbarous decimation were marched to the city of Mexico, ironed, and compelled to work in the streets.

if he was "*dead enough to bury!*" Singular as was this expression, I believe I have given the captain's own words. He had heard of the horrible barbarities practised between San Miguel and El Paso—knew that the ears of some of our unfortunate comrades were cut off by Salezar before they were yet dead, and that their bodies were thrown by the roadside unburied, to be devoured by wolves—he had heard all this, and the kind-hearted man was anxious to pay every respect now that one of the prisoners had died while he had charge of us. Poor Larrabee was buried by the roadside at Saucillo, and sorrowful enough were the faces of those present at his funeral; but the eyes of kindred, of those who would have bedewed his grave with tears, were far from the scene.

After a tedious day's march, we reached, just at night, a corn-field near La Cruz, and here encamped. During the evening we were visited by a young lad from a rancho close by, who brought with him a harp of his own manufacture. He had learned to play upon this instrument without a teacher, and although he could not be more than ten or twelve years of age, his execution was really good, and his style that of a master. The Mexicans generally are extremely fond of music, and great numbers of the men can strum the mandolin, a species of small guitar, and give the rude airs of the country with much skill and effect. They play from the ear alone—not one in a hundred of them, in all probability, could tell a note of music from the hieroglyphics on some of the old ruins of his country.

About noon, on the 3d of December, we arrived at Santa Rosalia, a pleasant town situated upon a pure, swift-running stream of water. As was universally the custom, the entire population—men, women, and children—assembled in the streets through which we passed, and gathered in great numbers in the plaza where we were ordered to encamp. We had scarcely halted, before the alcalde arrived and invited our little party of officers and merchants to a dinner at his own house. He was evidently a poor man, and his dinner was far from being as sumptuous as many I have seen; but we were waited upon by his two daughters, one of whom was a blooming, blushing, bouncing girl of sixteen, and the *tortillas* and *frijoles* held out until all of us were satisfied.

Next morning, and just as I had saddled my horse, a couple of Mexicans stepped forward and claimed him as belonging to them. They said that he had been stolen some two months before, and after proving property, were about taking him off without paying me any of the charges or expenses I had been at on his account. I appealed to Captain Ochoa, and told him the circumstances of my purchasing the horse of an American friend at Chihuahua. That the animal belonged to the two men who claimed him there was not the least doubt—they pointed out brands, marks, and numbers, and proved the fact of his having been stolen, by a statement under the *alcalde's* own hand and seal—but Captain Ochoa decided the case in my favour, told me to mount him, and turning to his owners, gave them leave to whistle for their property, or look to the person who had sold him to me. I am far from justifying the decision of Captain Ochoa, although I profited by it; I only mention the circumstance to show that the military power in Mexico tramples upon the civil—that there might makes right.

I was extremely fearful that the fellows would follow us and steal back their property; but Captain

Ochoa placed a special sentinel over the horse at night—had it not been for this watchfulness, I should probably have found myself on foot the next morning.

By making an early start from Santa Rosalia on the 4th of December we were enabled to reach a small rancho before nightfall, encamping in the open field near the roadside, for we had no desire to enter the miserable adobe huts of the inhabitants. Immediately in the rear of the place stood four or five crosses, new and recently put up, marking the places where that number of the little population had been killed by the dreaded Apaches some week or two before.

The traveller on the great thoroughfare between Santa Fé and the city of Mexico, in fact on every road throughout the country, meets numbers of these rude wooden crosses on every day's journey. Whenever a man is murdered his friends erect a cross, and frequently the name of the murdered person is cut with a knife upon the transverse part, together with his age, the date of his death, and any little circumstance of note attending it. Around the foot is a heap of small stones, brought thither by friends; and the importance of the murdered person, as well as the number of prayers which have been said for his repose, may be learned by the size of the pile. Many stories of romantic interest were told us, by our gossiping guard, of these roadside graves and their occupants, but I have now forgotten them. Should the traveller treasure up all the strange tales, wild legends, and superstitious traditions related to him in Mexico, he would soon have his head full. For the most part they are entirely destitute of foundation, for the Mexicans have very fertile imaginations, and are sadly addicted to dealing in the marvellous and romantic.

## CHAPTER IV.

Arrival at Guajuaquilla.—An Invitation.—Inhospitable Hospitality.—A little Mexican Lawyer.—His Self-importance.—A disagreeable Night.—Our Companions fare better.—Again on the Road.—Rejoicing at Guajuaquilla. —Tricks of a Wag.—Amusing Anecdote.—Montezuma's Brother.—Arrival at El Rio Florido.—General Pike.—The Hacienda of La Noria.—Its former Wealth and present Condition.—Inroads of the Apaches and Camanches. —A young Irishman.—Visited by pretty Girls.—A well-informed Mexican Lady.—Musical Soirée and Dancing.—Change of Scene.—Arrival at Cerro Gordo, in the State of Durango.—Our new Commander, Colonel Velasco, pointed out to us.—His sinister Appearance.—Visited by a French Woman. —A Fandango and Cock-fight.—Departure from Cerro Gordo.—A general Turn-out of the Inhabitants.—Suspicions in relation to Ochoa's Integrity. —Our new Guard of Dragoons.—Their Treatment of the Prisoners.—Honourable Conduct of Ochoa.—A roadside Camp.—Colonel Velasco's Character begins to develope itself.—Excellent Provisions provided.—Large Droves of Horses passed.—An immense Hacienda.—Former Wealth of the Proprietress.—Condition of the Peons, or Working Classes of Mexico.— Farther Insight into the Character of Velasco.—The Texan Officers allowed their Parole.

The night of the 6th of December was passed, agreeably enough, by a majority of the prisoners, at the town of Guajuaquilla, a place of no inconsiderable note in this section of Mexico—but a small party of us were made extremely unhappy by the misnamed hospitality of a whipper-snapper of a lawyer. When within five miles of Guajuaquilla, this little fellow rode up from a rancho near the roadside, and after selecting General McLeod, Messrs. Navarro, Falconer, Van Ness, and myself as his victims, invited us, with much importance, to his dwelling close by, at the same time promising the little major who had charge of us that he would be responsible for our appearance on the following morning. There was something haughty and repulsive in the aspect of the man, and I should have preferred taking the chances of procuring a good dinner and lodging in Guajuaquilla; but we were all obliged to accept his proffered hospitality, and I have little doubt the fellow thought he was doing us great honour and conferring a high favour by inviting us to his house. Be this as it may, he made us very uncomfortable.

At home, we found him a vain, pompous, talkative braggadocio, with a very limited education, and not the least real knowledge of the world. He did not think so himself, of course; but he thoroughly convinced us of the fact by his desperate endeavours to elevate himself in our opinions. He recounted the different offices he had held—said that at one particular time he was a colonel of the militia, an alcalde, a lawyer, and a judge —and that he had put seven men in the stocks in one single day, for daring to disobey his orders. As he thus ran on, he raised himself on tiptoe at every fresh demonstration of his own importance and power, and being naturally but about four feet and a half in height, seemed endeavouring to elevate himself to the ordinary standard of humanity. He gave us a miserable dinner, worse chocolate in the evening, a shuck bed to sleep upon, a breakfast in the morning which would have been spurned by a dyspeptic Grahamite, and then had the cool impudence to ask us if we had ever been treated so well before, and hoped that we might recollect him. I can assure him that he has not been forgotten. In almost every instance where we were invited to the houses of the Mexicans of the higher order, we found them gentlemanly in their deportment and extremely good livers —the little coxcomb I have just mentioned was a signal exception.

After our scanty breakfast he accompanied us into the town, where we found that our companions had passed a very agreeable night. They had been extremely well lodged, and had been invited to a fandango attended by all the beauty of the town. This incensed us more than ever against our ignorant, conceited, and mean-spirited host, but there was no help for it.

Shortly after the arrival of our little party in Guajuaquilla, the march was resumed. The journey that day was short, as we had reached, before noon, a noted stopping-place, where there was a spring in a grove of cotton-wood trees. After sundown it was evident enough that there was a great rejoicing in the town, where our main body had slept the night before. Rockets were seen shooting in the air, the report of muskets was heard, and everything denoted that the appearance of such a body of Texan prisoners was enough to arouse the patriotism of the inhabitants, and induce them to celebrate the unusual occurrence by fireworks and other demonstrations. The hand, too, of the little lawyer who had annoyed us the night before, was plainly to be seen in this outpouring of the public feeling; and I have little doubt he was very officious among squibs, India crackers, Chinese-wheels, blue fires, and sky-rockets. While I was enjoying what he called his hospitality he gave me his name. I did not think, at the time, that I should ever forget it; but it has entirely escaped my memory. I hope he will excuse me for not giving it in full, more particularly when he is informed that it is far from being an intentional slight on my part.

In a party so large as ours, numbering some hundred and seventy, and composed of persons from almost every Anglo-Saxon settlement under the sun, as a matter of course there were many originals—fellows up to all sorts of mad pranks, and ever ready to play off their tricks when opportunities occurred. Conspicuous among them was Captain H., a man with great powers of imitation, an inexhaustible fund of humour, and a dry manner of telling stories and playing off his practical jokes. Poor fellow! he is now dead; but the memory of his queer conceits still lives.

Among us, at the time, was a good-natured, easy, quiet sort of personage from the Western country, whom I shall call D. While nearly every one of the prisoners had picked up Spanish enough to "get along," as the saying is, D. never could learn the name even of the commonest utensil or article of food, and the same may be also said of Captain H. The latter, however, in mere fun, had induced D. to believe that he spoke the purest Castilian, and was always ready to interpret everything for him at a moment's notice. As a consequence, the most ludicrous scenes were of almost daily occurrence, and the translations of Captain H., while interpreting for his friend, would often drive from our minds the thousand melancholy reflections our forlorn situation could not but suggest. One or two little circumstances I will relate, which created great mirth at the time.

We were encamped in the plaza of a small town, the name of which I have forgotten, when a poor woman approached D. with two loaves of bread to sell. She had a reboso on her head, one end of which, drawn over her left shoulder, fell down in front. An infant, not more than three months old, was plainly seen resting upon her left arm, while the hand which held the bread was entirely concealed under the reboso. Addressing D. in Spanish, she asked him if he wished to purchase her bread.

"What does she want?" said D., turning to Captain H.

The latter knew just as little of the wishes of the woman as the former; but his ready wit at once saw that fun could be extracted from the circumstance. Mixing up, therefore, some half dozen unintelligible words—a speech of which D. knew as little as himself, and of which the poor woman was as ignorant as either—he mumbled them over as though addressing the Mexican in her own language. With an inquiring look she asked H. what he said, while he, without the least knowledge as to the meaning of her question, turned to D. with,

"She wishes to know if you don't want to buy that child."

"The unfeeling brute!" ejaculated D., evidently believing every word of his waggish friend. "Tell her 'No.' Tell her I've got a wife and three children already, and the Lord only knows how they are provided for. What upon earth does she think I want with her child?"

I turned away from the spot to conceal my laughter, as did several who were present, and who understood the joke. The perfect seriousness with which the wag carried the whole affair through completely deceived D., and I doubt not he really and honestly thought the woman wanted him to purchase her child.

But the anecdote to which I allude occurred on the morning when we left our encampment under the cotton-wood trees, the 8th of December. We had travelled but a few miles before we reached a large monument by the roadside, erected, a year or two previous, to the memory of some colonel in the Mexican service. On the side fronting the road was a long inscription in Spanish, detailing the services the occupant of the tomb had rendered in the Mexican Revolution, his exploits in ridding the country of the Spaniards, and his many heroic, patriotic, and virtuous deeds. While two or three of us were looking at the monument, the two actors in the scene above mentioned came up to examine it. Had the inscription been in Chaldaic, it would have been equally intelligible to either of them; but D. had the most implicit reliance in H. as a translator of Spanish.

"What is all that reading about, captain?" said D.

"On the monument there?" queried H., evidently studying some kind of speech.

"Yes, on the monument there."

"You want me to translate it, D., do you?"

"I do."

"Well, it amounts to this—Here lies the body of Montezuma's brother."

"His *what?*" said D., opening his eyes.

"His brother," coolly replied the imperturbable H., "who came to an untimely end, on the 15th of November, 1598, by the bite of a rattlesnake. This monument is erected as a testimonial of the high esteem in which he was held by *his aunt.*"

"His *aunt?*" inquired D., with emphasis.

"By—his—aunt!" answered the wag, slowly and deliberately uttering each word as though there could be no mistake about it.

This was too much, and I was obliged to put my horse into a brisk canter in order to reach a place where I could have my laugh out, without raising suspicions in the mind of D. that the whole thing was "got up" expressly for his benefit. Not a smile could be detected on the countenance of H. while he was giving his extremely free translation, and to judge from outward indications his friend swallowed every word of it.

That night we reached a small hacienda on the Rio

Florido, the place where General Pike left the main road when he was conducted through the interior of Mexico. From this point he was escorted out of the country by a detachment of Spanish troops, taking Saltillo, San Antonio de Bexar, and Nacogdoches in their route.

On the next afternoon we arrived at the old and well-known hacienda of La Noria,* where is a deep and never-failing well. From this well the immense herds of sheep, cattle, and horses raised on the estate are supplied, the water being drawn by two mules attached to an apparatus for the purpose. The hacienda of La Noria was formerly very wealthy, yielding a heavy revenue to its proprietor; but of late years the Camanche and Apache Indians have stolen large numbers of horses, cattle, and sheep, as well as grain, from the neighbourhood, and but a week or two previous to our arrival they had made a descent in the vicinity, killed three or four of the *peons*, or labourers, and carried off a large quantity of plunder. All over the States of Chihuahua and Durango the inhabitants live in continual dread of these savages.

At La Noria we met an Irishman, a lad of some eighteen or twenty years of age, who lived at a small village one or two leagues from the road. Two or three young ladies were also on a visit to the hacienda, having come expressly to see us. Their father was an Irishman who had settled early in the country, but their mother was of Mexican birth, and they could speak no other language than hers. All of them were pretty— one was extremely beautiful. She had the dark, expressive eyes, the long, silken lashes, and the rich bru-

---

* Signifying, in English, *the water-wheel*, or wheel by which water is drawn from a well.

nette complexion of her mother, while from her father her cheek derived that rosy, healthy tint, which seemed to gain something richer than its native charm when seen struggling, like sunlight, through the soft and beautiful brown of a Castilian skin. We at first supposed they could all speak English, but afterward ascertained that such was not the case. After spending an hour or two at the hacienda they went away, accompanied by their mother and the young Irishman, for their home at the village.

The lady of the house at La Noria was a well-educated woman, having spent some time at an academy in Durango. She also sang very well, and played upon the guitar admirably. When night came she gave us a fandango, which, before it ended, was turned into a musical *soirée*, and we really passed a very agreeable evening. She gave us several Spanish ballads with much feeling, and sang, in Italian, an aria from one of Bellini's operas, showing herself equally conversant with his music and his language. We had several very tolerable singers among ourselves, and from the song, mirth, and hilarity which prevailed, a spectator could not have supposed that we were prisoners in a strange land, and profoundly ignorant as to the fate that awaited us. So it was all the way through Mexico. One night we were enjoying ourselves with music and the dance—the next we were shivering over a scanty fire in the open air, and sleeping exposed to such inclemency as the ruler of the elements might see fit to bestow.*
The very night after the scenes I have described above

---

* Neither the Mexicans nor Indians, even where wood is abundant, build large fires. It is a common remark with the Indians, that the Americans make such large fires that they cannot approach near enough to warm themselves.

we were encamped upon a cold hillside within a couple of miles of Cerro Gordo, not a sign of human habitation in sight.

It was with feelings not a little excited that we entered the miserable town of Cerro Gordo the next morning. At this place Ochoa was to leave us, and we were to be consigned to a new guard. We were to enter a new state, too, that of Durango, and were ignorant as to the treatment we might receive from the governor. During our journey through the State of Chihuahua, a distance of some five hundred miles, we had been treated comparatively well; whether we were to find a continuance of such usage was a matter of great uncertainty, and hence our uneasiness.

As we were taken through the long street upon which the greater part of the town is built, our new commander, Colonel Velasco, was pointed out to us. At the time, I thought him the most unprepossessing specimen of humanity I had ever met with. He was dressed in a light blue roundabout or short jacket, with a small red cord along the seams and three rows of small silver-plated buttons in front, while his pantaloons were of cloth of the same colour, foxed with green morocco, to prevent his saddle from chafing and wearing them. He wore an enormous pair of whiskers, upon which he had apparently bestowed no attention, and his upper lip was disfigured or ornamented—I leave this point for my reader to decide—with a pair of huge, grizzly, coarse mustaches, which stuck out in almost every direction but the right one. His head was covered with a profusion of long, iron-gray hair, but partially covered by a small, rakish cap, drawn over his eyes as if to conceal any sinister expression they might have. Such is but an imperfect picture of the man who was to have charge of us, and not a person in our party could look at him without a shudder, or without thinking we had fallen into the hands of a second Salezar.

We were taken entirely through the town and confined in an old deserted building. Here, upon the walls, were the names of Cooke, Brenham, Frank Combs and others, written by themselves a short month previous. During the afternoon we were visited by numbers of the inhabitants, and also by a lively little French woman, who invited several of us to dine at her house. Her husband was dead, having left her a large property, and she evinced the greatest commiseration for our unfortunate condition, as well as a desire to alleviate it as far as lay in her power. At night several of us went to a fandango and cockfight, accompanied by two or three Mexican officers only as a guard. Everywhere we were treated with the greatest civility, and at a late hour we returned to our quarters and took up our hard lodgings upon the cold earth floor. There was something in our treatment, so far, that gave us some hopes we had fallen into humane hands; but whenever the picture of Colonel Velasco, with his mustaches, whiskers, and iron countenance, was called to mind, the hopes of being well used in a great measure vanished.

As some little preparation was necessary, in procuring bread-stuffs and other requisites for our journey, it was not until near the middle of the day on the 12th of December that we took up the line of march. We had been led to suppose that we were to be taken through Durango, the city of pretty women and *alicrans;** but

---

\* I believe that the city of Durango is somewhat celebrated for the beauty and talent of its women—I *know* that it is noted for the numbers and venomous qualities of its *alicrans*, or scorpions. Frequently, while travelling

as Colonel Cooke's party had gone by that route, we were ordered to proceed by a more easterly road. Before our departure, nearly all the officers of our guard who had accompanied us from Chihuahua came to take their leave of us, and bade us a kind farewell. Ochoa was not among the number, and as he owed several small sums to the Texan officers—money which he had borrowed at different places on the road—for the first time suspicions of his integrity were aroused. These suspicions were farther increased when the trumpet sounded an advance, and we were ordered to proceed.

The signal for our departure was also the signal for the entire population to rush to the street through which we were to pass, and as usual we found either side

through the State of Durango, were we regaled with Mexican stories of the swarms of poisonous alicrans which infest the capital. Of course I can say nothing of these insects from personal experience, not having been within thirty miles of the city which they inhabit; but if half the tales told me were true, the inhabitants must be kept in continual fear and much trembling on account of them. To children and to elderly persons the bite or sting of the alicran is said to prove fatal, while to the middle-aged they cause suffering the most intense. A bounty of some three or six cents—I have now forgotten the precise sum—is paid by the authorities for each insect secured, and according to some of the stories told us, no inconsiderable business is carried on in the way of catching and bottling the much-dreaded scorpions. As it may not prove uninteresting to many of my readers, I will quote a short paragraph in relation to these singular insects from the narrative of General Pike: "The scorpions of Durango are one of the most remarkable instances of the physical effects of climate I ever saw recorded. They come out of the walls and crevices in May, and continue in such numbers that the inhabitants never walk in their houses after dark without a light, and always shift or examine the bedclothes and beat the curtains previous to going to bed, after which the curtains are secured under the bed, similar to the precautions we take with our moscheto bars. The bite of these scorpions has been known to prove mortal in two hours. The most extraordinary circumstance is, that by taking them ten leagues from the city of Durango they become perfectly harmless, and lose all their venomous qualities!" Such are the stories told of the much-dreaded alicrans of Durango. Of their size and appearance I could learn little, save that they are an inch or more in length, have many legs, and move with much celerity.

thronged with a crowd of the most motley description—priests, robbers, peons, loafers, soldiers, half-dressed girls, naked children, high and low—all eager to obtain a last sight of *los Tejanos*. In the throng we observed many of the girls we had seen at the fandango the night before, waving their hands and murmuring their "*adios, caballeros*" as we passed. Our new guard was composed of about one hundred men belonging to Colonel Velasco's regiment. They were tolerably well mounted, it being a cavalry regiment, and known by the name of the "Frontier Guard of Durango." Their uniform is a blue woollen coatee or jacket trimmed with red, with velvet trousers of the same colour, and instead of a common cavalry cap they all wear a coarse, wide-brimmed wool hat, with a plate of tin some two inches in width entirely circling the crown. Their arms consisted of a carbine, slung to their saddles on the right and with the breech up; on the left side of the saddle is fixed a lance, to the end of which a strip of red flannel or woollen stuff is attached, which flutters gayly as they ride along; a heavy cavalry sword, which clatters at every movement of their horses, completes their equipment, for although a pair of holsters were attached to the pommels of their saddles, I never could see that they contained pistols. All were excellent horsemen, and at a little distance their appearance was decidedly showy and gallant; but a closer inspection convinces that they must prove ineffective men when hard blows and knocks and heavy service are required of them. They rode on either side of us in regular order, and evinced a degree of discipline far superior to that of the raw militia who had heretofore accompanied us; but they were old soldiers, and we augured very favourably as to our future treatment from their politeness, and the many little acts of deference which none but the veteran soldier exhibits to those whom chance may throw in his power. Throughout our long and tedious march we were almost invariably well treated by the regular troops, while the young and undisciplined recruits and raw militia were overbearing and insolent in their general deportment.

We had reached the confines of the town, and were about striking out into the open country, when a servant of Captain Ochoa came riding up in haste, and delivered a note and small parcel to Mr. Navarro. The note was written in Spanish, very courteously worded, and the purport of it was that Captain O. could hardly trust his feelings in bidding us farewell in person. He however sent his best wishes for our health and happiness while upon the road, and his hopes that we might be speedily liberated on reaching the city of Mexico. In the same note he stated that, in the parcel which accompanied it, would be found the different sums of money he had borrowed of our officers on the road, with a regret that he had been unable to repay them sooner. Nothing could have been more delicate or more gentlemanly than the tenour of this note. The clouds which had been rising over his fair fame were at once banished, and Captain Ochoa again stood out in the broad, clear light of an honourable man. I know not whether these remarks may ever meet his eye, but if they do, he will see that he has not been forgotten.

There being no settlement within some fifteen leagues of Cerro Gordo, we encamped, the first night, in a little mesquit valley, near a spring of water. Here the true character of Colonel Velasco began to develope itself. He asked the quantity of beef which had been given to each of the prisoners upon the march—apologized for the quality of that he ordered to be killed on the occasion—said it was the best he could procure at Cerro Gordo, and wound up by assuring us that, so long as we were under his charge, we should have the fattest meat and the best bread that could be obtained on the route, and as much as we wished for. Generally speaking, the character and disposition of a man may be read from his countenance; but in this instance we were all deceived. It may have been, however, that the huge whiskers and mustaches of Colonel Velasco completely hid all the better qualities of his mind as reflected in his face, for, unprepossessing as was his countenance, we ever found him a kind-hearted, gentlemanly officer, and disposed to grant us every indulgence in his power.

On our first day's journey from Cerro Gordo we passed a large number of horses and mules, herded on either side of the road in small droves not exceeding forty or fifty in each gang. The pasturage, as far as the eye could reach, was excellent, with no other trees than an occasional mesquit not much higher than a common thornbush. And here I might mention a fact which may not be generally known to my readers. Those at all conversant with Mexico know that it is far from being a wooded country; but few are aware of the extreme sparsity of trees to be seen while travelling through it, and more especially along the high table-lands. I have seen more trees in one day's travel in the United States than during a journey of three months through Mexico. In fact, every tree met with on the route between Santa Fé and the city of Mexico, with the exception of those which have been planted by the inhabitants, could be set upon twenty square miles in the United States and find a sufficiency of room to grow. The tops of some of the mountains are partially covered with stunted oaks, cedars, and pines, and from these the poorer classes and Indians make charcoal, which ever finds a ready sale in the larger towns and cities. They have no other use for it than to cook their food, fireplaces being nearly unknown after getting as far south as Zacatecas.

We were told, by some of our guard, that the horses we met during the day all belonged to a single hacienda, which we should reach on the following night. The Mexicans related stories that appeared almost incredible in relation to the former prosperity and richness of this hacienda, and the immense number of horses and mules owned at one time by its proprietor. They even went so far as to say, that but a short time prior to the Revolution no less than *three hundred thousand horses* were in the possession of the lady who was then the owner of the estate. Whether this story was true or false I am unable to say; but however incredible it may appear, the story is robbed of much of its extravagance when it is stated that her possessions extended some fifty miles on either side of the road.

Our second day's journey from Cerro Gordo was one of some twenty-five miles, yet we were constantly in sight of horses and mules. They were generally in droves of about fifty, each gang herded by a single Mexican, whose only business it was to see that none of them strayed away. Towards nightfall we reached a large hacienda by the roadside, an estate owned by the mistress of the immense tract upon which the horses were pastured. She is a widow, I believe; and although comparatively poor when the immense wealth of some of the former proprietors is taken into consideration, is still the owner of fifty thousand horses and mules, large herds of cattle and sheep, immense fields of corn and wheat, and has several thousand *peons* at her different haciendas.

To show the immense wealth of one of the former proprietors of this estate, who, like the present, was a widow, I will relate one little anecdote told us while we were there. A short time previous to that revolution which resulted in the separation of Mexico from Spain, and while the estate I have just alluded to was at the zenith of its prosperity, a regiment of dragoons arrived from Spain and landed at Tampico. This regiment was one thousand strong, and of course the men did not bring their horses with them. The colonel of the regiment happening to be a friend of the family of the wealthy proprietress, and well known to her deceased husband, she immediately sent him a thousand white horses as a present, for the use of his regiment. There was hardly a month's difference in the ages of these horses, and every one of them had been raised upon her estate. While we were there, a number of horses were brought to our encampment to be sold, and two or three were disposed of at prices ranging from seven to ten dollars—horses that would readily command from sixty to eighty dollars in the United States. A very well-made and showy bay, of fine action, and not more than five years old, was offered for twenty-five dollars. I am confident he would readily command two hundred dollars in any part of the United States.

And how, it will be asked, is the labour on this immense estate, and others of its kind, effected, and who are the workmen? I have already said that the mistress of the estate had several thousand peons or labourers upon its different branches, and to these unfortunate vassals, for they cannot be called by any other name, are the rich proprietors of Mexico indebted for all their wealth.

The Constitution of Mexico guaranties, to all classes and colours, the greatest liberty and equality—the poorest peasant is protected, by the glorious panoply of the law, from every infringement upon his personal liberty—and the most abject beggar in the land has rights and privileges which cannot be trampled upon by his neighbour, be he ever so powerful or wealthy.* So much for the law and Constitution in theory—the practice is an entirely different matter.

The traveller who visits one of the larger estates in Mexico, finds, in the centre of it, a village, or collection of houses, large or small in proportion to the quantity of land owned by the proprietor. Occupying the most conspicuous situation is the church, generally a strong stone building surmounted by a tower or cupola, with a clear, silvery-sounding bell. The interior is decorated, perhaps, with statues of our Saviour, the Apostles, the Virgin, and the patron saint of the hacienda, executed in wood, and frequently arrayed most fantastically; the walls are covered with wretched copies of Scriptural paintings. Close by the church is the residence of the haciendero, or owner, a massive, strong, roomy, but comparatively unfurnished dwelling, in one of the front apartments of which is his store. Here the poor peons purchase their liquor, their cigars, and the little cloth that furnishes their raiment, and at prices the most exorbitant. Adjoining this house are the *trojes*, or barns, where the produce of the estate is stored—strong, substantial buildings. Then come the rude adobe hovels of the common labourers, frequently having but one

* Such was the case while I was in Mexico : as the Constitution is changed, on an average, every six months, a different state of things may exist now,

room, in which the whole family, father and mother, brothers and sisters, sons-in-law and daughters-in-law, huddle together upon one common earthen floor.

And what relation do these people bear to the haciendero? They are many of them slaves—slaves to all intents and purposes, although they may enjoy a nominal liberty. A large proportion of them, probably, are in some way indebted to the proprietor, the law giving him a lien upon their services until such debts are paid; but most especial good care does he take that they never pay him their obligations so long as their services are in any way profitable. They are in his debt, and are kept so until age or infirmity renders their labour unproductive; then the obligation is cancelled, and they are cast upon the world, to beg, steal, or starve, as best they may.

Should some one of the peons, more active, ambitious, or enterprising than his fellows, chance to accumulate money enough to repay his debt and regain his liberty, how then? He offers his master the price of his redemption, but the latter, upon some flimsy pretext, refuses to take it—he has not yet done with the services of the vigorous servant. The latter flies to the alcalde for redress. The law is on his side, equity is on his side, but the functionary who administers them is very likely a creature of the proprietor, and will not listen to the case of the slave, be it ever so just. The latter attempts to purchase justice by a bribe, but he is outbid by the haciendero. The alcalde shuts his eyes upon justice, opens his hand to the longer purse of the proprietor, and the unfortunate serf is once more driven to bondage. Such, so far as I could see and learn, was the state of things at many of the haciendas we passed upon our journey. The immense wealth, which has fallen into the hands of the few in Mexico, has given them a power over the numerous and abjectly poor which amounts nearly to that of the English barons under the feudal system—never will there be a change in favour of the lower orders until a thorough and radical revolution takes place in the very natures of the inhabitants, or until the country falls into other hands.

To resume my narrative. On the 14th of December, our men now much improved and invigorated by the substantial and bountiful supply of food furnished them, we passed the Palo Chino, encamping at a hacienda a few miles farther on. It was at this place, the name of which I did not ascertain, that we had still farther reason to admire the conduct of Colonel Velasco. Calling the officers and merchants together, amounting to some eighteen or twenty, he told us that he had every confidence in our words, and that while in his charge we should be permitted to go where we pleased on our parole of honour. No guard was to accompany us—the only exaction he made, and even that was in the shape of a request, was that we should all be in attendance every morning when the trumpet sounded an advance.

From this time we enjoyed the greatest liberty. When night came, we could select any meron, at the place where we were halted, to sleep in, and could roam about at will. The same liberty would have been granted our men, but that among them were several drunken, worthless fellows, ever ready to abuse every privilege allowed them. The larger portion of the Texans were well-educated, intelligent men, possessing all self-respect; yet they were obliged to suffer from the bad conduct of a few of their associates in imprisonment.

## CHAPTER VI.

Arrival at El Gallo, or The Cock.—Singular Names for Towns.—A rich Silver Mine.—Scenes at a Fandango.—The Well of El Gallo.—Arrival at Dolores.—Guadaloupe.—The Prisoners reach Cuencamé.—A small Party of us quartered at the House of a Castilian. — Hospitable Treatment.—Strange Superstition in relation to a Statue. — Gullibility of the Poorer Classes. — We are turned over to a new Guard. — Selling a Watch. — La Señorita Juana.—Colonel Velasco takes leave of the Prisoners.—Captain Roblado.—Story in relation to him.—Superiority of the Bread of Cuencamé. —Our Departure.—Hacienda of Juan Perez.—Roblado, and his Treatment of an Alcalde.—A tedious March.—Arrival at San Sebastian.—Frightened Girls and wounded Dogs.—Freaks and Endurance of the genus Donkey. —Arrival at Saenea. — Picturesque Situation of the Town.—The Maguey Plant; its Uses and Abuses.—One Drink of Pulque sufficient.—A Gang of "Involuntary Volunteers."—Mode of Recruiting for the Mexican Army.—Rancho Grande.—Decay in Mexico.—An American Traveller.—Arrival at Fresnillo.—The Mines in the Vicinity.—Meeting with an Englishman.—The *Tienda del Gato.*—Stories and Egg-nog.—More "Involuntary Volunteers."—A Stage-coach, and Thoughts of Home.—La Caleta.—First Appearance of Small-pox among the Texans.

EARLY on the afternoon of the 15th of December we reached the small village of El Gallo, or The Cock.* It is situated at the foot of a rough and precipitous hill, on the sides of which, it was said, a rich vein of silver ore had just been discovered. This, I wish it to be understood, was but a Mexican story; I give my authority, lest some mining adventurer should be drawn to the spot in search of treasure, which probably has no existence, save in the imagination of the ignorant and gossiping inhabitants.

At night, a fandango was given at the house of the alcalde, attended by some half dozen of the prisoners as well as the very élite of El Gallo. One of the girls was

---

\* The Mexicans give queer names to some of their smaller towns. I recollect sleeping one night at the town of Wheelbarrow.

dressed in a yellow-white tunica, or modern gown, of French cut, and brought probably from the city of Durango. She undoubtedly wore it in honour of *los Señores Tejanos* and their customs; but there was no necessity of her punishing herself thus severely on our account. That she felt stiff, awkward, and ill at ease under the infliction of the frock was evident, and it would have been all the same to us had she appeared in the common loose dress of her countrywomen. There were others in the room arrayed with the usual Mexican regard to physical liberty and comfort, their easy and graceful movements forming a pleasing contrast to the constrained and straight-jacketish carriage of their companion.

The evening passed pleasantly away, and had a spectator, unacquainted with our true situation, been present, and seen the Texan officers dancing and waltzing with the Mexican señoras, he would not have suspected that we were prisoners. A dance, executed by a Mexican sergeant and one of the girls, afforded much amusement. The name given to it was *danza de la espada*, or sword dance, the difficult and dangerous feats of the sergeant completely eclipsing the tricks of any juggler of the sword-swallowing genus I have ever seen. That he would not only take his own life, but that of his brunette partner in the dance, seemed inevitable; for he cut and slashed about, fell upon his sword, balanced it upon his nose and eyes, and so pointed it at the breast of the girl, that we all felt relieved when the dance was over and ascertained that both had escaped unhurt.

This exhibition gave infinite delight to a score of girls of the poorer class, seated upon the floor at one end of the room. And here I would mention one circumstance, which must have been observed, but appears to have been forgotten or suppressed by all travellers and writers upon Mexico—the singular faculty the women have of bestowing themselves upon a floor. I have frequently seen a dozen girls seated upon a space too small for even three of any other nation. How they dispose of their nether limbs is a mystery—I only know that they group themselves so closely together, and sit so bolt upright, that one might imagine they had been cut in twain, and the upper portion placed upon the floor after the manner of so many barrels in a storehouse.

At El Gallo is a deep and clear natural well of warm water, from which the town is supplied. Like our negroes, the Mexicans can carry immense loads upon their heads, and processions of girls were seen passing to and from the well at all times, carrying large earthen jars with the greatest steadiness—not spilling a drop, even though the jars were filled to the brim.

The night of the 16th of December we spent at a poor rancho, the name of which I have forgotten. The next afternoon we reached the very wealthy hacienda of Dolores, where we saw a very pretty girl, and where we found every comfort. The night of the 18th we passed at the hacienda of Guadalupe, without any incident worthy of note occurring. On the 20th we reached Cuencamé, the largest town we had yet seen with the exception of El Paso and Chihuahua.

We had no sooner entered the plaza than a little Spanish merchant invited three or four of us to spend our time at his house. He was a proud and fiery little Castilian, fond of relating the exploits of his countrymen, but entertained us with the utmost hospitality and kindness. A very pleasant rest we were allowed at Cuencamé. Some of our officers, not liking the quarters provided for them, hired rooms in the town for the two nights we were to pass there, and during the day we roamed about the place, visiting the churches, cockpits, and tiendas with which it abounds. In the principal church is a singular curiosity, religiously kept and worshipped by the ignorant and superstitious inhabitants of the vicinity. It is nothing more or less than a rude wooden statue of our Saviour. The marvellous story related of it is as follows: Some centuries ago, when the good people of Cuencamé were surrounded and likely to fall into the hands of their enemies, this statue suddenly appeared in their midst, and by wondrous deeds of prowess gave them the battle and rescued them from their foes. The statue was then borne in triumph to the town, a niche set apart for it in the church, and from that day to this it has been held in especial reverence, and looked upon as the guardian and protector of the place.

It was not without regret we now learned that Colonel Velasco was to leave us, the jurisdiction of the State of Durango extending no farther, and his men being required on the northern frontier to guard the inhabitants against Indians. We knew, however, that his influence would have considerable effect upon the officer who was to take charge of the prisoners as far as Zacatecas, and this fact partially consoled us for the loss of one who had ever acted towards us with kindness and consideration.

The pert little Castilian with whom I was quartered had two or three pretty and well-dressed daughters, girls perhaps of sixteen, eighteen, and twenty years, one of whom saw my gold watch lying upon a table in our sleeping apartment, where I had accidentally left it. It was a pretty watch enough to look at, but the rough wooden statue in the adjoining church was just as good a chronicler of the passing hours, it having been injured in my fall before leaving Texas. The girl fell in love with it, however, and mentioned her ardent desire to become its possessor to her father, who hinted to Van Ness that he would be glad to purchase it for her sake. He approached this subject very delicately: I was an invited guest at his house, and his lofty Castilian pride revolted at the idea of asking me to sell him the article, or at all events he pretended that it did. Van Ness at once communicated to me the wish of our host, adding that he wanted the watch for one of his daughters. I had no desire to dispose of the trinket, but told my comrade to inform the Spaniard that he might have it for a hundred dollars. I thought the price would frighten our host out of all idea of purchasing, but its effect was quite the reverse. He immediately counted out the sum in good Mexican dollars, and with many protestations hoped I would excuse the liberty he had thus taken in asking a guest to sell his private jewelry. Considering the injury the watch had sustained, the price was far above its worth; still I was very unwilling to part with it. It had been my companion for several years; I had carried it thousands of miles, and had succeeded in saving it from the hands of the rascal Salezar. Yet I could not retract; and the next morning I saw the watch gracing the girdle of la Señorita Juana.

The morning after we reached Cuencamé Colonel Velasco called us together and took his leave, at the same time introducing the commandante of our new guard, Captain Roblado. The latter had a face even more sinister in its expression than that of Colonel V., and in this instance the actions of the man did not belie his features. He had been many years in the Mexican service, possessed naturally a sour and morose disposition, with a petulance and ill-humour he but half concealed, even if he attempted so to do. If one anecdote told of him was true, he certainly had no reason to entertain any uncommon friendship for the Texans. It was said that he had received a severe wound from one of Colonel Jordan's men, in the celebrated retreat of the latter from Saltillo, after having been treacherously betrayed into the hands of the Centralists by the Federal General Canales. In the retreat of Jordan, Roblado commanded a company of dragoons sent out to cut him off. By a single fire from the Texans, but little more than a hundred in number, some fifty or sixty Mexicans were tumbled dead from their horses, Roblado receiving a wound in the leg which crippled him for life. Although Colonel Velasco, his superior in rank, had ordered him to treat us with every civility, which order he obeyed to a certain extent, it was invariably with a spirit of reluctance.

The bread of Cuencamé is noted throughout Mexico for its whiteness and sweetness, and probably a better article is not made in the wide world. Of this Colonel Velasco ordered a large quantity for our use on the road, and he also ordered the fattest oxen to be purchased and killed on the journey. This was the man we had supposed a tiger in disposition, until his actions proved him a liberal, mild, and courteous officer.

Every preparation having at length been completed, we left Cuencamé on the morning of the 22d of December. We passed the first night at a poor rancho by the roadside, and the next evening reached the hacienda of Juan Perez. An American physician, a resident of some town near the city of Durango, had accompanied us the first day's march from Cuencamé. He could give us no other information in relation to

Colonel Cooke's party than that they had been tolerably well treated on the route they had taken.

After a long and extremely fatiguing march, over a gravelly and stony road, we reached a poor village late on the afternoon of the 24th. Many of our men were very foot-sore and completely tired out with the long march, so much so that they declared themselves really unable to pursue the journey on foot the next day. To allow them a day's rest was deemed utterly impossible by Roblado, and he immediately sent an order summoning the alcalde before him. That functionary soon appeared, when Roblado told him that he must provide a hundred jackasses for the use of the men. The alcalde replied that the place was extremely poor, and that he could not furnish more than ten of the animals required.

"I am a man of few words," answered Captain Roblado. "I want one hundred jackasses for the men to ride to-morrow. If they are not here by six o'clock in the morning I'll make a jackass of you, Señor Alcalde, pack you with the heaviest man in the crowd, and make you carry him to San Sebastian."

"Si, Señor," said the terrified alcalde, and the next morning the requisite number of animals were on the spot in readiness. Here was another instance of the supremacy the military power exerts over the civil in Mexico. Not a cent was paid the poor owners of the animals for services thus extorted, and Roblado manifested as little compunction on the occasion as a bear would while robbing a beehive. I will not give the man credit for having thus mounted our men through feelings of humanity, believing him to have been actuated by no other motive than that of getting us on as fast as possible.

Vol. II.—L

A tiresome march of some thirty-five miles, over a rough and uneven country, brought us to a dirty, miserable little hole which is dignified with the high-sounding name of San Sebastian. This place is situated in a small, sterile valley, amid barren hills, the only vegetation appearing upon their sides being a few stunted prickly pears and thornbushes. How the two or three hundred inhabitants obtain a living is a perfect mystery; in fact, they do not more than half live. Their little huts are built of small stones and mud, without doors or windows—they have neither chairs nor beds, nor in fact furniture of any kind—in fine, are infinitely worse off than Choctaw or Cherokee Indians, not only as regards clothing and food, but habitations and all the necessaries of life.

It was on Christmas day that we reached San Sebastian, and anything but "a merry Christmas" did we spend in the wretched hole. Many of us had intended to "keep" the day and night somewhat after the manner of our country, but we could not procure eggs and milk enough in the town to manufacture even a tumbler of egg-nog. We were therefore compelled to make our Christmas dinner of a piece of beef roasted on a stick, with no other than bread and water accompaniments.

While roaming about the town after nightfall, in company with one of our officers, and inquiring for milk and eggs of every man, woman, and child we met, we at length encountered a couple of half-dressed girls, standing within a few steps of one of the houses. We stopped, and were about to ask them if they had the articles we were in search of, when they set up a terrible scream, and scampered into the hovel as though frightened out of the little sense that had been vouchsafed them. Some half dozen starved curs issued from the doorless entrance and commenced yelping at us, and this appeared to be a signal for every dog in town to join the chorus. Fortunately for us, there was no lack of stones, of a suitable size for throwing, in the vicinity, and I am strongly inclined to believe that several of the barking whelps had good reasons for regretting that they had attacked us—one, I know, must have required careful and unremitting nursing before he could ever hope to raise another bark at a stranger.

On returning to our quarters, some half an hour afterward, we found that an exceedingly grave charge had already been entered against us by the relatives or friends of the frightened girls, the complainants informing Roblado that we had not only insulted but chased them, and that had it not been for their faithful dogs it was impossible to imagine where we might have stopped! This was too rich. We told Roblado the circumstances exactly as they occurred, with one exception: as there was a remote probability that the plaintiffs might obtain a bill for damages sustained by their dogs, we did not even hint to Roblado our knowledge of the virtue possessed by stones, or that either of us had ever thrown one in our lives. Thus ended our Christmas frolic at San Sebastian.

At an early hour the next morning we were on the road. I looked around me, as we filed through the narrow and crooked lane leading from the town, expecting to see an occasional dead dog, or a limping one at least; but the search was fruitless. A thousand open mouths were grinning, growling, grinding their teeth, and barking at us at every step—the killed and wounded had probably been provided for. Has any one of my readers, in his journeyings, ever noticed that the poorest towns and families always have the most and the meanest dogs? If he has not, I have, often.

We had proceeded a mile, or probably less, when suddenly one of our men was seen rising in the air, somewhat after the manner of a rocket, and then descending with even greater velocity. He had only been hoisted by one of those peculiar kick-ups which no animal but a donkey can give, but fortunately was only slightly injured. Many of the animals which had been pressed into the service by Roblado, although the forced contract with the alcalde extended no farther than to San Sebastian, were still retained to carry our more lame and infirm comrades; had it not been for this, many of them would have suffered dreadfully, as the march was nearly forty miles in length. How these animals sustain themselves is unaccountable; for they had nothing to eat for the thirty-six hours they were with us, and then had to retrace their steps over the same ground, and with the same nourishment. They stopped over night at San Sebastian, going and coming; but there was not food enough in the vicinity of that town to afford a respectable maintenance for a small flock of killdees.

Just at dusk we entered the town of Saenea, deep in a narrow but fertile and beautiful valley, which is bordered on every side by frowning hills and mountains. The location of this town, which contains some two thousand inhabitants, is picturesque in the extreme, and in addition it is one of the cleanest places we met with in the country. Here, for the first time, we saw the orange-tree in full bearing. Although we had been travelling for near a month in the latitude in which that delicious fruit arrives at perfection, the elevation of the table-lands we had journeyed over made the air too cold for it to thrive. At Saenea, too, we for the first time saw the celebrated *maguey* plant, from which *pulque*, the principal beverage of the country, is extracted. The process of gathering this fluid is by cutting off the centre shoot of the plant, in the hollow of which, holding about a pint, the pulque finds a basin. This little basin fills two or three times a day with the sap of the plant, which, after being slightly fermented, is drunk in immense quantities by the natives.

The process of extracting the sap from the basin is primitive, and not well adapted to make it palatable to all tastes. The person to whom this part of the business is intrusted has a long tube made expressly for the purpose, one end of which he inserts in the basin and the other in his mouth, and then, by exercising what is generally termed the power of suction, he draws the liquid from the fountain-head to his own. It next finds its way to some skin or trough, and after being allowed to ferment, is considered fit to drink. Foreigners become extremely fond of it after much use, and many of them drink it to even greater excess than the natives. For myself, one swallow was quite sufficient—I never tasted it a second time. Some of the Mexican officers insisted that it was very refreshing, and palatable withal, and pressed me to try another cup. I told them I had little doubt it was a very fine drink to those who liked it, but that it did not exactly suit my taste—and here the matter ended. To me it had the flavour of stale small-beer mixed with sour milk, and the odour of half-tainted meat as it approached my nose. Moreover, the system of hydraulics by which the suckers first extracted it was not altogether such as met with my approval. I am not sure that I should have taken a single swallow, had I not been assured that it had first undergone a ten days' fermentation.

Of itself, *pulque* is slightly intoxicating, but by distillation a very strong liquor is made from it, called *mescal*, or *aguardiente de maguey*. This is also a very common drink among the lower orders of Mexico, who are much addicted to intemperance. The soldiers will almost invariably get intoxicated upon mescal whenever they have the opportunity, regardless of the severe flogging they are certain to receive for the transgression.

The abuses of the *maguey* end with the *mescal*, but its valuable uses do not cease with the *pulque*. From its leaves, which are frequently eight or ten feet in length by one foot in width, not only thread but rope is made, both strong and durable. The fibrous part is first twisted into thread, which is useful for an endless variety of purposes, and this can at any time be manufactured into rope of any size. Immense plantations of maguey, where it is planted in rows some ten feet apart, and cultivated with great care, may be found in the vicinities of Guanajuato, Queretaro, Mexico, and Puebla, and yield large revenues to their proprietors.

As we were about starting from Saenea, some thirty miserable, half-dressed, and, to judge from their appearance, half-starved wretches, were taken from a prison adjoining our quarters and marched into the plaza. Who or what they were we could not imagine, but that they were arrant knaves and cut-throats was plainly visible in their countenances. The officer who had charge of them immediately produced a long rope, with shorter ropes attached to it at intervals of about a yard. Each end of these shorter ropes was made into a slip-noose, the distance of the noose from the main cord being eighteen inches or two feet. While we were alternately watching this singular contrivance and casting our eyes at the group of ragged wretches around it, the officer called upon one of them to advance to the head of the rope. His right arm was then drawn through the noose, the officer roughly pulling it tight. Another of the jail-birds was next made fast by his left arm to the opposite end of the short rope, and in this way the whole gang were strung together, and marched off under a strong guard directly upon our route.

On inquiry, one of the Mexican officers told us they were *volunteers*, on their way to the city of Mexico to join the army. The real truth was, they were convicts of the worst description, murderers and thieves, on their way to the capital to be manufactured into soldiers: yet abandoned as were these wretches, some of them had mothers and sisters who clung to them until the last, and were with difficulty forced away. With tears, they gave their vagabond sons and brothers the last remnants of tortillas and chile in their possession, and followed them with their eyes until lost in the distance. How strong is a mother's or a sister's love!

After being washed and cleaned up, and having uniforms put upon them, these convicts are drilled until they become familiar with the use of arms; but they can never make good soldiers. Our own men, who were in every way better treated, and guarded with far less strictness, made themselves not a little merry at the expense of the different strings of "*Involuntary Volunteers*," or "*United Mexicans*," as they were pleased to term them, whom we afterward met on our journey.

Immediately on leaving Saenea, our road led us up the steep sides of a mountain, difficult to climb, and of tiresome length. Once at the summit, however, we were partially repaid for our toil by the prospect below us. Cleanly and neatly built as was the town we had just left, and beautiful as we thought its situation while gazing from the plaza at the bold and rugged mountains on every side, distance now certainly lent an enchantment we had not perceived before. Irrigating canals were seen extending in every direction; small patches of maguey, with their long, coarse leaves, gave a picturesque air to the scenery; the orange groves, now concealing, now disclosing the dwelling of some more wealthy proprietor, were clad in richest foliage, and yellow with golden fruit, although January was about closing the doors of the old year; the whole scene was mellowed by the distance, and was one of that varied and subdued beauty seldom met with in other lands than Mexico.

Our march, in the earlier part of this day, was over a country broken by rugged hills, and desolate from lack of vegetation. In the afternoon, however, we came to a more level tract, and ere nightfall reached a large and wealthy estate known as the Rancho Grande, having on it a neat church, and a new and commodious *meson* for the reception of travellers. In all my journeyings through Mexico, I do not remember having seen any other house bearing the evident marks of recent construction, or a single dwelling in progress. All presented the strongest tokens of age—many were crumbling and tottering under the influence of decay. In that falling Republic the traveller sees no new towns springing into existence, no improvements in those that are already built, none of that bustle and activity which indicate a healthy state; but on the contrary, such of the villages and cities as are not stationary are going to ruin, and will continue to do so, slowly, perhaps, but surely, unless wars and revolutions cease, or the country falls into other hands. Of the former there is little hope; for such is the nature of the population, and so jealous, selfish, and ambitious are the men by whom that population is handled and governed, that no confidence can be placed in the stability of any form of government that can be set up.

At Rancho Grande we met an American, who informed us that Colonel Cooke's party had passed through the large mining town of Fresnillo about three weeks before, and that we should probably reach the same place the next day. The name of this American I do not recollect; I only remember that he said he was making his way out of Mexico as fast as a good mule would allow him, but the cause of his hot haste he did not mention.

As our informant conjectured, we arrived at Fresnillo early in the afternoon of the next day. It is a town containing some fifteen or twenty thousand inhabitants, has a large square with a costly fountain in the centre, and several large and showy churches. Within a mile are the celebrated mines of Fresnillo, among the most profitable, at the present time, in Mexico, if we were rightly informed. They are worked by steam, and the general superintendence is in the hands of Englishmen, although an American gentleman has charge of the hacienda. I have forgotten the revenue of this celebrated mine, which is owned by a Mexican family; but it is immense. The entire population of Fresnillo derive their support in some way from the mines; yet the most squalid poverty is to be met at every turn.

During the afternoon and evening we were visited

by several of the foreigners, and after dark a small party of us spent three or four hours very agreeably with a young Englishman employed about the mines. His residence was at some distance—too far for us to visit —but he appeared to be quite at home at the " *Tienda del Gato*," or Shop of the Cat—a singular name this for a confectionery or coffee-house, but such has the owner given it. In it was one of the largest cats I ever saw, and over the door was a painting which the proprietor informed us was a likeness of the animal. The painting was a most atrocious daub, and absolutely required some key to explain the intention of the artist. Had the animal within been a kangaroo or a grizzly bear, the strange figure over the door would have done as well for either as for the cat.

After being comfortably seated, our Englishman manufactured a generous bowl of excellent egg-nog. Over this, and with the usual accompaniments of smoking, story-telling, and anecdotes of travel, we passed a very pleasant evening, forgetting that we were prisoners in a strange land. Not until midnight did we return to the quarters provided for us at a meson, our acquaintance promising to see us before we set off in the morning. He said that the foreigners of Fresnillo had made up a liberal subscription for Colonel Cooke's party, and that they would endeavour to do something for the more unfortunate among our men.

Although many of the prisoners were worn down by our long and tiresome marches, we remained at Fresnillo but one night. Roblado said that Zacatecas was only some fifty miles distant, and that there we should be allowed a rest of two days.

Mexican-like, the streets of Fresnillo were thronged as we left it. The prisons of the place had been delivered of sixty or seventy convicts, hardened malefactors, whose very aspect showed a knowledge of every crime in the calendar. These were pinioned after the manner of those at Sacnea, attached to the same rope, and driven under a strong guard before us. Not the least notice did the inhabitants of Fresnillo take of these wretches—it was no uncommon thing with them to see their fellow-beings tied and driven like brutes to the shambles; but Texans they had never seen before, and to catch a glimpse at us they rushed, squeezed, hustled, and crowded the streets, their curiosity raised to the highest pitch.

I will say one thing in favour of the Mexican population generally—they seldom manifested any feelings of exultation in our presence. On the contrary, the mild and subdued eyes of the poor Indians were turned upon us invariably in pity, while the crowds through which we passed, in all the large cities, appeared rather to be actuated by commiseration than triumph or hatred, Jews and heretics though they thought and termed us. With all their bad qualities, the Mexican people, as a body, are kind and benevolent, and disposed to grant every favour and indulgence to strangers who have been unfortunate. Let it be understood that I am speaking of the lower orders, and consequently the mass. In a journey of over two thousand miles through the country, during which we saw many of the largest towns and cities, I do not recollect that we were publicly insulted on more than one occasion after leaving El Paso. This speaks much for the lower orders, when it is understood that they might at any time have practised many acts of insolence towards us with impunity.

On our first day's march from Fresnillo, a mail-stage passed us on its way to Zacatecas. It was manufactured at Troy, New-York, was of the same class as the stages in use in the United States, and as it rattled by, full of passengers, forcibly reminded us of freedom and of home.

At night we reached a poor rancho called La Caleta, where we stopped to sleep. Here one of our men, who had been complaining for two or three days, exhibited unequivocal symptoms of that loathsome disease, the small-pox. Eruptions appeared on every part of his body, he became partially delirious, and although we hoped that the disease might prove one of a lighter nature than appearances indicated, all were disappointed. It was small-pox of the worst type, and as there was no guarding against the infection, each one of our party could only hope that he might not become its victim.

## CHAPTER VII.

Approach to Zacatecas.—Tedious mountain March.—Picturesque View.—First Sight of Zacatecas.—Its singular Situation.—Specimen of Roblado's Vanity.—Entrance into Zacatecas.—Character of the Inhabitants.—Passage through the City.—Arrival at a deserted Mining House.—Miserable Quarters.—Permission obtained to visit the City.—Inquisitive Urchins.—Arrival at an Irish Restaurat.—A sumptuous Breakfast.—Visit to a New-York Gentleman.—A Stroll through Zacatecas.—Dinner at the Restaurat.—Invitation to another Dinner.—A goodly Company.—Painting of Washington.—A pleasant Evening in Perspective.—Unrealized Hopes.—Again at our old Quarters at the Mining House.—Mr. Falconer in Trouble.—Mexican Justice.—Dr. Whittaker's Mode of getting rid of a troublesome Sentinel.—Subscription raised for the Prisoners.—Liberality of a Mexican Lawyer.—Departure from Zacatecas.—Convent of Guadalupe. — Santa Anna, and his Fight with the Zacatecans.—Sack of the City.—Refugio.—Arrival at Ojo Caliente.—A Bathing Scene.—Customs of the Mexican Women, and their Fondness for Swimming.—El Carro.—Arrival at Salina.—A Kentucky Circus Proprietor.—His Adventure with Roblado.—The Mexican House of Entertainment, or Meson.—The Foreigner meets with but poor Fare.—Modes of living, and Customs of the Lower Orders of Mexico.

On the morning of December 30th we commenced ascending the high range of mountains to the northward of Zacatecas. A very good road winds up the sides, but the ascent was steep and tiresome. Small parties of women, driving asses and mules from market, were passed as we toiled up, and exhibited no little astonishment as they gazed at us.

On reaching the summit we had a fine view of the valley through which we had just travelled, the distant smoke of the mines at Fresnillo being plainly visible, with the numerous little ranchos we had passed. Before us, and on different points of the mountain-tops, the silver mines of Zacatecas were seen—many of them deserted, while others were still in operation. As we descended the mountain, the parties of market-women became still larger and more frequent. We continued our winding way down the sides until within half a mile of the city, wondering where a spot could be found for the habitations of men in a vicinity so wild; for mountain was piled upon mountain on every hand, with no other passes between them than yawning *barrancas*, or deep ravines. We could not believe that we were near one of the richest and proudest cities of Mexico, until a sudden turn in the road brought it fully into view, with all its domes, spires, palaces, churches, and convents. A more picturesque or grander spectacle can hardly be imagined than the city of Zacatecas as entered from the north. It appears to be hemmed in on almost every side by high and precipitous mountains, and of course has but scanty suburbs. The deep ravine in which it is built is filled with houses, even to the very base of the mountains, which seem, in many places, ready to slide and fall upon the town below them. The streets are not very wide, but are almost straight, and many of the buildings are of large size, handsome architecture, and costly and elaborate workmanship.

Before we entered the city a halt was called, for no other purpose than that Captain Roblado might change his ordinary fatigue-dress for a gaudy uniform, and mount a dashing bay horse upon which to "show off" at the head of a body of ragged Texan prisoners. With a loud blast from the Mexican trumpets we were then ordered to advance. Housetops, balconies, doors, and windows were filled with women and children on either side of us, and a crowd so dense thronged the streets that every exertion of the dragoons was needed to force a way through the ragged, dirty, and squalid mass. On many occasions the lower orders of this city have manifested great hostility towards foreigners, not a few unfortunate heretics, or Jews as they are more frequently termed, having been hooted and stoned from its gates; but latterly this hostility has in a great measure subsided, and not an insult was offered to us by a single individual. It may be that our forlorn and destitute appearance, and a belief that the government would punish us with the utmost severity, chilled any feeling of hostility into silence. Many of the foreigners on the road openly expressed their fears that we might be ill used and insulted at Zacatecas, but such was not the case.

We were taken completely through the city, passing numerous churches, convents, and palaces, besides the *mineria*, or mint. One of the buildings we passed was a large quartel, filled apparently with convicts destined to swell the ranks of Santa Anna's army; and the wretches gazed at us, as we went by them, with malicious looks. After going by the *paseo*, a large enclosure set with trees, we reached the outskirts of the town, and then, after climbing a steep hill, were marched into an old deserted mining-house, and locked up. Two mouldy, dirty rooms were set apart for our use, and even these were not sufficiently large to accommodate us all with shelter; but as Roblado would not allow us to go out of the place without permission from the governor, there we were obliged to take up our quarters for the night.

To show how uncomfortably we passed our first night at Zacatecas, I will describe the sleeping apartment in which I was allowed such space on the floor as I could cover with my person—no more. The room was about fifty feet in length, by twenty-five in width, destitute of windows, had a broken and uneven tile floor, and from having been long deserted, the walls were damp, mouldy, and fast crumbling to decay. No air found its way into this gloomy hole save through the door, and as the night was raw and cold, even this we were fain to close to protect those immediately around it from the piercing blasts. There were seventy of us in the room, all rolled up in blankets upon the floor; and when I add that many of the men were covered with every species of vermin, others suffering with distressing coughs, and one in the worst stage of that loathsome disease the small-pox, the reader is under no necessity of racking his fancy to imagine that we passed anything but a comfortable or pleasant night.

Early in the morning Van Ness obtained permission for Falconer, Doctor Whittaker, and myself to accompany him into the city, we all promising Roblado that the confidence he placed in us should not be abused. Scarcely had we entered one of the principal streets before we were surrounded by a gang of half-dressed urchins—inquisitive little fellows who jogged along on either side of us, and examined us as closely as they would so many strange beasts in a menagerie. As we passed the houses, the cry of "*Mira! mira! los Tejanos!*" would be heard from the women and girls, and then a general scampering and rush to the doors and windows to obtain a sight of our little party.

In order to get rid of the constantly-increasing crowd of boys, we quickened our pace, and after turning three or four corners, reached a large and well-conducted *restaurat* kept by an Irishman. This we entered, and immediately called for a breakfast such as we had not seen or tasted for eight months. It consisted simply of beefsteaks, mutton chops, boiled eggs, Irish potatoes, coffee, and claret—all simple and common enough—but then we had long been unused even to such a variety, and having a table before us, with chairs to sit in, and knives and forks to eat with, we did ample justice to our breakfast. The wife of our host, or female superintendent of the establishment—I am uncertain which—made her appearance just as we had finished our meal. She was a stout, fresh, red-cheeked Irish woman, wore a clean, flowing, and neatly-crimped cap, and as she was the first female I had seen since we left the frontiers of Texas who naturally spoke my language, I could not but regard her as my countrywoman, although she had a brogue as rich as that of the lamented Power in Pat Rooney.

Leaving the restaurat, I went to a German tailor and ordered such articles of clothing as I stood most in need of, and then had my measure taken for a pair of boots by a Mexican shoemaker next door. They were all to be delivered at our quarters at the old mining-house on the following morning, and the prices of the different articles were about the same as are paid in New-Orleans and other Southern cities of the United States—a trifle cheaper, perhaps. My next visit was to the office of an American gentleman, a New-Yorker, who showed me every attention and kindness. After writing several letters to my friends in the United States, we visited the different churches and public buildings of the town, attracting all the while not a little attention from the inhabitants, although no rudeness was offered us. The day was cloudy and raw, with intervals of rain; but regardless of this, we roamed about the place until dinner-time. I may here add, that from the day on which we left San Miguel, in October, to the time of which I am speaking—the 1st of January—we had not been annoyed by an hour's rain.

At two o'clock we again visited the restaurat and ordered dinner, selecting corned beef, cabbage, and the like plain "substantials," instead of the tempting knick-knackeries, decoy birds, and other luxuries that were hanging in profusion in the windows, or otherwise displayed with that ostentation so characteristic of eating establishments, as well in Zacatecas as in New-Orleans or New-York. How much have restaurat keepers, the world over, to answer for in the way of leading gouty gourmands and dyspeptic subjects into temptation by these window exhibitions!

We had scarcely finished our meal when a servant arrived with an invitation from a Mexican gentleman, a lawyer, to visit his house and partake of his hospitalities. We found dinner over when we reached the house, the servant having been searching some two hours before he found us; but at a table, covered with choice wines and cigars, we joined Mr. Navarro, General McLeod, and two or three Texan officers, besides a pair of fat, jolly priests, and in such mixed but goodly company we passed an hour very pleasantly. Our kind host was a distinguished advocate of the place, extremely liberal in his opinions, as were also the priests. In the centre of the library, and occupying the most conspicuous part of the room, was a well-executed painting of General Washington, enclosed in a splendid frame. Before we retired, our entertainer delivered a neat eulogy, extremely well expressed, upon the "Father of his Country," manifesting the high regard in which his memory was held. This little incident over, our party took their departure, leaving our friends still at the table.

## A SAD DISAPPOINTMENT.

After a ramble of some two hours, we once more repaired to the restaurat and ordered a luxurious supper, determined to make the most of our time and commence the new year as happily as possible—at least in the way of eating. We had scarcely finished our meal when a party of Mexican gentlemen invited us into an adjoining room to partake of wine with them. Shortly after, an English gentleman arrived from Fresnillo, with whom we had become acquainted there, and who insisted upon our supping with him. This pressing invitation we were compelled to refuse; but we joined him in a glass of wine. There was to be a splendid New-year's ball given that evening, to which we had received an invitation. Just as we were going to it, with full anticipations of finishing a delightfully-spent day by a ball at night, one of the officers of our guard, a bustling, fretful little Mexican, rushed into the room out of breath, and ordered us instantly to accompany him to our disagreeable quarters of the previous night. From his excited manner we could easily perceive that something had gone wrong, but the nature of his mission was not revealed until we had reached the gloomy prison, which we had determined not to visit until the following morning. The night was rainy and pitchy dark, the hill we were obliged to climb was steep and so slippery from the moistened clay that we could with difficulty make the ascent. Three or four times we fell sprawling to the earth while clambering to the summit; and it was not until we were all covered with mud, and wet to the skin, that we passed the portals, and the heavy gates of the old mining-house were locked upon us—a sad termination to a pleasantly-spent day, but such ever appeared to be our fortune.

We were not long kept in suspense as to the cause

of this sudden and unlooked-for movement. It appeared that the Governor of Zacatecas had that evening received a letter from General Tornel, Minister of War and Marine at Mexico, ordering him instantly to place in close confinement, and under strict guard, Colonel Milam, Antonio Navarro, and Robert Foster. The former had been dead for years, having been killed at the Alamo of San Antonio. Mr. Navarro was then on the spot, but no person answering to the name of Robert Foster could be found, and Roblado questioned each one of the prisoners and examined the different lists thoroughly. The only name that came anywhere near Robert Foster was *Thomas Falconer*, and Roblado presuming that he must be the person alluded to, he was instantly sent for with the rest of us. We all told the captain that Mr. F. was not the man; but this did not alter his purpose, and poor Falconer was accordingly placed in a small, close room with Mr. Navarro, two sentinels being paraded before them, who shouted " *centinela alerta!*" every ten minutes during the dreary night, to keep themselves from falling asleep.

In the mean while, Van Ness, Whittaker, and myself were constrained again to occupy our disagreeable apartment, where we passed our New-year's night—now rendered doubly disagreeable to us by contrast with the expected pleasures of the ball, in which we had promised ourselves such delights as would have made some amends for the annoyances and hardships of our unwilling journey.

We were no sooner in the close and dreary room than new inconveniences presented themselves; for not supposing, until the Mexican officer came in such haste for us at the Irishman's fonda, that we were to pass the night at the old mining-house, we had made no preparations for our lodging before leaving it in the morning. On our return, therefore, we found that our blankets had already been taken and our places occupied by some of our friends, leaving us almost as badly situated as was poor Falconer. The night, as I have said, was raw, rainy, and uncomfortable, and we were obliged to take up our quarters near the door. A drunken sentinel, whose duty it was to walk outside and see that none of us left the room, finally opened the door and took his station within—and not content with thus annoying us, he howled the disagreeable "*centinela alerta !*" almost incessantly in our ears, until Dr. Whittaker took a summary way of getting rid of both his presence and his noise. The doctor told the fellow to shut the door and his mouth; the sentinel answered impudently; the next moment the doctor knocked him sprawling into the mud outside, musket and all, and then closed and fastened the door after him. We expected that the fellow would make a complaint, and that we should receive a visit from the officer of the guard for an explanation; but we never heard anything more of it.

An American gentleman promised to forward the letters I had written to my friends in the United States, in such a way as would ensure their safe delivery; and he kept his word, for every one of them reached its destination. I speak of this circumstance, as many of the letters I sent from different points in Mexico never left the country—at least they did not arrive in the United States. Generally speaking, the mail arrangements of Mexico are well conducted, and letters and newspapers are forwarded with promptness and great regularity; but the postmasters who stopped my letters doubtless knew that they were written by some one of the prisoners, and thought they were serving their country by detaining them; or perhaps they had orders to do so.

A subscription was got up among the foreigners in Zacatecas for the benefit of the Texan prisoners, and a sum exceeding one thousand dollars, besides no inconsiderable quantity of clothing, hats, and shoes, was raised for their necessities, the governor and some of the Mexicans subscribing liberally. The clothing was distributed, and also a small sum of money to each man; but the larger portion was applied to the hiring of two large American wagons for transporting the sick and infirm, as well as the blankets and small bundles of the prisoners. The lives of many of our men were. doubtless saved by the timely assistance of these wagons, as by this time numbers were ill with the small-pox, and neither Roblado nor the governor dared take the responsibility of leaving the poor fellows behind in the hospital.

At an early hour on the morning of January 2d, the wagons which had been hired arrived at the foot of the hill, below the old mining-house, and the sick were as comfortably stowed in them as circumstances would admit. Shortly after, five horses were sent to our quarters, saddled and bridled, being presents to some of the Texan officers from the Mexican lawyer who had treated us so kindly. After partaking of an excellent breakfast, sent us by a French gentleman, we were ordered once more to resume the march towards the city of the Montezumas.

The main body of prisoners were guarded with no more strictness than heretofore, but an extra guard was detailed for the special purpose of watching Messrs. Navarro and Falconer—riding close by their side and eyeing their every movement. There was something peculiarly hard in the case of the latter. He was more anxious than any of the prisoners to examine thoroughly such of the cities and towns as we might pass through, had never harboured a single hostile feeling against the country, was innocent of any inimical act, and was now kept a close prisoner, and debarred every little privilege granted the rest of us, for no other reason than that *Thomas Falconer* sounded more like *Robert Foster* than any other name on the list. Tornel had seen the name of the latter attached to some of the papers taken at the capture of General McLeod, and supposing that he was an important personage, and among the prisoners, had ordered him to be closely confined and strictly watched. The real personage, whose name, by-the-way, was not Robert, was all the while peaceably and quietly pursuing his avocations as principal clerk in the war office at Austin, Texas.

Some five or six miles from Zacatecas we passed the celebrated Convent of Guadalupe, an immense pile of buildings, enclosed within a large yard. We could plainly see a number of melancholy, pale-visaged monks, gazing at us from the small windows, doors, and balconies of the place. Near this convent, in 1835, the noted battle between Santa Anna and the Zacatecans was fought, which resulted in the discomfiture of the latter, and the subsequent sack of the city. It is said that both armies were defeated, and that both were on the point of retreating; but that Santa Anna, happening to see a panic among his opponents before they noticed that his men were wavering, was enabled to rally and turn the current in his favour. In the general sack, which soon after took place in the city, the houses of the foreigners, who had taken no part in the opposition to Santa Anna, were indiscriminately plundered with the rest, and two or three gallant Englishmen and Americans were killed while stoutly defending their dwellings. Indemnification for the losses sustained by the foreigners in this outrage has since been made by the Mexican government.

A short time after the sack of Zacatecas, Santa Anna was on his way to Texas; and in less than six months after, the man who had filled grave-yards with victims to his avarice and ambition was upon his knees, cowering like a hound, and with uplifted hands begging a life he had richly forfeited by his massacre of Fannin and his men at Goliad, if by no other crime. The ups and downs of this man, than whom no one better qualified can be found to govern his own countrymen, would form a singular history.

Leaving the Convent of Guadalupe, our road led us across level plains until we reached the village of Refugio, where we encamped for the night. Our nearest route to the city of Mexico would have been by a road more to the right; but as Colonel Cooke and his party had been taken in that direction, it was determined by the Mexican government to give the inhabitants of San Luis Potosi and Guanajuato an opportunity to see a portion of the Texan prisoners, and we were therefore ordered to visit those cities in our march. We had plenty of *leisure*, however; and as our route took us through the more interesting portion of the country, and gave us an opportunity of seeing several of the finest cities, we cared but little for the extra delay it occasioned.

Early in the afternoon of January 4th, after a pleasant march, we reached the town of Ojo Caliente. Here we were allowed to ramble about wherever we pleased, and there being a noted warm well on the edge of the town, several of our party visited it for the purpose of bathing. The water boils up in great quantities, and forms a large, deep basin from the very fountain-head. Several of the prisoners immediately divested themselves of their clothing, and dashed into the refreshing element, diving and swimming about in water just warm enough to be comfortable. Before they left the large natural bathing-tub the party was increased by the arrival of several Mexican girls, who, not in the least daunted by the presence of the Texans, immediately joined them in their aquatic sports. With merry and joyous laughter they commenced splashing the water about them; now diving to the bottom, and then rising to the surface, shaking the water from their long hair, and paddling about like Newfoundland dogs. It may not have been generally remarked, and may not be always the case, but nearly all the females I have seen swim—Mexicans, Indians, and all—paddle along after the manner of water dogs, and one of them makes more noise than a dozen of the other sex. In San Antonio, where the women are excellent swimmers and visit the river regularly once or twice a day, the noise a party of them make might be mistaken for that of so many porpoises or sea-horses.

That the females living upon many of the rivers and lakes of Mexico take to the water so naturally, and appear upon its surface divested of those loose garments with which our American ladies are wont to array themselves upon such occasions, may be looked upon as betraying a want of modesty by some of my fair readers; but with the girls of Mexico there is an absence of all thought that they are doing wrong, which should fully exculpate them from blame. The customs of the country sanction the occurrence of scenes such as I have just mentioned, and many others which would be deemed highly indelicate in other lands; and however much the foreigner may at first be tempted to doubt their strict correctness, he soon learns that no conventional rules forbid them. True modesty consists in the thought which governs every action; and viewed in this light, there was certainly no immodesty in the girls of Ojo Caliente indulging in a bath, even if they did appear "right before folks," as the philosophic Sam Slick would say.

On the ensuing night we reached El Carro, a fine hacienda belonging to the wealthy Count of Jaral. About noon on the 6th we were halted at the town of Salina, where there are extensive salt-works. Here, at the meson where we stopped, we found a stout Kentuckian, who was one of the owners of an American circus company then performing at San Luis Potosi. He was now on his way to Zacatecas, for the purpose of obtaining a suitable place in which to perform in that city, and at the same time the consent of the governor. As he had arrived at Salina a short time before us, he had, of course, selected the best room in the meson for his own use. This room happening to please Captain Roblado, he ordered the circus proprietor to leave it; but the latter told him at once that he had the best right, and should retain possession as long as he pleased. Roblado fumed and swore a little, and then left the place, threatening to bring the alcalde to his assistance. The Kentuckian went soon after to the alcalde's residence, but before he reached it he found that Roblado had been there before him, and had procured a writ of ejectment. The American was now forced to leave the room; but he remarked that if he had but reached the alcalde's first, and slipped a dollar into his hand, he could have retained possession of the room even though fifty Roblados had wanted it. The dollar is the most powerful weapon with many of the officers of justice in Mexico, and when it is employed law and equity must step aside.

The English or American traveller, used to the comforts and conveniences of his own well-kept taverns, meets with but a sorry reception and miserable fare at the Mexican house of entertainment, or *meson*, as it is called. They are all built in the same style, the entrance being through a large gate or passage-way which leads into a *patio*, or court, in the interior. On either side of this yard are the rooms set apart for the reception of travellers. Another passage leads from this into the yard which his beast occupies, and which has a large trough of water in the centre, with uncomfortable stalls on the sides. The tired wayfarer is conducted to his room; but no friendly bed meets his anxious gaze. He sees, perhaps, a species of form, built of adobes and mortar, upon which he can spread his *sarape*, or Mexican blanket, and himself; or, mayhap, a corner of the floor is pointed out to him as a favourite spot on which to establish himself for the night; neither bed nor bedding is provided by the landlord. The next care of every prudent traveller is to bring his saddle, bridle, and the other trappings of his horse or mule, together with all and singular his own personal effects, into his room. If he understands well the population, he contrives to sleep upon as much of his property as possible, to prevent the léperos and ladrones from appropriating it during the night; for every Mexican town has its band of petty pilferers, ready to steal the very strings from the traveller's shoes, should he not take the precaution to lie down and sleep with them on.

The wayfarer is now housed—his next care is for his inward man, and here new difficulties arise. The Mexican landlord sets no public table—provides no meal, and very likely keeps no provisions fit for his foreign guests. At the *cocina*, or kitchen, amid the steams of rank and highly-seasoned stews, he may esteem himself lucky if he can purchase a bowl of mutton broth, a coarse earthen platter of frijoles, or, perchance, a guisado so particularly high-seasoned with red pepper that the skin of his mouth is in danger of going down his throat at the first swallow. Ten chances to one if he is fortunate enough to find knife, fork, or spoon—articles by no means necessary in Mexican housekeeping. But what need of these when he has his own good fingers and a plate of those ever-accompanying and never-failing thin cakes, yclept tortillas, to fall back upon? The soup he drinks from the bowl; a spoon he manufactures by tearing off a piece of tortilla and doubling it into a species of scoop, and with this he is enabled to shovel up a mouthful of his frijoles or guisado and carry it to his jaws. Tortilla and all are swallowed, for with every fresh mouthful a fresh spoon is made. Should the stranger happen to swallow a bit of guisado so outrageously hot with red pepper that from very agony a freshet of tears starts from his eyes, some by-standing Mexican exclaims that it is "bueno por el estomago"—good for the stomach! Fine consolation this, especially for an American; for what does an American care for his stomach? We may all fume and rage against Mrs. Trollope and Dickens, and work ourselves into a most patriotic fury at their strictures; but it cannot be denied that too many of us impose terrible taxes upon our digestive organs by bolting our food in overhaste and half masticated. Too many of us, again, consult but our tastes. We make a hopper of our mouths, feed it to overflowing with the richest dishes until that trough or reservoir called the stomach is running over, stop suddenly in our eating, rush to business as though life and death depended upon our exertions, and spend half our lives wondering why we are troubled with indigestion and dyspepsia! I hope my countrymen will pardon the truth and the episode, while I go back to the tavern.

There is one thing the traveller in Mexico gets in all its perfection, and that is chocolate. They may have it as good in Spain—but in no part of the United States, or of the British possessions upon its borders, can anything approaching it be made—so fragrant, so rich, so delicious. But when he has swallowed his chocolate, there is an end to everything like perfection. The traveller, if anywhere in the vicinity of the *tierras calientes*, may eke out his dinner with the fruits which grow there in endless variety and profusion, and of most delicious and nutritious quality; but nowhere need he look for the roast beef, the boiled mutton, the potatoes, the pies, the puddings, or the thousand-and-one substantials and delicacies to which he has been accustomed. Such is tavern life in Mexico, at least at a majority of the *mesones* and *fondas* scattered through the smaller towns and cities. What the charge is for the lodging of a man and the stabling of his beast over night, I do not know—the Mexican government paid all my bills of this nature during the interesting tour I made through that country. The prices are moderate, however, especially away from the larger cities. A dish of frijoles, or of guisado, with a stack of some half dozen tortillas to match, seldom costs more than six or nine cents; and as upon these the traveller is generally obliged to subsist, his expenses are light. With a dollar and twenty-five cents or thereabout per diem, I should suppose a man could pay his own expenses and those of his beast on the principal routes of the country, and live through it, unless some of *los señores ladrones* should see fit to stop his breath for the mere love of whatever plunder might be got from him.

Should the traveller happen to be at a village where there is no meson, it is considered the duty of the alcalde to furnish him with accommodations; but if night overtakes him at a poor rancho, where there is no alcalde, his situation is truly deplorable. He alights at the door of the best-appearing hut in the group, and after kicking and quieting some half dozen yelping, worthless curs, which seem inclined to dispute his passage by threats only—they never go so far as to bite— he at length effects an entrance. The room serves for all purposes—kitchen, parlour, and sleeping apartment.*

---

\* The reader must bear in mind that I am now speaking of the dwellings of the very lowest and poorest classes, although a large majority of the inhabitants have but a common room in which to eat and sleep. Attached to this apartment, in many instances, may be found a small room which serves as a kitchen, and in which the little cooking of the family is done. In this kitchen the tortillas are made, and as the process may not prove uninteresting, I will quote Madame Calderon's description of the manner in which they are manufactured: "They first soak the grain in water with a little lime, and when it is soft peel off the skin—then grind it on a large block of stone, the *metate*, or, as the Indians (who know best) call it, the *metatl*. For the purpose of grinding it, they use a sort of stone roller, with which it is crushed, and rolled into a bowl placed below the stone. They then take some of this paste, and clap it between their hands, till they form it into light round cakes, which are afterward toasted on a smooth plate, called the *comalli* (*comal* they call it in Mexico), and which ought to be eaten as hot as possible." I agree, most decidedly, with the fair authoress, that they "ought to be eaten as hot as possible," *if at all*—for from all such tough, heavy, and unsavoury cakes I beg to be delivered. Most excellent bread do the Mexicans make—white, light, and sweet — and why they spoil their corn by converting it into tortillas is a mystery. Two women or girls are always engaged in making them—one to grind the grain, the other to form the cakes—and pass by a hut, either at night or morning, the traveller is sure to hear the patting of hands which denotes the progress of manufacture. When cooked, if the Mexican has no frijoles, he besmears the tortilla with a composition of

There is no floor other than the hard-trodden earth; it is bedless, furnitureless, comfortless. The tired wayfarer looks around for some friendly evidence of food and rest—his beast without neighs aloud for corn, shelter, and some one to relieve him of his heavy load of saddle and baggage. Upon the rough walls of the room are to be seen, neatly enough arrayed with garlands of flowers and boughs, a collection of badly-executed lithographs, gaudily coloured, and intended to represent different scenes in the life of our Saviour and the Holy Mother. The centre of the little group is occupied, perhaps, by a rude wooden cross, trimmed with faded flowers. Beneath is probably a lithograph—sometimes an old engraving—of the Virgin of Guadalupe, while over it is suspended a picture representing the ascension of our Saviour. The crucifixion occupies a conspicuous place, then a print of the Virgin and Holy Child, and then an ingeniously-wrought crown of thorns, or a rosary and crucifix. A brass medal of Nuestra Señora de Guadalupe, and probably a lithograph of the patron saint of the country, will be seen in the collection, the former suspended by a red or yellow riband. A little bit of looking-glass generally completes the arrangement, for this piece of wordly vanity almost always has its station, in a Mexican cottage, in close proximity with the rude symbols of the faith of its inmates. On other parts of the walls the traveller sees little save strings of dry red peppers, perhaps a few ears of corn, and the coarse earthen bowls and dishes of the occupants.

Turning his eyes to the floor, in one corner he sees

red pepper and mutton fat, and always appears perfectly contented if he can procure a sufficiency of this singular food, with *pulque* enough to wash it down.

the universal *metate*, or stone instrument upon which the corn is mashed or ground before it is made into tortillas. In the next corner, probably, a fighting cock is tied by the leg, giving an occasional crow of defiance to some brother chicken tied in the same way in the adjoining or opposite house. Another corner is occupied, perhaps, by an elderly hen sitting upon a nest of eggs, while in the last stands a coarse box or chest, containing the little odds and ends belonging to the family in the way of dresses and ornaments. In this room, which is not more than ten or twelve feet square, live, sleep, and eat some eight, ten, or perhaps twelve persons, large and small, male and female, and with these the traveller is obliged to make his bed, or take up with lodgings upon the ground outside, which is every way preferable if the weather permits. "If a man lies down with a dog he gets up with fleas," says the old proverb—if he lies down with Mexicans of the lower classes he gets up with something worse, say I.

But sleep is a secondary, an after consideration—the wayfarer must have something to eat. He asks the master of the establishment if he has any meat. Nine times out of ten the answer is, "*No hai*"—there is none —accompanied by raising the right hand to a level with his nose, closing it with the exception of the forefinger, and then, with the palm turned outwardly, wagging the upraised finger directly before the face. Bread is next asked for. The answer this time is another wag of the forefinger, which is to all intents and purposes a negative; but frequently the word "*tampoco*" is uttered, signifying that there is neither bread nor meat on the premises. The traveller asks for milk or eggs. "*No hai nada*"—no, there is nothing here—is the answer, unless, by some turn of good fortune, his host happens to own a goat or a cow, or has had extraordinary luck with his poultry. It is only when the hungry wayfarer is driven to the strait of asking for tortillas or frijoles that the welcome " *si hai*"—we have them—greets his ear. With these he at least stays the cravings of hunger, and after having made such provision for his horse as the poverty of the rancho allows, he gathers his property as nearly under him as possible, rolls himself in his sarape, and seeks forgetfulness and rest in sleep.

The above is a picture of life in Mexico, among the lower classes of the inhabitants, the fidelity of which will be attested by all who have travelled over the country. Flying tourists, who have confined their trip to Puebla, Mexico, Queretaro, Guanajuato, and such places as they could reach in stage-coaches, can learn little from their own personal experience; for with the introduction of this mode of travelling came regular stage-houses, where regular and more bountiful meals are served up. They must journey upon the backs of mules, and through the less-frequented highways, before they can come to a proper understanding of the country and the modes of living of its inhabitants.

## CHAPTER VIII.

Departure from Salina.—Last Speech of the Kentucky Circus Proprietor.—His Wishes in relation to Roblado.—Arrival at Espiritu Santo.—Pass a pleasant Evening.—A Contrast.—La Parada.—Wild mountain Scenery.—The Organo.—A picturesque View.—First Sight of San Luis Potosi.—A beautiful Valley.—Innumerable Wells.—Large Prickly Pears.—The Peruvian Tree.—Our Approach to San Luis heralded.—Arrival within the City.—Beauty of the Women.—Description of San Luis.—Its Churches, Convents, and public Buildings.—Convent of the Augustine Friars.—Benevolence of the Brotherhood.—Wants of the Sick provided for.—An evening Stroll through the City.—Market Scenes.—Encounter with a Company of Equestrians.—A droll Specimen of the Yankee Genus.—" Old Hundred" in San Luis.—Return to the Convent.—Visited by the Foreigners.—Our Yankee Wag and his Stories.—Subscription for the Prisoners raised.—Allowed our Parole.—An interesting Scotch Lady.—Visit to the Circus.—Appearance of the Audience.—An Invitation to Supper.—Find ourselves in the wrong House.—Apologies unnecessary.—Supper at last.—An Opportunity to write to my Friends improved.—Departure from San Luis.—A new Guard and new Commander.—An interesting Incident.—Las Pilas.—Arrival at El Jaral.—Anecdote of General Mina.—Wealth of the Proprietor.—A singular Funeral Procession.—A " Hog on Horseback."—Description of the Arrieros of Mexico.

As we were about departing from Salina, the Kentucky circus proprietor rode up to take his leave of us. Just as he was turning his horse's head, in the direction of Zacatecas, Roblado passed by on a gallop, the Kentuckian simply remarking that he would like to have him, and six more just like him, in a close room for about ten minutes, the door to be locked on the outside, and the windows strongly barred. He entertained what he called a private opinion, but which he expressed publicly, that the whole of them would " find themselves most essentially chawed up" in less than that time. After uttering this short but emphatic speech, he too put spurs to his horse and galloped off in an opposite direction. I have little doubt that such odds as even seven Roblados would have fared badly in his hands, for the Kentuckian was a well-made, stalwart specimen of our Western men, and had that determined expression of countenance which plainly indicated that he meant what he said.

In the afternoon we reached Espiritu Santo, a noble hacienda, having a fine church and a very well-informed and gentlemanly priest. Here, too, we met with a good blacksmith, and as the road beyond was reported to be exceedingly rough and rocky, several of our party embraced the opportunity of having their animals shod. Fortunate it was that we did so, for we found the road even worse than had been represented.

Our night at Espiritu Santo was one of the most pleasant on the whole route. A Mexican gentleman residing there had two or three very pretty daughters, girls who had been educated in Europe and seen much of the world, and there were also several well-informed and intelligent ladies attached to the priest's family. At night a *tertulia*, or party, was given to the Mexican officers by the former, to which a number of the Texans were invited. One of the young ladies, in particular, waltzed gracefully, and played upon the guitar with excellent skill. A generous supper was given during the evening, and thus, amid music and the dance, feasting, and the charms of well-bred society, the night wore away at Espiritu Santo—the next we passed in miserable quarters at the poor and worn-out hacienda of La Parada. Surely, the hours of our captivity were checkered.

The country between La Parada and San Luis Potosi is wild, mountainous, and exceedingly picturesque. Often the traveller finds himself winding along through deep, dark, and dreary barrancas, or mountain passes, surrounded on all sides by high and rugged precipices. Many of these passes are not more than twenty or thirty yards in width, having pure streams of swift-running water dashing through them, and enlivened here and there by the rude mud dwelling of some family that has chosen the secluded retreat for a home. On either side the mountains rise in abrupt and precipitous masses, shutting out the sun almost entirely except for an hour or two in the middle of the day. Wild flowers of almost every variety and hue, sending forth delicious fragrance upon the pure mountain air, are to be seen on every side; orange and other fruit trees grow luxuriantly, and in one of these passes we for the first time met with the tall and symmetrical *organo* plant, a species of the cactus. It is about six inches in diameter at the base, tapering upward very gradually, from eighteen to twenty-five feet in height, and almost entirely destitute of limbs or leaves. As it is an evergreen, and grows perfectly straight, it is in many parts of Mexico planted closely in rows, and when it attains its full size and height makes a neat and strong fence—as symmetrical in every particular as though the hand of man had fashioned it. This singular production of nature receives its name from the resemblance a row of the trees has to the pipes of an organ. The prickly pear was also seen growing upon the almost perpendicular mountain sides, and here goats and ragged, rough-coated donkeys were picking a scanty subsistence from the thorny herbage. The climate in these mountain passes, for they scarcely deserve the name of valleys, is delightfully mild, and the limited wants of the scattered inhabitants are easily supplied by the vegetables that grow upon a few square rods of land. Ignorant of the wide world from which they are shut out, its cares and its vanities, the poor Indians here pass their days in peace and quietness, and in apparent unconsciousness of the wild sublimity with which they are surrounded.

Emerging from one of these passes, the traveller finds himself climbing the rocky sides of precipices that at first sight seem impassable. By slow degrees the mountain summit is reached, and then he is amply repaid for his toil by the scenes below him—scenes full of calm repose and quiet beauty, for distance has softened the harshness of the rugged barranca and subdued the asperities of the wild precipices by which it is hemmed in. Our wagons with the sick had been sent by a different road, it being utterly impossible for aught save man or beast to make the passage through these mountain gorges.

After toiling some six hours in gaining as many miles, we finally reached the summit of the mountains which overhang the beautiful valley of San Luis on its northern side. In our rear was a rude and broken country—a country formed by nature in one of her wildest freaks—before us was spread out a boundless and peaceful valley. In the distance the numerous domes and steeples of San Luis Potosi were seen rising, while all around were rich and fertile fields teeming with vegetation, and this, too, in the month of January. Innumerable well-sweeps were seen rising and falling in every part of the valley, for here there are no irrigating canals, and the inhabitants are compelled to depend on wells for water to moisten the earth.

Descending the mountains by a rough, zigzag path, in many places so steep that we were obliged to dismount and lead or drive our animals, we at length gained the valley in safety. Here we found a wide, straight road, skirted, on both sides, by huge prickly pear-trees, and

Vol. II.—O

leading directly into the city, now distant some six or seven miles. Those who have never seen the prickly pear as it grows in Mexico can hardly believe accounts of the immense size which it attains. I have seen the trunks of some at least two feet in diameter, growing eight or ten feet in height without a limb, and then branching off in every direction. As we drew nearer the city, the roadsides were planted with rows of Peruvian trees, a species of pepper or spice, their wide-spreading limbs and rich green foliage forming a shady arbour over our pathway, while pendent clusters of red berries, of aromatic fragrance, were hanging gracefully from every little twig and bough. Here and there a dwelling-house would be seen, the front yard fenced in by the towering *organo*, which completely cut off all view of the habitation save through the vacant space left in front for an entrance.

The self-important Roblado had sent on his trumpeters, as usual, to herald our approach, and the principal streets through which we passed were thronged with dense masses of the inhabitants. San Luis is one of the best-built cities of Mexico, regularly laid out, and with an air of cleanliness not common in a Mexican town. The women, too, are somewhat famous for their general beauty—they certainly have small and perfectly-formed feet and hands, large and lustrous eyes, and hair more black and glossy than any other females I saw while travelling almost three thousand miles through the country. The windows and balconies of the better houses were filled with the fashionables, while the girls of the poorer classes, who seemed as though they had run from their houses half dressed in their great haste to see *los Tejanos*, were gathered on either side the streets in countless numbers.

The city of San Luis Potosi, with its immediate suburbs, must contain some fifty thousand inhabitants. Like Mexico, it is built in a wide valley, much of which is fertile in the growth of Indian corn and wheat, besides affording excellent pasturage for immense herds of sheep. The city was a place of great wealth while the adjacent gold mines were productive; but since the working of them has ceased it has lost much of its former consequence. The inhabitants, however, appear to be engaged to no inconsiderable extent in the manufacture of clothing, shoes, hats, and different articles of iron, and a quantity of grain is raised in the valley far exceeding the wants of the population. The churches, convents, and public institutions are magnificent, and will vie with those of any city in Mexico—a country abounding with the grandest specimens of religious architecture.

Passing through the principal plaza of the city, which is surrounded by stately churches, palaces, and residences of the higher orders, we at length reached the convent of the Augustine friars. This is a rich establishment, and the holy and benevolent brotherhood kindly appropriated two or three large rooms in their convent to our use. Here our sick were attended to, visited by Mexican physicians, and several of those who were in the most hopeless condition were taken to the hospital to be better attended. How different this from the unkind treatment we had experienced but a few days previous at Zacatecas!

No sooner had dark set in than Van Ness, who had no little influence with the Mexican officers, from the fact of his speaking their language, obtained permission to leave the convent without a guard, accompanied by one of the Texan officers and myself. First ascertaining the name of the street in which our quarters were situated, we strolled off at random into the heart of the city. A walk of but a few squares brought us to the market, which was now filled with the venders of every species of eatable, drinkable, and wearable article. Seated upon the ground, a female might be seen with a few chiles colorados, or red peppers, for sale, her merchandise dimly lighted by a small fire beside her. But a few steps distant another woman, with a scanty supply of frijoles, would be quietly awaiting a customer, and her next neighbour was probably sitting by the side of an earthen pot of chile guisado, kept hot by a small charcoal fire beneath. In her lap would be a small pile of tortillas, and ever and anon, as some hungry customer gave her a call, she would throw two or three of the tortillas upon the fire to warm, dip a saucer of the guisado from the pot before her, and after receiving her *quartillo* in advance, hand over the eatables to the purchaser. The quartillo is a copper coin about the size of one of our pennies, but passes for three. There is a small portion of silver in the Mexican copper coins— just enough to make it an object to counterfeit them— and it is said that large quantities of spurious quartillos have been manufactured in the United States and in England expressly for the Mexican market.

The market-place of San Luis occupies a large square, and every part of it was in some way put to use by the females. Twenty-five cents would have purchased the whole stock in trade of a large portion of them; yet they seemed perfectly happy, and would chat away, while smoking their cigarritos, with the greatest vivacity and cheerfulness. There may not have been as many languages spoken as in the New-Orleans market, but there was as much talking, and even more bustle and confusion. The square was filled with soldiers off duty, loafers, market-women, girls, monks, gamblers, léperos, venders of oranges and other fruits, robbers, friars, fellows with fighting chickens under their blankets—in short, one of those miscellaneous collections always to be found about a Mexican market square. The adjoining buildings were occupied as drinking and cigar shops, retail fancy stores, and dwelling houses of the poorer orders. Around the liquor shops were seen a few drunken Indians, the husbands or brothers, probably, of some of the market-women, who had spent one half of their hard earnings in the purchase of mescal or aguardiente.

Entering an *estanquillo*, or shop licensed to sell cigars, we met two or three faces so decidedly Anglo-Saxon in complexion and feature that we at once accosted them in English, and were answered by one of the party with a drawl and twang so peculiarly "Down East," that Marble, Hackett, or Yankee Hill might have taken lessons from him. We soon ascertained that they belonged to the American circus company then performing at San Luis, and on telling them who we were they at once invited us to their *meson* to supper. The first speaker, who proved to be a regular Vermonter, was not a little surprised to see us out without a guard, and asked if we had received permission to that effect. His astonishment was removed when we told him that we were allowed to leave our quarters on parole.

In five minutes after our arrival at the hotel of the equestrians, I found that our Vermont acquaintance was one of the quaintest specimens of the Yankee race I had ever seen, and not a few examples had I met previous to my encounter with him. He had a droll impediment in his speech which gave to his actions and gestures a turn irresistibly comic, and then he told an excellent story, played the trombone, triangle, and bass viol, spoke Spanish well, drove one of the circus wagons, translated the bills, turned an occasional somerset in the ring, cracked jokes in Spanish with the Mexican clown, took the tickets at the entrance with one hand, while with the other he beat an accompaniment to the orchestra inside on the bass-drum, and, in short, made himself "generally useful." After partaking of an excellent supper, we spent an agreeable hour in his room, listening to story after story of his adventures. He "come out" to Mexico, to use his own words, by way of Chihuahua, accompanying the traders from Jonesborough, on Red River, in the first and only expedition across the immense prairies. They were some six or eight months on the road, and suffered incredible hardships for want of water and provisions. Our Yankee was a stout man when we saw him, but he told us that he was a perfect transparency when he first arrived at the Mexican settlements—so poor, in fact, that according to his own account "a person might have read the New-England Primer through him without specs."

When ten o'clock came we rose to depart; but the droll genius insisted that we should first partake of a glass of egg-nog with him, and then help him to sing "Old Hundred" in remembrance of old times. There are few persons in the New-England States who cannot go through this ancient and well-known psalm-tune after some fashion, and although neither time nor place was exactly befitting, we all happened to be from that quarter, and could not resist complying with his comico-serious request. He really had a good voice, and, for aught I know, may have led the singing in his native village church. After humming a little, apparently to get the right pitch, he started off with a full, rich tone; but suddenly checking himself in the middle of the first line, said that the thing was not yet complete. Taking a double-bass from its resting-place in one corner of the room, he soon had the instrument tuned, and then recommenced with this accompaniment. Never have I heard a performance so strangely mingling the grave and the comic. It was odd enough to see one of his vocation in a strange land thus engaged—and then the solemnity and zeal with which he sawed and sang away were perfectly irresistible. I did not laugh; but thoughts arose in my mind very little accordant with the earnest and devotional spirit with which our strange companion went through his share of the performance. This curious scene over, a scene which is probably without a parallel in the history of San Luis Potosi, we took leave of our singular acquaintance, who promised to call at the convent early the next morning, and do everything in his power to assist those among the Texans who were the most destitute.

During the forenoon of the day which followed this strange night adventure, we were visited at the convent by a large number of foreigners—Scotch, Irish, English, German, French, and American. Our Yankee acquaintance also made his appearance, with several of his companions, and for an hour or two the old cloisters fairly rang with laughter at his merry jokes. The mad wag had an inexhaustible fund of humorous anecdote, and one great charm about his jokes was, that while his hearers' sides were shaking at their recital, his own face was as solemn as that of any of the Yucatan idols which grace the volumes of Stephens or Norman. A faint twinkle of humour, enough to show that he felt the full comic force of his story, might be seen lurking about the corners of his eyes; but farther than this he did not indulge in outward expressions of mirth.

Among those who visited our quarters during the day were several of the wealthiest foreign merchants of the place. As Colonel Cooke's party had not taken San Luis in their route there had been no call upon their charity, and they immediately set about raising a handsome subscription of money and clothing for the more destitute among the prisoners. It was laughable to see some of the latter, who had for months been arrayed only in rags, now suddenly transformed into shabby-genteel dandies by the timely assistance of a suit of fashionable, although second-hand garments.

At night a small party of us were again permitted to visit the town without a guard, and the next day the commandante of San Luis permitted all the Texan officers to ramble about the town on their parole. In the forenoon I visited a very gentlemanly Scotch merchant of the place, and was introduced to his lady. She, too, was a native of Scotland, but had been many years a resident of San Luis, and was very affable and lady-like in her deportment. She was also very liberal in her gifts to the prisoners—especially to such of them as were her countrymen.

A performance was given in the afternoon by the equestrians, the large arena in which the bull-fights take place having been neatly fitted up by the company. To this performance we were all invited, and some eight or ten accepted the invitation. We found the arena tolerably well filled with the better classes of the place, and among the audience were many extremely well-dressed ladies. They wore not a little jewelry, and many of them had rich and showy mantillas; but by far the greatest charm about them was their large, liquid, black eyes, so full of deep and impassioned feeling. The riding of the American equestrians appeared to be new to the audience, and was greeted with repeated shouts of applause, while the antics, eccentricities, and jokes of the Mexican clown, all of which had been drilled into him by the wag of a Yankee who managed the concern, proved highly diverting to the crowd of ragged urchins in attendance.

A small party of us had received an invitation to supper that evening, with a German who had lived in Texas and who spoke English, and while seeking his dwelling we accidentally entered the house of another German, who was one of the wealthiest merchants of the place, and lived in a style of great splendour. Some five or six of us found ourselves suddenly in a richly-furnished drawing-room, in which were seated several Mexican ladies. They manifested not the least constraint, but invited us to be seated at once, and entered into conversation with such of our party as could speak the Spanish. The master of the house, too, politely invited us to take wine with him, and although we did not see the gentleman, whose invitation we had accepted, in the room, there was nothing in the deportment of those present to denote that we were unwelcome or even uninvited guests. After we had spent some half an hour in this way, the real individual of whose hospitality we had intended to partake arrived in search of us, and then for the first time we discovered our mistake. After a profusion of apologies on our part, which were deemed entirely unnecessary by the parties upon whom we had thus unceremoniously intruded, we took our leave, but not until we had been urged to take another glass of wine. Even the ladies joined in saying that all apologies were unnecessary, and fairly laughed the thing off as a most excellent joke.

Arrived at length at the house for which our visit was intended, we there found an excellent supper and wines of the choicest description waiting for us. After passing a couple of hours in their discussion, and in speculation as to what disposition the Mexican government would make of us after our arrival at the capital, we returned to our quarters in the convent. Here we ascertained that we were to renew our march the next morning, and as I found Falconer, who had not been allowed to leave the convent, busily employed in writing letters, I embraced the opportunity again to address Mr. Ellis, then our minister at Mexico. I also wrote numerous letters to my friends in the United States, all of which, through the assistance of the friend who took charge of them, arrived in safety.

It was on the morning of the 12th of January that we took our departure from San Luis Potosi, leaving six or seven of our sick in the hospital—men who were down with the small-pox and other diseases, and utterly unable to travel. A large supply of clothing was distributed among the more destitute the evening before, and also a small sum of money to each man—contributions which had been raised principally among the liberal foreign residents.

Roblado, much to the satisfaction of the prisoners, left us at San Luis. Among our unfortunate men he had obtained the cognomen of "Salezar the Second," and by his acts of petty tyranny and cruelty to such as were on foot, had doubtless well earned the title. Our new guard was composed entirely of cavalry, whose commander was a polite and gentlemanly person, disposed to grant us every favour and indulgence. I have forgotten the name of this officer, but he had been a prisoner himself in Texas, and frequently spoke of the excellent treatment he received while in that country. An incident extremely interesting occurred when he first appeared among us. It seems that at the retreat, after the battle of San Jacinto, this officer was wounded in the chase, captured by a Texan, and afterward quartered by him at the house of a gentleman, who dressed his wound and bestowed upon him every attention. In the person of Lieutenant Casey, one of our officers, he immediately recognised his former captor and benefactor, and the nature of the meeting between them it is easier to imagine than describe.

Passing through a fertile and thickly-settled country, the fields many of them fenced in with the organo and prickly pear, we reached the hacienda of Las Pilas early in the afternoon, and halted there for the night. I recollect but little of this place, other than that I hired a very pretty girl to wash a shirt and handkerchief. The next day we continued our journey through the beautiful valley of San Francisco, one of the most fertile in Mexico. On the 14th of January we arrived at El Jaral, the celebrated residence of the count of that name, who is deemed one of the wealthiest proprietors in all Mexico. The town, which is owned by Jaral, has a fine church, and an immense slaughter-house, where about a thousand sheep and goats are said to be killed daily for their hides and tallow alone. The residence of the count himself is a large and imposing building, although destitute of architectural beauty.* The dwellings of his peons, or labourers, and there are some two thousand of them, are mostly rude adobe huts, destitute of

* Ward, in his useful work upon Mexico, says that the live stock owned by the Marquis del Jaral at one time numbered three millions, including horses, mules, horned cattle, sheep, and goats. The famous General Mina, with his small but gallant force of Americans, took this town in 1817, and, according to the statement of the proprietor, robbed him of $300,000 in specie.

furniture and every comfort. You may call them by what name you will—Mexican citizens, freemen, or what not—many of them are to all intents slaves—serfs, subject to the will and pleasure of the lord of the immense manor.

We had proceeded but a short distance from El Jaral when we encountered a singularly grave, and, at the same time, ludicrous procession. Borne on the shoulders of four men came first a litter, on which a corpse was lying. This was decorated with flowers of different species, and the bearers were carrying it to El Jaral for interment. Not a creature, save the four men who bore the litter, was attached to this singular funeral procession, but immediately in the rear, and as if enjoying such protection as it afforded, was a female driving a little scrubby, half-starved donkey in the same direction. Upon the back of the ass, with his head turned towards the animal's tail, a large and extremely fat live hog was riding—the first of the swinish race I had ever seen mounted. His four legs were confined, two on either side of the animal which was bearing him along; and the hog was ever and anon changing the position of his head from one side to the other, in order, apparently, to take the greatest possible comfort under the circumstances. I cannot say that his equestrian performance was altogether as graceful as some I have seen, or that he had that dauntless bearing which gives to feats of horsemanship their greatest charm; but he certainly manifested a resignation and stoical indifference which could hardly have been expected, and we laughed outright as the dwarfish donkey, with his whimsical rider, trotted past us, chief mourner, as one of our men remarked, for the person borne upon the litter. I have often heard of a "hog in armour," but never expected to see a hog on horseback.

It is singular enough, and a matter which strikes every traveller with wonder who journeys through Mexico, with what facility the *arrieros*, or muleteers, can confine almost any burden upon the backs of asses and mules. Frequently we met moving fodder-stacks along the road—many of them nearly the size of a common load of hay—and as no living thing could be seen about them, their appearance at first struck us as curious in the extreme. Large bodies of wheat-straw, square and compact, and reaching within an inch of the ground, could be seen approaching us, and it was only when we bent close to the earth that their locomotive power could be seen. By looking in this position the four feet of the animal beneath the stack could be discovered—head, body, ears, and all being alike concealed under the bulky load which was packed, with the greatest regard to symmetry, upon his back. Almost the entire transportation business of the country is carried on in this way, and the traveller sees boxes, bales, barrels—in short, every species of merchandise—carried from one point to another securely packed upon the backs of mules and asses.

The *arrieros* of Mexico are the most hardy, brave, generous, and trustworthy of her inhabitants—a class of men in whom the utmost reliance can be placed, and whose calling, requiring them to be constantly roaming from point to point and mixing with the world, supplies them with a fund of anecdote and the legendary lore of the country, and renders them well-informed and exceedingly entertaining companions. From what I saw and heard of them they are universally to be trusted with any charge, and their word may invariably be depended upon—which is a good deal more than can be said of any other class, as a body, in Mexico, whether civil, military, or ecclesiastical.

The dress of the arriero is a pair of green or blue broadcloth pantaloons, foxed or trimmed with velvet or morocco, and slashed from the knee downward, while the sides are ornamented with a profusion of bright bell-buttons. Under these he wears flowing linen drawers, and both are confined around the waist by a gay sash. The bosom of the shirt is often elaborately worked, and over this a close-fitting jacket, decorated with a large quantity of bell-buttons and braid, is worn. Attached to his heels are an immense pair of iron or steel spurs, the rowel of a circumference equal to the palm of his hand, and having little steel ornaments at the sides, which tinkle at every step. A wide-brimmed hat, partially pointed at the top, covered with oiled silk, and around which gold or silver braid and tassels are confined, sits jauntily upon the head; and thus equipped, and mounted upon his richly-caparisoned horse or mule, the Mexican muleteer is one of the most picturesque, as well as showy horsemen in the world.

The stock in trade of the arriero consists of as many mules as he has money to purchase, with an *aparejo* for each. The latter is nothing more than a heavy, clumsy pack-saddle, confined to the mule's back by a hair-girth, and kept from slipping too far forward by a wide crupper, which is frequently embroidered, and has the name either of the mule or his master, or, perhaps, a couplet of poetry or some old Spanish proverb applicable to the calling of the arriero, worked with thread upon its sides.\* At night, the mules are formed

---

\* On the crupper of a pack-mule I remember reading the following: "*Between women and wine the poor arriero gets nothing.*"

in line and unpacked, and then either driven to pasture or fed at the corral attached to the meson. In the morning, the animals walk directly up to their saddles, and there stand patiently until packed. Not unfrequently does it occur that each mule knows his own particular aparejo, and unerringly picks it out from a hundred ranged in a row; should one of them, more stupid or careless than his fellows, chance to take his stand in front of another's saddle and load, the real owner soon convinces him of his mistake by a shower of well-directed kicks; and as if all felt it a duty to punish stupidity, the unfortunate animal generally has a dozen pairs of heels flying at him before he finds his own aparejo.

The work of packing, when, as I have before stated, boxes, bales, barrels, and every species of merchandise are thus transported in Mexico, occupies an incredibly short time, the arriero superintending his *mozos*, or servants, and directing them how and upon what mules to pack the heavier articles. When all is in readiness for the journey, he leads the procession, followed by some more steady and aged mule, which is looked upon by his followers as the bell-wether of the gang. So tightly drawn are the girths, that the animals are not only galled, but frequently find much difficulty in breathing, and in the early part of a day's journey manifest not a little pain and uneasiness by tossing aloft their heads, and giving utterance to loud grunts or groans; yet it is deemed impossible to fasten their loads securely without thus torturing them, their backs and sides, when unladen at night, giving painful evidence of their sufferings during the day. When on the road not one of them can be coaxed or beaten into passing their leader, and when he comes to a halt they also stop until he moves again. Whenever anything breaks, or a pack becomes loose, the mozo is at hand with a blind to place over the mule's eyes, and a piece of raw-hide in his pocket to repair damages. Thus the whole business is reduced to a system.

Such is the arriero of Mexico, and such he will continue to be until the mountains of his country are cut down, and the steep, craggy, and difficult paths are turned into beaten and open thoroughfares. He looks to the interest of those who employ him with scrupulous care; takes every precaution to guard the goods intrusted to his charge from being either stolen or damaged. He has a nod and a sly wink for every pretty girl he meets in his many miles of travel, can carol every rude madrigal known in the land, loves his honour and his religion, hates the ladrones and léperos, and despises lying and deceit. Would that all the inhabitants of Mexico were arrieros, or as honest as are these roving landsmen.

## CHAPTER IX.

A Night at San Felipe.—Meeting with one of Mina's Soldiers.—Santa Anna, and the Estimation in which he is held by his Countrymen.—San Juan de los Llanos.—Sickness and Suffering.—Tedious Mountain March.—Picturesque Scenery.—Arparos; its romantic Situation.—Arrival at Silao.—An American Physician.—Kindness of an English Gentleman and his Lady.—Approach to Guanajuato.—Singular Entry.—Laughable Scenes.—Arrival within the City.—Visits from the Foreigners.—Fitzgerald and others taken to the Hospital.—Liberal Contributions.—Opportunity to escape.—Departure from Guanajuato.—Singular Location of the City.—La Puerta.—Arrival at Salamanca.—System of Recruiting Volunteers.—Celaya.—Generous Conduct of Cortazar.—Sunday at Celaya.—The Cathedral.—Singular Customs of the Indians.—Cock-fighting at the Theatre.—"El Campanero de San Pablo."—A Spanish Play.—Lady Smokers.—Departure from Celaya.—Fertility of the Baxio.—Calera.—An early Morning March.—Distant View of Queretaro.—Arrival within the City.—Singular Currency and amusing Anecdote.—Soap a legal Tender.—A Stroll through Queretaro.—American Prisoners.—Spanish System of Shaving.—Texans Stoned in the Market-place.—A Mexican Restaurat.—Adventure with a Friar.—Return to our Quarters.

THE night following our departure from El Jaral we passed at San Felipe, the second town taken by Hidalgo in the early part of the Mexican Revolution. At that time it was said to contain sixteen thousand inhabitants; there are not half that number now, unless I am much deceived. At this place several of our party were treated with much attention by a Mexican gentleman, who had been one of Mina's soldiers. Of Santa Anna, and his ambitious projects, he was far from speaking in complimentary terms; but this was the case among all classes. From the best-bred gentleman down to the lowest lépero, all were loud in their curses of the despot and his schemes, and the question was often asked our men why they did not kill him when he was in their power!

On our next day's journey we passed a small rancho known as La Lorn, and at night reached the once wealthy but now insignificant hacienda of San Juan de los Llanos, or St. John of the Plains. By this time, although all of us had set out from San Luis in good health, several of our party were down with the smallpox, and suffering incredibly from being compelled to travel, and from want of proper medicines. There was no way of leaving them behind, however, and the poor fellows were carried along in the wagons furnished at Zacatecas, receiving such attentions as it was in the power of their companions to bestow.

After an exceedingly long and tiresome mountain march, through deep and ragged barrancas and up steep and rugged precipices, such of us as were on foot or had animals reached the little mountain rancho of Arparos late on the afternoon of the 17th of January. The wagons were taken by some roundabout and more level road, and did not join us until late at night; yet even they had been several times upset, and were much shattered by the roughness of the journey. The little adobe church at this rancho was cleared of its holy furniture to accommodate some of our party, while three or four of us hired a room of one of the villagers in which to pass the night.

Nothing can exceed the grandeur and picturesque beauty of the site which has been chosen for the little rancho of Arparos. The road to it, in both directions, leads through rugged mountain gorges and across swift-running streams—now climbing steep acclivities, and then descending into deep and secluded barrancas—dark and dreary except when the sun is at his meridian.

The prickly pear, or nopal, here attains much perfection, but other than this there is scarcely a blade of vegetation save here and there a small patch of corn, found in some little valley where the wash from the surrounding mountains has formed a soil.

The next day we reached Silao, a town containing some four or five thousand inhabitants, and situated in a fertile plain. Here we met an American physician, and an English gentleman to whose house a small party of us were invited to supper. He was a resident of Guanajuato, and a very influential man in that city; but during a portion of the year he made Silao his residence on account of the superior salubrity of its climate. We found his wife, who was an English lady, a kind-hearted, interesting woman, disposed to render every attention to such of our party as were ill with the small-pox, and there were now some twelve or fifteen on the list. She sent them a large quantity of hot tea and such other necessaries as she thought they would stand most in need of, while her husband said that he would leave for Guanajuato early the next morning, and use all his influence with the authorities to induce them to allow such as were really unable to travel permission to remain at the hospital in that city.

By making an early start on the morning of the 19th, we were enabled to reach Guanajuato before the middle of the day. Our approach and entry into that city were characterized by one of the most laughable exhibitions that occurred on the whole route from San Miguel to Mexico. It is almost impossible so to describe the scene as to give it full effect, but I shall make the attempt.

When within some five miles of Guanajuato numerous market-men were encountered, driving before them the donkeys that had borne their produce to the city.

As many of our men were foot-sore from the tedious mountain march of the previous day, the officer who had charge of us immediately pressed the animals into service, and told the Texans to mount them. It was in vain the owners of the animals expostulated, and told our captain that they were in haste to return to their homes—he not only reiterated his order for our men to seize the unsuspecting donkeys by the ears and mount them at once, but commanded their owners to assist in driving them. As we gradually approached the city the number of asses increased, and before we entered the suburbs every Texan was perched upon the back of a donkey, without saddle or bridle, and of such low stature were many of the animals, that their riders were fairly compelled to draw up their legs to keep their feet from dragging on the ground.

The whole scene was ludicrously rich, and afforded infinite amusement not only to the guard of dragoons who accompanied us, and the throngs of men and women gathered upon either side of the streets, but to the Texans themselves. In fact, all appeared to enjoy the comical appearance of our procession, save the donkeys and their unfortunate owners.

Shouts of every description rent the air as we thus journeyed along. "Here comes the Texas heavy light cavalry," some fellow would cry aloud, and the next moment, perhaps, he would measure his length upon the ground by one of those peculiar pitches and kicks understood and practised only by animals of the donkey race. At every step some one of the animals would take it into his head to run away—his next neighbour, very likely, would at the same time make up his mind not to move at all; an obstinate whim which it is extremely difficult to beat out of a jackass. Shouts of

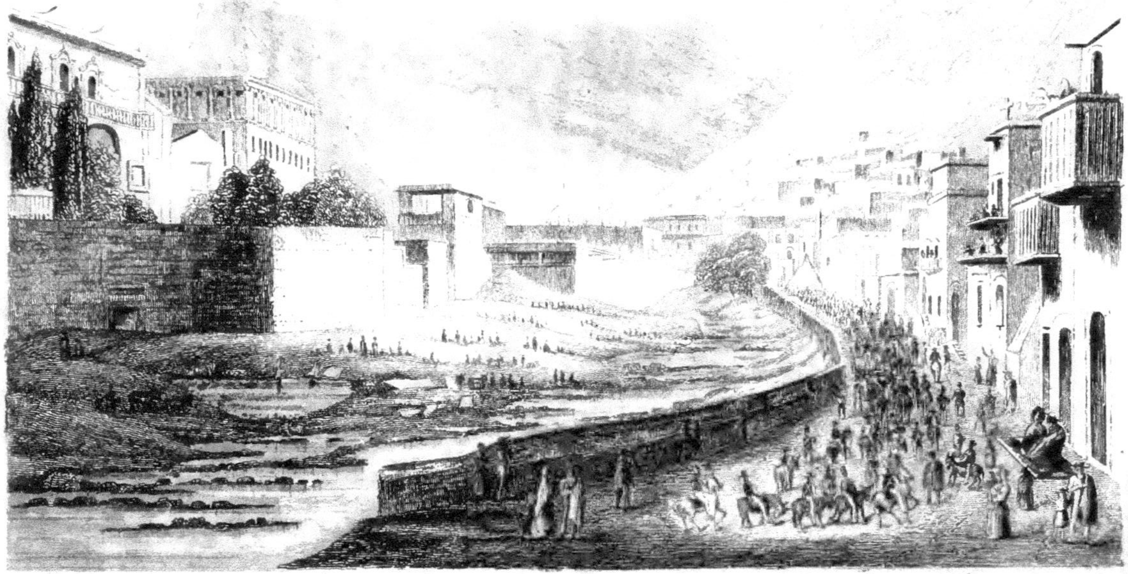

CITY OF GUANAXUATO.

NEW YORK, HARPER & BROTHERS

R. Miller Printer.

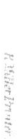

laughter from the Texans would ensue as some one of the animals indulged in an extra freak of eccentricity, and mixed with the laughter the muttered curses and deep imprecations of the owners could be distinctly heard. They were anxious to be relieved as soon as possible from this extra duty which had been imposed upon them, and accordingly pressed their overburdened animals along by those incentives a Mexican knows so well how to use. "Hip-ah! burro!"* resounded on every side, accompanied by blows and kicks—"Tchew, tchew, tchew," an unmeaning sound, but used as an encouragement for the animals to move faster, was freely administered at every step.

When once within the city, among its dark and narrow streets, the services of the donkeys were dispensed with, and their unfortunate owners set off for their homes in no good-humour. We were then taken completely through Guanajuato, and finally lodged at the soldiers' barracks—clean and airy quarters. My description of our singular entry into one of the proudest and richest cities of Mexico falls far short of the real scene itself—it is utterly impossible to draw a correct picture of a performance which not one of those who took a part in it, either as spectator or actor, can ever forget.

We had scarcely reached our quarters before we were visited by numerous foreigners—English, Irish, and American—who at once inquired into the wants of the prisoners, and promised to render every assistance. As was the case at San Luis Potosi, Colonel Cooke's party not having passed through the place, the foreign residents had not been called upon to contribute and render assistance to their countrymen in distress.

* *Burro*—the Spanish name for a jackass.

Accompanied by the Mexican physicians attached to the hospital, several of the foreign medical men examined such of our party as had the small-pox or other diseases, and permission was granted for eighteen of them to be taken immediately to the hospital, there to remain until their recovery, or till death should release them from their sufferings.

Among those more severely affected with the loathsome malady, now rapidly spreading among us, were Captain Caldwell and poor Fitzgerald. The latter was delirious when we placed him in the litter which bore him to the hospital, and strong fears were entertained that he would sink under the disease; but he recovered, and was shortly afterward liberated through the exertions of the British minister; he has since been retaken by the Mexicans, and shot while heroically assisting his comrades to escape. Captain Caldwell also recovered from the small-pox, and was released by Santa Anna with the rest of the Texan prisoners, but, as I have before mentioned, has since died in Texas. Of the eighteen left at Guanajuato, five died and were buried at the place—the remainder were sent to Mexico on their recovery, and confined with their comrades at the Convent of Santiago. They described their treatment as extremely kind and attentive while in the hospital, and on their arrival at Mexico they were all well dressed.

An attempt was made by our foreign friends to induce the commandante to allow us to remain at Guanajuato one day; but as all the sick had been taken care of, and the governor was not in the city, he did not feel at liberty to grant the request. Finding themselves unable to delay our departure, our friends redoubled their exertions in obtaining contributions, and the next morning a large sum of money and a generous supply of clothing were distributed among our men. At no place on the route did the foreigners contribute with greater liberality to the relief of the unfortunate Texans than at Guanajuato, and among those most indefatigable in obtaining these necessaries was the gentleman at whose house we had taken supper at Silao.

It was at Guanajuato that I first heard of the arrival, at the city of Mexico, of one of my associates in business, although the gentleman who gave me the information could not learn his name. Before I received this news I had half made up my mind to accept an offer made me to escape, an American gentleman I had met on the road suggesting a feasible plan, and proffering me every assistance. I was to be provided with a horse, a servant who spoke English, and a passport, and could take either the route to Tampico, or to Mazatlan, on the Pacific, the escape to be made at some town or rancho between Guanajuato and Queretaro. The gentleman appeared, according to promise, at the place appointed; but by this time I had heard of the arrival of my associate, and in addition to this I was allowed my parole by the officer then in charge of the prisoners. To run away under these circumstances would have involved an honourable officer in difficulty, and brought more rigorous treatment and closer confinement upon my companions; and taking these circumstances into consideration, I gave up all thoughts of escaping. Had I anticipated the sickness and loathsome imprisonment yet in store for me, I should not have visited the city of Mexico, and should have saved the United States and Mexican governments reams of correspondence in relation to my humble self and case.

About ten o'clock on the morning of the 20th of January we took our departure from Guanajuato, our route conducting us through the same streets by which we had entered—I am not certain that there is any other outlet to the place. The city is built in a deep but narrow ravine, some two miles in length, while its greatest width is perhaps not more than three or four hundred yards. On either side high and precipitous mountains rise—so steep that the very goats can hardly find a road up their sides. There are but two or three main streets; but these run the whole length of the city, are very narrow, and the houses extremely high, so that a large population is congregated in the deep and dark barranca. A more singular site for a city probably does not exist in the wide world, and nothing induced the early settlers to select it but the fact that the surrounding mines were among the richest and most productive in the country.

After crossing, some twenty times, a little stream of water which runs through the principal street leading into the city, and after passing the suburbs, we began the ascent of the mountains at the only point where a road was practicable. A single turn shut the city we had just left completely from the sight, and I doubt whether there is more than one spot within half a mile from which even the highest of its numerous domes can be seen, so completely is Guanajuato hidden from the world.

At night we halted at La Puerta, where we slept, and the next afternoon we reached the city of Salamanca. This is a neat and tolerably well-built place, containing several colleges, besides convents and churches. As we were leaving it the next morning, I had an opportunity of seeing a *volunteer* for the army *caught*. The man's crime I did not learn, nor in fact could I ascertain that he had committed any: be this as it may, he was seized and tied in front of the meson where we had passed the night, and dragged onward by two dragoons detailed for the special purpose of preventing his escape. The fellow had a mother, who, with tears and prayers, begged the commander of the dragoons to release her son. The officer turned a deaf ear to her entreaties, pushed her from him, and strode onward. With frantic shrieks the woman sprang after him, fell at his feet, and while clinging with convulsive grasp to his knees, besought him, in accents most piteous, to allow her son to remain with her. Again the officer threw the woman from him, and jumping upon his horse, was soon out of hearing. The last I saw of the mother she was flying about from one person to another, wringing her hands in the very phrensy of despair, and beseeching all to intercede in behalf of her boy. This in a republic which boasts of its freedom, and cannot issue the most trifling despatch without tacking "God and *liberty*" to some part of it!

In the afternoon of the 22d we reached Celaya, a neat and busy, but small city. The residence of General Cortazar, the gentlemanly and liberal governor of the State of Guanajuato, is at this place. From him and his officers, not only our party but that of Colonel Cooke, invariably received the best treatment; and even the common soldiers of our guard, while within the limits of Guanajuato, appeared to partake of the better qualities of the generous commandante and his officers.

Cortazar had us all quartered in a clean and airy convent, gave us the full liberty of the city on parole, and sent word that we might remain thirty-six hours in the place to rest and recruit ourselves. This favour was the more agreeable to us, as the following day was Sunday, and we thus had an opportunity of seeing the religious observances and public amusements by which this day is celebrated in a Mexican city.

At an early hour on Sunday morning a small party of us left the convent. Our first stopping-place was at a meson near the market square, where we partook of as good a breakfast as the tavern afforded. Our next movement was to the principal cathedral of Celaya, to observe the religious ceremonies of the morning. A party of Indians were in attendance, in addition to the regular worshippers, and the strange mingling of some of their own customs with the rites of the established Catholic Church, formed a picture of striking singularity. The early Spanish missionaries were never able entirely to eradicate the superstitious ceremonies of the original inhabitants, but by allowing them to ingraft some of their own rites upon Catholicism, they partially brought them over to their faith. This state of things still continues, and the religion of a large portion of the mixed classes is to this day but a blending of whimsical and grotesque ceremonies with the solemn and imposing observances which appertain to the religion of the Romish Church.

After twelve o'clock the innumerable liquor-shops of the city were thrown open, and in the afternoon cock-fighting commenced at the theatre. The pit seats were taken out for the purpose, and on visiting it we found a large assembly of gamblers, loafers, gentlemen, soldiers, and priests assembled to enjoy the sport. The Mexicans of all classes are passionately fond of it, and will frequently stake their all upon the result of a single fight.

The amusements of the cockpit over, the seats were replaced, and every preparation made for the production of "*El Campanero de San Pablo*"—the Bell-Ringer of St. Paul's — by a Spanish company of actors then playing at Celaya. This performance we also attended, and found the house well filled with many of the more fashionable families of the place, and among them that of General Cortazar. Ladies and all, as is the custom in a Mexican theatre, kept up an incessant smoking between the acts, and the rising of the curtain even was no signal for them to throw away their cigarritos. The drama was a translation from the French, but is founded on a story of the reign of Charles I. of England, and is extremely popular in Mexico. The actors were all perfect in their parts, but the play dragged heavily enough along to those who but imperfectly understood the language, and after seeing three acts of it, and inhaling cigar and candle smoke until we were half suffocated, we returned to our quarters. Thus did we spend our Sunday at Celaya.

On the next morning we took our departure from this hospitable town. As we were about starting, it was ascertained that young Curtis Caldwell had broken out with the small-pox.* He was not more than fourteen years old, but an extremely intelligent and active lad for his age, and Cortazar had him taken to his own house and treated with every possible attention. On his recovery he was sent to his father at Guanajuato, and finally returned to Texas with him.

In the afternoon of the 24th we reached a miserable rancho called Calera. During the palmy days of Guanajuato, when the mines of that district yielded their richest treasures and employed immense numbers of men, the Baxio, or fertile valley in which Salamanca, Celaya,

---

* His father, it will be remembered, had been left at Guanajuato with the same disease.

and innumerable rich haciendas are situated, found a ready market for the corn and wheat grown upon its surface; but now that the demand has been in a great measure cut off, the estates are gradually sinking in value and going out of cultivation.

In one part of this valley—I think between Queretaro and San Juan del Rio—the traveller passes through an immense corn-field, or rather a succession of corn-fields, miles in extent, the produce of which supplies the neighbouring cities. During a march of nearly two days nothing could be seen on any side but stacks of Indian corn, the husks still on, and each stack surmounted with a rude wooden cross. The owners of the grain had taken the latter precaution, so it was told us, to prevent the ladrones from preying upon their property; for it is said that nothing can induce the most hardened thief, in that country of petty pilferers, to touch aught which is thus guarded. Whether this is true or false is a point upon which I do not intend to decide; if true, I can say that it is much the cheapest and safest method of preventing theft that could be devised in Mexico, and I would prefer having my property under the guardianship and protection of one wooden cross than of twenty armed men. Robert Macaire would have starved to death had his lot fallen among Mexican ladrones, and the noted "Pony Club" of Georgia might have found valuable members by sending to Mexico.*

* The candidate for admission into this "Club" was obliged to pass through the following ordeal successfully before he could receive his diploma, or certificate of membership. A committee of passed members conducted the tyro to a secluded place in the woods, placed a hat upon a stump or rock in a conspicuous position, and then arranged themselves around it in such situations that all could plainly see the hat. If the candidate was successful in stealing it, while all were watching, he was at once admitted into full communion and fellowship; if not, he was dismissed with advice to practise still farther his "slight-of-hand" tricks, and by untiring industry endeavour better to qual-

Finding that he could procure no food for the prisoners at Calera, the officer who had charge of us determined upon an early start in the morning, with the intention of reaching Queretaro by breakfast-time. We were all in motion by two o'clock; and so raw and cold was the early morning air, that such of us as were mounted dashed onward at a brisk gallop, with the hope of thus obtaining warmth and a circulation of the blood. The days, at this time, were delightfully warm and pleasant, but the extreme height of the table-lands made the nights raw and chilly. To show how negligent were the dragoons who accompanied us as a guard, I may add that the little party with whom I made the morning ride did not see one of them from the time we set off until we had nearly reached the city gates.

We were but a short league from Queretaro when the sun rose—within sight of a city whose numerous public buildings and works, whose lofty and imposing domes, towers, and steeples, present to the view of the traveller, enter it from what quarter he may, a sight than which one more grand and magnificent can hardly be imagined. The city is in part encircled by lofty mountains, and as the rising sun first kissed their towering summits, the gray and sombre-shadowed town, lying far beneath them, was buried in profound repose. Anon, as the sun's rays came flashing from the mountain tops and lit up the higher domes of the place, the scene assumed an appearance of light and life. Soon the sun itself rose from behind those mountain barriers, and the whole city was at once aroused by its animating pres-

---

ify himself for the high station to which he aspired. So adroit is the veriest dunce among the Mexican thieves, that he could steal the hat from the very head of a sharp-sighted man without being detected, even if the latter had friends on the look-out to prevent it.

ence. To forget that morning's dawn and its effect upon Queretaro were impossible. Now a blushing ray would linger and play upon the loftiest peaks of the surrounding mountains; the next moment it would flash across the plain, dispel the deep shadows from the mountain sides, and gild some towering dome with a flood of light. To watch the bright beams reflected from tower to tower and from dome to dome—to see the dark shadows disappearing, as if châsed from their retreats by the vivid flashes — and then to behold the entire city lit up as by enchantment—all combined to form a spectacle of almost inconceivable grandeur. The morning was now bright, beautiful, and balmy, and the stillness which surrounded us was only broken by the distant deep-toned bells calling the dwellers to mass, and that busy but undefinable hum which betokens the awakening of a great city to the labour of another day.

As the last straggling loiterers of our party came up, we were formed in regular order, and then marched through the city. Quarters had been procured for us at an old convent on the side of the city opposite to that by which we entered—a vile, dismal hole at the best—but our commandante said that no other could be obtained.

A circumstance of a very amusing nature occurred while the officer of our guard was absent at the house of the commandante, for the purpose of obtaining permission for us to roam about the city on parole. We had scarcely been ten minutes in the convent when we were visited by the usual crowd of venders of oranges and other fruits, women with tortillas, frijoles, and guisado, all anxious to dispose of their little stock in trade. Mr. Falconer picked out some half dozen oranges and sweet limes from the basket of a fruit-girl, and in payment handed her a dollar. There was not small coin enough among them all to change the dollar, and Falconer sent it out by a corporal, telling him to get it changed. The fellow shortly returned with *sixty-four cakes of soap*, tied up in a handkerchief. Falconer told the corporal he wanted *change*, not *soap*. The corporal replied that it was the currency of the place—legal currency—and that there was no other. Such proved to be the case; and however singular it may appear, soap is really a lawful tender in the payment of all debts, and our companion was compelled to keep this singular substitute in the way of change for his dollar. He could not very well pocket it, as there was nearly a peck in bulk.

The cakes are about the size of the common Windsor shaving-soap, and each is worth one cent and a half—in fact, a fraction more, as eight of them pass for twelve and a half cents, or sixteen for a quarter of a dollar. Each cake is stamped with the name of the town where it is issued, and also with the name of the person who is authorized by law to manufacture it as a circulating medium; yet Celaya soap—for it also circulates in that city—will not pass at Queretaro. The reason I cannot divine, as the size and intrinsic value appear to be the same. The municipal authorities of either town appear to have made no provision for equalizing the exchanges between the two places, and there are no brokers' offices for the buying and selling of uncurrent soap in Mexico.

Many of the cakes in circulation were partially worn, and showed evidence indisputable of an acquaintance with the wash-tub; but all were current so long as the stamp was visible. Frequently I remarked that our men would use one of these singular bits of currency in washing their hands and faces, and then pass it off for a plate of frijoles or an orange. Much amusement, too, did we have among ourselves while in the district where it passes as a legal tender, and "Are you out of soap?" and "How are you off for soap?" were expressions continually passing from mouth to mouth. The same cant phrase is common enough in the United States, and has been for years; but how it originated is a matter of which I am most profoundly ignorant. At all events, it is applicable enough in some parts of Mexico.

In the afternoon we received permission to roam through the city without a guard. As we passed a prison, we were hailed from its gloomy, grated windows by a voice in our own language. There were two Americans—natives of Philadelphia, I believe—in the prison, who had been employed to work a woollen or cotton factory near Queretaro at a stipulated sum. Their employer had in some way broken his faith, and they had left him; but his power was superior, and he had thrown them into prison to gratify a mean spirit of revenge. We told them that we, too, were prisoners, unable to afford them assistance, and then left them with wishes for their speedy release.

We next strolled through the principal streets, entering some of the stores, taverns, cigar, and barber shops. In one of the latter I noticed two men busily employed in grinding and sharpening gaffs for fighting-cocks, showing that this amusement is common among the denizens of Queretaro. One man was shaving a customer, but instead of lathering him after the French or English fashion, he placed a large composition or silver basin, having a hollow in one side to fit the neck, directly under the chin of the customer, and then soaped his face with his hands. It is a vile Spanish custom, this; but, like thousands of others of that anti-go-ahead race, is persisted in. I thought of Don Quixotte and Mambrino's helmet the moment I set eyes upon one of these basins.

In our stroll we passed the walls of an immense convent or nunnery, said to be a large village of itself. We could only see the tops of the buildings above the walls, for no one is allowed to pass the gates. We entered a large dry and fancy goods store, having for a sign "Tienda de los Palomos," or Store of the Doves. Why the Mexicans name their shops and stores after cats, dogs, doves, and other birds and beasts, is a mystery to me. Their fondas and mesones all have religious names, or nearly all. It was quite common for us to stop at the tavern of the Holy Ghost, or Hotel of the True Cross, and others, a translation of which would appear irreverent and almost blasphemous to my countrymen.

Just as dark was setting in, and while three of us were crossing the market-place in the direction of a little Mexican restaurat, several stones were thrown at us from the dense throng at that hour congregated in the square. Fortunately not one of the missiles hit us, although they whizzed by close to our heads. Who the authors of this outrage were we did not ascertain; but they were probably some of the very lowest class, who only insulted us in this way to show their pitiful spite at our nation and religion. It was almost the only direct insult offered us south of El Paso, for generally the lower orders looked upon us rather as objects of pity than of hatred or revenge. We immediately entered the restaurat, after the outrage had been committed, and called for a supper, the perpetrators not following or molesting us farther.

While we were waiting for our meal, a monk or friar, of some poor and abstemious order, entered the apartment with a noiseless step. Tied about him with a piece of rope was a coarse blanket or gown, of a grayish yellow colour; his head was bare, the top of it being close shaven; and he may have been barefooted, for I do not recollect seeing either boot, shoe, or sandal upon his feet. In his hand he had a small tin box, resembling, in many respects, a lantern. At all events, I took it for a lantern; for as the room was but dimly lighted, and as he silently held the box close to my face, I thought he was endeavouring to scrutinize my countenance with the hope of recognising me by some mysterious and hidden light it might contain. A *galopina*, or kitchen girl, standing by, soon explained the business of the holy brother by dropping a quartillo into the box through a hole in the top, which I had not previously seen. Now the mystery was solved—the friar was holding the box in my face for alms. Fearing that I might have insulted him by rudely, although innocently, staring in his face, I resolved upon purchasing forgiveness to such extent as a quarter of a dollar would obtain, and accordingly dropped a coin of that value into the box. The amount purchased my pardon, if he thought I owed him one; for, making a low bow, he gave me his *benedicte*, and then, with dignified meekness, left the room.

Weary from our long walk, and the early morning ride, we remained no longer than to obtain our supper, and then retired to our quarters at the old convent, meeting with neither obstruction nor insult on the way.

## CHAPTER X.

Departure from Queretaro.—A stupendous Aqueduct.—View of Queretaro from a Mountain Summit.—Number and Magnificence of its Churches.—Meeting with Englishmen.—News that Colonel Cooke's Party were in Chains.—The Diligence.—Letter from Mr. Lumsden.—Liberation of Frank Combs.—Arrival at San Juan del Rio.—Escape of two of our Companions.—They are retaken and punished.—The Indian Village of Tula.—Strange Celebration.—Queer Characters.—Crackers and Sky-rockets.—Approach to the City of Mexico.—Speculations as to our future Lot.—Mr. Navarro separated from his Companions.— Route altered. — "Quien Sabe?"—Kindness of the Indian Women.—Arrival at the old Palace of San Cristobal.—The Texans locked within its gloomy Walls.—Visited by Mr. Lumsden and other Americans.—A joyful Meeting.—Prospects of Release.—Description of San Cristobal.—Release of Falconer and Van Ness.—Visited by Members of the United States Legation.— Difference in the Policy of the United States and English Governments.— Cause of Mr. Falconer's Release.—Another Visit from the Americans.—File of American Papers.—A Letter from Chihuahua, and its Effects.—Gloomy Presentiments.—Our Men supplied with Clothing and Blankets.—Celebration in Honour of Santa Anna's Leg.—Supplies cut off.—Sufferings on the Increase.—Nothing to Eat.—Resorts of the Texans to obtain Food.—Singular Tribunals, with the Results.—A Humorous Witness.—Wild Revel in San Cristobal.

IMMEDIATELY on leaving Queretaro, our road took us directly under the immense aqueduct which supplies the city with water. This aqueduct is a stupendous work, having been built many years since, by the Spaniards, when money was abundant and Indian labour easy to command. Pure water is carried by this means across a wide valley, the head spring being on a mountain side at a distance of some six or eight miles. The arches which support the stupendous fabric are of stone, lofty yet light, and of graceful proportions. Far as the eye can reach, the aqueduct is seen stretching across the valley; now rising high above the surface of the ground as some low place is crossed, and again all but touching the higher undulations. At the point where we passed under one of the arches, and we were on the direct road to the city of Mexico, the water must have been forty or fifty feet above us—perhaps more.

After proceeding but a few miles, we commenced the ascent of a steep and lofty chain of mountains. Once at their summit, the view of Queretaro, and the beautiful valley in which it lies, is one of the finest and most lovely in all Mexico. The number of inhabitants in the city we had just left does not probably exceed fifty thousand, but as is the case in every large town of the country, there are churches enough to supply the spiritual wants of six times that number in the United States. These churches, too, are built upon a scale, both in size and magnificence, to which we are perfect strangers, and give an appearance of splendour to their cities which without them would sink into comparative insignificance.

While stopping for a short time to rest, during the middle of the day, the diligence drove up on its way from the city of Mexico to Guanajuato. Among the passengers were two or three Englishmen, who informed us that in consequence of the escape of two of the men attached to Colonel Cooke's party, they had all been placed in irons. As to what disposition Santa Anna would finally make of them, they could give us nothing but mere speculation and idle rumour.

During our next day's march we again met the stage ascending a high, steep hill. The driver stopped to allow a passenger, an American gentleman, to alight for a moment. He inquired for me, and gave me a letter which I at once knew was from Mr. Lumsden. I have already mentioned that I had heard, while at Guanajuato, of one of my partners having reached the city of Mexico for the purpose of obtaining my liberation as speedily as possible, but my informant could not give me his name, and until this moment I did not know which of my associates was thus exerting himself in my behalf.

It will be readily supposed that I devoured the contents of this letter with no little avidity. It was to the effect that young Frank Combs had been liberated, and that every exertion should be made to effect my speedy release on reaching the city. I had all along supposed that the Mexican government could not possibly detain me twenty-four hours, after a statement of the manner of my arrest and the circumstances attending it was properly laid before those in authority by Mr. Ellis, our then minister; but in these anticipations I was destined to be most grievously disappointed. Santa Anna had no idea of letting me off so easily.

We arrived at the town of San Juan del Rio on the evening of January 27th. This place is situated upon a small river, and is the last town of any note before the traveller reaches Mexico, although the remainder of the road runs through a succession of villages. We met two or three Americans at San Juan, who only corroborated the story that our comrades in Mexico were chained in couples and compelled to toil in the streets.

We had proceeded but a short distance the next day before it was discovered, among ourselves, that two of our men had made their escape—frightened to this step probably by the stories of chains and servitude. We said nothing about it at the time; but when our guard counted us at night the fact of their having escaped became known. They were afterward retaken by a small party sent out for the purpose, closely guarded to the city of Mexico, and there thrown into that vilest of holes, the *Acordada*, as a punishment for their offence. With but a single exception, this was the only unsuccessful attempt made to escape while we were in the country.

Early in the afternoon of the 1st of February we reached the large Indian village of Tula, some ten or twelve leagues from the city of Mexico. Scarcely had we entered the quarters which had been provided for us, at a commodious meson fronting immediately upon the market-square, when a confused shouting was heard in one of the streets leading into the plaza—a hubbub as of boys following a military volunteer company in the United States. Before we had time to reach a corner of the square, whence the shouting appeared to come, we encountered a medley and most singular procession of ragged Indians. Preceding them was an eccentric and oddly-attired personage, who appeared not only to act as master of ceremonies, but took it upon himself to sell invitations to join in the grand procession and a mass which accompanied it. One of these invitations I purchased. It was written on a page of foolscap paper, the edges embellished with a wide and gaudy border, within which was a quotation in Spanish from the twenty-sixth chapter of St. Matthew, thirty-ninth verse —" O my father, if it be possible, let this cup pass from me." Then followed a short sketch of the sufferings of our Savior, of his great love for our fallen race, and of his betrayal by Judas, while at the bottom of all was an invitation in terms somewhat like the following: "Captain Don Lauriano Rodea and friends supplicate your assistance on the 1st and 2d days of February," and the invitation which supplicated for this assistance was sold for *dos reales*—twenty-five cents.

In advance of the procession walked, or rather jumped, two grotesque and diabolical figures. Of the sex, colour, or condition of these actors in the crowd we could form no opinion. Their faces, save the eyes and teeth, were completely hidden by hideous masks of black crape, while their bodies were covered with a dingy, dirty black dress, fitting closely to the skin. They did not walk, but crooked their knees, crouched their bodies as close to the ground as possible, and then hopped about after the manner of orang-outangs or kangaroos. Whenever a door was passed, at which stood some girl fairer and better clad than usual, one of those grotesque figures would hop hurriedly after her, grin hideously with his white teeth, and so frighten the pursued that she would instantly seek shelter within the house. These little innocent eccentricities on the part of the gentleman in black, who performed the most wonderful feats of agility while hopping from point to point, were much relished by the crowd of boys and idlers in attendance upon the procession. I was unable to make out the characters sustained by these imps of darkness; but whether devils or Judases, they certainly well sustained their parts, in action and appearance.

Immediately in their rear followed some four or five swarthy, dirty-faced, half-grown boys, dressed to represent angels, although they were like almost anything else. Their once white robes were soiled and stained until they had become a dirty yellow; their wings were unhinged, broken, discoloured, and draggling; their thick, uncombed hair was filled with withered flowers, or encircled with faded wreaths; their gait was awkward and swaggering, and, take them altogether, a sorrier set of angels were probably never let loose upon earth. Had they been personating angels of darkness, their aspect certainly would have been appropriate, to say nothing of their acting. It was shrewdly suspected that one or two of these good spirits had been partaking rather more freely of aguardiente than became their calling. The tail of the procession was a rabble of men, women, and children, the latter improving every moment in letting off squibs and crackers among the throng.

At the church, whither we followed the crowd, a short service appeared to end the ceremonies, at least for that day; for after it was concluded, the good and evil spirits broke up the order of march, and mingled promiscuously with the swarthy populace. So far as the sending up of rockets, and other exhibitions of the like nature, went—for, without fireworks, a Mexican celebration is incomplete—the strange mummeries were kept up until a late hour. Such were the performances at Tula on the 1st of February; what they were on the 2d I know not, although I had purchased an invitation to take part in them.

With the supposition that we were that evening to be marched into the great city of the Montezumas, we left Tula at an early hour in the morning. We had now been some three months and a half upon the road, journeying through twenty degrees of latitude, and exposed to hardships and privations innumerable. The fate of all, whether good or evil, was soon to be decided. Upon the flimsy pretext that one or two of their companions had escaped, we knew that Santa Anna had chained Colonel Cooke's men, and what was worse, had sent them to work in the streets and ditches—a punishment awarded only to criminals. Was our fate to be the same? The mind of each man was racked to answer the question—speculation only ended in doubt and uncertainty.

We had supposed that we were to be marched directly into the city, which, by the middle of the day, was only concealed by a mountain, when at a fork of the road a halt was called. At this point Mr. Navarro was separated from us, for what reason no one could divine. Under a strong guard he was conducted directly towards the city, while we were ordered to pursue the left-hand fork of the road, which led we knew not whither. We asked the dragoons, riding on either side of us, as to our destination. Our only answer was the eternal "*quien sabe?*" The Mexicans of the lower classes, if unable to answer a question, instead of giving a decided negative, invariably use this exclamation of "*quien sabe?*" the literal meaning of which is " who knows?" thus answering one question by asking another. The expression is, however, equivalent to "*I don't know*" in English.

Our route now took us through a thickly-settled and tolerably well-cultivated country, although squalid poverty was to be seen on every side. The half-dressed, swarthy Indian women, with their black but mild and pensive eyes, came running from the adobe houses, many of them in tears at our sad and wretched appearance; for by this time some twenty of our party were down with the small-pox and other diseases. Murmuring the universal exclamation, *pobrecitos*, they would divide tomales,* tortillas, fruit—in short, their little all —among men whom they must have supposed to be on the road to execution.

About noon, and after passing a poor village with a large and once magnificent church, the celebrated lake of San Cristobal appeared in sight. A few hundred

---

* The *tomale* is made of meal, with a slight mixture of red pepper and meat. It is then wrapped in the husks of corn and boiled.

yards farther we were halted in front of the old Palace of San Cristobal, once a celebrated summer residence of the Spanish viceroys, but long since deserted, and now fast crumbling to decay. We were ordered to enter its wide doorway; but why we were brought to a place so desolate and gloomy no one could imagine. The captain of our guard shrugged his shoulders when interrogated as to the cause of this singular movement, and after saying that he had been ordered to lock us up in San Cristobal, briefly remarked that he had obeyed his orders.

The key had hardly turned in the lock when three or four horsemen, evidently foreigners from their style of dress and riding, were seen galloping towards us across the plain. They pulled up in front of our miserable quarters, and on alighting I for the first time recognised Mr. Lumsden as of the party. After a short conference with the captain of our guard, and leaving their pistols and knives with the sentinels at the door, for no traveller ever rides to the outskirts of the city of Mexico without arms, the party were allowed to enter.

That I was overjoyed at meeting with Mr. L. may easily be imagined. His companions were American gentlemen, residing in the city of Mexico. Learning early in the morning that the prisoners were approaching, they had ordered horses and immediately come out to meet us. Finding that we had taken a different road, on reaching the fork where Mr. Navarro had been separated from us, they followed upon our track until they at length found us securely locked up within the crumbling walls of the old Palace of San Cristobal.

As regarded my own prospects of release, my friends gave me every encouragement. They appeared sanguine that but a few days would elapse before I should regain that liberty of which I had been so unjustly deprived for nearly five months; and as the afternoon was now far advanced, and the distance some twelve miles to the city, they took their leave, after promising to visit us again the next day.

The Palace of San Cristobal is pleasantly situated upon a plain, and immediately in front are the lake of the same name, and one of the canals to be met with in the valley of Mexico. In the immediate vicinity there are no buildings, save the miserable mud-hovels of a few poor wretches, whose means of procuring an honest livelihood must be precarious indeed. Directly in front of the palace, the range of mountains which divides the valley of Mexico from that of Puebla was seen in the distance, while to the right one of the high and snow-capped volcanoes, which give to the scenery of Mexico its grandeur and sublimity, was seen rising far among the clouds. In clear weather the mountain-top is plainly visible, as is also the volcano upon its side; but on the day of our arrival the atmosphere betokened rain, and its summit was covered with a fleecy veil of clouds.

The building in which we were confined may have been a very respectable palace in its day, but when we were there it would hardly afford shelter for the bats our presence frightened from their retreats. It is two stories high, and built in the fashion of nearly all the large houses of Mexico, in a quadrangular form, having a pat'o or court-yard in the centre. The entrance was through a large gateway. The ground floor of the front part of the building contained four rooms, while in the second story was a large dining hall, flanked by a bedroom at one end and a small kitchen at the other.

The only apartment in the house having any pretensions to being habitable was the bedroom I have just mentioned, and this the captain of our guard appropriated to his own use and that of his brother officers. The dining hall was given to the Texan officers and merchants, while the poor soldiers were compelled to take up their quarters in the yard below, and in such of the dilapidated rooms of the first story as were in any way tenantable. The ravaging tooth of time had eaten away almost the whole interior of the building, leaving the outer walls alone untouched, and into these cold, dreary, and miserable quarters were some hundred and fifty of us thrust—into a hole which would not afford even tolerable shelter for half that number of brute beasts. Another thing which served to render our quarters far more disagreeable was the fact that by this time eighteen or twenty of our number had the small-pox, and many of them were delirious. In this situation we passed our first night at San Cristobal.

At an early hour the next morning a Mexican officer arrived from the city, bringing orders for the immediate release of Van Ness and Falconer. The former was liberated entirely through the influence of the Mexican Secretary of War and Marine, General Tornel, who was well acquainted with the family of Van Ness at Washington, and who had received from them many favours; but with Falconer the case was different. He had been demanded, as I understood at the time, by the British minister, and this demand had been followed by his immediate release. Afterward, I heard a different version of the story.

Our liberated friends had scarcely departed for the city, in a coach provided for the purpose, when we were visited by Brantz Mayer, Esq., United States secretary of legation, and by the American consul at Mexico, Mr. Black. Mr. M. inquired of me the circumstances of my arrest and all the information I could give relevant to my case, as also to that of several others who claimed American protection. I told him that I had given Mr. Ellis, in several letters that I had written while upon the road, full particulars in relation to myself; that my case was much clearer than that of Mr. Falconer, inasmuch as I had joined the expedition with the previously-expressed intention of travelling through Mexico, had provided myself with a passport before leaving New-Orleans, and had entirely separated myself from the expedition previous to the time of my capture. In addition, I told Mr. Mayer, that while I rejoiced with Mr. Falconer upon his happy deliverance from the worst of bondage, I certainly thought it very singular, and by no means flattering to that country from which I claimed protection, that while a British subject, who was in a greater degree implicated than myself, was immediately liberated, I was held a prisoner even for a moment.* He expressed every sympa-

* In comparison with the English government, and with not a little reluctance do I say it, that of the United States is notoriously slow in interfering for its citizens when their personal liberty has been infringed upon—a statement the truth of which will be attested by every American who has travelled in Mexico or other foreign countries. The British government looks upon the *liberty* of the subject as paramount to all considerations—that of the United States will promptly enough interfere when a barrel of flo·.r is unjustly taken from one of its citizens, but let him be deprived of his liberty, and the matter requires, to use the words of the old diplomatist in one of Power's plays, "a mighty deal of nice consideration." So well is this policy of the United States government understood in Mexico, that while an American is allowed to remain for months in a loathsome prison, a single word from the British minister will give immediate liberty to a subject of that government, incarcerated for the same offence and in every way equally culpable. The Americans, all over Mexico, openly speak of the insults they receive and the little personal security they enjoy, and many of them even told me that were they to enter the country again they would carry British protections in their

thy, said that Mr. Ellis would exert himself to the utmost to effect my release, and after offering me any assistance I might require, left the prison.

In the afternoon I was again visited by Mr. Lumsden, who was now accompanied by Lieutenant Blunt of the United States navy, Mr. McRae, who had but recently arrived with despatches from the United States, and several other American gentlemen, residents of the place. They brought us out a liberal supply of cigars, fruit, and other refreshments, and what to me was of far more value and interest, a number of American newspapers. In the Picayune I read, for the first time, a letter from Chihuahua, which directly implicated me as connected with the expedition, it being incorrectly

---

pockets. An American citizen, who boasts of his birthright and of the great liberty he enjoys at home, hears these mortifying admissions while abroad with wounded pride; but hear them he must, and, in addition, will feel and know that they are founded in truth. Since the arrival in Mexico of our present minister, General Thompson, and the powerful and decided papers of Mr. Webster have appeared, the tone of the Mexican government may have changed somewhat; I allude above to the state of feeling existing while I was in the country.

After my return to the United States I saw and read a letter from Judge Ellis, to our then Secretary of State, Mr. Webster, in which the suddenness of Mr. Falconer's release is accounted for. By this document it would seem that Mr. Pakenham, the British minister, immediately on the arrival of Mr. F. at San Cristobal, called upon Santa Anna and presented him with a letter from Queen Victoria announcing the birth of the Prince of Wales. His excellency, the Provisional President, as an act of courtesy usual on such occasions, released Mr. Falconer the moment the British minister mentioned that he was a prisoner. Now, this was all right enough; but it is certainly unfortunate for us poor Republicans that no such door is open for our release when confined under similar circumstances. A corresponding increase to the family of one of our presidential ladies might take place, although such an event can hardly be looked for, and not a whit should we be gainers by it, while any addition to that of the august sovereign of Great Britain is a "walking paper" to her incarcerated subjects. We boast much of our freedom, and the perfect equality we enjoy, both at home and abroad, as compared with the people of other nations: surely, some provision should be made for us in contingencies like the above.

stated that I was one of the *avant courriers* sent forward by Colonel Cooke on approaching the settlements of New Mexico. Knowing that the Mexican government would eagerly seize upon any pretext to annoy one for whom, from the general tone of the articles in his paper in relation to Texan affairs, it could entertain no friendly feelings, I at once declared my belief that the publication of the letter would cause me months of imprisonment. My friends thought differently, and before leaving endeavoured to convince me that I should regain my liberty in a day or two; but I had a presentiment that no such good luck would befall me, and with this feeling passed my second night in San Cristobal.

During the first five days in the old palace we received regular visits from the Americans and other foreigners of the city. For the more destitute they brought blankets and different articles of clothing, and by their many acts of kindness endeavoured to make all as comfortable as they could be under the circumstances. It was during one of these visits that our friends gave us the particulars of a celebration in the city in honour of Santa Anna's leg—the one he lost when San Juan de Ulua and Vera Cruz were taken by the French. On the present occasion, a general holyday was given, and the limb was borne about in procession with great pomp and ceremony. Santa Anna makes much capital out of this affair—enough to console him, probably, for the loss of the limb. On several occasions it has been carried about in procession, and I have little doubt that the leg, *in pickle*, is of infinitely more service to him than when attached to his own proper person.

The day after our arrival at San Cristobal, a sum of

money was sent out, by the Mexican government, of sufficient amount to distribute twenty-five cents to each man: the same sum was also furnished the next day. With this the men could procure for themselves food enough, in the shape of frijoles, tortillas, chile guisado, and other articles which the Mexican women brought to our quarters, to appease the keen demands of appetite—it was all they were allowed. On the third day the supplies from the city were stopped. The fourth day came, and still no money; the fifth, likewise, and with it no succour. By this time the sufferings of those who had no money were severe in the extreme, and the tricks they resorted to in order to obtain food were ingenious to a degree, and occasioned not a little merriment.

Among the prisoners were a number of lawyers, doctors, and other professional men—persons who, either from a love of wild adventure or because they could obtain no professional employment in Texas, had originally been induced to join the expedition. Then there were several comedians among them, mad wags, who, finding that the drama yielded them but slender support in the new Republic, had shouldered the rifle and taken to the prairies for a better. Out of such materials it may readily be conceived that the richest fun and frolic could be extracted, and the story of one of their maddest pranks I will relate.

The wags knew that among the officers and merchants there were some who had money, and to levy a tax upon such pockets as were best filled these fellows commenced a game which, in the end, not only proved every way successful, but afforded infinite amusement to all. They in the first place fitted up an old, dilapidated apartment as a court-room. With two barrels and as many boards they made a kind of platform, upon which, as a bench, a claret-box was placed, and upon this the jokers seated the largest prisoner in the whole collection as judge—a half lawyer, who, in addition to having all the gravity of the Grand Turk himself, wore whiskers, mustaches, and hair in quantity sufficient to supply wigs for an entire bench of English justices. A sheriff, crier, and clerk—men who well understood their business—were then appointed; an eccentric comedian, who could speak for hours upon any subject, and possessed the keenest wit and the strongest imitative powers imaginable, was chosen prosecuting attorney. As principal witness in any cases that might be brought they fell upon a little Irishman named Jimmy Tweed. Jimmy was born and bred a soldier. He first drew breath in the barracks of a recruiting regiment in Ireland, and in process of time, after having picked up a fair education among the officers, joined the regiment as a soldier. The term of his enlistment he served principally at Gibraltar, where he obtained a name, to use his own words, " for being up to all manner of diviltry," and where he also learned a smattering of Spanish. On being discharged, he visited the United States, joined the army, served two or three campaigns in Florida, and was finally discharged regularly at Baton Rouge, in Louisiana. To finish his education, as he said, he then went to Texas, and after various campaigns, was finally taken prisoner in New Mexico. He had all the wit of his countrymen, and a fund of dry humour which was inexhaustible.

Thus organized, the court proceeded to the trial of such cases as they thought might be turned to their own profit. More decorum, more order, or more gravity of deportment was never seen in any court of justice. The crier in some way procured a small bell, and in regular form called the court together and issued his proclamations—the sheriff, with all the dignity imaginable, commanded silence, compelled all to take off their hats, and was very efficient in preserving the best order.

The first action upon their singular law-docket was brought against a young and very worthy man, a merchant, who was charged with being a " great fool generally"—I am not altogether positive but that the first word in the indictment may have been a much more forcible adjective than the simple term " great." The judge remarked that the charge was one extremely grave in its character, and admitted that he could not, at the time, think of any precedent that might guide him in his decision, which, he wound up by saying, should be a just and a righteous one. The prosecuting attorney, after a few pertinent remarks, brought up several witnesses to sustain the charge. Their evidence, which of course was made up and suited for the meridian of this particular court alone, all went to support the prosecution. The case, as made out, was clear enough—not a doubt arose as to the truth of the charge set forth in the indictment—but to make all sure, Jimmy Tweed was brought up to the stand. After kissing a brickbat with due gravity, there being no Bible in the court, Jimmy proceeded with his testimony. He instanced several particulars in which the accused party had evinced very little foresight—mentioned several of his actions which manifested great lack of judgment and knowledge of the world, and finally wound up by saying that the fact alone of his being found in company with the Santa Fé Expedition was ample evidence against him.

At this point of the trial symptoms of uproarious laughter were manifested in court, all which were instantly quelled by the sheriff, and the judge then proceeded to give his decision. Drawing himself up, throwing back his head, and clearing his throat with a preparatory "hem," and then raising one leg over the other with all becoming dignity, he remarked that all the evidence bore strongly against the accused, but that the testimony of the last witness, in particular, view it in what light he would, clearly sustained the charge that the arraigned party was slightly afflicted with a weakness known as "the simples"—troubled with not being so particularly wise as he might and should have been. He admitted that the charge which had been thus proved was a misfortune rather than a crime; but inasmuch as the times were hard, and victuals scarce, he should impose a fine of two dollars upon the accused. The latter, who enjoyed the joke as much as any one, interposed no motion in arrest of judgment, but paid the fine at once, and thus ended the first trial.

The next action brought, although not quite so grave in its nature, produced an infinite degree of merriment. One of our officers, Captain H., was charged with bad singing, or rather, as the indictment read, "with attempting to sing and making out badly at best." A number of witnesses testified, that at different times they had been most excessively annoyed, even to the losing of sleep, by the attempts of the accused at divers songs. They all admitted, during a process of cross-questioning, that they were not exactly good judges of music; still, they considered themselves blessed with ears which taught them to distinguish between the warbling of a canary and that of a crow—thought they could discover a soothing influence in the notes of a nightingale which they missed in the braying of a donkey. But as the testimony of Tweed went directly to prove the charge, and was a perfect gem in its way, I shall give it as nearly as possible in his own words.

"Yer oner," said Jimmy, with a ludicrous mock-gravity and quizzical leer of his dexter eye, "yer oner, as I was walkin' acrass the corral last evenin', I heerd sthrange, mystarius, and most unnath'ral sounds issuin' from the officers' quarthers up stairs—sounds resimblin', yer oner, those made by a sawmill, whin in the full tide of manufacthuring boards. Well, me curiosity bein' excited, I bethought meself I'd be after investigatin' the thing; so whin I was *abajo*, yer oner, which is the best Spanish I have at prisent about me for the foot of the stairs, I heerd the sthrange sounds louder and louder than iver. Up the steps I wint, and whin I was *arriba*, which manes, yer oner, the head of the stairs, divil a bit did it stop at all, at all. What in the name of all the saints, thinks I to meself, has put a sawmill in operation here away? for I still thought it was one, yer oner; so I opened the door cautiously, poked me head in slyly, and what should me own eyes see and me own ears hear but Captain H. himself, essayin' a bit of a ditty, yer oner."

"Doing *what?*" questioned the judge.

"Essayin' a ditty, yer oner—attempting a stave of a song—and—"

"Enough," interrupted the high functionary upon the claret box. "If you mistook the singing of Captain H. for those sounds ordinarily produced by a sawmill, the case is clear enough that he has undertaken a task which neither nature nor cultivation fits him to carry successfully through, and I shall fine him one dollar and fifty cents for the attempt."

In this way a number of cases, some for bad singing and others for speaking bad Spanish, were disposed of, and with the proceeds the merry wags procured a sufficiency of provisions and *chinguirite*, the latter a species of common rum manufactured from the sugar-cane, to hold a wild revel that night among the ruins of San Cristobal.

## CHAPTER XI.

Supply of Money received.—Our Sick examined.—Visited by a large Party of Americans from the City.—Hopes of Liberation still offered.—Reflections as to the Nature of my Case.—Departure from San Cristobal.—Start for the City of Mexico upon Asses.—The easy Gait of the genus Donkey.—Arrival at the Shrine of " Our Lady of Guadalupe."—Flimsy Imposture which caused its Erection.—Anecdote from Latrobe.—Nuestra Señora de los Remedios.—Mexican Beggars.—Tiresome Travel across the Plains.—The Garita.—Mexico, as seen in the Distance.—Arrival within the City.—Forlorn appearance of the Texans.—Commiseration of the Women.—Anecdote of Major Bennett.—Arrival at the Hospital of San Lazaro.—Hideous appearance of the Inmates.—A dreary Night.—Visited by the Hospital Physician.—His Prescriptions.—Description of San Lazaro and the unfortunate Lazarinos.—Speculations as regards the Leprosy.—Happiness among the Lepers.—New Sports and Dances.—We are visited by Mr. Mayer and other Americans.—Our Food at San Lazaro.—Kindness of the Mexicans in their Hospitals.—Smuggled Food.—Visits of the Physician.—Removed to other Quarters.—Worse and Worse.—Find our Room overrun with Chinches.—Our Friends gain Access by Bribery.—Departure of Mr. Lumsden and Friends for the United States.—Thoughts of an Escape.

On the day following that on which the singular and laughable trials took place, and the wild feast that followed them, a sum of money was received from Mexico for our men. On the same day, two or three physicians were sent out by Santa Anna to examine our sick. A report now obtained currency to the effect that such of the prisoners as were able to walk would be escorted immediately to Puebla, or the castle of Peroté, in the direction of Vera Cruz, while those who were unwell would be taken to some hospital in the city. The physicians pronounced eighteen unfit to travel, and as I was labouring under cold and fever at the time, I was placed on the list. Of the others, almost all were afflicted with the small-pox, in some stage of the disease.

The day before our removal from our miserable quarters at San Cristobal, we were visited by a large party of Americans, among them Mr. Henry E. Lawrence, of New-Orleans, who had but recently arrived from the United States with despatches for Mr. Ellis. They all gave me every hope that I was speedily to be liberated, and seemed confident that I should return to my home in company with them; but I was led to believe differently. The publication of the Chihuahua letter, I felt assured, would be used by the Mexican government as a pretext to detain me, and at the time I could not think the measures taken by Mr. Ellis to effect my release as efficient as they should have been. I knew that a temporizing policy would never procure my liberation, and that so long as the subject of my imprisonment was left open to argument, I might be kept until my head was as white as the summit of Popocatepetl. I looked upon my own case in this light: I conceived that I had not in any way forfeited my claim to American protection, and that therefore an immediate demand for my release should be made. On the other hand, if I had lost my rights as a citizen of the United States, and should our minister view my case in that light, I neither wished nor expected that he would say or do anything in my behalf. I was a citizen either of the United States or of Texas—if of the former, my imprisonment was unjust; if a Texan, I only hoped that nothing might be said in reference to my case, and in that event I should immediately set about making my escape. But while all this was passing through my mind, my friends told me that Mr. Ellis was using every exertion to procure my release, and that I was wronging him by harbouring a different opinion.

Will the reader, for one moment, place himself in my situation? He will then, if an American citizen, be better able to judge of my feelings. I had left New-Orleans, as I have before stated, with the openly-avowed intention of making a tour through both Texas and Mexico. I had armed myself, previous to starting, with a passport and other documents plainly defining my position, and on reaching Texas had still farther fortified myself with letters from influential gentlemen in that country, in which it was expressly stated that I had no connexion whatever, civil or military, with the Santa Fé Expedition—was subject to no control. On approaching the confines of New Mexico I had left the command, determined to take no part in whatever might occur. The first settlement I entered peacefully and openly—I attempted no disguise, for in the honesty of my intentions I could see no necessity for dissimulation or concealment. I was arrested, searched, robbed not only of property, but all my papers, and then, without a hearing or without a trial, forced to undergo the fatigues and dangers of the long march to Mexico. Arrived in the vicinity of that city, I made known my case to the United States minister; I informed him of the circumstances of my having left the Texan expedition upon the prairies, of my having been robbed of my papers and liberty on first reaching the settlements of New Mexico, with other important facts, and referred him to Messrs. Van Ness and Falconer, then at liberty, for the proofs. I also mentioned Colonel Cooke and Doctor Brenham, who, although they had lost their liberty, still retained their honour, as gentlemen who would corroborate my statements. I knew that in *thought* I had committed no offence whatever against the Mexicans, and that even in *deed* my actions could not, by the wildest and broadest construction, be perverted or magnified into crimes at all adequate to the punishment I had already received.

Such were my thoughts whenever my own case passed in review before my mind; and when to these are added the facts that an English companion, whose position had certainly been more inimical than mine, had at once been liberated by the Mexican authorities, and that the imbecility and inefficiency of my government were a theme for the constant taunts and jeers of the Texans by whom I was surrounded, the American citizen, proud of his birthright, will be brought to see and feel the full bitterness of the situation in which I was placed. The fault lies not with the *people* of the United States, but with the *rulers;* for the fact is notorious that a fear of losing political influence has induced those in power to sacrifice the independence and jeopard the honour of the country on more occasions than one. Full well does the Mexican government understand this weak point in our foreign policy, else we never should hear of our countrymen being arrested, robbed of all their evidence, denied a hearing, thrust into loathsome prisons among malefactors, compelled to labour in chains, and all to gratify the caprice or feed the revenge of some such tyrant as Santa Anna.

On the morning of the 9th of February, and in a frame of temper by no means amiable, I was ordered to prepare for the march to the city of Mexico. But a short time previous, General McLeod, and such of the prisoners as were able to make the journey, were marched off in the direction of Puebla, on foot and under a strong guard. They had scarcely gone when fifteen poor but hardy donkeys were driven up in front of San Cristobal for us to ride—three of our party being so weak that litters were provided to transport them. Mounted upon the donkeys, and with a gang of beggarly léperos to drive them, were put *en route* for the great city of Mexico, distant some twelve or fourteen miles. In mere jest, and to cause uneasiness among the more inexperienced, we had frequently, while upon the road, spoken of the probability of our being compelled to enter that city mounted upon asses, as a species of punishment: little did I think, when I was giving all credit and colouring to these stories, that I was actually thus to make my own entrance—ride into the city of the Montezumas upon an unsaddled and unbridled donkey!

Than a jackass there is perhaps no animal with a gait more easy; but to see a full-grown man mounted upon the back of one of them, without bridle or saddle, and with no other means of guiding and directing his course than by pulling his ears, is ludicrous in the extreme, to say the least of it. The patient animals, however, jog quietly along, their noses close to the ground, ready to pick up any bit of orange-peel or chance blade of grass, and in the situation in which I then was I would hardly have exchanged the sluggish little animal on which I was perched for the proudest charger in Christendom.

After we had passed through a succession of poor villages, and across an arid plain, the lofty and imposing dome of the Cathedral of Our Lady of Guadalupe appeared in sight. We soon entered the little village which surrounds the cathedral, our commander ordering a short halt to rest and obtain water and refreshments.

I did not enter this noted church, but its history was told us, and is interesting as showing by what nonsensical superstitions and barefaced impostures the poor Indians were originally gulled by a crafty priesthood. There are different versions of the story, but they agree in the main circumstances. Some three hundred years ago not a solitary hut was standing in a village which now contains its thousands of inhabitants, and probably one of the richest and most magnificent religious establishments in the world. Near the site of the church, shortly after the conquest by Cortez, a poor and simple shepherd was tending his flock, not a dwelling in sight save those in the distant city. Suddenly the Holy Virgin appeared to this wandering shepherd, clad in celestial raiment, and with a face of pure and heavenly beauty. She pointed to a small hill near, and then told him to go forthwith to the city and tell the bishop it was her will that a chapel should at once be built upon the spot, to be dedicated exclusively to her. The affrighted man went to the city that night, but fearing the bishop would not believe his story, he did not communicate the holy errand upon which he had been sent. The next day the Virgin again appeared to him. With much trembling he told her that he feared to open her message to the bishop, lest that dignitary might ridicule him as a fool or an impostor. She again commanded him to communicate her desire to the bishop, and on his second visit to the city the shepherd made known to him all the circumstances. The bishop laughed at the man as an impostor, and desired him to bring some token that he had communicated face to face with the Holy Mother. He returned to his flock on the third day, and was again visited by the Virgin. She asked him if he had well performed his holy mission, to which he answered by telling her the result of his conference with the bishop. "Go," said she, " to yon barren rock," at the same time pointing to the desolate hill, " and bring me a bouquet of roses which you will find there." The poor shepherd, albeit knowing full well there were no roses or flowers of any kind upon the spot, obeyed her mandate. What was his surprise when he found the roses as she had described them? He gathered a beautiful nosegay, and on returning to his singular visiter she told him to proceed with it at once to the bishop, and place it in his hands as an evidence of the truth of what he had seen and heard. He now cheerfully obeyed, and presented the flowers as commanded. On receiving them, the bishop discovered, imprinted upon the roses, an exquisite miniature of the Holy Virgin—a miniature of such surpassing loveliness and finish as at once convinced him that other than the hand of man had painted it. Its divine origin, as the legend goes, now seemed to him unquestionable.

With unwonted pomp and ceremony he had the miraculous bouquet borne about in procession, the request of the Holy Virgin was at once obeyed, and a temple dedicated entirely to her service was immediately erected on the spot she had pointed out. The fame of the miracle spread far and near, and rich presents came flowing in from all quarters. The reigning monarch of Spain endowed with costly furniture and religious trappings the sacred cathedral of *Nuestra Señora* *de Guadalupe*, she was ordained the patroness of Mexico, and to the present time her temple is noted as among the richest in the world. Such the flimsy imposture, and such the result. The lower classes of Mexico still believe that the Virgin really appeared to the shepherd, and flock in thousands to her shrine at Guadalupe.* As I have before stated, I did not visit the interior of the temple, but those who have describe it as gorgeous and magnificent beyond comparison. The exterior I can answer for as being of grand dimensions and admirable architecture—partaking, so far as I was able to judge, of the Moorish and Gothic styles. A crowd of poor wretches—léperos, mendicants, and females in tattered attire—were lounging about the spot, and several of them even went so far as to ask alms of us, a party of sick, ragged, and miserable objects—calling upon every saint in the Mexican calendar to shower down prayers and blessings upon us in a torrent of abundance if we would but give them a solitary *claco*.†

* The entertaining writer Latrobe, in his work entitled "The Rambler in Mexico," says that there is only one rival to the dominion of Our Lady of Guadalupe in the affections of the common people of the valley of Mexico, and that is *Nuestra Señora de los Remedios*, whose shrine is to be seen in a village near the base of the mountains west of the city. The léperos and poblanitas, the latter the more common girls of the city, pin their faith, in case of any impending danger, upon the wonder-working image of her of Los Remedios; and in cases of great emergency, as during the prevalence of the cholera in 1833, she is brought with great pomp into the metropolis. On one occasion it was settled that she should pass the night in town, as the weather was unfriendly, and a suitable lodging was provided: but when morning dawned, "Our Lady" had vanished! The fact was, that nothing could keep her away from her own flock at Los Remedios, where, accordingly, she was found at dawn in her usual place, covered with mud, however, from having walked a number of leagues in a dark and rainy night! And this miracle is believed! Alas! poor human nature!

† A piece of copper money, worth one cent and a half. An immense batch of *clacos* were coined in 1842, but whether their intrinsic value was one cent and a half I have my doubts. Santa Anna, with some of the other government officers, probably made a "pretty penny" by the copper war which raged in Mexico during that year.

The road from Guadalupe is a wide, straight thoroughfare, planted on either side with trees of rich foliage, and leads directly into the heart of the city of Mexico. As the hospital to which they were escorting us was situated at the extreme end of the city, near the point where the Vera Cruz road enters, the captain of our guard struck off across the arid and desolate plains which lie between Guadalupe and Mexico, with the intention of finding a much nearer route. We were not in the least annoyed at this change, as not one of us felt anxious to show off our donkey-estrianism, if I may be allowed to coin a word, in the heart of one of the proudest cities of the world. All, or nearly all, too, were extremely unwell, and we were anxious to reach our quarters, roll ourselves up in our blankets, and obtain rest and sleep after the fatigues of the march.

Had we proceeded directly by the road, instead of endeavouring to find a shorter route, we should have reached our destination much sooner; for we found the plains cut up by gullies and partially-dry canals, with here and there a small lake or pond by which our course was obstructed. After turning and buffeting about three or four hours to gain as many miles, we were at length fortunate enough to reach the Vera Cruz road, and following this, we soon passed the *garita*, or gate, and entered the great city of Mexico. While upon the sandy plains, the immense number of domes, steeples, and towers of the proud metropolis of the New World, as its inhabitants are wont to term it, were plainly visible, presenting a view than which nothing can be more grand and imposing.

A more forlorn, wretched, ragged, and pitiable set of Christians surely never before entered the place. Three or four were in the very worst stage of the small-pox and borne along upon litters, while the rest were seated upon jackasses, and nearly all had the earlier symptoms of that disease plainly developed in their countenances. The clothing, too, of the majority, would have disgraced a party of beggars—a description of the different costumes were impossible. No wonder, then, that our appearance excited deep sensation among the women as we entered the city, for they crowded about us in groups, wondering at the sight of a party of strangers in plight so melancholy, guarded like criminals upon the road.

Although suffering severely from headache at the time, having but partially recovered from an attack of fever at San Cristobal, I still could not help laughing at a little circumstance which occurred before we had advanced twenty yards into the city. Among our party was old Major Bennett, our quartermaster before the capture of the expedition. The major was some fifty-five or sixty years of age, hale and hearty naturally, although suffering much at the time from the severe headache and pains incident to the small-pox in its earlier stages. He was a native of Massachusetts, born and educated among the descendants of the Puritans, knew the Bible almost by heart, and was always ready with a passage from that book with which to illustrate or point his discourse. The major was a young man at the breaking out of the last war between the United States and England, immediately enlisted in the service of his country, and was a lieutenant at the celebrated and hard-fought battles of Bridgewater and Lundy's Lane. In the earlier conflicts of Texas he was also engaged, and was wounded in several places at the battle of Victoria. He was now sick and a prisoner, but nothing could depress his spirits or prevent him from quoting Scripture, in or out of season.

The anecdote I am about to relate showed the character of the man, and would have provoked a smile from Niobe herself. The major was drumming, with his heels, the flanks of a lazy donkey upon which he was mounted, when three or four women came out of a house immediately before him. Struck by his wretched appearance, the kind-hearted creatures clasped their hands with pity, uttered their common expressions of compassion, while their lustrous eyes became instantly suffused with tears. The major saw the effect his wobegone aspect had created, and instantly resolved upon a speech. Seizing his donkey by the ear and pulling his head round—the common way of stopping the animal—he looked steadfastly in the faces of the poor women who had marked his appearance. He then raised his other hand, as if to impress more forcibly what he was about to utter, and ejaculated, "*Weep not, daughters of Mexico, your rulers are coming, seated upon asses.*" This slightly-altered quotation from the Scriptures he uttered with a mock-gravity truly ludicrous, and then, pulling his donkey's head back to its original position, by dint of much kicking forced it into a mincing trot, and soon overtook our party. I had paused to hear the major's speech, well knowing, from his character and the unwonted preparation he had made, that it would be something uncommon; but little did I think he would force from me a laugh so hearty as that which followed the winding-up of his address. What the women thought of us I know not; they of course did not understand a word of what he said.*

* Some strange fatality appears to have attended my more intimate friends of the ill-fated Santa Fé Expedition. The ink with which I recorded the deaths of Fitzgerald, Brenham, Whittaker, Seavy, Holliday, and Old Paint Caldwell had hardly dried, before I was compelled to add Major Bennett to the list. He died during the fall of 1843, in Texas.

After crossing a canal immediately in the outskirts of the city, and proceeding some three hundred yards, we were drawn up and halted in front of the old church and hospital of San Lazaro, or Saint Lazarus. Enclosed within a wall were several buildings, devoted to the uses of the sick and also of the priests and hospital attendants, while in the centre was a small garden, in which were a fountain and a profusion of roses and other flowers. To the right of the main entrance stands the old church, which, with the department of the male *lazarinos*, or lepers, forms nearly one side of the establishment, and has no wall around it. In fact, the walls are only placed in the rear of the buildings.

Up to the very time of our arrival we were ignorant of our destination, and as we now gazed upon the hideous countenances that peered at us from the front building, we were still at a loss as to what manner of place had been selected for our new prison; that it was disgusting and horrible was evident enough.

A short conference with some of the attendants at the front door being over, our guard escorted us into the interior. Although the shades of evening had by this time set in, we could still see that the walls in the interior were hung with badly-painted pictures, the subjects all religious. Arriving at a species of anteroom, looking in upon a long and dimly-lighted hall which was filled with cots, we were ordered to stop, and there take up our lodgings for the night upon the floor. Within the hall, though it was now nearly dark, we could plainly see wretched figures hobbling about, many of them upon crutches, and several of the unfortunate creatures who came and looked at us were entirely bereft of noses, and their faces otherwise horribly disfigured with sores. Our guard informed us that the inmates were suffering under that dreadful disease, the leprosy, an affliction almost unknown in the United States; but although we had much speculation on the subject, it was not until the next day that we were made fully acquainted with "the secrets of our prison-house."

After an indifferent night's sleep, for the passage-way in which we had been compelled to take up our quarters was cold, dreary, and uncomfortable, we rose the next morning to a full sense of our wretched situation. I was half dozing, when a slight shake of my shoulder aroused me to full consciousness. The regular physician of the hospital was standing by me, accompanied by the major-domo and several attendants. The former asked me my disease, felt my pulse, looked at my tongue, and then prescribed a dose of glauber salts and a light diet. In truth, I was in good health enough, only requiring quiet and nutritious food for a day or two to recover my strength; but the Mexican physician probably thought that salts could do me no harm, and accordingly prescribed them. I tried to beg off when the attendant brought me the medicine, but was compelled to swallow it to the very dregs. I have no peculiar partiality for salts at any time, and now to take them when there was not the least necessity appeared to give the dose an additionally bitter flavour. To all the other prisoners a particular medicine and diet were prescribed; those who were more severely afflicted were provided with cots in the long hall, while the rest of us were compelled to remain in the dreary passage where we had spent the first night. This not one of us regretted when we had an opportunity of seeing the companions with whom we should have been compelled to associate in the large hall of San Lazaro.

The room in which the men afflicted with the leprosy

are confined is nearly three hundred feet in length, by about thirty-five in width. The windows are large and numerous, admitting a sufficiency of air during the heat of the day, and are all grated. At first I could see no reason why the windows of a hospital were grated; but afterward learned that when a person is known to be a *lazarino*, or leper, he is at once taken to San Lazaro, and there confined as a kind of prisoner until liberated by death—for I believe that none ever recover from the horrible disease. At the time when we were confined in the hospital the male department contained some fifty or sixty inmates, while in the female part of the establishment, which was in another building, there was a still greater number.

I feel not a little reluctant to attempt a picture of the unfortunate wretches who inhabit San Lazaro. The disease with which they are afflicted is unknown in Anglo-Saxon countries, or if there are any cases they are very rare. Other than those afflicted with the leprosy there were no occupants of the hospital until our arrival, and the reason assigned by the Mexican government for confining us there was said to be that we had a contagious disease among us. The appearance of the unfortunate lepers is loathsome and hideous to a degree that beggars description. It makes its first appearance by scaly eruptions on different parts of the face and body of the victim, and these eruptions are never perfectly healed. The limbs of many, and more especially the hands, at first appear to be drawn and twisted out of all shape. Gradually the nose and parts of the feet are carried away, while the features become distorted and hideous. The voice assumes, at times, a husky and unnatural tone, and again the doomed patient is unable to articulate except in a shrill, piping treble. With many, when near the last stages, all powers of speech are lost, and vainly do they endeavour to make known their wants by sounds which belong not to this earth of ours. Death steps in at last to relieve the poor creatures of their sufferings, and to them at least it would seem that the visit of the grim tyrant must be welcome.

Whether the leprosy of Mexico is contagious I am unable to say. With many I have little doubt that it is to a degree constitutional—being, in fact, hereditary, and perhaps never entirely eradicated from the blood. The climate may have some effect in engendering and keeping alive the disease, but of this, too, I am uncertain. The common belief among the lower classes is, that it is communicated by contact; and indeed I am inclined to think that the only risk a person runs of taking it is from touching the person of one afflicted with it in its worst stages. The families and friends of the *lazarinos* would frequently visit them, bringing many little luxuries to add to their comfort. They would sit and converse with them, too, for hours, apparently regardless of danger; but for myself I took particular care not to come in too close contact with the unfortunate lepers.

Notwithstanding their lot would seem to be most melancholy, as a body they appeared well to enjoy themselves. Afterward, and while confined among them for some two months, I had every opportunity to observe them closely; and one who has had no such opportunity can hardly imagine how much happiness and hilarity prevail among beings doomed to a lingering but certain death. Many of them were continually playing at draughts or cards, taking the most intense interest in the games. On many occasions I saw parties of four engaged at cards who had not a single nose or entire finger among them; and any little success of one of them would be hailed with every demonstration of delight. Their dexterity, too, in shuffling and dealing cards, when bereft of fingers, was astonishing. Many of them were musicians, performing on both the harp and mandolin, and after nightfall they usually had a dance among themselves. Frequently they were visited by some of the female inmates of the hospital, who would join their merry-makings. To describe one of their dances were impossible. A set of them would take the floor, composed of one or more couples. Some of the dancers were upon crutches, and almost all were in some way lame or disabled. The music would strike up, and then would follow some monotonous Mexican dance, accompanied by singing from voices which were excruciatingly harsh and discordant. The weird sisters around the magic caldron never made a more grotesque or frightful appearance than did these lepers, and had Macbeth encountered the latter upon the heath he would have run outright, without even exchanging a word of parley. The wretched inmates of the hospital enjoyed themselves, however, at these dances, and but that their loud laughter was grating and discordant it would have sounded joyous enough. The true feelings of merriment were there, but no midnight revel of witches or hobgoblins, or of the misshapen dwarfs romancers have created, could compare with the horrible manifestations of mirth that fell upon our ears, or could in any way shadow forth the strange orgies we frequently beheld within the gloomy walls of San Lazaro.

We were visited, the first day of our imprisonment here, by Mr. Mayer and a large number of Americans, all manifesting not a little disgust at the horrible situation in which they found us. Among the Mexicans themselves this hospital is looked upon with a feeling akin to terror—as a receptacle that never gives up its victims—for those who once cross its gloomy threshold seldom or never retrace their steps. Whether there are other patients than those suffering with the leprosy admitted within its walls I know not—the regular hospital for the small-pox is situated in a different part of the city, and why they did not take us to it was a matter of some surprise with all.

As regards our food, we had no reason to complain. In their hospitals the Mexicans are invariably kind and attentive to the sick, administering to their wants with unsparing hands. While at San Lazaro, four loaves of fine, well-baked wheaten bread were given to each of the Texan prisoners every morning—an ample supply for the day. For breakfast a tin cup of tea, made of some herb to which I am a stranger, was brought us. It was well sweetened, had a small quantity of milk boiled with it, and although weak and rather insipid, I have little doubt it was extremely wholesome. During the day a generous supply of orangeade was given us, cool and refreshing. At noon our dinner was brought to us in three tin cups, accurately made to fit one within the other. The upper one was covered and served as a cover for the second, as did the second for the one at the bottom. The lower cup was generally filled with mutton broth, having a piece of the meat left within it, and also a quantity of *garbanzos*, or large Spanish peas. In the second, they generally sent us a small piece of baked mutton, and in the upper cup we found alternately boiled rice and fried potatoes. Each cup was numbered with the figures attached to some cot in the hospital, and seeing the numbers on my dinner utensils staring me in the face from the couch of a leper, my appetite for the contents was gone at once. Afterward, when we complained of this carelessness of the hospital waiters, the cups corresponding with the numbers of our cots were invariably brought to us. Neither knife, fork, plate, nor spoon was sent with the dinner, but as we had been accustomed to eat without such conveniences, their non-appearance gave us but little annoyance.

Many of the Texans had no appetites. Others, again, swallowed their food with much apparent satisfaction; but there were those among us who could not be induced to eat the plain but nutritious food offered them on the first day—the appearance of everything around was too revolting. Some of us succeeded, however, although against positive orders, in bribing our guard to smuggle in a quantity of fried eggs; and watching an opportunity when no one of the hospital attendants was observing us, we stealthily made a very good dinner. At night another cup of tea was brought us, and the bill of fare of our first day in San Lazaro was not altered during the stay of any of the Texans, except that a lighter diet was ordered for those who were deemed unable to eat meat.

On the second morning we received another call from the physician. He examined us all as on his first visit, prescribing for such as he thought needed medicine. When my turn came I told the doctor that I was much better—a little weak only—and that I thought rest alone was requisite in my particular case. I was anxious to escape taking his vile medicines, and this time I succeeded.

In this way the first four days were spent, the doctor paying us regular morning visits, and our American friends calling upon us during the day. I was led to believe, in the mean time, that our minister might have obtained my release upon parole, until my case should be finally acted upon and decided by the Mexican government; but in this I was disappointed. I told my friends that I would always hold myself subject to the disposal of the American minister or the government of Mexico, and be in readiness, when called upon, let my sentence be what it might. Whether Mr. Ellis ever made an attempt to procure my release on parole or not I am unable to say; he may have thought it unadvisable to make any such solicitations while a correspondence was pending in relation to myself. Had I been imprisoned in any other place than San Lazaro, I should not have been so anxious to obtain a liberty only nominal; but to be compelled to breathe the air of that horrible place, and to have no associates but lepers and small-pox patients, was at first annoying to a degree that rendered the confinement almost insupportable. Some of my friends advised me to report myself well at once, in which case I should have been immediately taken to Santiago and confined with Colonel Cooke's party. There I was confident I should be put in chains and compelled to work in the streets—by no means a pleasant anticipation to a person undergoing an imprisonment than which nothing could be more unjust. While halting between these opinions, and hardly knowing which to choose—San Lazaro, and all its horrors of association, or Santiago and the chain-gang—such of us as could not be provided with cots, were ordered to take up our beds—a blanket each—and prepare for instant departure.

There were eleven of us in all who were now ordered to leave the hospital, seven of the original eighteen being unable to move. Under a strong guard we were escorted some three or four squares directly towards the heart of the city, in utter ignorance of our destination. Arrived in front of a gate having a mud house on either side, and a small, gloomy church in the rear, we were halted. An old Mexican in a ragged blanket soon appeared at the gate, and ushered us into a small room, upon the floor of which, stowed almost as close as they could be, were a coarse mattress and two clean blankets for each of us. Although the place seemed anything but comfortable, and in fact was in a condition hardly fit to shelter a brute, we still thought it a palace in comparison with San Lazaro—we could now breathe freely. Little did we then imagine the serious annoyances to which we were to be subject in our new quarters.

At dark, our rations of tea and bread were sent us from San Lazaro. The tea was brought in the regular hospital cups; but as the hideous inmates of that horrible place were no longer in our presence, we drank the beverage with far less reluctance. A regular guard of soldiers was now stationed over us, one of them marching up and down in front of our door. The old Mexican with the ragged blanket offered to do any little errand, and after sending him for candles we retired to our mattresses, firmly impressed with the belief that we were to sleep comfortably enough. The luxury of even a mattress we had been strangers to for nine months, a single blanket and the hard ground or floor having been the bed of each during all that time; but now that we had been provided with an apology for a place of rest—now that a coarse husk mattress was between us and the floor—we considered ourselves fortunate, and stretched our limbs upon the humble beds, confident of sound and refreshing sleep.

How bitterly were we disappointed! Scarcely had we touched the mattresses before we were visited by myriads of chinches! From every crevice and cranny of the walls they poured in thousands—the cracks of the floor appeared to send forth their legions to the onslaught. I thought of our quarters at San Miguel; but there our tormentors came only by hundreds, while here we were literally eaten alive by thousands. The room we were in had been unoccupied, probably, for months, and our assailants were as bloodthirsty as hyenas. The witty little Irishman, Jimmy Tweed, who was of the party, declared that he would willingly change his situation for a den of half-starved, royal Bengal tigers, while old Major Bennett alluded to the locusts and other plagues of Egypt as trifling in comparison with what we were compelled to endure. To obtain a moment of sleep was utterly impossible, and after a night spent in tossing and rolling about we were rejoiced when daylight came, for it drove our annoying visiters to their hiding-places. We made a complaint the next day, and asked to be removed to any place—back even to San Lazaro and all its horrors—but our request was unheeded. After this, and while confined in our present quarters, we slept much during the day, and our nights we passed in reading and conversation.

The colonel of the regiment from which our guard was detailed gave orders to the different sergeants that no one was to be allowed to visit or hold any conversation with us; but this did not prevent our friends from gaining access. A dollar, slily slipped into the hand of any of the guard, would gain an admittance readily. Books and writing paper, besides many little luxuries, were brought by my friends; the old Mexican who had charge of the premises was always ready to bring us any article of food we might wish, and but for the vile chinches at night we really should have passed our time agreeably enough. The sergeant of one of our guards, a light mulatto, was invariably attentive. He was born in New-Orleans, but at an early age emigrated to Mexico, where he had joined the army. Having picked up an education, just enough to read and write, he had been promoted, and ever when he was on guard we were well treated. He was particularly partial to me; learning that I was a resident of his native city, he asked me innumerable questions of the place and its older inhabitants, and invariably called me his *paisano*, or countryman.

On the 18th of February Mr. Lumsden, with a party of United States naval officers, among whom were Lieutenants Blunt and Johnson, left Mexico in the stage for Vera Cruz, on their way home. They had by this time nearly given up all hope of my being liberated through the intervention of Mr. Ellis, and Mr. L., in particular, was anxious that I should at once attempt an escape, either by bribing the guard or slipping past them in the night. The undertaking would have been fraught with little danger; but I was advised by friends, so long as my associate in business was in the country, to make no attempt of the kind. His movements were said to be closely watched by the authorities; and had I escaped while he was in the city, the circumstance would, in all probability, have involved him in difficulty, and very likely caused his arrest as in some way accessory. Under these circumstances I determined to make no attempt at an escape, at least until my friends were safely out of the country.

## CHAPTER XII.

Taken ill with the Small-pox.—Washington's Birthday.—A Patriotic American.—An excellent Dinner.—More of the Small-pox.—Ordered to move our Quarters.—Once more among the Lepers of San Lazaro.—Eight of our Companions marched to Santiago.—Philosophy in Chains.—The Irons nothing *after* one gets used to them.—Fresh Air and Exercise.—Determination to forego them.—System of Anointing in San Lazaro.—Anecdote of Lieutenant Burgess.—Visit from Mr. Lawrence.—His Departure for the United States.—Death of an unfortunate Leper.—A midnight Funeral in San Lazaro.—Its imposing yet gloomy Character.—Mass in the Church of San Lazaro.—Decorations of the Establishment.—Disgusting Figure of St. Lazarus.—A Procession and a Present.—Don Antonio.—The Fruits of Mexico.—A File of American Newspapers.—Present from Mr. Ellis.—Visited by Mr. Falconer.—Beauties of the "Vicar of Wakefield."—Death of another Leper.—Five of our Companions marched to Santiago.—Preparations for a Celebration.—The 11th of March in San Lazaro.—The Hospital visited by Throngs.—Compelled to receive Alms.—Dinner provided for us by a Party of Ladies.—Take an Account of Stock.—Strange Present from a Mexican Lady.—"Charles O'Malley" in San Lazaro.—Another Celebration among the Lepers.—Fondness of the Mexicans for Flowers and Ornaments. — A dolorous Chant.—The Celebration closes with a Dance.—Wild Revels of the Lepers.

On the 19th of February, the day after Mr. Lumsden left for New-Orleans, I was taken with a slight fever, pains in my bones and head, and other symptoms of the small-pox. I had been previously vaccinated, and therefore cared little for the disease except as it occasioned annoyance and severe suffering. On the 22d, Washington's birthday, a lithographed portrait of the " Father of his Country" was brought to each prisoner by a warm-hearted and enthusiastic American resident, and accompanying these were a generous chicken pie and several bottles of excellent wine. I was much too ill, however, to partake of these luxuries ; in fact, I was unable to sit up from extreme dizziness and pain in my head. I took little or no medicine for the disease, and after suffering greatly for some six or eight days, finally recovered, and without being in the least marked. Those who had never been vaccinated suffered incredibly, and were badly pitted if they survived; but many of them died of the disease. In such as had been vaccinated, the disease was mild in comparison, although they endured the very extreme of pain from bad attendance and the want of comfortable apartments and beds to sleep upon. That any of those recovered who had the disease in its worst form while upon the road, is certainly remarkable—their sufferings were horrible, and numbers of them were not only pitted to a great degree, but one or two were so unfortunate as to lose an eye.

On the 25th of February, without a word or hint of previous warning, we were all ordered to pack up and remove to other quarters, our guard not even informing us whither we were to be taken. By this time I had almost entirely recovered from my illness, and as Judge Ellis had kindly sent me an excellent mattress and cot bedstead, I was very comfortable. My companions, who still slept on the floor, were exceedingly annoyed by the legions of chinches that infested the place, but I was enabled to keep the tormentors from my immediate premises during the greater part of the night, and began fairly to conceive a liking for our prison-house, dirty and dreary as it was. The anticipation of being placed in worse quarters, for we heard horrible stories of the prisons of Mexico, may have induced this feeling.

After being formed in front of our prison, with the soldiers of our guard stationed on either side, we were ordered to march. Our course was in the direction of San Lazaro, and a walk of a few minutes found us once more safely housed within the walls of that gloomy establishment. Five of my convalescent companions were now ordered to be in immediate readiness for a move, together with three of those who had been left at San Lazaro when we were first taken thence. It was now evident that some of us were still to be retained within the hospital—the disposition to be made of our companions was shrouded in Mexican mystery, the most impenetrable of all. Under the usual strong guard the eight Texans were marched off, each man carrying his blanket and little wallet.

The next day, a Mexican girl called at San Lazaro with news of Colonel Cooke's party. Watching an opportunity, when no one was observing us, Francisca, for that was the girl's name, slipped a note into my hand. As soon as I could open it without attracting the notice of our sentinels, for one or two of them were continually marching before our cots, I found the billet to be from one of our companions who had been separated from us the preceding day. He said that they were all with Colonel Cooke's party at Santiago, *and in chains:* but that wearing the "trinkets" was nothing after a person *got used to them!* This was philosophical, to say the least of it. In addition, the writer informed me that a number of the prisoners were about to be taken to Tacubaya, a small but pleasant village some five miles from the city, to work upon the road in front either of the archbishop's or of Santa Anna's palace, and that I could probably join the delightful party by reporting myself well! Here was an opportunity to *get used to chains,* and to obtain fresh air and exercise; but feeling that I had no highway taxes to work out in Mexico, and not being particularly anxious to appear in public with one end of a long, jingling, clanking chain made fast to my ankle, and a man at the other end, I took all the pains in my power to decline the polite invitation of my friend. I was in no very enviable situation, to be sure, confined in San Lazaro among hideous, unclean wretches, whose very aspect was enough to frighten a man into almost any measure; but as in the hospital they would not place me in chains, and as I would have a far better opportunity of making an escape while there, I resolved to remain and forego all the fresh air and exercise I might obtain while working upon Santa Anna's roads, and in the fetters of a criminal. To remain at San Lazaro was a matter easy enough, at least so long as real sickness might detain any of my companions; for the hospital physician was a worthy, good-natured man, not disposed to investigate too closely a chronic rheumatism I "got up" especially as an excuse to stay. The only prescription he ordered in my case was a warm bath in the morning, and an occasional greasing at night. The former was agreeable enough; the latter I infinitely preferred to taking his vile glauber salts, *cosamiento blanco*,* and other inward remedies. This practice of anointing the prisoners from head to foot, with a preparation of hartshorn, lard, and other ingredients which I could not detect, was very common in San Lazaro.

I remember laughing heartily one evening while Lieutenant Burgess, one of the Texan officers, was rubbed with the liniment by a broad-shouldered, large-mouthed Mexican. The former was a man of less than the medium size, while the operator was one of the largest Mexicans I had ever seen. He had just finish-

---

* The *cosamiento blanco* appeared to be a very common and very innocent medicine—to judge from its appearance and taste, a mixture of magnesia and water.

ed rubbing the shoulders of the lieutenant, and had ceased his operation for a moment, when Burgess, looking him full in the face, with a ludicrous expression of mock-gravity and well-counterfeited alarm, exclaimed, " I wonder if the fellow is going to swallow me alive !"

On the 26th of February, Mr. Lawrence, who was to depart the next morning in the stage for Vera Cruz, called at San Lazaro to take his leave of me, accompanied by a gentleman who is a Corsican by birth, but who is a naturalized American. They were not admitted into the hospital, express orders having been given that no foreigner should be allowed to visit us; but the sergeant of the guard permitted me to see them at the front entrance. Lawrence's face gave me little encouragement as regarded my liberation. He endeavoured to offer some hopes of a speedy release, but I could plainly read that he hoped rather than believed such would be the case. After I had told him to inform my friends in the United States that I would contrive some way to escape if the government did not effect my liberation, that I had already gone through much and could endure a great deal more, my two friends took their leave. Why I know not, but during an imprisonment of seven months I never felt so dispirited, so ill at ease, and so restless as on this occasion, and determined to embrace any opportunity to escape that might occur.

The night Lawrence left us, a poor leper died in our room. To pass away the long evening I was engaged at a game of piquet with one of my fellow-prisoners, when an attendant came and requested us to speak only in whispers, as there was a man dying a few yards from us. He said there was no objection to our continuing our play; but as a priest was in close communion with the sufferer, loud talking might disturb him in his holy office. We ceased playing when the game was over, and immediately after retired to our cots.

I could not but indulge in a train of serious reflections upon the singular objects by which we were surrounded. In the same room, and but a few steps from me, an unfortunate *lazarino* was receiving the last consolations the religion he professed offers to the dying, while close by, a party of his companions, themselves within a few short steps of the same grave which was soon to receive the dying man, were busily engaged at a game of *monte!* So used to scenes of this description were the inmates of San Lazaro that they would have indulged, even at this time, in their usual boisterous and most unnatural mirth had not the priest forbidden it. In a far corner of the room a musical leper was strumming some lively air on a mandolin; and although he played in a low and suppressed tone, many of the notes of glee must have reached the ear of the wretched sufferer. Directly opposite my cot, an aged and gentlemanly Spaniard, in the last stages of leprosy, and who, in fact, died a few weeks after, was ever and anon striking a light and smoking his cigarritos with cool and philosophical indifference. Around a small charcoal furnace, in the centre of the room, a knot of lepers were heating their atole and tortillas—and they, too, with the perfect consciousness that one of their number was about to leave them forever, were chatting busily and tittering with the half-suppressed laugh some story of merriment might elicit —a laugh which would have been boisterous had it not been restrained by the presence of the man of God. Even among ourselves, we could not look upon the scene with those feelings of awe and deep solemnity it would have awakened in other days; for the heart becomes callous by familiarity with affliction, misery, and death. While surrounded by the humanizing influences of society, it is difficult to conceive how the warmest feelings of our nature may become chilled by exposure to hardships and acquaintance with suffering; and confident I am that not one of the Texans then confined in San Lazaro can now look back upon the scenes he there beheld, without actual astonishment at the cold indifference he manifested at the time—scenes which, were he to encounter them at home, would arouse all becoming sensibility.

In the midst of a train of reflections, as singular in their nature as the associations around me, I fell asleep. About midnight I was awakened by the ringing of a bell and a tramp of men, and on opening my eyes beheld a procession of priests and attendants, bearing lighted candles, and preceded by a boy with a small bell, passing my cot in the direction of the dead leper—for he had now breathed his last. There is something touchingly solemn and impressive in the funeral rites of the Catholic Church, even at ordinary times and on ordinary occasions; but a midnight funeral, in such a dreary place as San Lazaro, gave an additional solemnity to the ceremonies. As the procession passed me, the members of it were muttering inarticulate prayers and crossing themselves. The brilliant light from the numerous candles showed the inmates in different attitudes of prayer near their cots—now muttering a few words, and then beating their breasts as in deep grief for the loss of their companion. Arrived at the corpse, it was placed in a rough coffin, all knelt around, a prayer for the rest of the departed spirit was said by one of the priests, and then, with incense burning and the bell ringing, the procession marched in regular order from the room, leaving all again in darkness. Thus ended the impressive and melancholy rites, but the memory of those midnight ceremonies must still haunt all who were spectators—I can never forget them.

The morning after the events I have just related happening to be Sunday, we were all aroused at an early hour by the ringing of a small bell, calling the inmates of the hospital to mass. On this occasion I rose, and hastily dressing myself, attended the celebration. The church formed one side of the establishment, and to prevent all means of escape, a guard was stationed at the outer door. The interior of the church was decorated with numerous paintings illustrative of the sufferings of our Saviour, and especially those of the patron saint of the establishment, St. Lazarus. These paintings were generally badly-executed copies, but a wax figure of the saint, lying in a glass case and representing him as dead, was revoltingly natural. The artist had represented his subject as covered with sores, and so faithfully that the beholder could not but instantly turn from its contemplation with feelings of deep disgust. The marble floor of the church, for in Mexico there are no seats in the religious establishments, was covered with kneeling lepers, crossing themselves, beating their breasts, and telling their beads. After standing a short time in the church I left it for my quarters in the adjoining hospital, resolved never again to attend mass unless compelled by those in whose power I was; and as the priests of San Lazaro were so liberal as not to enforce our attendance, I did not a second time enter their church. In other places the prisoners were forced to attend the religious ceremonies, and in chains.

From the church I returned to my quarters, and began writing long letters to my friends in the United States, having learned that a packet was shortly to sail. At dinner-time, and before I had yet finished a letter upon which I was engaged, we were visited by a procession of priests and young lads, the latter being engaged in a course of studies before taking holy orders. The visit was not intended for us alone, but for all the inmates of the hospital. The procession made the entire circuit of the room, one of the lads handing each of the unfortunate prisoners a *medio*\* and a small bunch of paper cigars. Our dinner, which on Sundays was a little better than during the week, although served in the same cups, was brought to us by the lads, and each knelt upon one knee as he gave it into our hands. After this, there was some little ceremony in relation to the poor leper who had died the night before, and this over the procession left the room.

The old major-domo of the hospital, Don Antonio as he was called, allowed the fruit-women to visit us at all times, and this served to render our situation much more endurable. A person can live entirely upon the delicious and almost endless varieties of fruit which abound in Mexico, and little did I care for the boiled meats and broths—the regular hospital fare—when I could buy the fruit, which is there sold at a trifling cost. Not a day passed in which we could not purchase bananas, granaditas, oranges, melons of various kinds, pine-apples, cayotes, chirimoyas, different species of a delicious fruit called the zapote, mangoes, and other tropical productions, many of which I have never seen in any part of the United States. Some of these fruits are raised in the vicinity of Mexico, but the larger portion are brought from the *tierras calientes*, or hot countries,

---

\* Six and a quarter cents.

the great elevation and consequent coolness of the climate in the neighbourhood of the city not allowing them to be cultivated in their full perfection.

On the 2d of March, the secretary of legation, Mr. Mayer, who was ever attentive to me during my confinement, called with a bundle of American newspapers. No one, unless he has undergone a close imprisonment in a foreign country, can appreciate such a treat as a file of newspapers affords. I read and re-read them, advertisements and all, and the different familiar names I saw carried me back to other and happier days.

The next morning Mr. Mayer again called with a box of excellent cigars and several bottles of wine, a present from Mr. Ellis. Mr. Falconer, too, who had been on a visit to Real del Monte, made me a call, regardless of the danger he incurred of contracting the contagious diseases which prevailed in San Lazaro. I cannot too highly appreciate the kindness of Mr. Mayer, Mr. Black, and many other Americans who called upon me while at that loathsome prison—their visits, which certainly were fraught with no little peril to themselves, served to beguile many a heavy hour, and alleviate an imprisonment which would otherwise have been insupportable.

Mr. Falconer brought me a number of excellent books—among them several of Miss Howitt's simple but beautifully-written tales, and Goldsmith's Vicar of Wakefield. I had read the latter frequently, but the circumstances under which I was now placed imparted to it unwonted charms. Surely I never before had appreciated this *chef-d'ouvre* of that great master of English composition. The simplicity and graceful ease of the style, its quiet and playful humour, its touching pathos, and the interest of the narrative quite enchained me. I almost forgot the painful situation in which I myself was placed while reading the trials and afflictions of the pure and pious vicar.

From the 4th to the 8th of March our time passed without any incident worthy of note occurring. On the night of the last-mentioned day, about the middle watches, another unfortunate leper died in our room. He had suffered much during the twenty-four hours previous to his death, his groans filling the air, and rendering the situation of all more gloomy than ever. Again the procession of priests and assistants was in attendance, the usual ceremonies were performed, and the body was carried from the hospital and placed in the adjoining church.*

The next morning, a Mexican officer and guard of men arrived, with orders to escort five of my companions to Santiago. I expected that I, too, should be ordered to "take up my bed and walk" with the rest; but the hospital physician had not as yet reported me well, and I was allowed to remain. I was by no means desirous to change my quarters, miserable as they were;

* If all the Mexican inmates of San Lazaro were afflicted with leprosy, and we were told that such was the case, there must be three or four different species of the disease. The faces of some of the lazarinos were covered with blotches and eruptions, while their hands and feet were unmarked. Others, again, had complexions exceedingly fair and unblemished, yet their feet and hands were distorted or decayed. Some of the victims of the dreadful scourge were covered, from head to foot, with sores and ulcers hideous to look at—and then there were two or three cases where the patients presented no other marks of the disease than the loss of a nose. But the most singular case of all was that of the old Spaniard—I think he was a Spaniard—whom I have previously mentioned as continually smoking his cigarritos. His flesh appeared to be entirely gone—dried up—his skin turned to a bluish purple—and his whole appearance was so strangely changed and distorted, that he more resembled an animated mummy than aught else I can compare him to. His senses he still retained, while his actions and conversation convinced us that he was a well-informed and gentlemanly man.

for I felt assured that I should at once be put in chains, and sent into the streets to work, if taken to Santiago. Still I was anxious to see the different members of Colonel Cooke's party, but San Lazaro had, by this time, lost many of its horrors—we can soon familiarize ourselves with any spectacle, however revolting—and I preferred remaining there, at least until I was assured that better quarters awaited me elsewhere. Only seven of our original party were now left in San Lazaro, four of whom were slowly recovering from severe attacks of the small-pox.

The 10th of March was spent in cleansing and preparing the hospital for the imposing ceremonies of the day of San Lazaro, which were to take place on the morrow. The large folding doors opening to our apartment from without were closed and fastened, two small side doors only being left open to admit the immense throng who on this anniversary visit the hospital. A Yankee, with a strip of board, a hammer, and half a dozen nails, would have securely fastened this large door in half an hour—it took half a dozen Mexicans, with tools and timber enough to build a small dwelling, an entire day to perform the same operation. Not one of us could possibly divine what object these Mexican carpenters had in view all the while, until one of them told us they were fastening the door. This little circumstance will serve to show the state of many of the mechanic arts throughout Mexico. No improvements, no labour-saving machines are ever brought into requisition, but the same means to effect an object two hundred years ago are all that are known at the present day.

In the mean time, while the clumsy workmen were busy fastening the doors, the lepers were engaged in decorating the interior of the room; and here the Mexicans excel. Festoons, flags, and devices, cut in paper of all colours, were hung about the walls, and the lamps were decorated in the same way. The word "*caridad*"—charity—was also neatly cut in paper and pasted about on the different utensils, and in places where it would readily strike the eye of visiters. The floor was stained with a yellow tint, and on the ceiling long strips of red, white, and blue muslin were tastefully arranged in bows and different fanciful forms, giving relief and beauty to the general appearance. Flowers also were entwined about the cots, and, considering the material with which the lepers were provided, I doubt whether any other people under the sun could have given the room an appearance as beautiful as ours presented on the occasion of which I speak.

At an early hour the next morning the clothing on the different cots was changed, and the lepers began arraying themselves in all their finery. It was indeed strange to see these unfortunates—many of whom were standing almost upon the brink of the grave, and whose forms and faces were revolting to such a degree that the first sight could not but create the most sickly sensations—I repeat, it was most wondrous strange to see them equipped in their glaring holyday finery, apparently as vain as giddy drawing-room belles, their self-esteem leading them into an extravagance of display that would have been irresistibly comic had not the circumstances of their position been otherwise so melancholy and deplorable.

As the hour of nine approached the visiters began to assemble. Entering by one of the side doors, they would slowly walk the entire circuit of the room, examine the different inmates, bestow such presents as they had brought with them, and then depart by the door on the opposite side. This method of entering and departing was adopted to prevent that crowd and confusion which would otherwise have taken place.

By twelve o'clock the throng was immense, a continual stream of visiters pouring into the hospital. There were gentlemen and léperos; priests, with their shovel-hats, and soldiers; girls with the Poblana dress—short and gaudy petticoats, fancifully-worked chemises, gay satin shoes, and no stockings—and girls with hardly any dress at all; monks and gamblers; beggars in rags and ladies richly attired in satin, and brilliant with diamonds; friars and vagabonds; in short, a general assortment of a population than which one more diversified does not exist. The cots occupied by myself and companions were in the corner of the room near which the throng entered, and all stopped to gaze at us with intense curiosity. Finding that almost all brought with them some present to bestow, and that we were to receive every claco, cigar, loaf of bread, or whatever was offered, I endeavoured to assume as independent an air as possible, and let them know that I did not in any way stand in need of their charity. I cordially disliked the idea of sitting, like a poor beggar at a corner, and receiving the pitiful alms of every passer; but to avoid it was impossible. To prevent wounding the feelings of those who were certainly actuated by the kindest motives, I took everything that was offered—loaves of bread, cakes, oranges, flowers, fruits, puros, cigarritos, money, and all.*

* The *puro* is the common cigar of Mexico. The ends are not pointed, as are those manufactured in Havana, but are cut square and the puros are then put in papers of eight, twelve, or sixteen. Many of them, when well cured, are very fair cigars, yet all lack the coolness and fragrance of those made in Cuba.

Among the throng was a party of exceedingly well-dressed ladies, evidently belonging to the first society of Mexico. They scrutinized the Texans closely, and appeared at a loss to know who we were, and by what singular chance we happened to be confined within the dreary walls of San Lazaro. Upon our satisfying their curiosity, one of the ladies immediately sent off two of the servants who accompanied them, who returned in about an hour with a sumptuous dinner, provided expressly for us. The ladies themselves did us the honour of waiting upon us, bringing the different courses with their own hands, and appeared to take a lively interest in our unfortunate situation. Who they were I was unable to ascertain—I never saw one of them afterward.

It was not until near dark that the immense throng began to diminish in the least, and as this is the only day in the year when San Lazaro is visited, all Mexico appeared to have turned out. Occasionally I mixed in with the crowd, and took the circuit of the room, but arriving at the front door invariably found one of our guard standing there to invite me back to my cot. I wished to avoid, as I said before, receiving the simple presents of the visiters, and for this reason kept away from my cot as much as possible; but when night came, and I took an account of stock, I found that I had received almost enough bread, oranges, and cakes to load a hand-cart, a hatful of cigarritos and puros, besides several dollars' worth of clacos and medios, the smallest coins of the country. These, when the kind donors were out of sight, I gave to such of my companions as really stood in need, who were sincerely thankful for such a godsend. When night had finally set in our room was again deserted except by its unfortunate inmates, and thus ended the 11th of March in San Lazaro.

Two days after this great celebration, a present was sent me from a Mexican lady, such as probably never before was made in the country. She is the wife of an American resident of Mexico, pretty, and exceedingly intelligent, and is well known in the city for her great vocal abilities—having frequently given concerts, and appeared with much success at the Italian opera. She had called upon me twice while in San Lazaro, and with the customary Mexican politeness had offered me anything and everything in her house. The moment a person enters the dwelling of a well-bred Mexican he is told that all it contains is at his disposal—is his. In truth, one enjoys hospitalities in that Republic he does not find elsewhere; but should the traveller accept every offer of houses, furniture, horses, guns, and jewelry that is made him while journeying through Mexico, he would make a very profitable speculation by a tour in that country. Admire a horse upon which a Mexican is seated—he is yours: remark that a ring or breastpin is rare or beautiful—it is at your disposal instanter. Such is Mexican etiquette—polite, but unmeaning.

The present to which I have alluded was neither more nor less than a large dish of codfish and potatoes, well cooked, and in quantity sufficient for a score of half-starved Yankees. I happened to be "raised" far enough "Down East" myself to have a natural fondness for this dish, a common and favourite one in that section of the country, and nothing the fair señora could have sent me would have been more acceptable. I warmed and rewarmed the savoury compound, morning, noon, and night, and day after day, for it lasted more than a week, and during this time the regular hospital fare found no favour in my eyes. The husband of the lady, who was a native of the seacoast of Massachusetts, was doubtless a great lover of this Cape Cod luxury, and as I was a *paisano* of his, the señora supposed that I too was fond of it. She was certainly right in her conjectures, although I doubt whether my partiality for it would have been as great under other circumstances. The farther we find ourselves from the scenes, the customs, and the *dinners* of our childhood, the more do we enjoy anything resembling them, especially the latter, which we may chance to meet in our wanderings.

On Friday, the 18th of March, one week before Good Friday, they had some kind of celebration in our room, the object of which I did not learn. I had received a copy of "Charles O'Malley" from Mr. Mayer during the day, and was busily engaged in its perusal; but even that laughable book could not entirely withdraw my attention from the scenes enacted around me.

During the day a full-length picture of our Saviour, nailed to the cross, was hung upon the wall at the opposite side of the room from where my cot was placed. Around this picture were hung several smaller ones, exhibiting the Virgin in different scenes, and also a painting of St. Lazarus. These were decorated with wreaths and festoons of flowers, and at the foot of all was an altar having a small figure of our Saviour executed in wood, and dressed in a fashion partaking more of the modern than of the ancient or classic style—statues of the apostles, and I believe even of their great Master himself, are sometimes seen in Mexico clad in military uniforms, with cocked-hats upon their heads! Upon the altar I have alluded to, in addition to the figure, were a number of massive candlesticks containing large wax candles, and the beauty of the grouping was tastefully enhanced by flowers, oranges stuck full of glittering flags and covered with gold leaf, and many ingenious devices that no other people than the Mexicans know so well how to get up and arrange.

When dark came, the female lepers, dressed in all their finery, began to assemble, the numerous candles were lighted, and after all were collected, the ceremonies of the night commenced. The hospital attendants with their families, the priests attached to San Lazaro, with a few visiters, were present, and took part in a long and discordant chant, the like of which I am confident has never been heard beyond the walls of San Lazaro. Every line in this wild hymn appeared to end with "*Dolores!*" and certainly more dolorous sounds can scarcely be imagined. All the lepers joined in the chorus, their harsh, croaking, and discordant voices giving an effect horribly grating to the ear. They did not sing through their noses, for many of them had none to sing through; but they gave utterance to screams and screeches which seemed not of this earth. Their appearance, too, kneeling about in groups, and with their disfigured and hideous faces lit up by the glare of numerous candles, combined with the strange and most unnatural chorus, gave the whole affair a strong resemblance to some monstrous dream of a disturbed imagination—to some midnight revel of witches and hobgoblins, held within a charnel-house. Had the lepers been arrayed in habiliments befitting their unfortunate lot, and their deportment been of a character more consonant with their condition, the effect of the whole scene would have been different; but to see the wretches flaunting in gaudy apparel, and many of them joyous under the most horrible affliction which has ever been entailed upon humanity—all this formed a picture which may be imagined, but cannot be described.

The long chant over, the priests and attendants left the room, and now commenced a performance which was even more singular. One of the lepers brought forth a harp, and a wild and strange dance was immediately got up opposite our cots, and within ten yards of us. Many of the dancers were cripples, and the performances consisted of alternate singing and dancing. Out of such materials the reader may, perhaps, imagine the kind of exhibition we were compelled to gaze upon. I had heard of a hornpipe in fetters—here was one on crutches. The horrible orgies were continued until near midnight, and as the actors in the scene were well supplied with liquor, the wild revel grew louder and more boisterous as the hours sped along. One by one, exhausted by their efforts, they dropped off, and by the time the numerous city bells had tolled the hour of twelve, all again was quiet in our room save the groans of some more unfortunate lazarinos, who, from pain and infirmity, had been unable to join in ceremonies at once partaking of the grotesque and solemn.

## CHAPTER XIII.

Another Dance in San Lazaro.—Mexican Improvisatores.—Accident to a couple of Dancers.—Fondness of the Mexicans for Music.—American Visiters.—An agreeable Afternoon passed.—Good Friday, and a better Dinner.—Fasts preferable to Feasts.—A drunken Lazarino.—Touching Incident.—Visits of our Friends prohibited.—Speculations as to the different Modes of escaping from San Lazaro.—Several Plans agitated.—The Foreigners once more permitted to visit us.—News of the Appearance of an American Fleet upon the Mexican Coast.—Advised not to attempt an Escape.—A severe Epidemic in San Lazaro.—Horrible Colds and worse Coughs.—Death of another Leper.—A second midnight Funeral.—Rarity of the Atmosphere of Mexico.—A regular Uproar in San Lazaro.—José Maria and his inhuman and vicious Conduct.—Mexican Gamblers.—Farther Annoyances from José Maria.—An early morning Visit.—Prospects of Release.—Santa Anna's Reasons for not liberating us immediately.—General Thompson at Vera Cruz.—Santa Anna anxious to shuffle out of a Dilemma.—Bright Anticipations of being once more at Liberty.—More American Visiters.—Arrival of General Thompson in Mexico.—The Annoyance of Suspense.—A File of American Papers.—Visit of General Thompson to San Lazaro.—Letters from Friends.—A Visit from Mr. Perrin.—Prospects of Liberation again clouded.—An Opportunity of Escape thrown in my Way.—Determination to improve it.—Anxiously await the arrival of Assistance from without.

On the Sunday night following the strange events related in my last, the lepers had another dance in the hospital, accompanied, as usual, by singing. The Mexicans are great *improvisatores*, and can rattle off rhymes at a moment's warning. A stranger is frequently struck with surprise, at a fandango, when he hears one of the dancers commence a song the words of which relate exclusively to himself, and which, of course, is "got up" expressly on his account. The copiousness of the Spanish language gives the greatest facility to rhymesters; but the verses of the lower orders are generally made up of senseless jingle, abounding with unmeaning tropes, absurd metaphors, or the most outrageous inconsistencies.

One little incident occurred during this evening which may be worthy of notice. While a couple were dancing face to face, with a species of shuffling, breakdown step, the plank in the floor upon which they were performing their *pas de deux* suddenly gave way, and amid screams and scrambling both disappeared in the dark and gloomy cellar beneath. After some little exertion on the part of their friends they were extricated, and fortunately neither was so much injured but that they immediately chose a fresh plank and recommenced their dance and song.

Out of San Lazaro I have heard singing among the lower orders of Mexicans which was extremely harmonious and pleasing. Without the slightest knowledge of music, as a science, the common people are still fond of carolling the little airs of the country in chorus, and have ears exquisitely correct in singing the different parts. Frequently, while upon the road, might the closely-tied and strictly-guarded Mexican prisoners, or *volunteers*, be heard giving their native songs and choruses with most pleasing effect. One would think that these unfortunate men, after a long day's march, would be more inclined to sleep than to sing; but such was not the case. On the contrary, some dozen or fifteen of them, seated upon the ground after their scanty supper, would join in a melody which floated sweetly on the evening air. The different voices, from the highest falsetto to the deepest bass, were many of them of purest and softest quality, and blended together with a harmony at once musical and soothing. Madame Calderon de la Barca, in her entertaining work upon Mexico, speaks frequently of the fondness of the lower classes for music, and of their rare gifts and great taste in singing. The fair author considers music a sixth sense with the Mexicans, and really it would seem that such is the case.

On the afternoon of the 23d of March I was visited by Mr. Mayer, accompanied by Mr. Elliot, who had been chaplain to the United States exploring expedition, and a young American named Weed, who had been travelling some two years in Mexico and the South American republics. They passed the whole afternoon with me, and so far as regards myself, three or four hours have seldom been whiled away more agreeably. We all had many anecdotes of travel to relate, most of them amusing, and night had fairly set in before my friends were admonished that it was time to depart. That quarter of the city in which San Lazaro is situated is notorious as being frequented by robbers of the worst class, fellows who would have little hesitation in taking life for a few dollars; hence there is danger in traversing it after nightfall, unless well armed; and as my visiters had not taken that precaution on setting out, they now hurried their departure. Should any of them chance to peruse this chapter, they will recollect the afternoon they spent with me at San Lazaro, and the merry time we passed—I never once thought that I was a prisoner until I accompanied the gentlemen as far as the door, and was reminded by the guard stationed there that I could go no farther. Until some time afterward I was not aware that Mr. E. was a clerical gentleman, else there might have been more constraint and less hilarity.

Good Friday passed in San Lazaro with no incident to mark it, save that a better dinner was provided for us than usual. We had fish served in different modes, frijoles and other vegetables, all of them well cooked. The fast-days we always preferred to the feast-days; for in the absence of meats they invariably gave us far better fare in every other respect.

Here I will relate a little incident which occurred one morning in the hospital, and which occasioned me not a little annoyance. Among the unfortunate *lazarinos* was one poor fellow, fast verging towards the grave, who, for getting intoxicated and afterward quarrelling, was sentenced to wear a long and heavy chain. The leper had lost a part of his nose and almost all his powers of speech—in fact, was only able to articulate a few words intelligibly, and these in a tone harsh and frightfully discordant. While yet stupified by liquor and lost to all feeling of shame, he appeared to care little for the disgrace which had been inflicted upon him, but, on becoming sober, his countenance plainly denoted that the iron entered his soul, and occasioned him much distress, not only of body but of mind.

The chain was tightly riveted to his right ankle, and whenever he left his cot for the cocina or kitchen, where the lepers warmed their food and made their chocolate, he was obliged to drag it after him. While passing my cot, on the occasion I have alluded to, his face wore an expression unusually lugubrious—so grotesque yet piteous, that I had much difficulty in repressing a smile. It would seem no easy task to read a man's countenance when it wants a nose; but in the present instance the eye had a peculiar expression that was a complete key to his thoughts. He appeared to divine what was running in my mind, came to a halt, and turned upon me another look—a look which denoted that he deeply felt the disgrace of wearing the galling chain, and which it was evident he also intended as an appeal to my sympathy. There was something so ludicrous, however, although mournful, in this look—something in which the comic was so strangely mixed with the serious—that for the life of me I could not resist laughing. This was too much for the leper. He drew back the foot to which the chain was attached, gave me a glance full of reproach for my want of feeling, and then, by a violent kick, sent the instrument of his disgrace clanking across the floor. He then gave me another upbraiding glance, uttered with much effort the worst oath in the Spanish language, and stalked off, dragging his chain after him. Once only he turned his eye towards me, as if to ascertain the effect his singular movements had wrought; and if my own face betokened the workings of my mind, I am confident the leper was satisfied. I felt vexed with myself to think that I had unnecessarily wounded the feelings of one upon whom misfortune had laid her hand so heavily—one whose situation called rather for pity than ridicule—and I resolved never again to give him cause to reprove me for want of sensibility. The leper appeared to see contrition in my countenance; and as he afterward manifested no ill feelings towards me, I had the satisfaction of knowing that I had made him sufficient atonement.

From the 22d of March to the 6th of April not a person was allowed to visit us at San Lazaro, the authorities having taken some whim into their heads which induced them to forbid our friends holding any communication with us. During this long interval—long at least to one confined—I determined upon making an escape if possible. So long as my friends were permitted to have personal interviews with me, and daily held out hopes that I should be speedily liberated, so long my situation was endurable, although my better judgment taught me to believe many of these hopes delusive; but now that I was *incomunicado*—now that all intercourse with my friends was cut off through some trifling caprice, my situation became irksome in the extreme.

There were three ways by which an escape could be effected from San Lazaro. The most feasible plan, or rather the one that would require no Mexican accomplices, would be the most perilous; but liberty was then worth all the hazards I should be compelled to run. The plan was this: attached to the hospital was a small yard which we were allowed to visit at all times during the day, and in fact until dark. At this time our guard was changed, the new sergeant locking the door which led to the yard for the night. The yard was surrounded by a wall about twenty feet high, and there was one place where the top could be attained, with little difficulty, by means of an out-building which had partly fallen to decay. Once upon the top, a person with sound limbs would run little risk in jumping to the ground; but as my ankle was still tender, from the effects of the severe injury I had received in Texas, I was fearful about hazarding the jump. Outside the walls was the immense plain stretching towards Guadalupe, San Lazaro being at the extreme edge of the city; yet a walk of a few steps would take me to the head of a street leading directly into the heart of Mexico. All I wanted was some friend to smuggle a rope into my hands, which I could in some way fasten to the wall, and thus let myself down in safety. At dusk, and just as the new guard were about locking us in, I could slip stealthily into the yard, effect my escape over the wall, and then, by having a friend at the head of the first street next the hospital to conduct me, reach some safe quarters in the city. This plan gave every promise of success. Should I be missed immediately, all would be over with me; but with five minutes' start, I could reach an asylum secure from the guards.

Another plan I agitated in my own mind was to bribe the guard to let me pass out during the night, and still another was to induce the old major-domo of the establishment to leave a door, which led from the upper part of our room into the street, open at night. This door had an alphabetical lock, the secret of which was known only to him; had it been secured by an ordinary lock, I could find means to procure false keys, in which case it would afford an easy and safe means of escape. In the mean time, I had had a map of the Mexican country in my possession for several weeks, which I had studied so thoroughly that I was well acquainted with the geography of every section. My intentions were, instead of endeavouring to escape by way of the Atlantic, to make at once for Acapulco or some port on the Pacific, thence by some of the coasting vessels to Callao, where I should be able to find a vessel up for the United States; but in the midst of all these calculations circumstances occurred which for a time drove all thoughts of effecting an escape from my mind.

On the 6th of April several foreigners obtained permission to visit us, bringing with them a number of papers from the United States, and also news that a large American naval force was concentrating in the Gulf, and that several men-of-war were already lying off Sacrificios, near Vera Cruz. From the tone of the journals brought me I could plainly see that my friends throughout the United States were moving with great spirit in my behalf, and pressing upon the government the necessity and justice of making an immediate and imperative demand for my release. This was all I wanted. I was anxious that some definite action in my case should be at once resorted to, that I might know what to expect, and that the annoying uncertainty which now pressed me down might be removed.*

I mentioned the fact of my contemplating an immediate escape from San Lazaro to my friends. They advised me to give up all thoughts of the attempt, at least for the present. Should circumstances render it necessary to escape, they promised me every assistance; but as now there certainly was a probability of prompt action being taken in my case, they recommended me to give up the idea until the result should be known. With this advice, they left me to pore over the files of papers they had brought for my amusement.

About this time a severe epidemic broke out in the hospital, and I believe was general throughout Mexico, in the form of a cold, accompanied by a distressing cough. Every leper was more or less affected, and the Texans, too, came in for a full share of the malady. There is nothing interesting about a cough, even when a person has a good set of lungs and other appointments to give it full effect; but among the unfortunate lepers, many of whom were destitute of noses, and whose throats were severely affected by the disease which

* While all my editorial brethren throughout the United States spoke as with one voice in my behalf, during the unjust imprisonment I was subjected to, it may appear invidious to single out one as more deserving of my gratitude; yet I cannot, while returning my warmest thanks to all, resist mentioning the name of Mr. Bullitt, the able and warm-hearted editor of the New-Orleans Bee. He, perhaps, knew more of my intentions on first starting for Texas and Mexico, was better enabled to judge of the injustice of imprisoning and detaining me, than any of his compeers, and as a consequence he was more strenuous and untiring in his endeavours to procure my release.

was fast hurrying them to the grave, the strangling noises uttered were of a nature the most horrible. Night after night I was kept awake by sounds the most distressing, the poor fellows apparently in strong convulsions during the paroxysms, and some one of them appearing at all times ready to commence the moment another would obtain a short relief. In this way a continual din and harassing clamour were kept up, and the nights we now spent in San Lazaro were among the most annoying of all our imprisonment.

From the 6th to the 14th of April our time passed heavily and drearily. One poor leper died in our room during this interval, a dreadful cough cutting short days to which his deplorable malady would inevitably have soon put an end. Whether he had more money or influence than some of the unfortunates, who had here ended the journey of life before him, I know not; but the night ceremonies on the occasion were upon a scale more grand and imposing than were those which took place at the death of any other leper who died during my imprisonment in the hospital. The procession of priests and attendants was larger, there were more candles burning, and they appeared to shed even a more lurid glare upon the wan and gloomy countenances of the lepers in the farther parts of the room. At every interval when the paroxysms of coughing left them, the lepers muttered prayers for the repose of their departed comrade, and smote their breasts violently, as if in penance for their own unconfessed transgressions. Amid low, murmured prayers, the burning of incense, and the monotonous ringing of a bell, the procession left our room, and again all was gloom; a dismal quiet reigned, broken only by the frightful coughs which were heard on every side — the sufferers apparently half strangled with the paroxysms. There is a rarity in the atmosphere of Mexico, at certain seasons, which makes respiration difficult; and in addition to a slight cough which I had at the time, I suffered from a difficulty of breathing closely allied to the asthma, which gave me much annoyance.

During the afternoon and evening of the 14th of April there was a grand uproar in our room, in which one of our guard received a severe flogging from the corporal. The duty of the soldier on guard was to walk, with his musket at a shoulder, directly in front of our cots, both day and night. On the afternoon I refer to, a gambling leper, on the opposite side of the room, had opened a game of *monte* upon his cot, and as the guard had that day been paid off, he found ready customers and patrons in every one of them. A knot of soldiers and lepers were congregated around him during the afternoon, and among them the corporal of our guard had taken a hand and finally lost, not only his own pay, but that of such of his men as were willing to lend him.

A more ill-natured, morose, and vicious fellow than this corporal I had not met during all the intercourse I was forced to hold with the soldiery of Mexico. His features and expression proclaimed him a petty tyrant of the worst description; for there was a lurking malice in his eye, a sinister expression in his mahogany-coloured countenance, that as plainly denoted his character as a sign over a grocer's door tells the passers-by that sugar or coffee may be purchased within. The fellow took every occasion to annoy us—would prevent our friends from entering our room when they called—deprived us of every liberty in his power, and, in short, made himself odious to all. His name was José Maria;

and here I would remark that José Maria is the John Smith of Mexico. Call the name in almost any crowd you may meet, you will find José Marias ready to respond.

When the wretch had lost his own money, and could borrow no more, he appeared to lose all command of his bad passions. One of our party, against whom he had some ill will, he drove to his bed, and soon after ordered his own men to leave the gambling cot of the leper, and by this means "blocked the game;" but no sooner had he left the room for a few moments than the cards were again produced, and the game resumed. On returning, and finding his men once more engaged, he drew the stick which all the corporals in Mexico carry, and belaboured them most unmercifully—and all to gratify his own malicious passions. This closed the game a second time, but no sooner was his back turned than it was again recommenced. One of his men had won, by three or four successful bets, some ten or fifteen dollars, all of which he had staked on the turn of a single card. The game of *monte* closely resembles *faro*, and the leper had hardly commenced dealing before José Maria again made his appearance. Walking stealthily to the cot, the wretch raised his stick, and uttered a horrible oath. The poor soldier who had staked his all saw the impending blow, but, Mexican-like, his love of the game overcame all fears of the pain and disgrace of a beating, and he continued to watch the cards as the leper slowly turned them over, one by one. José Maria now struck him a violent blow upon the back. He shrugged his shoulders, but still watched the game with as much intentness as ever. Another and another blow followed in quick succession, and still the soldier made no other motion than a slight flinching as the stick fell heavily upon his head or back. The ungovernable passion of the corporal appeared to gain fresh strength from the stoical indifference of the soldier, and he now belaboured the poor fellow with blows that cut to the very quick; but still he did not move. His all depended upon the turn of a card, and neither blows nor threats could drive him from his watch of the game. An unlucky turn at length decided the bet against him, and now for the first time he turned his head. It was only to give a look of stern defiance at his cruel oppressor, for he did not dare strike back, and then coolly to walk off. Exhausted with his efforts, and pale from exertion and passion, José Maria also left the spot, and quiet was once more restored.

I have related this anecdote to show how deep-seated is the passion for gaming in Mexico. From the *lépero**\* to the highest dignitary—men and women—all, or nearly all, are alike afflicted with the passion. They manifest, too, the greatest indifference to loss, and instances are daily occurring where a man will lose his hat, shoes, blanket, and even the very shirt from his back, with a coolness and nonchalance which in any other situation would be highly commendable. He fears no pain or disgrace—starvation he looks upon with perfect indifference—in short, so strong and deep-seated is his passion for any game of chance, that the Mexican will stake a month's food in advance upon the single turn of a card, even were he to know that starvation would be the inevitable result of an unlucky deal. That there are many gentlemen in Mexico who do not gamble I have little doubt; but as a general rule, all classes are more or less addicted to games of chance.

\* The *lépero* is the *loafer* of Mexico, not one afflicted with leprosy, as many of my readers may imagine. The latter are called *lazarinos*.

For hours after the strange scene at the cot of the gambling leper sleep did not visit my eyelids. A continued succession of horrid sounds from the lepers around me—sounds intended for coughs, but which resembled more the last rattling struggles of dying men—would have prevented sleep; but to these were added an extreme difficulty of respiration on my own part, and the unceasing annoyances of José Maria. The wretch had seen that we took part in the general dissatisfaction manifested at his inhuman conduct, and sought his revenge by counting us every half hour un til after midnight. Not content with simply examining each cot closely, he held a lantern directly in our faces, so that the light could not but awaken us even had we been ever so much disposed to sleep. It was not until he himself became completely weary with too much watching that he ceased his annoying attentions, after which I was enabled to fall into a doze.

At an early hour the next morning, even before the sun had risen, I was awakened by a hearty shake of my shoulders. On opening my eyes, I was not a little astonished on seeing Mr. Mayer sitting by the side of me on my narrow cot. The unusual hour, and the fact that his face wore an expression of much satisfaction, convinced me that he was the bearer of glad tidings, and with not a little curiosity I inquired of him the news.

Mr. M. informed me that there was now every prospect of my speedy liberation, together with five or six of the other prisoners who had claimed American protection. He farther stated that Mr. Ellis had had an interview with Santa Anna, at which the latter manifested a disposition to give an order for our release so soon as certain movements on the part of the American government, and some of its citizens, could be satisfactorily explained. Among these, Santa Anna referred to the fact that a number of United States men-of-war had either anchored or been seen off Sacrificios, and to a rumour that young Frank Combs had entered Texas from the United States with a body of men, whose intention was to invade the Mexican territory. He farther mentioned the case of young Spencer, whose movements in New-Orleans and Texas at that time were of a suspicious nature, and that there might be some design against Mexico at the bottom of them.

That all these circumstances could be so satisfactorily explained as in no way to compromise the dignity of either Mexico or the United States, Mr. Mayer expressed himself confident, and at the same time congratulated me upon the prospect of once more regaining that liberty of which I had now been deprived for seven months. After informing me, in addition, that General Waddy Thompson, the new minister to Mexico, had arrived at Vera Cruz, and was then on the road to the capital, and promising to call upon me the next day, Mr. M. left San Lazaro.

That I was not a little elated by this favourable turn in my affairs may be readily imagined. I had all along believed that Santa Anna would keep me in confinement so long as he could find any pretext for such a course; but that the moment he found he could no longer detain me, he would find some excuse for granting my release. He now saw that the subject of our imprisonment had excited a lively interest in the United States; that meetings were held at different points, having for their object a call upon the government to demand the immediate and unconditional release of such Americans as were entitled to its protection; and that several of the state legislative assemblies had passed strong resolutions to that effect—resolutions which must, sooner or later, drive the naturally tardy General Government into other measures than mere argument in order to secure the liberation of its citizens. He moreover was aware that General Thompson, a gentleman whose character for promptness and decision was well known, was now on his way to Mexico as the accredited minister of the United States, and he naturally enough supposed, from the tone of the public journals, that he must bring with him stronger instructions in relation to our release than any which had been sent to Mr. Ellis. With all these circumstances staring him in the face, it was plain enough that Santa Anna was disposed to shuffle out of a dilemma in which he found himself involved; and to do it with as good a grace as possible, and to preserve the dignity of the great Mexican nation spotless, he now concluded to get rid of us on the best terms he could make. Hence his artful *ruse* to have the facts I have alluded to above—those in relation to the squadron, young Combs, and Spencer—accounted for, knowing all the while that there was really nothing in them to arouse the suspicions of his government.

But even should Santa Anna refuse to grant my release, I still had the satisfaction of knowing that my individual case would be definitely acted upon—that I must shortly know my fate, whatever it might be. Should the Mexican government still refuse to give me up, I had made every arrangement to effect an escape. In doing this, I had studiously avoided implicating any member of the United States legation, but had found friends among the foreigners who promised to assist me in any way. Money, that great talisman, I had at my command to an amount that would open any prison-door in Mexico; and in addition to this, the escape over the wall, a mode I have previously described, was open so long as I remained in San Lazaro. Under all these encouraging circumstances, it will be imagined that my spirits were not a little raised, and that my mind was relieved of many apprehensions by the bright anticipations of once more regaining my liberty, either through the influence of my government or by my own individual exertions.

It was on Friday, the 15th of April, that Mr. Mayer called upon me with the good news just related. During the day I received no other visits, but on the afternoon of the next Mr. M. again called, and this time in company with two or three American citizens. He said there had been no farther action in relation to my release, but that there probably would be that evening, and that I should be made acquainted with the result immediately.

From the Americans I learned that General Thompson was expected that evening in the stage from Vera Cruz, and that a large party of them had come out as far as San Lazaro, by which the stage passed, to meet and escort him into the city. While we were speaking of the circumstance, the distant rumbling of wheels was heard. My friends immediately retired, but not until they had promised to visit me again before dark.

Shortly after their departure I could plainly hear the stage, in which was the new minister with his suite, rattling by the hospital, and making its way towards the centre of the city. To me there was something unusually enlivening in the sounds, for I well knew that I was now soon to be relieved of the annoying suspense which had long weighed upon me like an incubus. There are few men who have had the opportunity of feeling the harassing annoyance of suspense to the degree I had experienced for the last two months. Imprisoned unjustly in one of the vilest holes in Christendom — surrounded by loathsome wretches, whose very aspect was enough to drive one almost to desperation—shut out completely from the world—taunted almost daily by my Texan comrades with invidious comparisons between my own government and that of Great Britain in looking after the rights of their subjects, and half convinced, as I was, that the former was not moving with that promptness the case demanded, I was also suffering under an indisposition which was far from inconsiderable ; and when to all this is added the circumstance that during much of this period I had little hope of a change, except such change as is found in chains and labour, the reader may easily imagine the irksomeness of my situation. But now the time had arrived when the dark curtain of suspense was to be raised—a suspense so torturing that a sentence to ten years' imprisonment would have been almost a relief—now my position was about to be defined in some way, and I certainly felt an elevation of spirits I had been a stranger to for months.

At sunset two of my friends returned, bringing me a large file of papers, and word from General Thompson that he would visit me early the next morning. I spent hours in poring over the papers from different quarters of the United States, and absolutely forgot my troubles as I read the many articles I found in them relating to my own case, and saw the warm interest taken in my behalf by my editorial brethren throughout the country.

Shortly after breakfast the next morning I was visited in San Lazaro by General Thompson himself. I was reading when he entered, seated with my feet resting against a large medicine-chest in the centre of the room. On seeing him at the door, I advanced to meet him. He inquired the nature of the diseases in the hospital, and on my informing him that we had none other than leprosy and small-pox, he obtained, through the assistance of Mr. Mayer, permission for me to walk with him as far as the front door of the building, where there were several benches or seats. Accompanying General T. were Lieutenant Faunce, of our revenue service, and Messrs. Coolidge of Boston, and Perrin of New-Orleans. These gentlemen brought me a large package of letters from my friends, and expressed the greatest confidence that I should return with them to the United States.

General Thompson asked me every particular in relation to my arrest and subsequent imprisonment—promised to exert himself to the utmost in procuring my unconditional release—and moreover said that he would endeavour, at least, to obtain an order for my removal to other and better quarters forthwith. If possible, he intended to procure my release upon parole until my case could be definitely settled one way or the other, pledging himself to give me up whenever the Mexican government might call for me. After a little farther conversation the new minister and his party took their leave.

With spirits elated I returned to my gloomy quarters, passing much of the day in perusing and reperusing the letters from my friends. There is something at all times soothing and grateful to the feelings in receiving one of these written tokens of attachment—something which convinces that you are not forgotten—that you still hold a place in the memory of those endeared to you by ties of friendship; but how doubly grateful to me were these kind evidences of regard—the first I had received for nearly a year. They carried me back to other and happier days—to scenes I had strong hopes of soon visiting—and I almost fancied myself free as I scanned their pages. But alas! how often is the cup of happiness dashed from our lips when we have it within our very grasp. Thirty-six hours after I was indulging in these pleasing anticipations, and while bright hope was opening to me a prospect of the most flattering nature, I was plunged into the very lowest depths of uncertainty—I may almost say of despair.

On the morning of the 18th of April, the day after General Thompson's visit, Mr. Perrin called upon me at San Lazaro. From his conversation, although he endeavoured to offer me hope, I could plainly enough see that the chances of attaining my liberty were not as favourable as they had been some two or three days before. The partial promise to release me, given to Mr. Ellis by Santa Anna on the 14th, the latter had probably found some means to evade entirely or to defer, and I was confident he would temporize to an extent which no other diplomacy than Mexican can ever hope to equal. In that particular branch of diplomatic science—deferring or "putting off" the main question—the Mexicans excel even the Chinese.

On leaving me, Mr. Perrin advised that I should make no attempt to escape, at least until General Thompson had been duly received as the accredited minister of the United States; but a circumstance which occurred soon after he left the hospital determined me to make the attempt at once. While walking in the little yard which we were allowed to visit during the

## PREPARATION FOR ESCAPE.

day, I noticed, standing against the wall, a long pole, strong enough to bear my weight, and at equal distances, and about one yard apart, were placed pegs. For what use this pole was originally intended I am at a loss to conjecture; at the time I looked upon it as a special interposition, as by means of it I could easily enough climb to the top of the wall, and then, after dragging it over, let myself down, without danger, on the other side. Watching an opportunity when I supposed no one was observing me, I removed the pole to one of the corners of the yard, and then returned to my quarters in the hospital. I am confident not one of the guard observed my movements, as on entering the hospital I found them all engaged in conversation with the inmates, where they could not possibly have seen me.

The fact of my having either seen or moved the pole I did not disclose to any one, not even my friends. My plan was, in case any of the foreigners called upon me in the afternoon, to divulge the circumstances I have mentioned to some one of them who knew the city well, and ask for his assistance in enabling me to escape. All I wished him to do was simply to name either the first or second street, running from San Lazaro, that led directly into the city, and place himself at the head of it at dark, dressed in such a manner that I might easily distinguish him. I then intended to risk the danger of being observed while clambering over the wall. The attempt was to be made at twilight, and just before the time at which the door leading to the yard was generally locked for the night.

In order to be every way in readiness, I put all my money and valuables in my pockets, intending to leave my clothing, books, &c., to any one who might take them. All these arrangements made, I now awaited, with not a little anxiety, the arrival of some one of my friends, to whom I might confide my secret and upon whose assistance I might depend.

## CHAPTER XIV.

Hours of Expectation.—One of the Santiago Prisoners brought to San Lazaro, sick with the Small-pox.—Disappointed Hopes.—Arrival of a Guard of Soldiers at San Lazaro.—Mysterious Conduct of the Commander.—Ordered to prepare for Departure.—A vile Litter produced.—Refusal to enter it.—Leave San Lazaro.—"Farewells" of the Texans and "Adios" of the Lepers.—Gloomy and mysterious night March.—Interior of the City of Mexico.—Stared at by the Populace.—A Coach ordered.—Misery likes Company.—Dogs in the Outskirts of Mexico.—Arrive at our Destination.—Farther Uncertainty.—Ushered into the Presence of Women.—The Mystery unravelled.—Find myself in Santiago, and among Friends.—Ordered to make Choice of a Partner in Chains.—Select Major Bennett.—First Appearance in Fetters.—Congratulations of my Friends on the Occasion.—Major Bennett quotes Scripture again.—Determination to escape.—Santa Anna's Motives in the Removal to San Lazaro.—Action of the Mexican and United States Governments in relation to the American Prisoners.—Consider the Chances of Liberation as hopeless as ever.—Strange Conduct of Santa Anna.—No Difficulty in shaking off the Irons.—The "Secrets of our Prison-house."—Character of the old Commandante of Santiago.—Texan Tricks upon a Mexican Blacksmith.—The Blacksmith and Santa Anna in Converse.—Description of Santiago, and Chances of an Escape.—The Texans going out to labour in the Streets.—More Play than Work.

THE hours after dinner dragged heavily along, but no one called to whom I could make known my contemplated escape. About the middle of the afternoon a young man named Bowen, one of Colonel Cooke's party, was brought to San Lazaro from Santiago, very ill with the small-pox. He was delirious, giving incoherent answers to the different questions asked him.

Night finally set in, yet not a single foreigner made

his appearance. This was the more remarkable, as several of them had promised to call upon me that afternoon. There appeared to be a strange fatality in the circumstance, that at the very time when I most wanted to see the face of a friend, no one came; but there was no help for it, and I saw the door locked with a heart made heavy by disappointment. The only consolation I had was, that the same opportunity to escape would probably be open on the ensuing day, and with this expectation I retired to my cot and soon fell asleep.

About half past nine o'clock at night I was awakened by a heavy tramp, as of men marching past me. On opening my eyes, I saw eight or ten soldiers paraded directly in front of my cot, with shouldered muskets. Not a little astonished at a circumstance so unusual, I was about to inquire the cause, when the officer in command of the party, after asking my name, said I must immediately prepare to leave San Lazaro.

I asked him whither I was to be taken, but he gave me no answer. There was something mysterious in the air of this man that caused me much uneasiness, but I was completely in his power and could only obey his commands. While I was hastily slipping on my clothes, and packing my books and other articles in a carpet bag, the lepers congregated about me with not a little astonishment depicted in their dismal countenances. I had formed a kind of distant intimacy with many of the unfortunate wretches, and their surprise was equal to my own on learning that "Don Jorge," as they called me, was about to be taken from San Lazaro under so strong a guard, and at an hour so strange and unseasonable. I thought of my dealings with the pole, and for a moment supposed that this unusual movement might be caused by my having been discovered in the act; but of this I was uncertain.

After a few hasty preparations, I told the officer I was ready to accompany him; but first I asked him if he would allow me to ride. He immediately ordered his men to bring in a litter, and pointing to it, told me I could ride in that. The litter had a vile, filthy blanket in it, and had evidently been used to transport some worthless or wounded lépero to a hospital or dungeon; but what gave me more uneasiness than all were the words "*Carcel de Ciudad*"—city prison—painted upon its sides. That I was to be taken to some vile hole, and thrown alone among the most worthless and abandoned wretches, was now evident enough, and I could scarcely restrain a shudder at the thought of a fate so horrible.

Again I asked the officer if he would send one of his men for a coach, telling him that I had money to pay for it, and that one of my ankles was so weak that I was fearful, from not having taken much exercise of late, of its failure if I had far to walk. He only answered me by pointing to the litter. Determined, under no circumstances, to ride or be carried in a conveyance so vile, I told him I would endeavour to walk. My mattress and blankets, which were my own property, together with the carpet bag, were now thrown into the litter, the guard formed on either side of me, and amid the " adios" of the poor lepers, and the kind " farewells" of my companions, I was escorted out of San Lazaro. I turned one look, as I passed the threshold, at the companions of my imprisonment, but not a gleam of hope's sunshine could I discover in their sorrowful countenances. In moments of sudden trial or peril, how much of the mind's workings, how much of the inward emotions, can be read while hastily scanning the faces of those around us. I keenly scrutinized the features of the crowd gathered at the door to see my departure—commiseration, pity, all the kindlier feelings of man's nature were there, but not one glimmering of assurance as to the fate that awaited me could I discover, no key to unlock the mystery in which the movements of my guard were hidden. With a heavy heart I bade the inmates of San Lazaro farewell, and I doubt whether one of them, either Mexican or Texan, expected ever to see me again.

On reaching the front door of the hospital, the officer in command ordered a halt. He then took me into the small office connected with the establishment, and gave the major-domo a receipt to the effect that I had been regularly delivered into his hands. I once more requested him to send one of the guard for a coach—a request which he only answered by pointing to the litter.

Outside the hospital, the officer now formed his men, some five or six on either side of me, a trumpeter in the rear, and himself in front. In this order we marched from San Lazaro, the course taken leading directly towards the heart of the city. For the first four or five blocks my ankle gave me little or no pain, the uncertainty which shrouded my destination probably drawing my attention from all personal inconvenience; but as we entered the better portion of the city, and were leaving the low and miserable habitations which form the outskirts of Mexico, my ankle began to give way under the unwonted exercise.

Two or three times I asked the soldiers who were marching next me whither we were going: the eternal "*quien sabe?*" was the only answer.

We had now proceeded some half or three quarters

of a mile on our mysterious journey, and had entered the better part of the city, when my ankle began to pain me excessively. I stopped for a moment, and in eloquent bad Spanish told the Mexican officer my situation. He shrugged his shoulders, and still pointed to the filthy litter, which was borne by two of his men. Had my ankle been perfectly sound at this time, such were my feelings, I should most certainly have broken through the guard which surrounded me, and put the chance of an escape upon a run, regardless of their muskets. As it was, I could but hobble along, and submit to being guarded, I knew not whither.

As we approached the centre of the city, although it was now almost eleven o'clock at night, we met numbers passing. My dress plainly denoted that I was no countryman of theirs, for I wore a blanket coat I had purchased of an American at Chihuahua, and an American hat. The sight of a foreigner thus attired, and thus strongly guarded through the streets at an hour so unseasonable, excited not a little curiosity in the passersby, and they crowded under the lamps and peered inquisitively in my face.

We passed several churches, and once or twice we were halted for a few moments directly in front of large gloomy edifices, which I could not but think were prison-houses. I was not allowed to march upon the sidewalk, but was taken directly along the middle of the streets, where the walking was rough and uneven, and where my ankle was liable to be strained or injured at every step. Driven at length almost to desperation, not only by pain, but by the uncertainty with which I was surrounded, I forced myself between two of the soldiers who guarded me, and sat down upon the sidewalk directly in front of a large church. The officer ordered me to rise and continue the march, but I told him I could walk no farther.

Anxious, probably, to be relieved as soon as possible of his charge, the officer now consented to send one of his soldiers for a coach; and being near one of the great coach-stands of the city, he soon returned with the conveyance I was so much in need of. I immediately entered the heavy and clumsy vehicle, the officer following and seating himself by my side. The soldiers were then formed on either side, and at a brisk pace the strange night march was resumed.

On several occasions the coach stopped for a moment, probably to give the guard rest, and each time I scanned the buildings on either side with an eager gaze, expecting to see some dismal prison. Had there been a single companion with me, for misery *does* like company, I should not have been so oppressed by the sickly feelings I experienced; but I was alone, and could only brood over my singular and annoying situation in silence.

A half-hour's ride carried us almost entirely through the city, and after leaving the poorer habitations of the suburbs, we emerged into the open country. Passing now and then a small house, from which some score of noisy dogs would jump and bark at us, the coach finally drew up in front of a large and gloomy establishment, walled in on two of its sides, where a halt was called. It was now near midnight. I asked the officer what building it was; but he was stepping from the coach at the time, and either did not hear or did not heed my question.

I had hardly left the coach before I heard the startling "*centinela alerta!*" from a soldier directly over my head. The cry was taken up by another in a different part of the building, then by another, until at length I could but faintly hear the long-drawn-out and to me grating sounds feebly echoed and re-echoed from the more distant walls of the building. Around the passage-way which led to the establishment, groups of soldiers, rolled up in their cloaks and blankets, were lying asleep, and a regular guard was marching backward and forward in the entrance. I was soon taken, still strongly guarded, through the main door of entrance. Once within, I found a large yard, surrounded on all sides by buildings, and by the dim light of a lamp I could plainly read the word *castigo* — punishment — over a strong and gloomy door. In this apartment, I at once thought I should find a resting-place; but who were to be my companions, or what the cause of my imprisonment, I could not imagine.

Not a little overjoyed was I when the guard, who even to this time was stationed on either side of me, marched by this dreadful room and led me up a flight of stone steps on the other side of the yard. We now groped our way along a dark passage, the floor of stone, and every footfall sending up a doleful echo. Once, by the dim light of a distant lantern, I saw the gloomy figures of two or three monks, slowly wending their way towards their silent cloister, and again all was darkness.

Groping his way a few steps in advance of us, the officer who had me in charge at length reached a small door, at which he knocked. A female voice within asked him for the countersign. He gave it, the door slowly opened, and I was ushered into a small but neatly-furnished apartment, having a guitar and several pieces of music scattered about, while a sideboard and other articles of furniture graced the sides of the room.

Two females were present — one a lady-like woman some thirty-five years of age, the other a pretty girl of not more than sixteen, and both were undressed as if just from bed. After they had politely beckoned me to a chair, I asked the elder for some water, which she gave me after inquiring whether I would not prefer a glass of wine. The kindness of these women gave me hope, which was soon banished, however, by the entrance, from another room, of an elderly and grim-visaged officer, apparently some sixty years of age. He had a morose scowl upon his face, and his upper lip was decked with a pair of mustaches which might have been cut from a shoe-brush.

He asked my name, entered it in a book which was lying upon the table, and after telling the officer who had charge of me that all was right, ordered him, with a cold, business-like air, to march off and lock me up. By a different passage I was now taken to the yard below, and halted in front of a large and strong door. A key was applied to the lock, and while they were slowly turning it I could plainly hear the clanking of chains and the indistinct hum of voices within. This was the most trying moment of all, for I was profoundly ignorant alike of the place and of the companions I was to be associated with.

The door was at length opened. A loud shout arose as I entered the room, and my name was called by fifty voices in a breath. Never can I forget my own feelings when, with spirits but a few moments before depressed by a suspense the most harrowing, I now found myself suddenly and most unexpectedly in Santiago, greeted by Colonel Cooke, Dr. Brenham, Captain Sutton, and the friends whom I had not seen for seven months. The prospect of chains and servitude was as nothing—I was among my old companions.

By far the greater number of the prisoners were asleep when I entered the room; yet there were some twenty still awake, engaged at cards upon the stone floor, or reading by the dim light of Mexican candles. After half an hour's conversation with my friends, I spread my cot among them—a refreshing sleep following a day replete with excitement.

Immediately after breakfast the next morning, the Mexican who had charge of the Texan chain gang politely requested me to choose a partner from among the prisoners—some one to assist me in carrying the heavy fetters which were now to decorate one of my ankles for the first time. The recollection of the favourable opportunity I had to escape from San Lazaro the day before now flashed across my mind, and I deeply regretted that fate had prevented me from improving it; but as this was no time to speculate long on the past, or indulge in idle regrets, I commenced a survey of my fellow-prisoners with the intention of making a choice. It fell upon the veteran Major Bennett, of scripture-quoting memory. One end of his chain was vacant, owing to the sickness of his comrade at the time; but what induced me more particularly to make choice of him, was a sly wink he gave me, and a side speech to the effect that he had a way of ridding himself of the fetters which few of the Texans possessed.

We were now conducted to a small room, adjoining that in which the prisoners were locked up for the night. Here an anvil had been placed for the business, and the room was decorated with rings, rivets, chains, and other instruments of disgrace. I slipped a dollar into the hands of the Mexican whose duty it was to fasten the trinkets upon me. This I had been advised to do by my friends, as it would induce the fellow, either to give me a ring so large that I could slip it off, or so to fasten the rivet that I could remove it with but little difficulty. The dollar had the desired effect, for the Mexican selected a ring which I could easily remove after taking off my boot.

With as good a grace as I could assume—for this chaining a man excites any feelings but those of a pleasant nature—I now submitted to the operation. The chain was some eight feet in length, extremely heavy, and of the class used to draw logs with oxen—in other words, a log chain. After cutting the straps from a pair of fashionable, French pantaloons, which I had purchased at Zacatecas, I placed my foot upon the anvil, and the Mexican, although well knowing that I could shake myself free with ease, hammered away and made as much noise as though the chain was to remain upon my ankle for life.

A knot of my fellow-prisoners gathered about me during the operation, and made themselves exceedingly facetious at my expense. One of them, accompanying the remark with a shake of his foot that made his own chain clank again, assured me that I should find it agreeable enough *after* I got used to it. Another said it was not half so bad as pulling teeth; and still another remarked that chaining one's leg was far less painful than sawing it off. A musical genius commenced humming Bruce's Address, laying emphatic stress upon the line

"Chains and slavery;"

while another individual, gifted slightly with vocal abilities, essayed the ditty commencing with

"Liberty for me."

Even Major Bennett, although not much given to humorous remarks, could not resist the opportunity of being facetious. With a gravity which would have become a graven image, he pretended to comfort me with the remark that we all have our trials and tribulations, quoted a verse from Job to the effect that useless repining was of little avail, and wound up by saying that the time would yet come when our bonds would all be rent asunder.

While all this was in progress, I felt indignant enough fairly to eat half a dozen links of the chain attached to my ankle, but I still forced a laugh, and assumed a cheerfulness of demeanour when I felt much more like shedding tears from very vexation. Thoughts, too, of an escape, of an immediate escape, ran through my mind with such rapidity that twenty half-digested plans to effect my liberty were formed and abandoned in half as many minutes. I now considered myself cut off from all hope of release through the interference of my own government, and resolved to run every risk, and go to any expense, to achieve my liberation. In this frame of mind I went back to the main room in which the prisoners were confined, myself and companion dragging the heavy chain after us. My friends congratulated me upon my appearance in the "trinkets," and one of them, pointing to the chain, humorously remarked that I must now feel *bound* to the major by the *strongest ties!* This was on the morning of the 19th of April.

Up to this time I have never been able to fathom or ascertain Santa Anna's motives in having me removed from San Lazaro to Santiago. Clothed in mystery as the movements of the Mexicans generally are, and delighting as they do in a dark and covert policy, there was something unusually strange in the hour chosen, the strong guard sent to secure my safe conduct, and the fact that the officer who commanded the guard appeared studiously to avoid giving me any clew as to my destination.

But to show my readers in what a veil of mystery the whole affair was shrouded, I will here revert to the negotiations which had been pending, for the previous three or four days, in relation to the liberation of myself, and of six other Americans who had claimed the protection of the United States government.

On the 14th of April, Mr. Ellis, who was then shortly to leave Mexico, had an interview with Santa Anna in relation to the cases of these seven Americans. At this interview, Santa Anna expressed himself willing to release the prisoners, but not until certain acts of the United States were explained. He alluded to the fact that at that time the U. S. frigate Macedonian was off Vera Cruz, with another American man-of-war, and said that as soon as he received information, from the commandante at Vera Cruz, that these vessels had sailed, he would be pleased to give the prisoners up to Mr. Ellis. While the vessels remained he should be prevented from releasing them, as rumours were prevalent in Mexico that the frigate brought a *demand* for the prisoners, and the Mexican public might charge him with being influenced by their presence in granting a release—in other words, with being frightened into the measure. The result of this interview, which was considered at the time as very favourable to my release, induced Mr. Mayer to call upon me early the next morning with the news—a circumstance I have mentioned in the previous chapter.

On the 16th of April, two days after this interview, Mr. Mayer called upon the Mexican Minister of Foreign

Relations, José Maria de Bocanegra. This call was made about twelve o'clock, at the request of Mr. Ellis, and with the object of ascertaining the farther action of the Mexican government upon the subject of our release. M. de Bocanegra informed Mr. Mayer that he could not tell him at what time the prisoners would be set at liberty, as intelligence of a very disagreeable nature had just been received by the government, which might influence the mind of Santa Anna; but in the mean time the minister requested Mr. Mayer to call upon him again the same evening, when he might expect a more definite answer upon the subject.

About five o'clock Mr. M. called again at the Foreign Office, when M. de Bocanegra enumerated five points of difficulty as to carrying into immediate effect the promise made by Santa Anna, on the 14th, to Mr. Ellis. I give these points as they were taken down in writing by Mr. M., thinking they may interest some of my readers:

*First.* That young Combs had armed, and was at the head of, a body of hostile persons, under the name of *emigrants*, advancing upon Mexico.

*Second.* That a Mr. Spencer had been sent from the United States, with despatches to Texas, and that immediately afterward, and in strange coincidence, the Texan blockade of the eastern coast of Mexico had been proclaimed.

*Third.* That Texas had proclaimed this blockade.

*Fourth.* That *all* the vessels of war had not yet left Vera Cruz.

*Fifth.* That the publications in the papers of the United States against Mexico were most unfriendly, inflammatory, and hostile.

Not thinking it his duty to enter into an argument

upon these points, Mr. Mayer asked M. de Bocanegra whether the legation of the United States should consider the negotiations in regard to the release of the seven prisoners as terminated. The minister replied that they were *not* to be considered terminated. Mr. Mayer then wished to know whether the legation should consider the Mexican government as having withdrawn its word as to the release of the prisoners. The minister answered that such was not to be the interpretation —that his own government did not withdraw its word, but only "*suspended*" its operation upon the question— in short, that the "*suspension*" should only be momentary. Those acquainted with the artful, evasive, and temporizing policy of a skilful Mexican diplomatist may readily conceive that this "*momentary* suspension" might be spun out to ten years—and in this light I believe it was viewed by those who were acquainted with the circumstances. At all events, I judged, from the tone of such friends as called upon me the day after this interview, that my chance of release was as hopeless as ever, and this opinion induced me to attempt an escape over the walls of San Lazaro on the Monday following.

At the very time that I was thus contemplating an escape, and while I was anxiously awaiting the arrival of some friend at San Lazaro who would assist me, Mr. Ellis was holding an interview with the ministers de Bocanegra and Trigeros at the Treasury Department. At this interview Mr. E. answered the *five points* which had caused the "*suspension*" of our release, as follows:

*First.* That he had positive information that Combs had gone home with his father from New-Orleans to Kentucky, and was not engaged in the Texan war upon Mexico.

*Second.* That Spencer was not a bearer of despatches from the government of the United States to Texas; but had used the title (as was rumoured) to protect himself from, or to evade, charges affecting him personally.

*Third.* That the United States had no part, influence, or concern, in the Texan blockade, and, moreover, that if the government he represented entertained hostile designs upon Mexico (which it did not), they would be manifested openly by our own forces, and not secretly, through the navy of another power.

*Fourth.* That *all* the vessels of war of the United States had actually left Vera Cruz.

*Fifth.* That the prints of the United States were free —not under the control of the government—and not the organs of its opinions.

In answer to this, M. de Bocanegra wished Mr. Ellis distinctly to understand that the promise of Mexico, for the release of myself and the six other Americans, was given—it was an act concluded—and its operation only momentarily suspended. He farther stated, that he would immediately see Santa Anna, and hoped the conversation he had just held with Mr. E. would so far satisfy the President as to induce him to order the release of the prisoners previous to Mr. Ellis's departure from Mexico, and that they might then accompany him to the United States.

From all this it would seem that my release had been fully and finally determined upon, to take place immediately; yet but a few hours afterward, and late at night, I was escorted from San Lazaro under a strong guard, and under circumstances the most annoying and mysterious, and taken to Santiago. It could hardly be for my better security, and it would seem almost impossible that any person had seen me removing the pole in the hospital yard of San Lazaro; whence I can only conjecture that the whole proceeding was the result of one of those capricious impulses which appear to govern the conduct of Santa Anna. Perhaps he thought he had not already punished me enough, was anxious to make the most of the short time I was still to be in his power, and therefore sent me to Santiago to give me a taste of life in chains.

The floor of our room at this old convent was of stone, and in the way of furniture we had neither chairs, tables, nor beds. After receiving the *congratulations* of my friends, upon my first appearance in fetters, I threw myself upon a blanket in that quarter of the prison which had been appropriated by Colonel Cooke and Dr. Brenham. The latter immediately began scratching the earth from the chinks between two stones, and soon drew forth a small file which had been secreted there. This he gave me, with directions for filing the rivet that secured the chain to my ankle. I told him that a small bribe had procured for me a ring, which I could easily enough slip over my foot when night came. While this conversation was going on, old Major Bennett quietly released himself from his end of the chain, and stalked off to a corner to peruse some book upon which he was at the time engaged.

I was now initiated into some of the "secrets of the prison-house." The old commandante of the guard—the same person into whose quarters I had been taken the night before, and who had registered my name in the presence of two women—was tyrannical and overbearing in his disposition, and used his best exertions to keep the prisoners continually in chains. The younger officers of the guard, however, were many of them generous and kind-hearted to a fault, and not only furnished our officers with files with which to rid themselves of their irons during the night, but also winked at any trifling violation of orders, and allowed them to move about without the "trinkets" during the day—only requesting them to avoid being seen by the old commandante. The latter seldom visited the prisoners more than once during the day; and as there was always some one of them to give warning of his approach, the chains were apparently "all right and tight" whenever he entered our quarters.

Every morning a blacksmith from the city was sent to examine and fasten the chains upon each prisoner; yet such adepts had the latter become at "working in iron," that while the knight of the anvil was securing one couple, the pair who had just passed through his hands were very likely loose from their fetters, and performing various antics and exchanging significant nods at the old fellow's expense behind his back.

The blacksmith, it was said, received twelve and a half cents for each rivet he fastened, and as every morning he found nearly all of them loose, the job was an extremely profitable one for him. A good story was told—having, probably, as much foundation in truth as the thousand and one legends and traditions by which the Mexican population is gulled—of an interview the old blacksmith had one morning with Santa Anna. The latter had noticed that a heavy bill was paid daily for fastening the chains of the intractable Texans, and questioned the blacksmith as to the cause. He made answer that the Texans were difficult people to deal with, and had strange ways that he could not understand. Santa Anna asked him how it was that while the simple fastening of a chain upon the ankle of a Mexican was sufficient to secure him for a twelvemonth, without putting the government to farther expense, a Texan was sure to rid himself of the same irons once in every twenty-four hours. This was a question the blacksmith was entirely unable to answer, farther than by informing his Excellency, the Provisional President, that " while he was busily engaged, with hammer and anvil, securing one Texan, his comrade at the other end of the chain, and whom he had but just operated upon, not only worked himself free, but very likely *did so at him !*" This latter movement of the Texan the blacksmith explained to Santa Anna by putting his right thumb to his nose, and then performing certain well-known and fanciful gyrations with his fingers. As the story ran, which was of course a fabrication of some wag among the prisoners, the President and the blacksmith, profoundly ignorant of the meaning of a movement so mysterious, came to the conclusion that the Texans had dealings with the prince of darkness, and that it was labour lost to attempt to secure them farther. At all events, the blacksmith suddenly ceased his morning visits, and from that time until the Texans were liberated they were only submitted to an occasional visitation from the Mexican who had charge of the parties sent into the streets to work.

The reader may recollect that on the night when I was escorted from San Lazaro to Santiago, and while the guard who accompanied me were unlocking the door of the room in which the prisoners in the latter place were confined, I mentioned hearing a rattling and clanking of chains. It arose from the circumstance that the prisoners thought the old commandante was paying them a night visit, and on this supposition they commenced fastening their chains with all possible despatch. Upon seeing me enter the room, they shook them off with even greater celerity.

With the fastening of irons upon my ankle went all hope of my being released by Santa Anna. I could not conceive it possible, after subjecting me to this disgrace, that he had the most remote intention of giving me liberty, and accordingly made up my mind at once to attempt an escape. I openly told my friends that I would not remain in Santiago a week, let the risk be what it might, and deeply was I vexed when I recalled to mind the many unimproved opportunities to escape that had presented themselves.

Here I will attempt a description of the convent in which we were confined. It was originally intended for a religious establishment, and some ten or fifteen monks still dwelt within its walls. The front entrance was through a narrow passage-way, having heavy doors on the outer and inner sides, which were both closed at night. In this passage-way many of the soldiers forming our guard slept. It led into a large yard, having heavy stone buildings on each side, and a fountain of excellent water in the centre. The prisoners occupied rooms on two sides of the square below, the other rooms being used as a kitchen, apartments for storing, a hospital, and a room in which mass was said on Sundays. The upper stories were occupied by the monks, by the commandante and his family, and by a number of crippled, invalid, and aged soldiers, veterans in the Mexican service. Outside of the building, on the side next the city, was the balcony from which Lieutenant Lubbock and the Frenchman Mazur had jumped when they made their escape, but the entrance to this balcony from within had been immediately walled up to prevent others from following in their footsteps. On the same side, a flight of stairs led from the second story to a garden below, in which the monks walked or worked during the day. This garden was surrounded by a low wall, which would have offered but a slight impediment to an escape; but a soldier was constantly stationed at the door leading to the garden, to prevent others than the monks from passing in or out.

There was a passage-way in the rear, corresponding with that which led into the yard in front, but its doors were kept continually locked. This passage led, I believe, to a walled enclosure in which thousands of the victims of cholera were buried in 1833. The back part of our room was destitute of windows, and the walls were extremely thick, so that there was no hope of escape that way. The only means, therefore, of getting away from Santiago with any probability of success, were either to bribe the guard stationed at the front entrance; to procure false keys for the doors leading to the rear, in which case we should also have been compelled to bribe the sentinel at the door of our room; or to walk out of the door leading to the garden in open daylight, and in the disguise of a monk. The latter would have required no associate within the walls, either Texan or Mexican, and I resolved to undertake it, should no more feasible plan offer. I should have taken holy clothes, not holy orders, for a short time, or, in other words, procured a monk's gown and cowl from some one of my friends. Then, by cutting off whiskers and mustaches, of which I had cultivated a liberal quantity for the express purpose of disguising myself; by also shaving the top of my head in imitation of the holy brotherhood, and putting the gown and cowl over my other dress, I could have passed out for a respectable monk—at all events, I should have tried the experiment in case other plans failed.

I had not been in irons an hour before Dr. Brenham

and myself, with one of the Texan officers, had determined upon sounding some of our guard as to whether they would pass us out in the night for a liberal sum of money. Young Sully, one of the Texans who spoke Spanish, was also let into the secret, and would have ventured with us had the attempt been made. Sully was the interpreter of the prisoners, and from constant communication with the guard knew every officer and soldier belonging to it. He had frequently hinted the subject of an escape to some of them, and from their answers felt confident that one hundred dollars would open every door in the Convent of Santiago. Having thus made up our minds to escape, we all awaited, with not a little impatience, a favourable opportunity to carry some one of our plans into effect.

At eight o'clock in the morning the Mexican having charge of the prisoners who worked in the streets made his appearance, with orders for them to be in readiness. I had expected that Santa Anna would impose street duty upon me also, and compel me to work it out; but in this I was agreeably disappointed.

It was really amusing to see the Texans setting out for their morning's work. The orders from headquarters were, that all should be sent into the streets; but it was easy enough to avoid it by feigning sickness. The larger portion preferred the fresh air and exercise outside the walls to the confinement and closeness within, going to their labour with joyous laughs which contrasted strangely with the clanking of their chains. The latter they cared little for. Their limbs were fettered, but their minds were free; and a moment's reflection taught them, however much they might have been annoyed at first, that they had committed no act which as men they could be ashamed of, and consequently their chains were no disgrace. As to the work they did, it was all a mere farce: there was not one of them but could have performed the labour of a day in fifteen minutes by using mere ordinary exertion.

## CHAPTER XV.

Fare of the Texans in Santiago.—Their Companions at Puebla not as well treated.—The Latter compelled to work and associate with Mexican Malefactors.—Anecdote of the Old Commandante of Santiago.—The Texans achieve a decided Victory over their Oppressor.—The Puebla Prisoners at their Tricks.—Attending Mass in Chains.—Mad Pranks of the Texans in Church.—Additional Ceremonies ingrafted upon the Catholic Ritual.— The Reader taken back to Santiago.—Foreign Visiters.—Farther Thoughts of escaping.—Action of General Thompson in my Behalf.— The Foreign Policy of the United States — Its Weakness and Inefficiency.— Santa Anna " Laughing in his Sleeve."—Plan to bribe our Guard at Santiago.— Evening Amusements of the Prisoners.—Major Bennett and his Bible.— Agreeable Soirées.—Character of the Anglo-Saxon Race under Misfortune. —Anticipation worse than Reality.—The Texans taken to their Morning Work.—Reasons for Slighting the Author.—More Visiters at Santiago.— Advised to defer an Escape.—Preparations for celebrating the Anniversary of the Battle of San Jacinto.—The Texans at their Work.—Experiments as to the smallest possible Amount of Labour a Man can perform when he exerts himself.—The Mexicans Outwitted.—Decorations of our Room.— San Jacinto and Patriotism.—The Texans at their Celebration.—Close of the Anniversary.

The prisoners in the Convent of Santiago were comparatively well fed—far better than were their unfortunate comrades at either Puebla or Peroté, as I afterward ascertained. At Santiago, a pint of very good coffee was given to each man in the morning, with a dish of well-cooked frijoles and as much bread as he wanted. The latter was white, sweet, and brought to us fresh, the Mexicans being famous for the rare quality of their bread. For dinner, which was cooked by some of our own men, we had beef, rice, and vegetables, the former of inferior quality, as the cattle in the vicinity of Mexico are seldom fat. There was an abundance of everything, however, and seldom are prisoners of war better treated, as far as regards eating, than were the Texans at the city of Mexico.

At Puebla the case was said to be widely different, a niggardly economy prevailing in the *commissariat*. As regards clothing, too, the prisoners at Santiago were infinitely better provided for than their comrades at Puebla, for while the former were neatly and comfortably clad—I believe by the chief magistrate of the city of Mexico—the latter received little raiment other than that supplied to them by foreigners. They were confined, too, at the Presidio, in the same patio or courtyard with two or three hundred of the vilest malefactors, and at first were even chained to them—a Mexican and Texan at either end of a long and heavy chain: but from some cause they were afterward separated, and the Texans confined together by the same fetters. The Puebla prisoners were also sent into the streets under most oppressive taskmasters, and, in company with the lowest Mexican felons and malefactors, compelled to clean the streets, gutters, and filthy sewers of the city, besides undergoing other trials even more degrading.

Not so at Santiago. The old commandante, one morning, ordered the Texans to perform some debasing work, which they at once and peremptorily refused to engage in. A second time they were commanded to the task, but still they persisted in the stand they had taken. Driven almost to madness, the ill-natured officer next ordered such of them as refused the disgracing labour to step a few paces forward, at the same time muttering dark threats against such as should venture from the ranks. To his utter dismay, every man boldly stepped forward, determined to be shot at once rather than obey his orders. The old commandante fumed, fretted, and swore, and threatened to send an account of their refractory conduct to Santa Anna himself, but all to no purpose—the Texans were united and determined in the stand they had taken. This was the last time they were called upon to perform any vile office. The commandante really sent a report of the transaction to the functionary who was at that time the principal magistrate or mayor of the city; but the prisoners forwarded another account of it to the same personage, in which they declared their willingness to labour, but boldly added that they would be coerced to no debasing work. The magistrate, whose name I have forgotten, but whom all the prisoners must recollect as a gentlemanly and liberal man, admitted the justice of their conduct, and gave orders that they should never be called upon to perform such offices as the commandante had endeavoured to exact from them. Here was a decided victory gained over their oppressor, and the Texans improved it in such a way that the old and ill-natured fellow was sorry he had ever crossed them.

One would suppose the indignities and hardships heaped upon the prisoners at Puebla would break their spirits; but such was not the case—nothing could subdue their natural buoyancy of disposition. Many and amusing were the stories related of the fun and frolic they were continually " getting up" among themselves, and the tricks and jokes they perpetrated whenever an opportunity occurred. The wags who were instrumental in convening the mirthful courts at San Cristobal were still among them, ever ready to extract laughter let what would happen. One anecdote I will relate—a story which is entirely too good to be lost.

Every Sunday morning, the prisoners confined at Puebla were compelled to attend mass, in chains, at one of the churches. The floors of all the religious establishments of note in Mexico are of stone or marble, without seats of any kind, and those in attendance must either kneel or stand during the ceremonies. In the present instance, the Texans were paraded in rows before the altar, and compelled to fall upon their knees while mass was said; but they were not obliged to go through all the little forms and ceremonies which the Catholic Church in Mexico exacts of its votaries, such as crossing themselves, smiting their breasts, and other outward observances. Well drilled, however, were they in all the minutiæ of these demonstrations, and in addition one of the jokers, who had acted as the prosecuting attorney at San Cristobal, and who was a great mimic, taught them a few original "extras" and " fancy touches," which he had ingrafted upon the regular Catholic ceremonials. So well had he disciplined his brother prisoners, that they could go through all his ritual with as much promptness and precision as could the best military company in existence go through its simplest manoeuvres.

On arriving at the church, and after kneeling in front of the altar, the well-drilled Texans awaited the usual signal from the officiating priest to commence. There probably was not a Catholic among them; yet the assumed air of grave devotion to be seen in their faces would have done credit to the most rigid of that creed. At the given signal, and at the proper time, the chained prisoners would cross themselves with all seeming humility, closely imitating every motion of the priest and of the Mexicans around them; but instead of stopping with their Catholic neighbours, they wound up by placing the right thumb to the tip of their noses, and then, with a mock gravity which might have drawn a smile from an Egyptian mummy, circled the fingers about, and all this directly in the face of the officiating priest, and without a smile upon their countenances. When the proper time came for again crossing themselves, the mischievous leader of the Texans would pass the word for his men to " come the double compound action," as he called it. This resembled the first movement, with the exception that it was more complicated and more mysterious to the surrounding Mexicans. After the right hand had gone its usual round, from forehead to breast and from shoulder to shoulder, the thumb again settled on the tip of the nose; but this time the left thumb was joined to the little finger of the right hand, and then commenced a series of fancy gyrations with all the fingers, the like of which was probably never before seen in a Catholic church. Sam Weller, I believe, or if not he, some modern philosopher of his school, defines the movement I have just described as meaning something like " This may be all very true, but we don't believe a word of it." What the Mexicans thought of it, or whether they noticed it or not, I am unable to say: it may be that they considered it as simply " a way" the Texans had, and thought no more of it. Such is the story told of the pranks played by the prisoners confined in Puebla.

During the first day of my imprisonment at Santiago we were visited by numbers of foreigners, all manifesting not a little astonishment at seeing me there, and in irons. They had not even heard of my being removed from San Lazaro, and promised to inform Mr. Ellis and General Thompson of the circumstance as soon as they returned to the city. I told them, one and all, that I would not remain in the place a week, let the risk be what it might, and even requested one of them to smuggle me in a monk's habit, that I might have everything in readiness should a favourable opportunity occur of escaping in that disguise through the garden. Our friends left after a short visit, and the rest of the day I passed in dragging my chain over the stone floor, and in waiting, with not a little impatience, the return of Sully, who was in the street, with the men. I was anxious to know his success in tampering with the guard.

Among the Americans who visited us during the forenoon was Mr. Perrin. On returning to the city, he at once communicated the fact of my being in Santiago, and in irons, to General Thompson. The latter had not yet been duly received as the accredited minister of the United States, but he promptly interested himself in my behalf by calling immediately at the residence of Mr. Ellis and informing him of the facts, expressing not a little astonishment and indignation at the strange and uncalled-for conduct of the Mexican government. Here I will give an extract from General Thompson's official letter to Mr. Webster, narrating the circumstance of his visit to Mr. Ellis, which I find published in the Madisonian of the 30th of June, 1842:

"On my arrival in Mexico I was informed, and afterward learned from Mr. Ellis, that on the 14th of April, two days before my arrival in this city, and when I was hourly expected, he had an interview with the President, Santa Anna, and had been promised the release of the American prisoners. Mr. Ellis told me, at the same time, he had no hope of the fulfilment of this promise. It was natural that Mr. Ellis should desire these prisoners to be released to him, and not to me; and as I thought the Mexican authorities would prefer that the matter should take this course, I was disposed to aid Mr. Ellis in his negotiations by every means in my power—the liberation of the prisoners being the primary object. On Tuesday, the 19th, I was not a little surprised to learn that Mr. Kendall had been removed from the hospital of San Lazaro to the Convent of Santiago, and for the first time put in chains. I immediately went to the office of Mr. Ellis, and proposed that he should write a note to the Minister of Foreign Relations, or that we should address to him a joint note on the subject. He declined doing so, saying that he had seen the minister the day before, and that he did not think any good would result. I told him I thought the subsequent placing of Mr. Kendall in irons justified and demanded it, and immediately addressed to M. de Bocanegra the note No. 5."

I will also give extracts from General Thompson's letter to M. de Bocanegra, referred to at the close of the passage just quoted. M. de B., it should be remembered, was at that time the Mexican Minister of Foreign Relations. This letter, I believe, was written at the room of Mr. Ellis, and was despatched immediately to M. de Bocanegra. It is dated " Mexico, April 19, 1842," bears the signature of General Thompson alone, and appeared originally in the same number of the Madisonian:

" The undersigned had the honour, on yesterday, to address a note to your excellency, announcing the fact of his appointment as minister of the United States of America, near this government, and of his arrival in this city, and requesting to know when he could have the honour of being presented to the most excellent the Provisional President of Mexico. Not having received an answer to that note (of which he by no means complains), the undersigned as yet bears no official relation to this government. But having this moment been informed that a citizen of the United States, Mr. George W. Kendall, who has been confined in the hospital of San Lazaro, has been removed to the Convent of Santiago, and placed in chains, the undersigned hopes it will be his sufficient apology for his again addressing your excellency.

" The undersigned is in possession of testimony additional to that heretofore submitted to your excellency, which he believes will place beyond all doubt the facts of Mr. Kendall having had a passport, and that his purposes in his visit to Mexico were altogether pacific. The undersigned, relying (as he does) on the sincerity of the professions heretofore made to his excellency, Mr. Ellis, has no hesitation in saying that the Mexican authorities will be satisfied with this evidence, and will take pleasure in releasing Mr. Kendall."

These extracts I have copied, partly to show the effect my removal from San Lazaro to Santiago had upon my friends in Mexico, but principally to make known the deep interest taken in my behalf by General Thompson. Although at the time I had little hope of obtaining immediate liberty through the intervention of my own government, I still could not but feel grateful for the prompt and decided tone adopted by the new minister in an emergency to me so critical.

I could not, at the time, look upon the course pursued by Mr. Ellis as sufficiently energetic, yet even to this day I do not believe that a majority of our diplomatic agents would have acted differently. I am firmly convinced that a bold tone would have been the proper one, and that the assumption of responsibility would have met with the approval of the people of the United States; but the chief blame must lie at the door of the government, not at the minister's. That Mr. Ellis did not succeed better, in his efforts to procure the liberty of his countrymen, must be ascribed, in the first place, to the circumstance that it has almost become a settled policy with our foreign plenipotentiaries—a policy he did not feel disposed to deviate from—to avoid taking a serious and decided responsibility, in cases of sudden emergency, fearful that the interests of the party which has sent them may be injured, or its plans for future advancement frustrated by so doing; and herein lies one of the most serious deficiencies of our system of government. The foreign agents of the United States have nominally the same powers that are granted to those of England or France; yet while the latter can act promptly, and with the full confidence that they will be justified and supported at home in whatever stand they may take, the hands of the former are too often tied by the fear that their course may possibly run counter to the interests of that party or clique whose servants they deem themselves, and hence, in matters of really trivial importance, they are driven to write home for advice how to act. In the second place, the instructions at first sent to Mr. Ellis were such as allowed him no other alternative than a "war of words" with the Mexican diplomatists—a game at which the latter leave the Anglo-Saxon race entirely in the distance. They resemble Goldsmith's country schoolmaster,

"For e'en though vanquished, he could argue still,"

and so can they. If my reader would allow me one moment's digression, I would give it as my firm conviction that we have had but two administrations, since the days of Washington, that were properly bold and independent as regards their foreign policy—those of the elder Adams and General Jackson. Politicians can take no umbrage at this remark, as I have mentioned two extremes when the general policy of the country is taken into consideration. One great fault, with too many of the administrations by which we have been governed, has been the resort to protracted arguments in matters where not a word of debate should have been allowed—a policy but too well understood by every government with which we have had dealings, and of which all, as a matter of course, have taken advantage. When the powers at Washington are convinced that they are in the right, upon any question of foreign policy at issue, what necessity for dispute? If it is evident that any little patch of territory, no matter how insignificant, belongs of right to us, why not plant, occupy, and, in firm but dignified language, say that we will *keep* it at any and all hazards? If it can be made to appear that an American citizen, under protection of that flag of which we so much boast, is insulted in a foreign land, why not demand and *obtain* full satisfaction at once? In many, too many instances, such has not been the case, and every fresh demonstration of inefficiency or inattention to these matters is but granting a fresh license for some foreign power to repeat its aggressions and its insults. In the case of Mr. Alvarez, our consul at Santa Fé, who, in 1841, was wantonly attacked and severely wounded in his own house, and directly under the "stars and stripes"—in his case what has been done? Nothing whatever. I might mention even greater outrages, but this is sufficient.

Had Mr. Ellis been authorized to try the virtue of

"blows and knocks," as he undoubtedly would have been by General Jackson, he would have done so with promptness; but he seemed anxious in no way to transcend the limited instructions given him, and hence the long-protracted correspondence which took place in relation to the American prisoners.* Mr. E. might, and I believe should, have taken the responsibility, and made a positive demand, either for the prisoners or his passports, in which case, such was the state of feeling in the United States at the time, I am confident he would have been justified by nine tenths of the people; but, like too many others, he was a "strict constructionist," and disposed to obey rigidly the very letter of his instructions.

On the other hand, had General Thompson been then our minister, he would have stretched the instructions given him to their utmost—nay, would have shaken off the trammels a weak point in our government appears to have thrown over her agents—and by so doing, let what would come of it, received the warm approval and universal thanks of his countrymen. He might not have effected more than did Mr. Ellis, yet I am constrained to believe that he would — that our immediate liberation would have followed close upon a positive demand.

Such I conceive to be the difference between the two ministers, or rather between the course adopted by Mr. Ellis and that which undoubtedly would have been pursued by his successor; and although suffering and im-

---

* Had General Jackson been President of the United States at the time, I do not believe that one of the American prisoners would have been in bondage twenty-four hours after the first despatch in relation to them had been received at Mexico from Washington. The Mexican diplomatists know perfectly well with whom they have to deal—there would have been no " putting off the previous question" had General J. been in power.

prisonment without cause for months may have wrought prejudice in my mind, I cannot but believe that the latter course would have been the better and the proper one. Nor can I even now divest myself of the idea that Santa Anna, to this day, laughs in his sleeve when he remembers upon what flimsy pretexts he retained several Americans in prison, without the shadow of cause, and despite the remonstrances of the representative of the United States.*

But to return to the actual. When Sully came in from the streets, on the evening of the day which had first introduced me to the irons, we ascertained that he had made partial arrangements with some of our guard to pass four of us out secretly in the course of a night or two, or at the first favourable opportunity. The plan was to be more fully matured the next day.

At dark, the heavy door of our room was locked, not to be opened again until morning, and in the mean time a regular guard was placed before it on the outside. The closing of the door was but the signal for all the prisoners to divest themselves of their chains. Such as could slip the irons over their ankles and feet

---

* The fact of my having a passport, although denied, was so abundantly proved, that the Mexican government hardly urged it as an excuse by which to detain me; but the Chihuahua letter, thoughtlessly written by an American gentleman since dead, and in which it was erroneously stated that I was sent forward as an *avant courrier*, was used as a pretext to the very last. By a distortion of the sense of that letter peculiarly Mexican, I was implicated with the Santa Fé Expedition, and finding this a sufficient plea to continue me in prison, it was never lost sight of. I have little doubt, if the truth could be known, that the papers of which I was robbed by Armijo. passport and all, were quietly resting in the bureau of the Mexican Minister of Foreign Relations during the whole time of the negotiations in relation to the release of the American prisoners. The story that Armijo destroyed the passport in my presence was certainly erroneous, and as he sent all the important papers found upon the Texans to the capital, I have little doubt that mine found their way there in the same package.

were at once free, while others produced files from their hiding-places, and the work of cutting down rivets was commenced, with an assiduity and zeal, which soon resulted in the Texans ridding themselves of all encumbrances upon their comfort and free locomotion. In certainly less than half an hour the ankles of nearly every prisoner were loosened from the shackles, and it was only from indolence that all did not free themselves. The chains were then carefully placed in positions where they could easily be put on again, should the ill-natured old commandante by any chance take it into his head to make us a night visit, and this little precaution over, the varied entertainments which usually beguiled the long evenings commenced.

There were some fifty of us in the room in which I was confined, and in one quarter of it would be seen a party engaged at whist, all-fours, uchre, or some other game a knowledge of which they had brought with them from Texas. In another part some prisoner would open the game of *monte,* an insight into which he had picked up from the Mexicans since his confinement, and around him would be gathered a small knot of betters staking small sums upon the turn of the cards, for all appeared to have more or less money. By the same candle, probably, some two or three of the Texans were reading such books as the foreigners had sent us. In still another quarter a small party would be seen, half reclining upon their blankets, while one of their number recited some story of other days and lands; and should the story chance to be humorous in its nature, the joyous and hearty laugh which followed its termination showed plainly enough that the listeners were thinking of anything but chains and imprisonment.

Songs, too, enlivened the scene, and served to beguile

the hours, while several musicians in the party had found means to procure instruments upon which some of them played exceedingly well. But of all the modes employed to while away the evenings, the most common, perhaps, was reading, and conspicuous among this class was my yoke-fellow in chains, the veteran Major Bennett, who might be seen busily poring over a Bible which had been given him by Mr. Elliott, the chaplain of the United States Exploring Expedition, when in Santiago on his way from the Pacific to Washington.

Thus with books and song, cards and stories, the hours slipped away pleasantly enough to all, and the reader may feel not a little astonishment when I say that the nightly soirées in the old Convent of Santiago were as productive of mirth as are many of those held within the gay saloons of any land. There is something in the Anglo-Saxon character which buoys and sustains the spirit under adversity, a quality which appears to be inherent; and it was continually a matter of surprise to our guard, from San Miguel even to the city of Mexico, to see not only the indifference we all manifested under our misfortunes, but the gayety and good-humour which at all times prevailed among the prisoners. And I doubt whether any of the Texans, when memory now carries them back, ever think, without shuddering, of scenes through which they then passed, but which at the time they thought little of, or cared not for. The anticipation of any impending danger or difficulty is invariably worse than the reality; and when the dreaded reality arrives, and the full measure of our fear breaks upon us, the imagination so busies itself in fancying still greater peril and suffering in perspective that the present is lightened of half its burden. The much-dreaded future is an *ignis fatuus*, leading the mind to anticipate troubles and annoyances which, when encountered, are either not noticed, or only surprise us by their comparatively trifling importance.

When the morning of the 20th of April came, and the Mexican who had charge of the prisoners while at their work entered our apartment, I again expected that I should be ordered into the streets, and compelled to go through the form of labour; but I was once more fortunate enough to escape. The reason for thus *slighting* me may have been the circumstance that Major Bennett, my companion at the other end of the chain, was exempted from all outdoor work—partly on account of his age and rank as an officer, but principally because he was engaged a portion of his time in the cocina, attending to the cooking of our food.

In the course of the day several parties of foreigners visited Santiago. I told them all that I should attempt an escape, and that very night if a favourable opportunity offered. They advised me, by all means, to defer any attempt until after General Thompson was duly received as the accredited minister of the United States, and I partially consented to this course; yet had a door been left open, or the least chance of a successful escape offered, I should most certainly have bidden farewell to imprisonment, chains, and Santiago together.* The recollection of the many favourable opportunities to

* A Yankee friend of mine resident in Mexico—one of the old Bunker Hill stock—told me, while in San Lazaro, that he hoped I would "tough it out awhile"—I use his own words—in the expectation that our government might be driven into a " small skirmish"—his own words again—with Mexico. I know that one reason why many Americans were anxious that I should not escape through my own means was their desire for a war, and that they thought my farther detention would be just cause for one. The result of a war, they were confident, would place them upon an equality with the English and French residents—a position they said they were far from enjoying.

escape while in San Lazaro haunted and annoyed me excessively; and nothing short of a positive assurance of an honourable liberation within a week could have kept me twenty-four hours in Santiago, had there been a possibility of liberating myself.

At a late hour on the evening of the 20th two or three Americans called upon me a second time, and earnestly requested me to remain quiet another day—to hazard no attempt at an escape until I should hear farther from them. As the principal plan, adopted by myself and companions to effect our liberation, was still far from being matured, I consented to abide by the advice of the Americans, and with no little reluctance passed another night in Santiago.

Early the next morning there appeared to be unusual bustle and preparation among the prisoners—an excitement which I did not at first understand. On inquiry, I learned that it was the anniversary of the celebrated battle of San Jacinto—the great victory gained over Santa Anna—and that the Texans were determined upon celebrating it as brilliantly as possible. Some of the Americans then in Mexico, among them Mr. Coolidge, had sent the prisoners some half dozen turkeys, and other luxuries in the way of eating, besides a generous supply of wines and liquors of the choicest qualities. The Texans had also provided themselves, while in the streets the day before, with such little delicacies as they could purchase, determined upon having a grand dinner on the "glorious 21st," if nothing else.

On ordinary occasions the prisoners were taken from Santiago at about eight o'clock in the morning, conducted some half or three quarters of a mile from the convent to a ditch, and then compelled to go through the forms of pumping and digging. By as close a mathematical calculation as could be made, without instruments or figures, it was thought the water ran into the ditch they were clearing just as fast as they pumped it out—perhaps a trifle faster ; but the economy of effecting much with little labour is but ill understood in Mexico, and the fact that the Texans made no progress in the job upon which they were engaged created but little difference with the Mexican overseers. At twelve o'clock, or near that hour, the prisoners were conducted back to the convent for their dinners, all in chains, and after occupying some hour and a half or two hours with this meal, they were again conducted to the ditch. Not one of them ever hurt or tired himself with work, but on the contrary it was said that they amused themselves by experimenting on the smallest possible amount of labour a man could perform when he set his wits to work and tried his best ! I recollect a remark made by a facetious prisoner one evening—I think it was Jimmy Tweed—to the effect that he had *exerted* himself all day to ascertain how little he could do ; and the result, in round numbers, was, that he had thrown one shovelful of mud from the ditch, but in so doing he had contrived to *tumble three back !*

The great object with the Texans, on the morning of the 21st of April, was to obtain the consent of the old commandante to their remaining in-doors during the afternoon—they were anxious enough to be taken out in the morning, as it would give them an opportunity to increase their supply of liquor and other materials for the feast. A committee, composed of such as could speak Spanish, was accordingly appointed, whose business it was to wait upon the Mexican officers and inform them that the 21st of April was the patron saint's day of Texas, and also, in language most respectful and courteous, to ask permission to celebrate it in the afternoon with all becoming ceremony and rejoicing. In profound ignorance of the day, and the glorious battle the Texans wished to celebrate, the Mexican officers kindly gave their consent to every request made. By such stratagem the great object of the prisoners was accomplished, and they now set themselves about making every arrangement for the approaching festivities.*

Such of the prisoners as had any skill in drawing or painting feigned illness, and were not taken out in the morning with their comrades. They had obtained, by some means, a supply of red and white paint, and the result of their morning's work was the decoration of the walls of our room with Texan flags, and sea and land fights—the Texans of course triumphant, the Mexicans discomfited, and the "lone star" in the ascendant. An appropriate ode—full of patriotism, liberty, San Jacinto, love of country, detestation of tyrants, &c.—was written by some poet among the prisoners, and one of the Texan officers, known to be endowed with vocal powers, was appointed to sing it. A master of ceremonies, an orator of the day, toast-master—in fact all the requisite officers were appointed, and before the men came in from their morning's work, every necessary preparation had been made for a regular celebration.

The hour at which the dinner was to be served was three o'clock; but before that time a number of foreigners had arrived at Santiago for the purpose of taking

---

* It could not have been that the Mexicans were aware of the events which had transpired on the 21st of April. The younger officers of our guard were liberal and accommodating to a fault; yet they would not have dared grant the Texans permission to celebrate a victory which had lost their country one of its most valuable provinces, and this under the very nose of Santa Anna himself, who had been taken prisoner in that battle.

part in the celebration. One of them, who at this time was residing in the city of Mexico, was himself a member of the small but gallant band that achieved the great victory of San Jacinto, and related several interesting anecdotes of that desperate struggle—a struggle which resulted in the complete overthrow of the Mexican power in Texas. The dinner itself was excellent —I might almost say sumptuous. The "bill of fare" did not display that varied list of French inventions to be found at the noted St. Charles Hotel, in New-Orleans, or the Astor House, in New-York; but we had roast beef, turkey, and good appetites, and the whole affair went off with the greatest éclat.

After the "cloth was removed"—a performance which it took but about two minutes to execute, as there was nothing to do save to stow the bowls, plates, and spoons away in the corners—after this was done, the celebration of the great anniversary began in real earnest. The regular toasts were appropriate, the volunteers spirited, and the ode a very creditable piece, and given with much effect. An oration by Major Bonnell, one of the prisoners, followed, Dr. Brenham and several other gentlemen also making some very pertinent remarks. As the hours wore along, and the liquor circulated more freely, the hilarity and general good feeling increased. Some of the foreigners present placed the chains of the prisoners around their own ankles, and several fancy jigs and hornpipes were executed with jingling and clanking accompaniments. "Hail Columbia" and the "Star-spangled Banner," in addition to the Texan patriotic songs, were duly honoured by numerous voices, while the memory of Washington was drunk standing and uncovered. Even the younger Mexican officers took part in a celebration which to them must have been strange, drinking several toasts which were highly complimentary to the Texans.

It was not until dark that the joyous festivities ceased, and even after the prisoners were locked in their room for the night, wild catches of song and uproarious merriment helped still farther to enliven the scene. While Santa Anna, at his palace in one part of the city, was doubtless brooding over his misfortunes on the fatal field of San Jacinto, a crowd of jovial Texan prisoners were celebrating that very victory in another part, and in chains.

## CHAPTER XVI.

Intelligence of immediate Release.—Its Effect.—Close of the Celebration.—Night Visiters at Santiago.—Arrival of Mr. Ellis with an Order for our Release.—The old Blacksmith again.—His Services dispensed with.—Once more free from Chains.—Leave Santiago and Imprisonment.—Cheers of the Texans at our Departure.—Congratulations of the young Mexican Officers.—Another night Ride through Mexico.—Encounter with a religious Procession.—Arrival at the United States Legation.—The Gran Sociedad.—Comfortable Quarters.—Sleep impossible.—Change of Circumstances.—The Watchwords of Mexico.—Encounter with a Sentinel.—Early Morn in Mexico.—Strange Cries.—" Carbon."—Appearance of the Streets.—Picture of morning Life in Mexico.—Change of Wardrobe.—Visit to a French Barber.—A Shearing and Shaving Operation.—Improvement in personal Appearance.—Beggars in front of a Church.—Description of the wretched Throng.—Return to the Gran Sociedad.—A sumptuous Breakfast.—Visit to the British Minister, Mr. Pakenham.—Once more in Santiago.—Mexican Girls.—Visit to our old Quarters at San Lazaro.—Bribing a Sentinel.—Meeting with the Texans and Lepers.—Call at the Dwelling of a Mexican Lady, an old Friend.—Her musical Attainments.—Anecdote of her Spirit and Patriotism.

In the very midst of the celebration, and while the rejoicing was at its height, Mr. Coolidge called upon me with the intelligence that I was to be liberated immediately—in fact, that the order for my release was already given, and only awaited certain signatures to be carried into effect. This gentleman, in company with a number of Americans, had been at the palace of Santa Anna when Mr. Ellis took his leave and General Thompson presented his credentials and was duly received as the Minister Plenipotentiary of the United States. At this audience, Mr. Coolidge informed me, Santa Anna formally assured Mr. Ellis that he should give up to him young Howard, Sully, and myself, with four of the prisoners at Puebla who had claimed American protection. With a cunning characteristic of the Provisional President, he now saw that he had an opportunity to dispose of us without compromising his honour and dignity, and, placing our liberation in the light of a personal favour to Mr. Ellis, had consented to give us up to that gentleman. Santa Anna is never caught without some loop-hole through which to crawl when closely cornered.

The time had been when news that I was to be immediately released, coming in shape so authentic, would have filled me with sensations the most pleasing—now I received it with an indifference which even to myself appeared unaccountable. It may be that the numerous false hopes that had been held out to me partly induced this unconcern, for I should most certainly have received a present of a box of cigars with more pleasure; but the principal reason was, that I felt perfectly confident of making my escape within a few hours, or days at farthest. I say that I felt confident—I was *certain* of being free from chains and imprisonment immediately, and through my own individual exertions, and this certainly begat indifference to any other means. Another thing, which in some measure served to alloy the cup of happiness, was the circumstance that we understood our liberation was granted, not as a right, but as a personal favour. We all had that pride of country which induced us to hope that our government would peremptorily and unconditionally demand our release, and were every way prepared to bide the issue, be it what it might. We knew the *people* of our native land, and knowing them, felt confident that our wrongs would, if persisted in, sooner or later be redressed.

The door of our prison, on the night of the celebration, was locked a little after the usual hour, yet the rejoicing still continued. As the hours sped along, the prisoners, one by one, rolled themselves in their blankets upon the stone floor, and soon fell asleep. Suffering from a cold and slight headache at the time, I had followed their example and was already in a half doze, when a sound was heard at the door as of a key slowly turning in the lock. This was between nine and ten o'clock, and the unusual circumstance of a visit at that hour not only awoke such of the prisoners as were asleep, but induced all to begin fastening the chains about their ankles and take the necessary precautions in case the old commandante had chosen that strange hour to look in upon us. I had not taken off my irons on lying down—why I know not—so that my " toilet was made" for the reception of any company that might call at our quarters.

The door at length slowly opened, and the old commandante, accompanied by Mr. Ellis, Mr. Mayer, and two or three of the Mexican officers on duty at the convent, entered our prison. On seeing Mr. Mayer at an hour so unusual, I at once felt assured that I was to be released. He introduced me to Mr. Ellis, and afterward made him acquainted with Colonel Cooke and several of the Texan officers; and as he looked around him, as he heard the clanking of chains, and beheld such numbers of his countrymen in plight so mortifying and degrading, the kind-hearted minister was deeply affected.

He had brought the order for the release of Howard, Sully, and myself, and the old commandante had ordered a blacksmith to accompany him for the purpose of releasing us from the irons. Sully soon extricated himself without assistance, but with young Howard the case was different. His chain was almost the only one so securely fastened that it could not be got off without difficulty, and the old blacksmith was compelled to hammer away upon his anvil several minutes before the task was accomplished. I well knew that a single shake of my foot would release my ankle from the annoying load of iron; but anxious to astonish the Mexicans a little, even at this time, I allowed the blacksmith to place his anvil in a position near me. On his pointing to my ankle, and making signs that he was ready to perform the kind office of relieving me, I gave my foot a slight shake, which sent the chain clanking across the floor. The rivet, which had but partially confined it, fell near me. I quietly picked it up and put it in my pocket, determined to have some memento of Santiago and imprisonment more lasting than mere recollection, should that ever fail me. If the old commandante of the convent, in taking an account of stock, should happen to miss one of his rivets, he can charge the same to me.

In a few minutes, after promising to call upon our Texan friends on the following day, we left the lock-up room of Santiago, the prisoners giving three hearty cheers as we crossed the threshold. At the outer door the young Mexican officers crowded around us, cordially congratulating us upon our release, and expressing the warmest wishes that our still imprisoned comrades might soon be permitted to accompany us. From their actions, it appeared that our liberation gave them emotions even as pleasurable as our own.

Mr. Ellis had procured a coach to convey us to the city, which we now entered in company with himself and Mr. Mayer. Several buildings were passed which I recollected having seen, a few nights before, while on the gloomy midnight trip from San Lazaro to Santiago. On entering one of the main streets of Mexico we met a long religious procession, preceded by bells and lights, and probably on its way to perform some funeral service. Our postillion reined up his mules, and uncovering our heads, we remained still until the last stragglers had passed. A drive of some half a mile now brought us to the apartments of Mr. Ellis, at the United States Legation, in a street immediately in the rear of the cathedral and within a stone's throw of the great palace whence came all the decrees and vaunting proclamations sent forth to the Mexican people, and which has been the scene of revolutions innumerable. At the rooms of Mr. Ellis we found several of our countrymen collected, all congratulating us upon our happy release. Our next movement was to the Gran Sociedad, a large establishment where Mr. Mayer had provided rooms for our accommodation. I had intended to take lodgings at the *Casa de Diligencias*, or Stage Hotel, but my kind friends would not listen to any such arrangement.

Once in comfortable quarters at the Gran Sociedad, free again and at liberty to do as it might please me, I passed some two or three hours in reading a file of American newspapers which had just been received

At a late hour I retired to rest, but not to sleep. From the 15th of September to the 21st of April, more than seven months, I had been a prisoner—I had performed a toilsome and painful march exceeding two thousand miles—I had seen my comrades inhumanly butchered around me, had seen them die from exposure, from hardship, and from sickness—I had passed through an endless variety of scenes the most exciting; yet all this time I had slept well, except when illness or severe inclemency of weather prevented it. Now I had liberty and every comfort at my command, but sleep would not visit my eyelids. The very quiet around me, instead of being a provocative of slumber, seemed to keep me awake. I missed the hard stone or earthen floors, the knowledge that comrades were strewn close around me, the clanking of chains—the very groans of the unfortunate *lazarinos* were wanting. I missed, too, the eternal cries of our guard—the "*centinela alerta!*" the "*quien vive?*" and "*que gente?*"* which had rung

---

* These are the common watchwords of sentinels on duty in Mexico. If any one approaches, the sentinel shouts aloud "*quien vive?*"—who lives, or, rather, who comes? The answer expected is "*Republica*"—the Republic. The guard next cries "*que gente?*"—what people?—the party addressed, if a friend, being expected to answer "*paisano*"—a countryman. Not a little startled is the stranger, on arriving in Mexico, as he hears these watchwords ringing around him—I know that on one occasion, to use a nautical phrase, I "was thrown all aback" by the cry. I was passing the palace at a late hour of the night, not a living being within sight or hearing, and no sound breaking the stillness save that dull and heavy echo which follows every footfall upon a pavement. I had approached within six or eight yards of a sentry-box, standing directly in front of the palace, when a sentinel, who was probably asleep, suddenly awoke, and bringing his musket to a present, in a hurried manner gave the well-known "*quien vive?*" So sudden were his movements that I was even more astonished than himself. I flourished a cane which I held in my hand around my head, as if to ward off his musket, should he level it, and not thinking of the proper answer immediately, ejaculated "An Englishman!" Whether he understood me or not I am unable to say—I passed on without farther molestation or hinderance. It may

in our ears until the grating sounds had fairly become so many lullabies. Thoughts of home, of liberty, of once more visiting the friends and scenes of other days, came crowding and jostling each other through my mind in such rapid succession that my head was in a very whirl of excitement. Tired nature at length achieved the mastery, however, and towards morning I fell asleep.

At an early hour, and before the sun was yet up, I was awakened from my dreamy slumbers by a distressing and most doleful cry in the street, apparently under the window of the second story in which I lodged. To me the sounds resembled those of some unfortunate human being, suffering pain the most acute—so piteous were the cries, that I could not but think some poor fellow had been knocked down and run over by a coach, or met with some serious hurt, and with broken limbs was groaning aloud for assistance. Arising at once, I opened a glass door and stepped out upon the small balcony which is to be seen under the windows of the better houses in Mexico. No creature whose appearance indicated pain or distress could I discover, as I ran my eye up and down the street and along the side-walks on either side. Whence could the accents of suffering proceed? In the street, immediately under the balcony, stood a swarthy, badly-dressed, half Indian half Mexican charcoal vender, his entire stock in trade strapped to his back in a large, square basket. Not the

<sub>appear singular that I called myself "an Englishman;" to account for it I would state that on that very evening I had been told by an American, while conversing as to the greater respect entertained in Mexico for the English than for our own countrymen, that he invariably "hailed from England" whenever asked as to his origin. With this true but mortifying remark fresh in my memory, and in my haste to say something, I gave the sentinel that answer.</sub>

most remote suspicion had I that he was the author of the piteous cries, which had first startled me from repose, until the fellow raised his dark but subdued eyes to the balcony where I was standing, and drawled out a word which, with the key attached to his back, I now understood to be "*carbon*"—charcoal. Had it not been that I could plainly see the charcoal, I certainly never should have suspected the meaning of the strange sounds he uttered or his calling. In giving articulation to the word " carbon" alone, the crier had run through the entire scale, and really used notes enough to form an Italian bravura of no inconsiderable complication. Those who have visited Mexico must have been struck, at first, with the strange and most discordant cries which assailed their ears immediately after daylight.

The morning was bright, beautiful, and balmy—the ushering in of one of those delightful days of spring-time known only in the dry, pure climate of the Mexican *tierras templadas*—and I lingered upon the balcony to survey the scene below and around me. Crowds of women, of every class and nearly every shade, were seen either going to or returning from mass at the different churches, their rebosos or mantillas coquettishly covering their heads and necks, their gait inimitably graceful, while their brilliant yet languishing black eyes were wandering from object to object with those indolent but expressive and voluptuous glances which go straight to the heart—Castilian, but indescribable. Water carriers, with their large jars strapped to their heads, were hurrying to serve their morning customers. Fellows stooping and staggering under the weight of huge coops filled with chickens, strapped to their backs after the fashion of the charcoal baskets, were visiting the houses of their daily patrons—threading and jostling their way through the crowds of females who at this early hour thronged the principal thoroughfares, and crying aloud their calling as they passed. Fair doncellas, whose complexion bespoke their pure Spanish blood, were tripping along, followed closely by ancient and vinegar-faced dueñas, whose calling it was to prevent the charge intrusted to them by prudent mothers from falling in love or running away. Fruitmen and women, with immense baskets of luscious oranges, melons, sweet limes, bananas, and zapotes resting upon their heads, were hastening towards their stands at the market-places. Mexican girls, apparently half dressed, were watering the plants and flowers with which the opposite and adjoining balconies were adorned, while inside a window, seated cross-legged upon the floor and in dishabille exceeding loose and slight to say the least of it, was a young lady quietly sipping her chocolate, ever and anon turning her dark eyes with a dreamy expression towards the spot where I was standing, my presence not seeming in the least to disconcert her. Priests, with their long, shovel hats, monks, gentlemen, léperos, friars, mendicants, sisters of different charitable and religious orders, were mingled with the heterogeneous currents of people below me—and as if to diversify a scene already strikingly singular in the eyes of a foreigner, a gang of ragged *forzados** from some of the prisons, strongly chained and securely guarded, were sweeping or mending a street-crossing close at hand. Far off, in the distance, a string of the *voluntarios* of whom I have often made mention—convicts tied together, and on their way to some *presidio* to be manufactured into soldiers—were seen escorted onward by a detach-

---

* Literally galley-slaves, but by a free translation made to denote men forced to work against their will.

ment of dragoons: to enliven and still farther to vary the scene, a troop of cavalry, preceded by a dashing and showy officer and such music as a badly-blown trumpet produces, were riding past. Such were the strangely-assorted figures and groups which composed the picture spread before me the first morning after my liberation, and I continued to gaze until Mr. Mayer called at my door with inquiries as to whether I had passed as comfortable, as agreeable, and as quiet a night as I did while in San Lazaro, or more recently in Santiago.

That my wardrobe, after a seven months' imprisonment and a journey of three or four months without a trunk or portmanteau, was scanty enough, may be readily imagined; but my friend at once kindly offered me the free use of his, and I soon found myself arrayed in habiliments more befitting my new position. The purchase of a hat, at a shop in the Portales close by, still farther improved my outward man, and the patronage I bestowed upon a shoemaker in the neighbourhood, to the extent of a pair of boots, advanced the work of thorough change and renovation I had commenced. One thing was still wanting—my face required an introduction to a barber. While a prisoner, I had endeavoured to make myself as little like myself as possible, firmly convinced that I should recover my liberty in no other way than by escaping: in order, therefore, to disguise myself completely, I had assiduously cultivated whiskers, mustaches, and hair enough for a foreign prince, or even the Great Mogul himself. Now I had no farther use for these appendages, and to be relieved of them as speedily as possible I inquired the way to a French hair-dresser's in the Plateros, or street in which the gold and silver smiths, fancy and jewelry dealers, milliners and barbers pursue their different callings. No sooner had I passed through the hands of a lively and chattering but polite little Frenchman, than such was the change that I hardly knew myself. True, my acquaintance with my own face, for the previous eleven months, had been extremely limited, looking-glasses not being in common use among Texan campaigners or prisoners; but I had had an occasional opportunity of obtaining a glimpse of myself, and now that I had undergone the shearing and shaving operation, the alteration wrought in my personal appearance was not only astonishing, but, I am inclined to believe, altogether in my favour.

While retracing my steps towards the Gran Sociedad, I passed a large church, in front of which a crowd of wretched beggars had already taken their stand. Such an assortment of mendicants I had never before seen collected—such squalid misery as the mass presented—and although dreading contact with the unclean and hideous *mendigos*, I could not resist pausing for a few moments to examine the different characters. There were the lame, the halt, and the blind—sickly and distorted childhood, decrepit and palsied old age. A deformed living skeleton, with a face of bluish, ashy paleness, and borne in the arms of a strong man who doubtless divided such small pittance of copper as the ghastly object received, was stretching forth its shrivelled and skinny arms to every passer. Armless and legless objects, so dressed that their crippled situation must at once strike every beholder, were beseeching alms in accents most piteous. Mothers were holding deformed, rickety, pale, and sightless children up to the public gaze, imploring the prayers and blessings of every saint in the long calendar upon such as would give to their unfortunate offspring a single claco. Wretched cripples, their arms and legs contracted and twisted out of all shape, were peering, with bloodshot eyes and haggard faces, at the current of pedestrians as they passed, a gleam of satisfaction almost demoniacal lighting up their countenances as some more charitable person would throw a copper into their hands. No disguise, no concealment of their deformities, was attempted—on the contrary, it seemed as though a full exposure of their crippled limbs and repulsive distortions was the aim of all—as though they were expressly " got up" to set off their natural hideousness in the strongest possible light. Such is but a hurried picture of a portion of the miserable mendicants congregated in the vicinity of the church, and it was not without a shudder that I turned into a short street leading to my quarters. In former times the lepers of the city were allowed the privilege of begging, and it was even considered fortunate when a poor family numbered a lazarino in its fold. The wretch thus afflicted was paraded daily at some conspicuous stand, directly in the way of the passers, and the alms he or she was sure to receive would feed, clothe, and support a large family in idleness. Finding the number of lazarinos on the increase, or rather shrewdly suspecting that many of the wretches were but counterfeits, made up by the use of blisters and other applications, the city government ordered every one known to be afflicted with the disease to San Lazaro, there to be provided for; but this course was not resorted to until both foreigners and the most respectable Mexicans had openly complained of the increase of the repulsive objects to be met at every turn, and the disgrace they brought upon the city. This was the story I heard in relation to the banishment of the lepers to San Lazaro—if it be true, their places have since been filled by wretches wanting but little to make them equally loathsome in appearance, and equally objects of pity.

Before I reached the Gran Sociedad, I met several small parties of soldiers. A moment's reflection told me that I was free, and no longer subject to their watchful control; yet I could not feel altogether at ease in close proximity with these fellows. I was in momentary expectation, although there was not the least cause for it, that some one of them would lay his hand upon my shoulders, and ask me how it happened that I was "out without a guard;" and several days elapsed before I could divest myself of the idea that I was still in some way a prisoner — before I could feel and believe that I was indeed at liberty.

An excellent breakfast was served up immediately after my return to the Gran Sociedad, Mr. Ellis and several other gentlemen being already in attendance to partake of it. Most ample justice did I and the two companions of my recent imprisonment to the rich and dainty viands, for it was now almost a year since we had seen a meal so inviting spread before us, and hardly half a dozen times within that year had we seen all those trifling necessaries known in civilized countries as knives, forks, spoons, chairs, a table, and other useful and comfortable et cæteras, considered by the majority of my readers, perhaps, indispensable in every well-regulated household. Our coffee, too, was of rich quality and flavour, while excellent claret was cooled by ice brought from the adjoining snow-capped mountains. The remembrance of these luxuries, trifling as they might have appeared had I never been deprived of them, still clings to me. Those, and those only, who have for months spent their time upon the prairies, and amid scenes kindred to those through which we had passed, are able to appreciate the full blessings of civilization and the thousand and one comforts which before they heeded not.

When breakfast was over, I called upon Mr. Pakenham, the English minister, in company with Mr. Mayer. Two or three of my fellow-prisoners had claimed British protection, and I wished to relate to the minister of their government, in person, some of the circumstances connected with their arrest and imprisonment, which would show the justice of their claims in the strongest possible light. I found Mr. Pakenham a plain and unostentatious but agreeable and gentlemanly man, disposed to aid his countrymen in every way. A few days after this visit, through his intercession, my friends were released.

A small party of us, procuring one of the heavy coaches of the city, next visited Santiago—the miserable quarters from which we had been removed the night before. So great had been the change wrought in my appearance by Mr. Mayer's wardrobe, aided by the French barber in the Plateros, that many of my former fellow-prisoners with difficulty recognised me—a circumstance I mention as showing how thoroughly I could have disguised myself had I attempted the escape which I contemplated. After promising the unfortunate fellows another visit, we again turned our backs upon Santiago, but before entering the coach a couple of Mexican girls came running towards us to offer their congratulations upon our release. These kind-hearted creatures were of the lower class, fruit girls, who had formed strong attachments for two of the Texan prisoners, and who never left the vicinity of Santiago during the day. Wherever the prisoners were taken they were to be seen, carrying their blankets, washing and mending their clothes, and performing every act of kindness within their power. They now not only appeared much rejoiced at our liberation, but pressed us with questions as to the probability of the other prisoners being shortly released. After flattering them with hopes we were but too fearful would prove false, we put some silver into their hands, and then returned to the city to dine.

In the afternoon, after I had purchased several little articles of clothing of which I knew my companions in San Lazaro to be sadly in need, and adding a few bundles of puros with which they might beguile the dreary hours of their imprisonment, a small party of us rode out to that establishment. The sergeant of the guard at first positively denied us admission, saying that express orders to that effect had been received; but a dollar stealthily slipped into his hand, not only opened his heart, but the hospital doors at once. The steward of the establishment next made some objections to our entrance into the interior—but one of my companions, who spoke his language fluently, soon overcame his scruples, and we were permitted to pass without farther hindrance.

As I entered the long and gloomy hall in which I had passed some two months, the unfortunate lepers came hobbling from their cots, crowded around me, and at the same time expressed not a little satisfaction at seeing me in the possession of liberty. My former Texan companions, too, were overjoyed to see me once more; for the strange and unseasonable hour chosen for my removal, the strong guard that accompanied me from San Lazaro, combined with the appearance of the litter and the mystery in which the whole affair was shrouded, had raised suspicions in their minds that I had at

least been thrown into one of the lowest of the Mexican prisons, if no worse fate had befallen me. I believe that they were entirely ignorant of all the circumstances until I called upon them in person. After distributing our little presents, and promising to make them another visit, we left the hospital, the sergeant hurrying our departure. Whether the fellow thought we had got our dollar's worth, or whether he wished a farther bribe, is known only to himself.

Our next call was at the house of a Mexican lady—the same who had visited me while in San Lazaro, and who had sent me the present of fish I have mentioned in a former chapter. She informed me that she had heard something of my good fortune with pleasure, and was now doubly gratified that I had called upon her thus early to confirm the report of my release. At home, we found the señora a lively creature, chatty and of most agreeable manners, with a dashing, spirited way of expressing herself peculiarly pointed. An anecdote is told of her which goes far to show her character. During one of the more recent revolutions which have distracted Mexico, two or three gentlemen who had espoused the cause she favoured sought refuge, during a turn in affairs against them, in her house, anxious to escape the dangers to be encountered in the streets. So far as mere words went, they were most zealous and unflinching supporters and advocates of certain principles; but when blows came and balls whistled, they were not to be seen at the post of peril. Their party had met with various reverses, and, as they thought, everything was going directly against them, when suddenly the roar of cannon and the rattling of musketry without convinced them that their fighting friends were once more struggling manfully for the ascendancy. "Those are our cannon! those are our cannon!" shouted one of the inflated patriots from his hiding-place, at the same time clapping his hands and skipping for joy. "Now we are gaining ground again!"

"*We!*" retorted the spirited señora, with ineffable scorn. "Fine patriots, *you*, to be sneaking and skulking here, among a parcel of women, when your friends are bravely exposing themselves in the streets for the principles you are so loud-mouthed in advocating, but which you have not the courage to stand up and protect. Would that *I* were a man. You would see me at those cannon whose music so delights your ears— not secreted among helpless women, and spending my time and breath in idle words. If those are your cannon, why don't you go and help work them, like true patriots and brave men?"

Such was the character given us of the señora, and I certainly passed a very agreeable hour at her house. Not a little is she celebrated in Mexico as a singer, and on this occasion she favoured us with a number of Spanish ballads in style most exquisite, accompanying her rich and powerful voice on the piano. The visit over, I returned once more to the Gran Sociedad, amid a shower of rain which flooded the streets, and at an early hour retired to try what success I could have in sleeping the second night after my liberation.

## CHAPTER XVII.

An early Morning Walk.—Beggars at their Work.—The Plaza Mayor.—The Cathedral and Stone of the Calendar.—Strange Belief.—Interior of the Cathedral.—Its Appearance.—Filthy State of the Establishment.—Agency of a Pair of new Boots in preventing an Examination of the Cathedral.—Shops of the Portales.—The Streets of Mexico.—Another Visit to Santiago.—The "True Blue."—More of Lieutenant Hull.—Encounter with Major Howard.—His Disguise.—Particulars of the daring Escape of Captain Hudson and Major Howard.—The Italian Opera.—Castellan.—Another Encounter with Major Howard.—Farther Particulars of his Escape.—Temerity of Captain Hudson.—Mexican Pickpockets.—Their Dexterity.—Mexican Modes of Salutation.—Cordiality of Greeting.—Anecdote of a Meeting with a fair Mexican.—The Mystery solved.—An excellent Trait in Mexican Character.—Hospitality of the Lower and Middle Classes.—Their Benevolence towards the Sick.—The present Priesthood in Mexico.—Domestic Relations of the Padres.—Influence of the Priests.—Their Reluctance in resigning Power.

WITH body and mind strengthened and refreshed I arose the next morning, for although some of the objects and scenes I had beheld during the day passed in review before the eye of the slumbering mind, my sleep had been sound and unbroken. Hastily dressing, as I had resolved upon attending early mass, I descended to the street and took the direction towards one of the principal churches.

The beggars of Mexico must be an industrious class, and very early risers, for before even the sun had made his appearance I found them up and stirring—many of them already at their stands in front of the religious establishments to be met at almost every turn, and with outstretched arms reciting their well-conned prayers for charity. Determined upon going to the celebrated cathedral at once, as the headquarters where I should probably see more than at any other place devoted to the showy religion of the inhabitants, I passed two or three churches of most imposing appearance with merely an examination of their exteriors. A short walk brought me to the Plaza Mayor, or principal square, on the eastern side of which, and surmounted by two ornamented towers, rises the noble Cathedral of Mexico. I paused, for a few moments, to examine the great Stone of the Calendar, resting against the southwestern corner of the cathedral. It is of immense size, weighing more than twenty tons, the entire face of it sculptured with strange, but well-executed hieroglyphics. By means of the carved figures upon this stone—some twelve of which, it is pretended, represent the signs of the zodiac—the ancient inhabitants are said to have divided and computed time — the years into months, weeks, and days, and the latter into hours—and even to this day the traveller is told, and with much appearance of sincerity, that the ignorant Indians can tell the hour of the day to a minute by examining this singular calendar. They might as well say that the natives can tell the time by consulting the face of a common burr millstone, or a pair of hay-scales.

Satisfied that I could make nothing of the hieroglyphics, which were every way as unintelligible as the figures on a Chinese tea-chest, I turned and entered the cathedral. The walls, paintings, statues, balustrades, and different ornaments, were rich even to magnificence—the floor dirty, covered with kneeling groups of all classes and conditions at their devotions—while an odour, disagreeable and prison-like, caused by the filthiness characteristic of all Mexican churches, pervaded the spacious and imposing interior, perceptible even above the fumes of burning incense. Dogs were either lying asleep in different parts, or walking about so noiselessly that it almost seemed as though they were fearful of disturbing the deep stillness of the immense apartment—a stillness broken only by the hum of half-muttered prayers and the low pealing of an organ the position of which I could not discover. Anxious to examine the farthest recesses of the cathedral, to note its paintings, statues, gilding, costly panelling, and exceeding richness of adornment, I doffed my hat and advanced towards the interior. The first step I took drew the eyes of those immediately in front towards me; the second attracted the attention of a still greater number of the kneeling worshippers. I now found that the boots I had purchased the day before were yet unbroken, and sent up a loud creak from the stone floor at every step. I attempted to advance on tiptoe—the creaking seemed to grow louder the more I endeavoured to prevent it. I paused, with the hope that I might advance under cover of the noise made by the arrival of a party of fresh worshippers who were approaching —they were either barefooted, or else their well-worn shoes gave forth no sound. One more attempt I made; but it was as unsuccessful as the others—every step appeared to draw additional attention, and even the dogs seemed to eye me rebukingly as a disturber of the solemn stillness which reigned around. It may seem a simple matter, but I was compelled to put off an examination of this noble establishment solely on account of a pair of new and creaking boots; for finding that I could not advance without annoying the assembled congregation, I retraced my steps and left the cathedral as quietly and silently as possible.

By this time the stores and shops in the *Portales*, on the opposite side of the plaza, were open, the gay Mexican sarapes and other gaudy merchandise displayed in front presenting a brilliant and showy appearance. The walls of many of the houses, in this quarter of the city, bear indisputable evidence of the various revolutions which have distracted the country and paralyzed its energies, for the marks of cannon balls are still plainly visible, let the eye range where it will. After getting lost once or twice, and travelling three or four blocks out of my way in consequence of what I conceived to be the wrong directions I received from such of the passers as I asked for information, I finally reached the Gran Sociedad in season for breakfast. In Mexico the more important and principal streets have a new name for every square—a single straight and continuous thoroughfare having perhaps a dozen different titles—and hence the difficulty the foreigner at first meets in finding a location.

During the forenoon I made another visit to Santiago, in company with several Americans. Before leaving the convent, one of the prisoners, a young man named Grover, presented me with a copy of a neatly-written paper, published weekly in Santiago, entitled the "*True Blue.*" It contained a regular report of the proceedings of the 21st of April—speeches, toasts, songs and all. Among the contributors were Mr. Grover himself, a young man named Mabry,* and others, and, in newspa-

* I have been told that Mr. Mabry, after his return to Texas, obtained a midshipman's warrant in the navy of that country, and that he was lost on board the ill-fated war-schooner San Antonio, Captain Seger. It may be remembered by the reader, that a man with nearly the same name—Mayby—lost his life when Lieutenant Hull was killed, being a member of the unfortunate party first massacred by the Caygüas. Since the first volume of this work passed through the hands of the stereotyper, I have learned farther particulars in relation to the melancholy deaths of Lieutenant H. and his men. Mr. Phillips, a young man attached to the Santa Fé Expedition, who saw the whole affair, informs me that the party did not retreat an inch, as I have previously stated, but on the contrary simultaneously threw them-

per parlance, the "whole affair was exceedingly well got up." Again promising our friends another visit before leaving the country, we entered our Mexican coach and returned to our quarters in the city.

It was while walking through one of the principal and most densely-thronged streets, and in the middle of the day, that I met my old companion, Major Howard, of whose escape from Puebla I had already heard, but of whose present whereabout I was ignorant. He was disguised, it is true; for his naturally light and curly hair was coloured to a more than Mexican blackness, and combed and pomatumed down until it lay as straight as a Quaker's; yet there was no mistaking his florid complexion and his walk, and I crossed the street and accosted him at once. He informed me that both himself and his companion in escape, Captain Hudson, although a price had been set upon their heads, were then boarding openly at a Mexican meson, as a place where they would be least likely to be suspected or sought, and that they were both determined to see the

selves from their horses on discovering the approach of the Indians, formed the animals in a circle, and each man knelt inside to await the charge of their enemies. Suddenly, and as if by magic, the Caygüas were on every side, their heavy buffalo-hide shields held before them, and after a short but desperate struggle, the Texans were overpowered by the fearful odds, and slain. The names of the men thus massacred, in addition to those of Lieutenant Hull and Mr. Mayby already mentioned, were Sergeant Flenner, Dunn and Woodson. Many errors, but principally of omission, have of course occurred in this narrative. On leaving Austin, I provided myself with a note-book, in which I entered not only every little incident on each day's march, but the course, the distance travelled, as near as it could be kept by dead reckoning, with a description of the country, soil, and general appearance. Of this book I was robbed by Salezar, and hence I have been compelled to depend almost entirely upon memory in making up my "travel's history." The reader who will but reflect for a moment, will see the disadvantages under which I have laboured, and, I am confident, will overlook and excuse any discrepancies, omissions, or errors which must necessarily occur in a work written under the circumstances.

"sights" in the city before attempting a return to Texas or the United States.

At the Italian Opera, whither I had gone to see "*Il Templario,*" on the same evening I again met Major Howard, listening to the rich, full voice of the Castellan with much apparent satisfaction. Between the acts, in the coffee-room attached to the theatre, I once more met him, in conversation with a Mexican officer, and on taking him aside, and remonstrating with him upon the risk he ran in thus exposing himself, he contended that the best way to avoid suspicion was to frequent the most public places, and mix with the Mexicans themselves. He then gave me a short account of the manner in which himself and his companion effected their escape. On account of either real or feigned sickness, they had been quartered in the hospital at Puebla, where, for some weeks, they were allowed to visit the town every night upon parole. So long as this privilege was granted them, they had no opportunity to escape, as they could not break their faith with the officers who had treated them thus generously; but on the night in question, through some whim for which they could not account, they were told that they could not leave the hospital walls without a guard of four men. With this guard they sallied into the streets, determined not to return if a shadow of opportunity to escape offered.

They went at once to a restaurat which they had frequently visited, their watchful guard attending them. But a short time elapsed before they contrived to turn the attention of the soldiers into an adjoining room, and no sooner was this effected than they slipped through a side door or window, and hastily fled to the house of a generous Mexican with whom they had become acquainted. At this place, although a large reward was offered for their apprehension, they remained safely secreted some ten days. Their next movement was towards the city of Mexico, by the regular daily stage. This conveyance they left when within some ten or fifteen miles of the city, and striking across the country, they were enabled to reach a factory village in safety. Here the foreigners, to whom they made known their situation, provided them with passports to enter the city, and taking one of the canals they were soon comfortably housed at one of the mesones of the capital. Such are the brief particulars of their daring escape from Puebla and arrival in safety at the city of Mexico.

If possible, Captain Hudson exposed himself even more than did his comrade. Not content with openly visiting all the walks, curiosities, public amusements, churches, and other general resorts of the population, he clambered into one of the towers of the cathedral, where he either carved or picked his name in the most conspicuous place he could find; and as if this was not enough, he even added " Of the Texan Santa Fé Pioneers" at the end of it, and this when a heavy reward was hanging over his head.

Fortunately both these young men reached the United States and Texas in safety, although the risks they were compelled to run were almost incredible. They travelled to the seacoast in the stage, entering Puebla in open day and the hospital from which they had escaped being but a few yards from the Casa de Diligencias where they were obliged to stop and sleep one night. They even saw, standing around the hotel on the arrival of the stage, several officers with whom they had become well acquainted during a confinement of nearly two months in the place; but they passed boldly by them, and under the disguises they had procured were not suspected. Such is a short account of the escape of these officers—an escape well conceived and bravely carried through from first to last.

After sitting out the opera, which as a whole was well performed, we returned to our quarters. I now found that during the day I had been robbed of two handkerchiefs and a penknife, besides part of a bundle of puros, but how, when, or where was a mystery. I had exercised, as I thought, all due caution—had kept an eye or a hand on my pockets whenever there seemed to be the least chance for the light-fingered gentry, who infest churches, theatres, and thoroughfares alike in the great city of Mexico, to ply their calling—but with all my watchfulness I had been eased of everything save a lead pencil, a little loose change which was in my vest pocket, and the clothes on my back. On informing my friends of these depredations, they appeared to think me peculiarly fortunate, inasmuch as to save anything was of itself an exceedingly rare occurrence with a stranger. As a "general average," they said that the robbers should at least have taken my hat and what little silver I had! This was certainly consoling; but to guard against the ladrones in future I determined upon carrying nothing with me that the rascals might covet. The Mexican *cortabolsas*, or pickpockets, have the name of being the most adroit in the world, and from my little experience I should say they had well earned the reputation. At all events, I do not intend to rob them of their foul fame.

For three or four days after my release—in fact, during the whole of the time I was in the city at liberty—I was continually meeting with Mexicans of my acquaintance—officers who had been attached to our guard at different places. They all appeared much rejoiced on seeing that I had regained my freedom, manifesting their pleasure by warmly embracing me, meet me where they would. This custom of throwing the left arm around each other, while the right hands are clasped as with us, is common, I believe, all over Mexico, alike when two men, or two women, or two of the opposite sexes meet who are well acquainted; and perhaps this cordial mode of reception from the females of the country may be considered as one of the strongest of those ties which certainly bind the Americans and English to the land of Montezuma. The cold and phlegmatic Anglo-Saxon, after a residence of some year or two in Mexico, leaves it with regret; for there are a grace, an ease, a fascination, and a cordiality of greeting among the señoritas of that country which cannot be forgotten. The American or Englishman reflects upon the stiffness and restraint imposed upon the actions of his fair countrywomen by cold, conventional rules—he remembers the distant bow, the formal shake of the hand, with which he will be greeted on his return, and contrasts them with his daily salutations from the dark-eyed daughters of the sunny land in which he is sojourning. The result is altogether in favour of the latter.

It is indeed a delightful thing to be ever greeted with the most cordial freedom, when we know that that freedom is entirely removed from forwardness—to have the person encircled by arms which are faultless in form —and a man feels that it is difficult to tear himself away from a people whose manners, in their daily intercourse, are in every respect more full of warmth and kindness than those of his own countrymen, and countrywomen, too; for while even the men are not wanting in natural and easy politeness, the Mexican señoras have a frankness of deportment, a kindness and singleness of disposition, which captivate the natives of colder climes, and frequently did I meet with countrymen whose love for their fatherland had become completely estranged by the fascinations of female society in Mexico. The women of that country, when married to any of the Anglo-Saxon race, have the reputation of making the best and most affectionate wives; and scattered through Mexico may be found innumerable instances where foreigners, induced by no other motives than the superior charms and excellent domestic endowments of the women, have settled permanently and are rearing families.

I have been led to these remarks by a little circumstance which occurred a few mornings after I had regained my liberty. While walking at an early hour through one of the principal streets, wondering whence came the incessant current of passers, and staring at the many strange sights which strike the traveller on first visiting one of the most magnificent cities of the world, I noticed a young and pretty girl approaching, who seemed to gaze at me with marked attention. Dressed somewhat after the fashion of the Poblana girls—a costume I have already described—her neat and gracefully-worn reboso but partially concealed her head, face, and well-turned shoulders, and I might have bestowed more than an ordinary passing look upon the fair gazer, even had she not so intently eyed me. Her face certainly seemed familiar—like that of one I had previously seen: but in a country where there is so great a resemblance between the women—where black hair, dark and lustrous eyes, great regularity of features, and the same fashion of dress are almost universal—it is difficult to recognise a face until one becomes well acquainted. On arriving directly in front of me, the girl paused for a moment, gazing earnestly and intently in my face; and at a loss what to make of conduct so singular, I also stopped, anxious to see how this pantomime was to end. The last look of the girl seemed to satisfy her; for suddenly casting her reboso from her shoulders, while it still remained hanging from her head, she threw both arms around my neck with even more than ordinary Mexican *abandon*, and embraced me with as much cordiality as though I had been one of her dearest friends or nearest relatives. That she was making herself extremely familiar, on an acquaintance which I felt assured must be very limited, was my first impression; but not to be outdone, either in politeness or cordiality, I too threw my arms around her after her own fashion, and *acted*, to say the least of it, as though meeting with one of my oldest and most esteemed acquaintances.

In the streets of New-Orleans or New-York such a meeting would doubtless attract some little attention—not so in Mexico. The passers went by almost without deigning to notice us, and glad was I that they did so; for I could not satisfy my own mind that the open street was altogether a befitting place for the enactment of such a scene. But who was my fair friend, and why did this accidental meeting afford her so much gratification? These were questions I now asked myself. I placed a hand on either shoulder of the girl, gently disengaged myself, and then intently scrutinized her features with the hope of recognising one who must certainly be entitled to an acquaintanceship. I had an indistinct recollection of having seen her somewhere, but at what place or under what circumstances it was impossible to recall to mind. The girl, however, was far from imagining the dilemma I was in, but on the contrary addressed me with as much familiarity as though we had known each other from childhood, expressing, over and over again, the great pleasure it afforded her to see me once more alive and at liberty, and then alluding to the time when I was first attacked by the small-pox with not a little feeling. This last remark was a clew to the whole mystery; for I now at once recollected that she was the sister of one of the sergeants of our guard, and had frequently brought her brother his dinner at the place where we were confined when I was ill with the disease I have just spoken of. In common with all the women of the country, she had manifested great solicitude in our behalf, had expressed her ardent hopes that we might all recover our liberty, and in addition to this, had, on several occasions, kindly invited me to partake of such food as she had brought her brother. To repay her, in some way, I had made her a trifling present; but it was one she had not forgotten, as was fully proved by the cordial manner in which she greeted me on my first meeting her in the street some two months after.*

As I was about shaking hands to leave her, for I did not much care about going through another scene quite so familiar as was that at our first meeting, she invited me to visit her at her mother's residence before leaving the country. With artless simplicity she told me that her relatives were poor—in circumstances humble—but

---

* Let not the reader understand that an adventure of this kind—a meeting so cordial—is a common or every-day occurrence in the streets of Mexico, although, as I have stated, it seemed to attract little notice from the passers. The girl was probably much astonished and highly pleased to meet with one at liberty whom she had last seen sick and in prison, and in the warmth of her heart threw a greater degree of cordiality into her actions at this first meeting than is common even with the impulsive women of her country.

that I should be welcome, and that her mother would feel pride if the stranger would but condescend to cross her lowly threshold. Promising to call upon her I turned from the spot, and the next moment, after repeating for the third time the exclamation, "*Ah! señor, quanto me alegro de ver a V. afuera de es a maldita carcel!*"\* she was lost to sight in the throng of passers which crowded the street.

The circumstance of the girl's telling me, openly, of the humble sphere and station in which she moved and lived, brings to mind one excellent trait in the character of the Mexican people—with them poverty is certainly no crime, is never insulted. The unfortunate mendigo, or beggar, is seldom or never spurned from the door of the rich; but on the contrary his misfortunes entitle him at least to respect if not to alms, and almost invariably both are bestowed. No concealment of poverty is attempted—the poor Mexican family, unlike that of the American or English in similar circumstances, never impoverishes itself still farther by forced endeavours to conceal its real necessities. Of such hospitality as the Mexican dwelling affords the stranger is always invited to partake; and while the master frankly admits his poverty, he at the same time uses it as an excuse for the scantiness of the repast to which he invites his guest. The stranger is not told that his presence is unexpected; that the butcher has neglected to furnish meat, with a threat to patronise him no more; that the bread has just given out and that there is no time to bake or send for a supply, or any of the thousand and one excuses a false and foolish pride invents in other lands to conceal its indigence—nothing of the kind is resorted to. "*Somos pobres*"—we are poor people—is

\* Ah! sir, how much it pleases me to see you out of that bad prison!

the honest admission made by the Mexican to cover any deficiency in his entertainment.*

As an offset to their many vices, the Mexicans certainly possess charity and hospitality in an eminent degree—virtues which cover a multitude of sins, and which are not only professed but practised in that country. The early Spanish missionaries, in their endeavours to convert the Indians to their faith, appealed to the heart and sense through the medium of the eye—spread before the natives the pomp and pageantry of their imposing religion with hands far from niggardly—and thus first estranged them from their idols and many of their more absurd ceremonies. Then, as I have before stated, by allowing them to ingraft some of their own superstitions upon the rites of the Catholic religion, they were enabled to bring them over to Christianity. Such the primary efforts, and such the results.

The early fathers next zealously inculcated that heavenly spirit of charity which teaches that we must clothe the naked, feed the hungry, and relieve the sick and distressed; and with such untiring ardour did they impress this article of their creed upon the natives, that it took root, and has increased and continued to the present day. For evidence, we have but to look at the hospitals for the sick in body and mind scattered through the country, to the institutions for relieving the distresses of the unfortunate, and to the different orders of sisters of charity, those meek handmaidens of benevo-

* Let it be understood that I am now speaking of the middle and lower orders. A concealment of poverty is no singular thing among such of the higher class as may have been reduced, and I have little doubt that many a family party may be seen rolling along the Alameda in the evening, in their carved and gilt coach, which is driven to great strait to procure a breakfast the next morning at all in keeping with the ostentation they outwardly assume.

lence, whose eyes are ever seeking the couch of sickness and whose hands are ever raised to succour with a beneficence that knows no tiring. It is not in Mexico alone that this holy feeling of charity towards the sick and helpless exists; but wherever the religion of Rome is known there do we find the same active benevolence exerted, the same attention to the wants of the suffering, and well would it be were other denominations of Christians to pattern after the Catholics in all that pertains to pity and compassion towards their sick and needy fellow-creatures—in plain terms, if they would make fewer professions and enter more into the real practice of charity.

I cannot close this subject or this chapter without a few words in relation to the present priesthood in Mexico—the faults of the holy brotherhood I shall allude to with reluctance, for from one and all I never received other than the kindest and most benevolent treatment. With whatever intolerant zeal they may preach to their congregations against the heretics, and with whatever vividness they may paint the purgatory to which all out of the fold of the true Church are destined after death, the Protestant stranger will seldom find other than a hospitality the most munificent within the gates of the padres. He will find them, too, men of liberal and enlightened views, well-educated and entertaining companions, tolerant and charitable, extremely good livers, and disposed to an indulgence in many of the luxuries and vanities of this lower world—in short, he will find that their numerous departures from the rule of conduct prescribed for them sit as easy upon their consciences as do their gowns upon their backs.

With the style of living and domestic relations of the Catholic priest we are taught to associate all that is abstemious, so far as relates to worldly affairs, and that such is the case in Ireland and in the United States, I know full well; but he who believes that such a state of things exists among the brotherhood of Mexico is either wofully ignorant or wilfully blind. At his table, as I have stated above, the Mexican padre is a *bon vivant*, delighting in the good things of this life; and however strongly he may inculcate upon his flock the necessity of strictly observing all fasts, his appetite frequently begets an obliviousness which turns every day alike into one of feasting while at his own table. Another thing: if all the male portion of the community in Mexico were attached to the priesthood, centuries would elapse before the race would become extinct unless some tremendous revolution in the morals of the brotherhood should take place; for it is just as well known that they contrive to break the bonds of celibacy strictly enjoined upon them, as it is that such bonds are prescribed by the Church of Rome. Were the pope to be put in a *clairvoyant* state, and willed to look into the domestic habits and relations of his agents in Mexico, a precious set of backsliding padres he would find.

That the good padres of that country have their *compañeras*, or female companions, is well known, not only to foreigners, but to their own people, and equally well known is it that they invariably make their selections with a discrimination which shows that they are most excellent judges of female beauty. They rear families, too, and with great care and attention; and although the unaccepted and more ill-favoured portion of the women constituting his flock may think their padre very naughty, he finds means to close their eyes and mouths upon his peccadilloes, and all goes on smoothly.

I trust that the kind-hearted curas, from whom myself and companions received so many favours and attentions, will give me full pardon for thus exposing some of their weaknesses and frailties—absolution for my tell-tale sins: they will not attempt to deny anything I have said of them. They will also excuse me, when I say to and of them, that they are a class of enlightened, generous, good-natured, discerning, hospitable, hail-fellow-well-met, penance-hating, women-loving men, prone toward the enjoyments of the table, holding fasts in great scorn, addicted to occasional gambling and wine-bibbing, and pretending no ignorance in matters of cock-fighting and sports of a like nature; more particularly when I repeat that I entertain the best feelings towards one and all of them. In describing them, I have not " set down aught in malice," but, on the contrary, have spoken of them precisely as I found them.

The influence and power exerted by the priests of Mexico, over the ignorant and superstitious population, are immense—a fact as well known to them, and even better, than to the intelligent foreigners who have visited the country. They know, too, that the population they govern is led and kept in subjection by impostures the most flimsy, by deception the most transparent—for not to know this would be proving them fools, a title they do not deserve. They farther know, that in order to sustain themselves in their past and present position, to retain their supremacy and their fat benefices, they must persevere in their impostures and continue to gull their simple flocks—to hold the down-trodden mass in the same ignorance in which they have so long been kept—and hence their open intolerance towards all other sects, and their zealous care that no other religion than their own shall be preached or inculcated in the land.* The almost countless number of ecclesiastics in Mexico are well aware that their expensive system of church domination inevitably tends to diminish the resources and retard the prosperity and advancement of the country; but it is not in the nature of men holding power, whether Protestant or Catholic, political or religious, to resign it willingly, or give up any office of influence or emolument already within their grasp, because it conflicts with the interests or liberties of the people; and to expect the priests of Mexico to abandon their sway or abdicate their ascendancy would be to suppose them more than men. All reformation of existing evils, either of Church or State, must come from the people themselves: whether the Mexican nation will ever be brought to know, feel, and exert itself against the powerful ecclesiastical and military establishments which are pressing and keeping it down, is a matter extremely problematical.

The Catholic reader must not construe these remarks into an attack upon his religion, for such is far from my

* No other religion than the Catholic is allowed or preached up to this day in Mexico, but a greater degree of tolerance is manifested towards the professors of other creeds now than formerly. I have read in some book—but its author I cannot call to mind—of a debate in the Mexican Senate in relation to the allowing Protestant foreigners a burial-place. No such privilege was permitted them until within the last ten or fifteen years, and it was only through the urgent remonstrances of the then British minister that the point was conceded. One of the Mexican Senators, when the subject was debated in Congress, made remarks something like the following: "There is one of four things we must allow these heretics who may happen to die in our land: we must eat, pickle and send them out of the country, throw them in the fields, or bury them under ground. To eat them would be most repugnant—not one of my colleagues would taste the flesh of a heretic; to send them out of the country would be expensive; to throw them in the fields would be pestilence-breeding, and otherwise exceedingly offensive. I move, therefore, as the easiest, cheapest, safest, and every way the best course for us to adopt, is to allow them a burial-place"—and the motion was carried-

intention—towards both faith and its professors I entertain no other feelings than of respect. My object has been to draw a rough picture of Catholicism in Mexico, and the power and means by which it is sustained, and in so doing I have confined myself strictly to the truth. In its essentials the Romish religion in Mexico is doubtless the same as it is in the United States, or in any country where toleration, that firm and enduring foundation of all political liberty, is known; but in its administration there is as much difference between the two as there is between the religion of the Pilgrims of New-England and that of the Hindoos or New Zealanders.

## CHAPTER XVIII.

Mode of passing our Time.—Herr Cline.—Mexico by Moonlight.—Note from Madame Calderon.—Rambles over Mexico.—A Dance.—The Jarabe.—Change of Scene.—A murdered Soldier.—Touching Instance of Grief.—More Moonlight.—"Quien Vive?"—A staggering Padre.—Release of Americans through the Exertions of General Thompson.—Visit to Tacubaya.—Cruel and mysterious Murder of Egerton and his Mistress.—Visit to the Acordada.—A Show-case of Murder.—Gloomy Entrance to the Acordada.—Some Description of the Interior.—Release of a Female Prisoner.—Mr. Navarro.—Story of his Wrongs.—Robbery and Crime in the Acordada.—Texan Prisoners within its dreary Walls.—Take Leave of Mr. Navarro.—Farther Description of the Prison.—Encounter with Dutch Broom Girls.—An old Acquaintance in the Broom Line.—The Balladmongers badly patronised.—Evangelistas, or Letter-writers of Mexico.—Their singular Calling.—Stock in Trade of the Evangelista.—Mexican Coaches and Mexican Coachmen.—Another Visit to Santiago.—More of the Mexican Coachmen.

Our days, from the 21st to the 27th of April, were passed in roaming over the city and environs, in rides through the Alameda and Paseo, and in occasional visits to our companions still in confinement at San Lazaro and Santiago, while the evenings we whiled away at the Italian Opera, at the monte rooms in the vicinity of the Plaza, where heaps of doubloons dazzle and allure gambling adventurers, at fandangoes, in midnight walks over the city, or mayhap in seeing the feats of a company of pantomimists under the direction of the celebrated Herr Cline, who had engaged the Italian Opera House on alternate nights.

No city in North America, or perhaps in the wide world, can vie with Mexico as seen under the softening influence of moonlight—can equal the sweet and silent grandeur with which her palaces, churches, and innumerable establishments, rich in architectural beauty and exterior painting, are clothed by the subdued beams of the queen of night—and on one occasion I spent hours in wandering at random through her streets, completely absorbed by the beauty of the scene.* Attracted by

* Madame Calderon draws a graphic picture of Mexico by moonlight. She says that it is the most flattering medium through which the city can be viewed, with its broad and silent streets, and splendid old buildings, whose decay and abandonment are softened by the silvery light; its ancient churches, from which the notes of the organ occasionally come pealing forth, mingled with faint blasts of music borne on the night wind from some distant procession; or with the soft music of a hymn from some neighbouring convent. The white-robed monk—the veiled female—even the ragged beggar, add to the picture: by daylight his rags are too visible. Frequently, as the carriages roll along to the opera, or as, at a late hour, they return from it, they are suddenly stopped by the appearance of the mysterious coach, with its piebald mules, and the *Eye* surrounded by rays of light on its panels; a melancholy apparition, for it has come from the house of mourning, probably from the bed of death. Then, by the moonlight, the kneeling figures on the pavement seem as if carved in stone. The city of Mexico by moonlight—the environs of Mexico at daybreak—these are the hours for viewing both to advantage, and for making us feel how

"All but the spirit of man is divine."

Such is the picture drawn of this splendid city, as seen under the influence of moonlight, by the author of "Life in Mexico"—a picture the strict fidelity of which I can attest.

the sounds of a mandolin, coming from an open door in a street near the market-place, I first took the precaution to gather such small amount of silver as I was possessed of at the time into my hands, placed my hands in my pockets, and entered the apartment. The dimly-lighted room was rendered even more obscure by a cloud of cigar smoke; yet I could plainly discern the faces of some dozen swarthy and blanketed léperos and the same number of scantily-clad girls, watching the movements of a party of dancers who were executing one of the rude *jarabes* of the country — a species of dance consisting chiefly of shuffling with the feet and singing, and at the termination of which the males are expected to treat their partners to refreshments in the way of dulces.* One of the girls politely made room for me upon a rude bench, but my stay was short—the fumes of cigar smoke, and the odour of pulque and mescal, drove me from the apartment at the conclusion of the first dance.

While passing a house but a few steps from this haunt of revelry, and certainly within hearing, I saw through the open door the face of a corpse, lying in a coarse box or coffin upon a table, and with some half dozen long candles burning on either side. Two or three females, their faces covered with their hands as if in deep grief, were seated upon the floor near the head of the table, while a single soldier was unconcernedly smoking on a rough chest in one corner of the apartment. Wishing to ascertain the circumstances attending the death of the man in the coffin, and to see any ceremony that might take place, I noiselessly entered the room. The soldier informed me that the unfortunate man upon the table

---

* *Jarabe* means, I believe, some species of sweetmeat, so that it can be called the "*Dance of the Sweetmeats.*"

was a comrade of his, who had been stabbed by a girl some two hours before in a fit of jealousy. The knife had reached the soldier's heart, killing him instantly, and one of the women on the floor was sobbing audibly her grief that he had died without the presence of a priest and unconfessed. Whether she was his mother or sister I did not learn—she lifted not her face while I was in the room.

The lateness of the hour, the sorrowful spectacle before me, with the attendant train of thoughts upon the insecurity of life in Mexico the scene called up, now admonished me to hasten towards my quarters at the Gran Sociedad. The moon was riding high in heaven as I once more found myself in the streets, and shedding her mild and subdued light upon the innumerable religious establishments—now kissing, with sweet radiance, a towering dome or steeple; and anon, as some wandering cloud would brush hastily across her face, flitting and spectral shadows, as of misshapen giants, would stalk silently across the plazas and thoroughfares, and dissolve or lose themselves as the vapory intruder which had created them resigned its momentary sway. The air was soft, pure, and balmy—such an air as would, in many countries, tempt thousands from their couches; yet the streets of Mexico were deserted—that stillness which can be heard, that indefinable hum which seems to be the breath of nature while asleep, reigned on every side—and I even essayed to advance on tiptoe, as if fearful of awaking the deep loneliness of night.

The startling "*quien vive?*" of a sentinel, after I had walked two or three squares without meeting a single living being, was a relief as I neared the Plaza Mayor. When within this noted square, the clattering of half a dozen horsemen, dashing over the rough pavement in hot haste as though to arrest some midnight assassin or quell some drunken brawl, was really a welcome sound —the previous quiet had been so intense that it was painful.

I crossed the Plaza and entered the Plateros. Ten steps farther, I encountered two servants assisting homeward a staggering priest. Charity induced me to hope that the padre was lame or infirm, but the strong light of the moon constrained me to believe that he had been dining or supping with some holy brother, and that his potations had been other than of chocolate or water. A walk of some few minutes brought me once more to my quarters, and still another five minutes added me to the list of sleepers within the Gran Sociedad; but the memory of that moonlight walk awoke with me in the morning, and the remembrance of the scenes which I beheld that night is vivid as was their reality.

On the morning of the 27th of April we were rejoiced to learn that three of our comrades in imprisonment—S. B. Sheldon, Allensworth Adams, and W. Tompkins—had been released through the interference of General Thompson. The liberated men were soon comfortably quartered in the city, and their wants provided for.

During the afternoon of the same day a party of some six or eight of us, composed of Englishmen and Americans, visited the garden of an Italian at Tacubaya, who kept a ninepin alley and provided refreshments for such foreign guests from the city as might visit the little village. Before we returned to the city, an English artist of great celebrity in Mexico, a landscape painter named Egerton, was pointed out to us by one of his countrymen, who also related several anecdotes referring to the many attainments of the artist.

While breakfasting the next morning, with an English gentleman in the city, we were shocked with the intelligence that Egerton, together with a female with whom he lived as his wife, and who possessed rare personal attractions and endowments as a landscape painter, had been cruelly murdered during the night. The whole city was at once thrown into the highest excitement by the startling news, and to increase still farther the commotion, many Mexican families, who had made Tacubaya their country residence, packed their furniture with all haste, and with their families returned immediately into the city, as if fearful of being massacred.

It seems that on the evening of the murder, Egerton and the unfortunate woman were walking in a large garden attached to their residence, as was their custom, and that while thus engaged they were attacked by some person or persons unknown, and both slain. The body of Egerton was found some distance from that of his companion, run through apparently with a sword, while by his side was a walking-stick much hacked, rendering it evident that he had fought to the last and made a stout resistance. The body of the female, who was on the point of becoming a mother, was also stabbed and otherwise horribly mangled, and this induced the belief that she too had resisted to the last. Her face was scratched and otherwise disfigured, a piece was bitten from her breast, her person had been abused, and the perpetrator of the outrage, as if fearing that she might not be recognised, had written her name upon a piece of paper and pinned it to a fragment of the dress that still remained upon her body, most of it having been torn off in the struggle which ended in her death. The formation of the letters was plainly English, a circumstance which went directly to prove that the murder was neither planned nor matured by Mexicans; and to corroborate this belief, the money and watch of Egerton, and the jewelry of his companion, were untouched —rendering it certain that the act was not one of the native robbers, but of deep revenge. Among the thousand reports and rumours circulating in Mexico the next morning, was one to the effect that the murdered man had a wife and two children in England, and that some two years previous he had visited his native land with the intention of bringing them to Mexico; but instead of returning with his wife, he had seduced and enticed away the murdered woman, who had since lived with him as his wife. Rumour also had it that the latter was engaged to be married to a young man in England at the time of her elopement with Egerton. Among the many speculations afloat among the countrymen of the unfortunate couple, the one which received the most credence was, that the murder had been planned in England, and effected by some acquaintance of the woman, as a matter of revenge. There was also a story that Egerton had been involved in a love affair with some fair Mexican; but this report received little credence. The British Minister, Mr. Pakenham, exerted himself to the utmost to ferret out and arrest the perpetrators, in which he was assisted by General Valencia and the Mexican police and authorities; but up to this time no clew to the authors of the horrible outrage has been discovered, and the whole affair remains a profound mystery.

Determined, if possible, to gain admission into the noted Acordada, and have one interview with my old companion, Antonio Navarro, before leaving Mexico, on the morning after the murder I have just hastily described I obtained the assistance of a young and influential Englishman, who spoke confidently of his being able either to coax or bribe his way into the interior of the prison. Arrived in front, my companion pointed, through a barred window, to a species of form built upon an inclined plane, on which the bodies of such persons as have been murdered during the night are exposed in the morning, so that they may be recognised by their friends! With a shudder at the thoughts of scenes of misery and deep wo which must almost daily be enacted in front of this revolting show-case of murder, by the wives, sisters, mothers, and other relatives of the victims, we passed onward.

After a few words of parley with a guard of soldiers stationed at the main entrance, we were admitted within the gloomy walls and commenced the ascent of a flight of solid but much-worn steps. Either side we found lined with ragged and squalid wretches, doubtless in some way related to the prisoners, and lounging about with the hope of being allowed to visit them. Arrived at the head of this dismal staircase, and after a few words of farther parley, we were admitted through a strong and massive door. Here we at once found ourselves involved in a labyrinth of gloomy galleries and dark passage-ways. Soldiers, keepers, officers of the courts, gentlemen and léperos, were hurrying to and fro; ponderous locks were turned in opening or closing heavy iron doors and gates on every side; curses and deep imprecations were heard in unseen quarters; while the clanking of chains, as they were dragged along the floors of the different apartments and across the stone pavement of an immense patio below us, were grating harshly on our ears.

My companion asked a young man, who appeared to be in some way connected with the dreary prison, if he could be allowed a few minutes' conversation with Señor Navarro. " Presently," answered the individual addressed, at the same time ushering us into a small office on the outer side of the main corridor. A hard-featured man, who seemed as though he might be a captain of the night watch, was reading the Diario del Gobierno in one corner of this apartment, while a clerk was making out what appeared to be arrest-warrants or subpœnas for witnesses, at a desk on the opposite side. Here we remained anxiously, for some half an hour, until *a* Mr. Navarro, but not the *right* one, stepped into the room and asked our business. On telling him that we had called to see another prisoner who bore the same name, he pointed to a heavy iron door or gate, leading to a species of anteroom, and said that we must inquire there. A word or two with a keeper through the grates sufficed to gain us admission, and no sooner had we entered than the door was closed and locked after us, with a clang that sent a shudder through our frames.

The young Englishman who accompanied me now again made known our wish to see the prisoner, Mr. Navarro, adding that we had received permission to that effect. The keeper, after telling us to wait a few moments, unlocked another grated door, which seemed to open into an inner corridor, and went in quest of my former comrade. During the few minutes that elapsed before his return, we had an opportunity of learning some of the secrets of this celebrated prison, and of seeing the cold, business-like air with which it is conducted. On every side it seemed as though we could hear keys turning in ponderous locks, the dreary sound of bolts, and the clanging of the heavy iron doors as they opened or were shut. On one side of the interior they appeared to be admitting prisoner after prisoner, crying aloud their names as the unfortunates crossed the gloomy thresholds: at an opposite side, the passage leading directly through the room in which we were standing, seemed to be the outlet through which the prisoners made their way on being liberated, for while we remained three or four were escorted through in the direction of the main entrance to the building from without. A sickly, deadly, prison-like smell, arising from damp and dirty walls and floors, ragged and filthy wretches covered with vermin, and a close and confined atmosphere, pervaded the apartment, and as if to make the air doubly offensive, the opening of a heavy door would bring in some freshly-foul current from the dismal interior.

Three times was the name of each liberated prisoner shouted aloud, and three times, it seemed to us, was the cry accompanied by sounds as of keys turning in the prison locks and of doors slowly opening. "Guadalupe Ribas" was heard, in low and muttered tones, from the inner recesses, followed by sounds almost indistinct, but which resembled those of a heavy door within doors as it swung upon its hinges. "Guadalupe Ribas" was again heard, in tones far more distinct, succeeded by sounds which it was now plainly evident proceeded from a key turning in some heavy lock and the opening of still another iron door. "Guadalupe Ribas" once more resounded in our ears, louder and more distinct, a strong door grated heavily upon its hinges, and Guadalupe Ribas was passed through the room in which we were awaiting. Who or what she was, or for what crime she had been confined, we did not learn; but for attempting the life of her lover in a fit of jealousy, or for some act of a like nature, she had probably been provided with lodgings within the gloomy walls of the Acordada. She was a pretty girl, of not more than eighteen, was neatly and cleanly dressed in garments brought probably by the friends who had procured her release, and with downcast eyes and hurried steps tripped from the place as the last door was opened.*

No sooner had she departed, than a ponderous iron gate, leading apparently into another part of the prison, was slowly opened, and Mr. Navarro stood before us. Three months' close imprisonment, combined with the horrible associations of the Acordada, had wrought terrible changes in the appearance of my old companion—his unshaved face was pale and haggard, his hair long and uncombed, his vestments ragged and much soiled. On first entering the walls, his fellow-prisoners, composed of the most loathsome and abandoned wretches, had robbed him not only of his money but his clothing, and with emotion he now told us that the only sustenance he received was the scanty allowance of tortillas and frijoles given to each of the immense horde of felons and assassins by whom he was surrounded—a pittance barely sufficient to sustain life. He spoke of his wife and children at San Antonio, of a son at college in Missouri, and with tearful eyes begged me to convey to them information that he was still alive and not without hope of ultimate release. Stealthily, and without being seen by the surrounding Mexicans, we gave the unfortunate man what money we had—shaking hands with him three or four times previous to our final parting, and at each grasp slipping a

* I may have mistaken the name of this girl, although I heard it pronounced three times.

few dollars into his possession: then, after expressing our ardent wishes for his speedy liberation, we left the Acordada, but not until I heard the ponderous iron door close, with a dreadful clang, upon my old comrade.

As we were leaving the building, I looked down into an immense patio, paved with stone, where some hundreds of male prisoners were sitting, lounging, working, and sleeping—the apartment for the females I did not see. Near the main entrance we found several of the men belonging to the Santa Fé Expedition—Englishmen, Americans, Frenchmen, and Prussians—who had been liberated through the intervention of the ministers of their different governments. They were now awaiting an opportunity to see several Texan prisoners, who had been captured on the Rio Grande in the vicinity of Matamoros. I, too, was anxious to give these prisoners a call, although unacquainted with them; but as my companion had an engagement to fulfil in the city, was compelled to hurry off without accomplishing it. Another opportunity to visit the Acordada did not offer while I was in Mexico.

A full description of this dreary prison might not prove uninteresting, but I am unable to give it. Hundreds of wretches, male and female, and of every grade, are confined within its walls—chained, ill-fed, dirty and ragged. In 1828 occurred the Revolution of the Acordada, and during some of the more recent pronunciamentos the prisoners, or many of them, have escaped; but in the spring of 1842 the place appeared to be stocked, even to overflowing, with murderers, thieves, counterfeiters, wives who had stabbed or poisoned their husbands, girls who had assassinated or attempted to assassinate their lovers—in short, a miscellaneous collection of every hardened class in Mexico, from the highest to the lowest. Some one of the guards, attendants, or keepers should have been provided with a chain and a lodging within the prison while I was there, for among them they robbed me of a handkerchief. This was a mere trifle, however, for it is impossible to turn a corner in Mexico without having your pockets picked. Even in the churches, it is said, the léperos ply their calling; for while their spiritual wants are administered to by the priests, the ragged rascals have an eye upon their temporal need by introducing their fingers into the pockets of their neighbours, and this with a dexterity unknown in other lands.

On our return to the heart of the city, I proceeded at once to the great coach stand in the Plaza Mayor for the purpose of hiring one of the clumsy vehicles to ride out to Santiago. In the Plateros I met a couple of Dutch broom-girls, with their "fader and big broder," squalling away at one of their street ballads, and with the usual tambourine, hurdy-gurdy, and dancing monkey accompaniments. One of the girls I recognised as a veteran itinerant, well known in the thoroughfares of every city of the United States. She spoke a little English, and on my asking her how she liked Mexico, she remarked that "dese peoples is very poor in dis city, so poor as we can't make de expenses." Presuming that the expenses of one of these families are far from heavy, it may be naturally inferred that the patronage they received in Mexico was not very extensive, and that the demand for brooms and ballads of Dutch manufacture is not sufficient to induce a farther exportation.

As I passed under the Portales, with the intention of examining a showy sarape exposed in front of one of the shops, I paused for a moment to watch the movements of one of the letter-writers of Mexico—*evangelistas* they are called—who was intently scrutinizing the countenance of a customer, seated upon a small box in front of him, as if to read his thoughts. If the customer was not an assassin, or a noted robber at least, his face certainly belied him; for a more hang-dog expression of countenance was never worn. As he whispered a few words in the attentive ear of the *evangelista*, I could not but think that the fellow was consenting to an offer made him to assassinate or rob some unfortunate person, and wished the letter-writer to make the fact known upon a note he was in the act of sketching.

These evangelistas, it is said, ply a profitable trade by writing letters for those of the inhabitants whose education, in the matter of expressing their thoughts by intelligible signs on paper, has been neglected—and of the entire population of the city of Mexico, I do not believe that five in every hundred adults can read and write. Where it is impossible, then, to communicate by verbal message, the professional letter-writers are called in requisition, and thus they are made the repositories of secrets innumerable, and secrets which it is well understood they will never betray. There, in the neighbourhood of the Plaza, do these evangelistas sit from day to day, their stock in trade consisting of pens, ink, and a few quires of assorted paper, with a small tablet upon which to write. As their principal customers are girls, it is more than probable that love and intrigue are the themes upon which their talents are oftenest called in requisition; but that they are ready, for "a consideration," to indite epistles in relation to treason, assassination, or robbery, there can be little doubt.

As I approached the coach stand, I suppose there

must have been something in my countenance which indicated that I could furnish a job, for twenty Mexican Jehus at once crowded around me, and each pointed out his establishment as in every way preferable to those of his fellows. Coachmen are the same the world over, and if you do not ascertain that their animals are faster, their vehicles newer, easier to ride in, and less liable to break down than any others, it will not be because these circumstances are not told you with open-mouthed vehemence. In the present instance I threw myself entirely upon the generosity of the assembled crowd of "whips," and after undergoing the usual amount of pulling and hauling, at last found myself in one of the coaches. In another moment the postillion mounted the "near wheel mule"—I believe that is the technical term—and I was whirled and jolted off on a short visit to my imprisoned friends. In an hour I was once more in the city, my hat suffering severely from the jolts of the coach as it crossed one or two of the gutters, while a new bump was developed on the crown of my head by sudden and forcible contact with the top of the vehicle.

A few words in relation to the appearance and construction of the Mexican coach, and I have done with this chapter. The superstructure, or body of the vehicle, is well enough, being somewhat after the fashion of our own light hackney-coaches; but the huge frame or scaffolding upon which it is swung is altogether a different thing, and gives the whole affair a clumsy, ill-proportioned appearance. The wheels are large, strong, placed at a distance of three or four yards apart, and were the immense platform upon which the top rests taken away, the American would at once suppose it to be a lumber carriage, such as timber and heavy stone pillars are transported on in his native land. The sides of the body are painted, the scaffolding upon which it rests elaborately carved with queer conceits, and not to speak far out of the bounds of reason, there is timber enough wasted in the construction of the whole to build a small class Western steamer of the lighter model. Such is a hasty description of the coach: the animals and driver require a few words. The latter is generally a swarthy, brigandish, dashing fellow, dressed in a leathern jacket not lacking in embroidery and bell buttons, stout trousers of the same, with a broad-brimmed hat covered with oiled silk, and frequently decorated with silver cord and tassels. This is perched in a jaunty, devil-may-care style upon his head, and thus arrayed, the stranger, who has read some life of brigands illustrated with plates, cannot but think the Mexican *cochero* an individual even more ready to attack and rob his coach than to drive it. His mules are often large and strong animals, and although encumbered with heavy and useless ornaments attached to the harness, and frequently with a leathern case which completely covers their hind quarters and tails, he contrives to get over the ground with a celerity which could hardly be expected. What the charge per hour is I have now forgotten—I only know that, like coachmen in other countries, the Mexicans get all they can, and almost invariably ask for more.

## CHAPTER XIX.

The Alameda.—Visit to that noted Pleasure-ground.—A Yankee Livery-stable-keeper in Mexico.—A Shower.—Paseo Nuevo.—Family Parties in their Carriages.—Mexican Cavaliers on Horseback.—Singular Gait of their Steeds.—Manner of training them.—Race with a Shower.—Santa Anna.—His Courtesy, Policy, Power, and ambitious Projects.—Reasons for the Decline of the Mexican Republic.—Our last Night in Mexico.—More of Captain Hudson.—Santa Anna's Benevolence!—Take leave of our Friends.—San Lazaro again.—Mexican Escort.—Mexico from the Mountain Sides.—Arrival at a Breakfast-House.—Arms and Equipments of our Party.—A Yankee Driver.—Roadside Crosses and Graves.—Stories of Robbers.—Robbing the Stages reduced to a System.—Señor Garcia and the Ladrones.—Rio Frio.—Mexican Dogs.—Cholula in the Distance.—Arrival at Puebla.—Visit to the Texan Prisoners at the Presidio.—Their unfortunate Condition.—The Cathedral of Puebla.—Its great Riches.—Anecdote of the Angels.—Superstition from which Puebla received its Name.—In Bed and Asleep.

In my last chapter I related the particulars of a visit to the Acordada. Although that prison is situated near the Alameda, a celebrated park or resort for all the fashionables of Mexico, up to this time I had not entered its gates or examined its beautiful fountains. The day was now approaching when Mr. Ellis was to leave the capital for Vera Cruz, with such American prisoners as had been liberated; and, determined to enjoy the pleasure of a ride through the Alameda before our departure, a small party of us procured horses after dinner, and sallied out with the intention of galloping over the pleasure-grounds of the *élite* of Mexico.

April seems to be a month of "smiles and tears" in Mexico as with us; for although the sky was bright and clear when we mounted the nags procured for us at the stable of a Yankee, who has found his way to

that city, and established himself in the business of
"hiring out" horses, before we had been ten minutes in
the saddle the heavens were overcast, and in five more
the clouds were discounting with a liberality which
threatened to lay the city under water. *Cargadores*,
with their leather trousers rolled up, were standing at
the different crossings, ready to carry any unfortunate
pedestrian, who might be "caught out," over the swift-
ly-running street currents caused by the shower. So
suddenly was the rain pouring upon us that there was
no chance of an escape by retreating, and we therefore
dashed on towards the Alameda. A few minutes more,
and rain, clouds, and all were over. The rapidity with
which showers come and go in these high mountain re-
gions, for Mexico lies some seven thousand feet above
the level of the sea, can scarcely be imagined.

We passed an hour pleasantly in the Alameda, and
in the Paseo Nuevo, which is but a continuation, admiring the beautiful fountains, groves, walks, and rides
with which they are adorned. Before we left the former, the carriage-roads which wind through it were
thronged with the lumbering but costly vehicles of the
higher orders, filled with ladies and children. At certain points the carriages would draw up in line, many
of the fair inmates smoking their *cigarritos* with much
apparent gusto, while ever and anon a dashing horse-
man would amble up on his prancing steed, exchange a
few words, and then canter off to exchange compliments
with the ladies in some other coach. The reader must
not suppose, however, that the cavalier starts off at a
rapid gallop—he does nothing of the kind. There is
little "go-ahead" in a spirited, showy, well-trained
Mexican horse—the old saying of the country is, that
" a true and devoted lover will ride and amble all day

long under the window of his mistress." If the animal "lifts" well, or, in other words, if he hoists his fore feet some ten or twelve inches at every step, and will make motions enough while going twenty yards to carry him half that number of miles, he is the horse for a Mexican's money. To train him to this showy but most unnatural gait, it is said that, while a colt, large and heavy clogs are fastened to the fetlock joints of the fore feet by means of straps—these straps allowing the clogs some twelve inches play. To move onward at all, the animal is obliged to hoist the weights entirely from the ground, and they are never taken off until the colt has contracted such a habit of lifting as cannot be overcome. To give him a farther shuffling gait, the Mexican gentleman covers the haunches of his steed with a large leather casing which reaches to his hocks. The edges of this casing are trimmed with little iron points, which not only tinkle at every step, but prick the horse's hind legs, so much to his annoyance, that he throws them as far forward as possible. Thus, what with lifting his fore legs and mincing with his hind, a gait is contracted which more resembles the dancing of a circus-horse upon a plank than aught else I can liken it to. A cruel bit, of Mameluke pattern, which causes the horse to curve his neck, champ, and froth incessantly at the mouth, completes the fit-out of the Mexican gentleman on a pleasure ride.

We had intended to make the entire circuit of the Paseo Nuevo; but a small cloud in the direction of one of the snow-capped mountains warned us that another shower was brewing, and that to escape it we must be moving homeward. Fortunately, our Yankee livery-stable-keeper had brought with him his inherent utilitarian principles of getting over as much ground as possible in the shortest time, and had taught his animals rather to annihilate miles than minutes—a circumstance which saved us a second soaking; for as we clattered through the streets at a rapid pace, the shower which had driven us from the Alameda was following close at our heels and gaining upon us at every step. The full weight of it was falling as we threw ourselves from our jaded animals under the archway which formed the entrance to our quarters.

We had now but one more day to remain in Mexico, and I felt that I had yet scarcely seen half the curiosities of which the proud city boasts. Santa Anna himself, the great man who has risen above reverses that no common intellect could have combated so successfully, I had never set eyes upon—he moved not from the palace while we were in the city at liberty, or if he did we were not aware of it. All the foreigners—American, English, and French—spoke of him as a man extremely courteous and affable in his intercourse; of polished and most agreeable manners; in short, the last person who could be suspected of the many acts of oppression, tyranny, broken faith, ambition, avarice, and treachery of which he has been accused. To obtain at least a glimpse of this man was the ardent desire of us all; but we were disappointed. His lady was lying dangerously ill at the time, which may have been one reason that prevented him from appearing in public.*

* Madame Santa Anna is spoken of by all as an estimable woman, of great kindness of heart, and it was reported that she was untiring in her exertions to have the treatment of the Texan prisoners mitigated. On the 19th of April she was thought to be lying at the point of death, and a solemn service in the cathedral was held and the last sacrament administered to the sufferer. It was said at the time, but with what truth I know not, that ten thousand dollars' worth of wax candles were burning within the walls of the cathedral at the same moment. The magnificence of such a spectacle can

No farther proof is wanting of the great talent—perhaps I should call it cunning—of Santa Anna, than the simple fact that he has been able, in the face of adverse circumstances apparently insurmountable, and in direct opposition to the known wishes of a large majority of the inhabitants, to regain and retain a supremacy which amounts to absolute power. With every variety of discordant element arrayed against him—with popular and powerful military men known to be inimical in different quarters, with a Constituent Congress opposed to him, with reverse after reverse and defeat after defeat staring him in the face—above all these he has risen, and at this time is really in the possession and enjoyment of a power such as the Autocrat of all the Russias would hardly dare to wield. That his arbitrary and despotic government is the best that could be adopted, to keep the people in subjection, can hardly be doubted by any one who has seen Mexico; yet not one jot of credit does Santa Anna deserve for thus ruling the land, as his own selfishness rather than a love of country actuates his every movement. There are many liberal, enlightened, and well-disposed statesmen among the Federalists of Mexico—men of great moral honesty, and earnestly desirous of placing the government of the country upon a republican basis—but they have an ignorant population to deal with, a population entirely incapable of governing themselves; to this may be added the influence and power of the priesthood; and as if this was not enough, the ambitious and selfish schemes of Santa Anna, and after him some half dozen military leaders who only lack his talent and

hardly be conceived, much less described—such a flood of light illuminating the rich adornments of the church, and the showy and imposing dresses and brilliant ornaments of the priests officiating on the occasion.

energy to make them equally opposed to the supremacy of civil power—with all these drag-weights upon their efforts, what hopes can the friends of free government entertain of even ultimate success? The day has gone by when a priest-ridden population, governed by a military despotism, can make headway in the great race of advancement which has been commenced by Anglo-Saxon toleration, and by the civil and religious liberty which the latter race enjoy. That Santa Anna, or such a man as Santa Anna, unless some tremendous revolution takes place in the very natures of the inhabitants, will continue to govern Mexico until she is swallowed in that vortex which appears to be yawning to receive her, is certain—a vortex formed by the liberal spirit of universal education, free toleration of religion, and that stern and inflexible love for equal rights now spreading through the earth, which compels ambition to sacrifice personal feelings to the public good.

The evening previous to our departure from Mexico was spent in cleaning and loading pistols, packing up, and making ready for the tiresome and hazardous journey to Vera Cruz. The exact date I have forgotten, as I took no note of time or circumstances after my release —but that it rained incessantly during the earlier part of the night I well remember. The diligence set off at three o'clock in the morning, and as we all had much to do no one retired to rest. About midnight, and while I was at the rooms of Mr. Ellis, a Mexican officer arrived in great haste, with an order for the release of Captain Hudson—Santa Anna, I believe at the request of the then Governor of Connecticut, having consented to give him up. Captain H., however, as is already known, had put it out of the power of the Provisional President to exercise another act of "*benevolence*" towards the United States, by taking the responsibility of liberating himself.*

At half past two o'clock in the morning we took our leave of General Thompson, who had been employed up to that hour in writing and making out his despatches, and set out with bag and baggage for the Casa de Diligencias, from which the stage starts. After some half hour passed in weighing and stowing trunks and valises, each passenger being compelled to pay extra if he is the possessor of more than an *arroba* or twenty-five pounds of baggage, we finally entered the coach, some eight or ten Americans in all, and once more shaking hands with Mr. Mayer and several of our countrymen, who had lost one night's sleep for the purpose of " seeing us off," the driver cracked his whip and we rattled over the pavements at a rapid rate.

---

\* In the published correspondence, in relation to the release of the American prisoners attached to the Santa Fé Expedition, it is openly asserted that we were released, not as an act of justice, but purely from *benevolent motives !* I will quote one or two passages from a letter addressed to General Thompson by M. de Bocanegra, and dated " Mexico, April 23, 1842." In this letter General T. is informed, " That his excellency the Provisional President, in consideration solely of the cordial friendship by which the Mexican Republic is united to the United States, has been pleased to accede to the repeated petitions addressed by Mr. Powhatan Ellis, conjointly with the other diplomatic ministers, by means of notes and private conferences, to the effect that those persons among the Texan prisoners from New Mexico should be liberated, who, according to the said notes, are citizens of the said States, and who, on incorporating themselves with the Texan force, had no intention to make war on the Republic." M. de Bocanegra next goes on to say that Santa Anna, " though he has on this occasion done an act of benevolence, in order to prove to the United States how much he desires to preserve the relations which now fortunately exist between the two nations, protests that for the future, every individual of any nation whatever, who may be found in the Texan ranks, and may be made prisoner by the Mexican troops, shall be subject, without ransom, to the laws of war." A very pretty piece of Mexican kindness, this, ingeniously interwoven with Mexican vapour! I certainly feel under great obligations to my own government for its *petitions*, and to Santa Anna for his exceeding *benevolence*, but I doubt whether I should ever tax either of them again were I arrested under the same circumstances and should the same opportunities to escape be within my reach.

As we passed the old Hospital of San Lazaro, which lies immediately to the left of the road leading to Vera Cruz, I could not resist taking a last look at its gloomy walls, now indistinctly seen by the dim light of morning. Not without a shudder did I recall the revolting scenes, dreary hours of imprisonment, wild orgies, and imposing night funerals, I had passed and seen within its long and dismal halls, nor could I think of my comrades still confined there, and of the horrible associations of the place, without a fervent hope that the Texans might speedily be released. Five minutes more, and we had passed the garita, and were speeding along over the open thoroughfare. An escort of dragoons, provided by Santa Anna for "El Ministro" and his party, were galloping on either side of the stage, their lances and sabres rattling at every movement of their horses.

The dull gray of morning was slowly dispersing as we commenced the toilsome ascent of the mountains which divide the valley of Mexico from that of Puebla, and long before the summit was reached the full light of day was shining far and wide over the scene below us. The arid waste which surrounds the great city we had just left was softened down, and served to heighten the magnificence of the innumerable towers and domes still plainly visible. The distant mountain sides were clothed with a fleecy covering of clouds, the wasted receptacles of the last night's shower; and as the sun gradually lifted the curtain of vapour the bold and precipitous sides were brought out in striking grandeur. As we were approaching the last turn in the road the sun suddenly shot up from behind the mountain tops; for an instant the valley was lit up as by enchantment, and the next moment a projecting cliff shut out the brilliant scene — we had looked our last upon the city of the Montezumas.

An hour's ride over the rough mountain country now brought us to the breakfast-house, a noted stand by the roadside, and kept, if my memory serves me, by a Frenchman. It was not until we had dragged our cramped and benumbed limbs from the stage that our full strength and imposing armament were brought to full view, and we ascertained that our diligence was a perfect arsenal of war's dread implements of destruction. Judge Ellis had a sword in his hands, while a belt stuck full of United States boarding-pistols was strapped around him. In the hands of some of my companions were double-barrelled guns—and the butt of a pistol or the handle of a bowie-knife was peering from every pocket. While in Mexico we had breakfasted, dined, and supped full of horrible tales of robbers and robberies upon the road to Vera Cruz; but as we now counted our strength, we felt a confidence in our ability to withstand a successful siege from four times our number of *los señores ladrones*, and would even have paid extra fare could we have been ensured a small brush with the lawless freebooters. "We're good for fifty of 'em, *sure*," was the remark of one of our companions, as we displayed our arms upon a table in the breakfast-house, and I have little doubt that such odds would have fared badly. The greatest risk we ran, in all probability, was of accidentally shooting each other; for while crowded in the stage it was impossible to look in any direction without seeing the muzzle of a loaded pistol staring in our faces.

After making a breakfast which mainly consisted of mutton, fowls, eggs, and frijoles, aided by chocolate and some excellent claret provided by Judge Ellis, and after hearing a much exaggerated tale of a party of robbers, recently seen prowling in the neighbourhood of Rio

Frio, we once more buckled on our armour and took our places in the diligence. The morning was mild and agreeably pleasant in this high mountain region, so much so that two or three of us soon took our seats outside with the driver, a well-informed, entertaining Yankee, who knew the history of every roadside cross which lifts its head over the remains of some murdered occupant of the rude grave below. With whatever skill the Mexicans may be able to manage a single horse in the saddle, the science of handling some half dozen from the box of a stage-coach is above their comprehension, and a feat they have not the temerity to undertake—and hence the owners of the different lines of diligences invariably procure the services of Yankees when they can be obtained.

Your stage-driver is an entertaining fellow go where you will; full of interesting stories, and ever prone to relate the history of every remarkable point upon his route. Ours we found unusually amusing, perhaps from the abundant material at his hand of perilous encounters with banditti and hair-breadth 'scapes on occasions innumerable. The driver of the Mexican diligence is a *neutral* in any attack that may be made, as it would be more than his place is worth should he side with the passengers against the ladrones; yet it frequently occurs that the latter blaze away at random at the stage, and on more than one occasion the driver has lost his life although it was not sought. His duty is—and nothing else is expected of him either by the highwaymen or the passengers—to jump from his box at the first onset, hold his lead horses by the head until the affray is over, and let it terminate as it will he is not molested intentionally. He knows every robber upon the road, yet never exposes them, for the very simple but satisfactory reason that his life would pay the forfeit if he did.

The business of robbing the stages is reduced to a perfect system in Mexico; and it is shrewdly hinted that many men, of respectable station in the larger cities, are in some way connected with the bands, and have no hesitation in taking to the road when other resources fail. A spy is almost invariably stationed at the stage-house as the coach is about starting, whose duty it is to take down a list of the passengers, their appearance, arms, and the amount of luggage with which they travel. If the stage happens to be filled with well-armed foreigners—Americans, English, German, or French—it is generally allowed to pass unmolested; for well do the ladrones know that they will not give up their property without a desperate struggle. On the contrary, should the travellers be chiefly Mexicans, with but a foreigner or two among them, the load is at once put down as legitimate game, as the former are almost invariably looked upon as non-combatants, who would rather be searched than shot. The moment the spy ascertains the character and condition of the passengers, with the chances of a successful attack, he gallops off to give the information to his companions, who are quietly waiting for him in some dark defile or lonely barranca.

Should an attack be deemed expedient, the diligence is suddenly waylaid in some well-known spot; the passengers, if no resistance is made, are compelled to descend from the vehicle, lie down with their faces to the earth, and then submit to a thorough searching. The baggage, in the mean while, is overhauled, and every article of value abstracted, after which the unfortunate travellers are permitted to gather themselves up and proceed on their journey. The robbers, whose faces are almost invariably concealed by black crape, have the reputation of being very gentlemanly in their conduct, treating ladies with much respect and consideration, and apologizing to the other sex for the trouble and detention circumstances have compelled them to cause. A friend of mine, who was unfortunate enough to be travelling this road in the spring of 1843 with no other than Mexican companions, was robbed near Rio Frio by a party of ladrones. Their captain, as he turned to ride off, touched his hat very politely, and before giving our American the customary "adios," said that he was extremely sorry thus to take liberties with and incommode a stranger, trusted that the money of which he had despoiled him would prove no serious loss, and after hoping that he had more where that came from, dashed off at a canter! The fellows never seem anxious to shed blood, firing into the stage only when they anticipate resistance; on no other occasion is the life of the driver placed in jeopardy.

A volume of interesting anecdotes might be written, filled entirely with accounts of the different robberies which have taken place between the city of Mexico and Vera Cruz. One only I will relate—a story told of the laughable indignities offered the celebrated Señor Garcia, Malibran's father, while returning from the capital after giving a series of successful concerts. I have now forgotten the exact point, but the very spot was pointed out to me where the lawless brigands first waylaid the great vocalist, as well as the stone or little hillock upon which they mounted him, after the robbery, and compelled him to sing several of his most popular pieces. It would seem that the rascals had been regular patrons and warm admirers of Garcia while in the city; for they not only knew him at once, but were well acquainted with his music. After searching and robbing him, they next perched him upon a little eminence, gathered around in a circle, and after taking off their hats, one of them called for a favourite air. It was in vain that the señor pleaded—told the brigands he was hoarse, out of voice, indisposed—nothing would do but he must give them a song. They openly told him that they had listened, with pleasure, to his surpassing efforts in the city, and that they could not think of allowing him to leave the country without giving a "farewell concert!"—the thing was impossible. Garcia, with piteous face, again begged them to excuse him, and was about to give a peremptory refusal, when a call for a favourite Italian aria, accompanied by a click of the lock of a carbine and a significant look from one of his tormentors, convinced him that he must sing now or forever after hold his peace.

With broken and tremulous voice he commenced his song. A shower of hisses followed, which plainly told that the strange audience would not put up with an effort so unworthy of the great vocalist. Another trial was made—better, perhaps, than the first, but still falling far short of what the rascals knew Garcia to be capable of—and again they manifested their disapprobation by hisses. Wound up to a pitch of desperation, and, it is even said, stung with mortification and wounded professional pride at being hissed, the señor once more attempted the aria. This time he was more successful, for applause rather than hisses greeted its conclusion. Another favourite piece was then called for, and this was given with even greater effect and met with more decided marks of applause: the rascals were connoisseurs of music. Garcia improved, as the story runs, with every fresh song, and after giving several pieces in a style which was perfectly satisfactory to the brigands, he was greeted, at the conclusion of the last, with a shower of " bravas" and three rounds of applause! Such is the tale related of the great vocalist and his audience of robbers.

We passed the Rio Frio without molestation, and early in the afternoon entered the valley of Puebla. Scattered along by the roadside were the adobe houses of the inhabitants, from each of which, as we rattled by, some half dozen worthless Mexican dogs would jump and dash at the stage. A shower of barks and yelps from the curs would be duly honoured by us with a shower of bullets and buckshot; and as several of them were seen to tumble over and commence kicking, it is fairly presumable that the sun did not rise the next morning on as many live dogs as on that of the day when we passed through the once rich and fertile valley of Puebla.

To the right of the road, in the distance, our driver pointed out to us the grand pyramid of Cholula, with what is left of that once sacred city. The vast mound is fast crumbling away, while the former magnificent city at its base, with its many inhabitants, is now said to be falling into ruins and depopulating more and more every year.

About four o'clock we entered Puebla, covered with dust and with our faces much burned by the hot noonday sun. As we rattled down one of the main streets, the Presidio where the Texans were confined was pointed out to us—a short ride farther, and the plaza, with the rich and imposing cathedral of Puebla, was in plain sight. With a crack of his whip, and faster pace of his horses, our driver dashed by the Portales—crowds of admiring urchins gazing with eyes open to the utmost, while groups of girls scampered far out of the way, as if fearful of being run over by the stage. A short and abrupt turn of the street, and a trot of but a few yards farther, and we were landed safe and sound at the Casa de Diligencias, the best public house in Puebla. Here we found the worthy American consul, Mr. Black, with Messrs. Snively, Torry, Houghtaling, and Buchanan, four of our former comrades in imprisonment who had been given up to Judge Ellis, all comfortably quartered, and awaiting our arrival.

No sooner had we washed the dust from our faces, and shaken and brushed the thickest of it from our clothes, than, accompanied by the late minister, we visited the Texan prisoners at the Presidio. Our unfortunate comrades were here confined in the same yard with hundreds of Mexican criminals of the worst class, chained together in pairs, employed during the day in the city cleaning ditches, sewers, and other dirty work; covered with every species of vermin, poorly clad, worse fed, and at night herded and guarded with the low wretches who surrounded them. No comparison between their treatment and that of the Texans in Santiago can be drawn, for the former were deprived of such comfort as is found in a sufficiency of food, comparatively clean quarters, and the absence of such vile association as the lowest malefactors afford. Thus were men, whom Santa Anna openly avowed prisoners of war, treated in Puebla. The population of this city are said to entertain more hostile and bigoted feelings towards "heretics and dogs," as many of them are wont to call the Americans and English, than those of any other place in Mexico—it may be that this bitter hatred induced the inhuman treatment bestowed upon the poor Texans.

After passing some half hour in the loathsome prison, receiving such messages and letters as the inmates wished us to convey to their friends in Texas and the United States, we took our leave of them and hurried back to our hotel to a late dinner which had been provided. I had wished to examine the interior of the rich cathedral, so celebrated in the works of every traveller through Mexico for its exceeding elegance and splendour of adornment; but the dusky shades of evening had set in before I reached the edifice—the light was shut out from the interior, and with it went my hopes of seeing the costly chandelier, the famous statue of the Virgin, which is described as almost crushed under the weight of diamonds and precious stones, with the other rich ornaments that decorate this temple—all which wealth would be infinitely better applied were the priests to open their hearts and devote it to the construction of railroads and canals, mending the thoroughfares, meliorating the condition of the lower classes, or even paying off a portion of the immense internal and foreign debt under which the country groans.

It was while this cathedral was in progress of erection that the miraculous aid of angels in the good work was discovered. Every morning, on the assemblage of the Mexican builders, they noticed with much surprise that unseen hands had been toiling through the night in the construction of the walls. That they must be angels was considered a matter of course—through no other agency could the heavy walls arise—and from that day to this the city has been called *Puebla de los Angeles,* or "City of the Angels." It is a neat, well-built place, containing some sixty or seventy thousand inhabitants, and of late has been gaining additional importance from the establishment of numerous factories in the vicinity. I roamed for some two hours through the streets, squares, and market-places, jostling my way through a crowd of ragged léperos on one occasion for the purpose of obtaining a closer look at a long and brilliantly-lighted religious procession. From a dark doorway I watched the kneeling groups of men and women congregated on either side of the street as the procession passed, the light from the numerous torches bringing out their swarthy features in bold relief, as with deep devotion they raised their eyes upward and moved their lips apparently in prayer. In half an hour afterward, knowing that the diligence was to start at three the next morning, I repaired to the hotel, and was soon asleep.

## CHAPTER XX.

Preparations for Departure.—High Words with a Mexican Stage-agent.—A Victory.—A Scotch Traveller.—No Room for another Passenger.—Leave the "City of the Angels."—Approach of an Escort.—Appearance of the Dragoons.—Arrival at El Pinal.—Roadside Graves.—Change of Horses.—A wild Mexican Steed and his Antics.—A rapid Start.—A noted Stand for Robbers.—Another doughty Escort.—The Mal Pais and Cerro de Pizarro.—Arrival at Peroté.—Visit to the Texan Prisoners.—Their Condition.—A vile Supper.—A French Lady.—Another early Start.—Coldness of the Mountain Air.—A false Alarm.—Colder and Colder.—Tierras Frias.—Arrival at Las Vigas.—In want of Refreshments.—"No hai" and "Quien sabe" again.—Wild Mountain Scenery.—Volcanic Formations.—El Cofre de Peroté.—Strange Indian Legend.—Leave the Region of Lava.—Remarkable Change of Scene and Climate.—Sudden Transition.—Halt at the House of a Mexican Lady.—Singularity of her Conduct.—La Guerra Rodriguez.—Examination of our Passports at the Garita.—Arrival at Jalapa.

We were awaked at two o'clock in the morning by a servant with the old announcement, which has annoyed so many thousands of travellers, "stage is ready, gentlemen." Huddling on our clothes as rapidly as possible, we descended to the patio of the hotel, stumbling over a sleeping Mexican rolled in his blanket in the passage-way, and treading upon one leg of a worthless cur, which went whining off on the other three.

Repairing at once to the stage, we found one of our passengers engaged in high words with the agent, a Mexican, who insisted upon sending a set of harness to Peroté upon the top of the coach. There were fourteen passengers belonging to our party, all good-sized men, and these fourteen were to be stowed in and upon a common, Troy-built coach, intended only to carry nine inside, with a seat for two on the box with the driver. Of course three of us were compelled to perch ourselves upon the extreme top of the coach, and as a heavy harness, with its strong iron buckles and other appurtenances, afforded anything but a soft or comfortable bed, its transportation by this particular stage, it was at first respectfully contended, was putting all hands to serious annoyance. The agent said this was a matter we must settle among ourselves—the harness he was obliged to forward by this conveyance. A passenger, who had already taken his station upon the top of the stage, now expressed a doubt whether the objectionable baggage would be allowed peaceable and quiet possession of its quarters in case the Mexican insisted upon giving it a berth—the latter, after a little frothy vapour, threw the harness upon the stage. The next moment a shower, very much resembling horse collars, traces, and girths, was falling upon the head of the agent, accompanied by a general laugh at his expense. Finding it impossible to carry his point, the fellow now slunk into the office, muttering a variety of unbecoming Spanish oaths as he went.

By this time our trunks were all safely stowed in the boot, and the inside of the stage was wedged with the substance of as many as could possibly crowd into the contracted quarters. Some of the younger passengers —harum-scarum fellows who were anxious that the ladrones might give us a call upon the road—recommended that we should all conceal our weapons under our sarapes and cloaks. A crowd of Mexicans were standing around the diligence, some of whom were evidently spies; and it was thought that if they should discover no arms about us they might give their companions such information as would draw them into a snare of guns, pistols, swords, and bowie-knives. But this plan was overruled by one of the older and more prudent travellers, on the ground that the robbers, should they see fit to attack us, would probably fire directly into the stage without previous parley, and thereby gain an advantage at the expense, perhaps, of the lives of some of the passengers.

As we were about leaving, a Scotchman came hastily down the stairs, dragging a trunk by the handle, and shouting that he was a passenger for Vera Cruz, and must have a seat. There are two stages running daily between the city of Mexico and Puebla, in one of which, with a party of Mexicans, he had made the trip on the previous day; but as this stage went no farther, the Scotchman was anxious to go directly on with us. He was a stout, healthy man, dressed in a suit of blue clothes, and as he well knew that we were all armed, no better chance for a safe transit to himself and chattels could possibly offer. We told him there was no room—no possible opening for another passenger: he said he had a sum of money about him, and that if we did not give him a seat he should be robbed of it the next day—he was sure he should. He even announced to some of the by-standing Mexicans, in their own language, the fact of his having money; for in his eagerness to obtain a seat with us he was drawn into a departure from prudence not very common with his countrymen. On finally ascertaining, to his own conviction if not satisfaction, that there was no room for him—not even a chance to hang on to any part of the stage—he reluctantly gave up all hope of prosecuting his journey until the morrow. As we left the place, after having shaken hands for the last time with Mr. Black, we could still see the sorrowful countenance of the poor Scotchman, as he stood in the patio with one end of his trunk resting against his knee, while his fingers were securely clasped around the handle.

After a short drive we passed the outskirts of the "City of the Angels," and struck into the open country. One of the most noted stands, or rather hiding-places, for the robbers, is within hearing of the town, and just as we were reaching the spot a clattering of horses' hoofs was heard rapidly approaching. Fourteen pairs of eyes were instantly peering into the darkness to ascertain the nature of the party, while at least twice fourteen pairs of pistols were pointing in the same direction to be ready for any emergency. The horsemen turned out to be a detachment of some half dozen dragoons, sent out from the barracks to protect and succour us in case of an attack from the ladrones. Muffled in their yellow military cloaks, for the early morning air was raw and biting, the fellows appeared well enough as their horses clattered along on either side of the stage; but we were now seeing them in the most favourable light. Long before the sun had risen above the eastern mountains, dispelling that darkness and chillness which precede daybreak, our doughty guardsmen had uncloaked themselves, and sat before us in all their inefficiency. Very respectable scarecrows I have little doubt they would have made, stuck about judiciously in a corn-field; but I have a better opinion of the Mexican brigands than to suppose, for one moment, that such a set of ill-appointed, badly-armed apologies for soldiers could in the least intimidate them if they had meditated an attack. We openly told them they might canter back to their barracks, and finish their morning nap; for no more dependance could be placed on them than on an equal number of the crosses stuck by the roadside. With the first appearance of danger they would undoubtedly have left us, and at a speed as great as their horses could conveniently accomplish, if not faster.

At a rapid pace we sped across the valley which encircles Puebla, passing the noted robbing-post without meeting other than the usual number of market people, wending their way to the city and driving their donkeys before them. Our driver allowed his horses to slacken their pace as we ascended the pine-clad hills known as the Pinal. This lonely forest is another noted haunt for the ladrones; but we passed through it seeing nothing more alarming than the numerous crosses which pointed to the spots where murder had done its work, and hearing naught more terrifying than the wind sighing mournfully in the pine tops—a sad requiem, it seemed, for the rest of the departed victims. Many thrilling tales did our driver relate of these roadside graves.

About the middle of the day we changed horses at a meson built near a large spring of warmish water. The circumstance I recollect from the fact that one of the fresh horses was a wild, vicious creature, not only disposed to break our necks, but having no apparent marked regard for the safety of his own. In Mexico they frequently hitch five horses to a stage, two on the pole as is the custom in the United States, while the three leaders are harnessed abreast. In the present instance one of the leaders acted as wildly as would a fresh-caught mustang; leaped entirely over the heads of his fellows, wound himself up in the traces, and reared, pitched, and kicked in such a manner, notwithstanding the efforts of half a dozen Mexican hostlers, that he was soon free from all encumbrances. After several attempts, the driver was so far successful as once more to place harness upon the vicious animal's back; but no sooner had the stable boys released him from the strong halters with which he had been held, than he jumped and dashed off at a furious pace, imparting his own fright to the rest of the team, and threatening us all with a dangerous upset. For some distance the mad steed pressed forward, the driver in vain attempting to check him; and it was only when much exhausted by his efforts that he slackened his onward course in the least. It was now the driver's turn. "You've run a spell on your *own* account," said the Yankee, addressing the tired animal; and then, after a loud crack from his whip, finished the sentence with " you've got to run a piece farther on *mine*." And run he did, and at a rapid pace too; for determined to subdue his vicious spirit, and break him of his mad pranks, the driver forced him onward until the reeking team could no longer withstand the killing pace. A short time after this occurrence, we approached still another celebrated stand for robbers—a dreary spot upon a wide, sandy plain, with a few scattering clumps of thornbushes and rocky hills in the vicinity, which afford a cover for the gentlemen of the road. As we drew near the spot an escort of badly-mounted dragoons came out to meet us from an adobe-built hovel some little distance from the road. As they formed themselves on either side of the stage they were told that we could dispense with their services; but the valiant fellows, thinking of the money which it is expected the passengers will pay them, and of the drunken frolic which is sure to follow, insisted upon seeing us *safely* through all dangers as far as Peroté.

It was about four o'clock in the afternoon, after we had crossed the *mal pais*, or bad country, as it is called, and taken a survey of the huge volcanic mass known as the Cerro de Pizarro, that we reached the stage tavern at this dreary and desolate place. As we entered the patio of the inn, a crowd of bad-visaged fellows congregated about us, scrutinizing our weapons and the general appearance of the party. If some of them were not robbers and cutthroats, their faces villanously belied them.

No sooner had we safely secured and locked up our baggage, than we inquired and took the way towards the castle in which General McLeod, and a party of the officers and men attached to the Santa Fé Expedition, were confined. A short parley with an officer at the ponderous gate of the fortress, and we were permitted to enter. Our former comrades had just returned from their work at a neighbouring stone quarry. They crowded around us, and knowing that our visit must necessarily be short, with eager inquiries asked intelligence in relation to their friends at Puebla and the city of Mexico—pressing question upon question in such rapid succession that to answer one half of them was impossible. Their situation, in many respects, was preferable to that of the prisoners at Puebla, for their quarters were cleaner and more comfortable, and the Mexican criminals were confined in separate apartments; yet the castle is but a cold and dreary place at best, being situated at an elevation far above the level of the sea, bleak and exposed, and where the biting winds from the surrounding snow-clad mountains have full and powerful sway. After receiving messages and letters innumerable from the poor fellows, and promising to make known their situation, we bade them farewell, and retraced our steps to the tavern.*

Here we found that the stage from Jalapa had arrived, and that our supper was ready—a vile, greasy repast, to which nothing lent sauce or aid save the remembrance of worse, and the hearty appetites we had contracted by our long ride. Among the passengers from Vera Cruz was a French lady with a little child, the mother on her way, without a protector, to join her husband at Zacatecas. We could not but admire the boldness of the lone female, who had undertaken a journey so long and so perilous.

After smoking our cigars, and watching the ice-incrusted sides of the towering mountain peaks in the vicinity, as the setting sun clothed them with silvery lustre, we retired to rest. At two o'clock in the morning we were aroused from sleep by a servant, and in half an hour, after swallowing a cup of chocolate in the dirty cocina attached to the tavern, we muffled ourselves in cloaks, greatcoats, and sarapes, and, shivering with the early morning cold of this bleak region, took our seats in the diligence and were again on the road towards Jalapa.

If the air was raw and chilly at starting, it was doubly so as we ascended the gradual slope which brings the traveller near the base of the celebrated Cofre de Peroté. We had entered the gorge of a gloomy barranca, such of us as were within the coach nestling close to each other for warmth and with the vain hope of finishing

---

* Notwithstanding the isolated situation and great strength of the castle of Peroté, several successful escapes have been effected within the past year by Texans confined within its walls. They suffered much from want of food, water, and sufficient clothing in the mountains, but eventually arrived safely, either in the United States or Texas.

the sleep from which we had been disturbed, when the report of a heavy pistol from the top, and the cry of "*Ladrones!*" "*Ladrones!*" startled us as with an electric shock. The loud laugh from the region of the driver instantly convinced us that it was a false alarm—an eccentricity, merely, of some wag on the top of the coach, who only wished to get up a little excitement. The place chosen was certainly well adapted for a joke of the kind; for a more dark, dismal, piratical haunt to all outward seeming was never chosen by freebooters.

As the morning advanced towards daybreak, and a higher region was attained, the cold appeared to increase. The air was damp and disagreeable to a degree—a chill fog rested lazily in the lower atmosphere—it seemed as though we were cutting our way through frozen clouds. On reaching the high mountain hamlet of Las Vigas\* we were directly in the *tierra fria*, or cold country, at an elevation of nearly eight thousand feet above the level of the sea. The driver halted for some ten or fifteen minutes, but whether to change or water his horses I am unable to say: I only know that we dragged our benumbed limbs from the stage, and by dint of much shouting, pounding, kicking, and knocking were enabled to arouse a Mexican family from their slumbers and effect an entrance within doors. No other refreshment could we obtain than rank Catalan brandy, as it is called, strong as alcohol itself, and with the flavour of ley or a tea made of potash. With teeth chattering we called for coffee, chocolate — for some-

---

\* The literal translation of Las Vigas is *the beams* or *timbers*. The houses of the village are constructed of logs—the first and almost the only dwellings of the kind I saw in Mexico—a circumstance from which the place probably received its name.

thing warm. "*No hai*," was the chilling answer. We asked the stupid, half-asleep master of the dwelling if he could tell us where we could obtain the desired refreshments. The eternal "*Quien sabe?*" was the only rejoinder. How the inhabitants of Las Vigas obtain a livelihood is a mystery. Of course we could see nothing of the face of the country in the vicinity of the village; but judging from the feeling of the cold mountain air, it would seem impossible for even Greenland moss to withstand it—so keen, so cutting, so penetrating.

Muffling again in our blankets and cloaks, we entered the stage and resumed the journey. As the sun began to disperse the mists and fogs of morning we were awakened to a full realization of the wild mountain grandeur which surrounded us. We were already at an elevation several thousand feet higher than the loftiest summits of the United States; yet it seemed to us, as we gazed upward to the cloud-capped peaks, that we were at the base of huge, towering mountains, thrusting their lofty heads even into the very vault of heaven. As we commenced descending the rough and rocky road which leads down the lower mountain sides, the prospect below us was concealed by an immense sea of misty, cloudy vapour, reaching far as human vision could penetrate—looking back, the fog was still above us—it appeared as though we were travelling directly between two stratas of cloud. Such of the country as we could see immediately around us, bore evident marks of its volcanic formation. In one spot a huge mass of rock, evidently the upheaving of some strong throe of nature, was plainly visible; in another, a bed of hard, black lava, with the appearance of having been poured down in a liquid stream and of having cooled as it fell, gave farther evidence of the mighty convulsions nature has undergone in this wild region in bygone times, and of the violent and tremendous efforts by which she has relieved herself of some burning, inward fever. The gnarled and stunted firs and oaks, which have found root among the different volcanic masses, show that they have wrestled powerfully for nourishment and growth.

With astonishment the traveller looks at the beds of lava, and masses of broken rock he sees on every side—so fresh and with such a seeming newness that he cannot imagine more than a few months, or years at farthest, to have rolled away since they were first deposited; yet even the oldest legends of the aborigines, their most remote traditions, carry him not back to the awful disruption which placed them there. The Indians point to the now extinct volcano upon the Cofre de Peroté as the point from which came the shower of burning lava and rocks that has rendered this section desolate, but offer no surmise as to the time when the crater belched forth its storm of destruction; and the mind, in attempting to trace the interval which has since elapsed, is soon lost in the wide and mazy fields of conjecture.

El Cofre de Peroté, or *The Chest of Peroté*—so called from the fact that its sides bear strong resemblance to a trunk or chest—was, ages since, a volcano, and the different volcanic formations over which we were now journeying were doubtless belched from its yawning but long-smothered crater. Awful must have been the throes, the mighty workings and convulsions, of the huge mass of mountain while in labour. Imagination shudders and turns pale, the mind is awe-stricken, as the immense rocks are reviewed by the eye — rocks which are of themselves hills, and which must have been quarried, torn, riven, and hurled upward from the bowels of the earth by the elemental fever within, and, after roaring high in air, descended, amid streams of burning lava, a red-hot deluge of mighty fragments.

I have said that the Indians have no tradition of the time when this terrible convulsion occurred, but they relate a story of its causes and effects—a story which I will here insert for its singularity and simplicity. Previous to the first eruption, the mountain was fertile, peaceful, and well behaved as its brother mountains, and was the joint property of a deer, a tiger, a leopard, and a bear. For a long time these animals, so discordant in temperament, lived in the greatest amity together, each roaming over a particular section which was set apart for him, and never trespassing upon the land of his neighbour; but by-and-by the bear, either from lack of forage within his own specified limits, or from a natural proneness to interfere with the just rights of his neighbours, crossed, after the manner of certain governments of more recent times, the prescribed boundary lines, and made inroads upon the domain adjoining his own territory. The deer, the tiger, and the leopard, upon learning this trespass, held public consultation, and warned their neighbour of his encroachments and of their determination not to submit to outrages of the kind. The bear threw defiance in their teeth, and insisted upon roaming the mountain-sides at will; whereupon the deer, the tiger, and the leopard made common cause against a common enemy, joined their forces, and declared war at once. What part the deer took in this struggle is not related, but among them they drove, worried, and chased the bear from point to point, giving no rest to the soles of his feet until he reached the summit of the mountain, where they encompassed and beleaguered him about with the full intention of starving him into terms. But the bear was not to be thus hemmed in by his adversaries; so, bethinking him that there was no other means of escape, he commenced digging through the mountain with his paws, firmly determined upon working a passage to the lower side. Deeper and deeper did he force his way, toiling diligently, until at length he came upon the evil spirit Tlacatecolototl, who was lying asleep in an immense fire cave. Not aware of this new danger, the bear still pawed and dug away, and not until he had scratched the slumbering fiend upon the nose did he cease from his labour. Tlacatecolototl awoke from his sleep, and instantly all was rumbling and commotion. The bear retreated upward; but the enraged fiend pursued him with a shower of fire, and drove him for succour to his former enemies. He hugged, with all love and familiarity, the deer, the tiger, and the leopard wherever he met them, and was successful in quieting their just displeasure; but the fury of the fire-fiend was not to be appeased. He pursued the bear with red-hot stones, with streams of burning lava, with an avalanche of fire—his rage waxed fiercer and more fierce—the fair mountain-sides were lurid and made desolate with the implements of his strange revenge—and never did the torrent of destruction slacken until a good Indian shot the bear and ate him: then was the mighty wrath of Tlacatecolototl assuaged, and he retired once more to his bed of fire. Such is the marvellous tradition of the simple natives in relation to this long extinct volcano.

As we left the region of lava, the morning air became more mild, vegetation of more luxuriant growth took the place of the stunted pines and firs, and the ocean of vapour far below us began to dissipate under the influence of the sun. Turning our eyes back, we could see scudding masses of fog and cloud creeping up the mountain-sides, and fast hiding and dispersing themselves apparently among the clefts and fissures. The stage rattled more rapidly down the winding road, and at every step new beauties presented themselves. Every revolution of the wheels seemed to bring us into a new climate—each succeeding minute brought with it an air more bland and balmy. Birds of bright plumage were seen crossing the road, and fluttering from copse to copse of deep-green foliage, while here and there a rude dwelling, surrounded by a small patch of ground richly cultivated, relieved the rugged asperities of the mountain cliffs. So sudden is the transition, that a short hour conducts the traveller from bleak and dreary winter to bright and sunny spring—a winter which it seems to him is unchangeable, a spring which is eternal. At one moment, as it were, he is shrugging, shivering, and rubbing his hands in the *tierras frias*—the next he is basking in the soft sunshine of the *tierras templadas*, or temperate lands, amid orange groves and flowers innumerable. A single day's travel in Mexico carries the traveller from the heat and verdure of unchanging summer, to the cold and sterile face of undying winter.

When within a few short miles of Jalapa, the morning fog had entirely dispersed, the sun was out in all his splendour, and the ocean of cloud had given way to a vast expanse of green—we were looking down upon the *tierra caliente*, the land of summer's heat and summer's verdure. The driver halted for a few moments at the house of a Mexican lady, and allowed us to alight. We entered the dwelling, the front of which was almost concealed from view by creeping vines and different species of rose and other flowering bushes. The mistress of this sylvan retreat, a stout, handsome-faced

woman, some thirty years of age, instantly beset us
with inquiries in relation to some American she had
known formerly—a colonel she called him, but the
name I do not remember. His hair, features, size, and
all were described with a minuteness which convinced
us that his image still lingered in the memory of the
fair questioner, but not one of us could give her information which seemed satisfactory. She kindly asked
us to partake of refreshments; but mingled with her
pressing invitations were farther inquiries about the
colonel—thoughts of one, who evidently occupied a
strong hold in her affections, never left her while there
was a ray of hope that some one of us might possibly
know him.

When we were again on the road, the driver informed us that for many years this woman had been earnest
in her inquiries respecting the colonel. In her artless
simplicity she had asked all foreigners alike for information—one whom she knew so well must surely be known
by others—but had never been able to gather a gleam
of intelligence of the long-lost one. Love, as a matter
of course, was at the bottom—was the mainspring
which actuated her in her inquiries. Some roving,
blue-eyed, light-haired American had won her affections
in early life, and those affections continue as warm as
ever for the *guerro*, as she called him. In Mexico all
light-haired men are termed guerros—yellow locks, blue
eyes, and a fair complexion, are so uncommon in that
country, that the possession of them is a passport directly to the affections of the opposite sex. Among the
celebrated beauties of Mexico, and one who held sway
as a reigning belle for many years, was La Guerra
Rodriguez, or *The Light-haired Rodriguez*. In Humboldt's time her empire over the hearts of all was su-

preme in Mexico; and although a beautiful and fascinating woman in every respect, much of her celebrity and ascendancy she owed to the circumstance of her having light hair. She is still alive, I believe, and her society is still courted by all, although her light locks have long since faded.

From the residence of the Mexican lady at which we had called—a place where the driver stops to water his horses and allow her to press her questions—the road runs through a cultivated country until it reaches Jalapa, distant some three or four miles. It was Sunday, and the road was filled, chiefly with pedestrians, on their way to the city to mass, to market, or some merry-making. The air was richly perfumed with the fragrance of innumerable flowers—the roadside was bordered with that luxuriant vegetation which appears to belong to this climate. We were compelled to halt a few minutes at the garita to show our passports—this examination over, we were again on the road, and in a short time were descending the steep declivity which has been chosen as the site for Jalapa. The stage wound slowly down the precipitous streets, passed through the crowded market-place, turned into the Calle Principal, and safely deposited us in the patio of the Casa de Diligencias in season for breakfast. We were now revelling in a soft and wooing climate, of spring-like temperature—two hours before we were shivering in an atmosphere which would freeze an Icelander.

## CHAPTER XXI.

The Cracovienne.—Large Body of Mexican Troops.—Their Inefficiency.—Speculations as to the Result of an Invasion of Mexico.—The *Vomito* at Vera Cruz.—Determination to remain at Jalapa.—The Scotchman we had left at Puebla arrives.—Work of the Robbers.—Indian Girls from the Tierra Caliente.—Picturesque and neat Style of Dressing their Hair.—A pleasant Ride.—Departure from Jalapa.—Description of the Litera.—Changing Teams.—Mexican Drivers.—Puente Nacional.—Night Ride through the Hot Country.—Residence of Santa Anna.—Fireflies.—Santa Fé.—Number of Dogs in the Vicinity.—Singular District.—The Gulf of Mexico in Sight.—Arrival at Vera Cruz.—A Conducta.—Sopilotes.—The Black Vomit again.—Arrival on board the Woodbury.—Commodore Marin.—Salutes.—Under Way.—Pleasant Passage.—The Balize in Sight.—Author's Leave of his Reader.

WE had no sooner alighted from the stage, stretched our stiffened limbs, and attended well to the safety of our baggage, than the enlivening notes of the *Cracovienne*, played by a large and well-organized military band, reached our ears from without. On going to the front doors and balconies of the hotel, we ascertained that there was a full parade of all the regular troops then stationed at Jalapa, several thousands in number, and for half an hour we watched the solid platoons as they marched past. A majority of the men, although they were now cleaned up and had uniforms upon their backs, were doubtless ragged and wretched convicts but a few months before, and driven to the capital tied in strings. Such men, destitute alike of moral principle, pride, and that love of country which is a main requisite, can never be manufactured into effective soldiers under any discipline; but when to their natural deficiencies is added the fact that the majority of their officers are taken from the higher classes and placed at once at the heads of companies and regiments, without either theoretical or practical knowledge of arms, little need be expected from a force thus constituted. In case of a foreign invasion, such a force could be crushed at once by one fourth the number of well-disciplined troops; but the invading army would encounter other difficulties than the meeting with such defenders. It is much easier to *say* that ten thousand well-appointed Americans or Englishmen can march from the seacoast directly to the city of Mexico than to *do* it. The ordinary troops of the country would offer but few obstacles, would be little in the way could they be brought to battle in the open field; the strong natural barriers against invasion in the shape of mountain fastnesses, a better class of troops to be met in the vicinity of the capital, the opposition of the hardy rancheros who would at once be drawn into the contest, combined with a religious phrensy which would doubtless be created and kept up by the priests—all these obstacles must be encountered on the road to Mexico. I do not say that they could not be surmounted—far from it—I only wish to offer the opinion that something more than mere holyday work might be expected by those who should set out on such an undertaking. Of the troops we saw that morning at Jalapa a large portion have since perished—some at Vera Cruz, but the greater number in Yucatan, where they were either cut off in the vain attempt of Santa Anna to subdue his refractory subjects during the years '42 and '43, or by the malaria and dreaded sickness of that unhealthy climate.

On arriving at Jalapa, Judge Ellis found letters awaiting him which gave the information that the *vomito*, or yellow fever, had broken out on board the cutter Woodbury, the vessel in which we were to sail for New-Orleans, and which was then lying under the Castle of San Juan de Ulua at Vera Cruz. One or two of the officers, besides several of the men, were down with the disease, and as it was deemed imprudent to sail with it on board, Judge E. was advised to remain at Jalapa until farther intelligence should be sent him. Several of the passengers determined upon proceeding at once to Vera Cruz, regardless of the fever; but the larger number remained behind, and took lodgings which the ex-minister procured for us at the hotel of an American.

On the arrival of the next stage from Puebla, we crowded around it to note the passengers and gather any intelligence that might be brought. There were but five travellers, three or four of them Mexican officers, and our Scotch friend for whom we could not make room the morning we left the "City of the Angels." His face wore a lugubriously comic expression as he alighted from the diligence, while his vestments gave token of a change of wardrobe other than the difference of climate called for. Instead of the substantial blue cloth coat, of goodly dimensions and excellent preservation, which had graced his upper man when we left him standing by his trunk, his arms and shoulders were now tightly encased within a yellow Nankin short jacket, a world too small, while his head was partially covered by a queer hat much the worse for wear. He recognised us immediately, and with a face half-sorrowful, half-upbraiding, exclaimed, "You see me," at the same time turning himself round so that we could be brought to a full realization of his unfortunate plight. "I told you so," he continued, " I knew it—I said so at first. Talk about Scotch mists—I came near perishing this morning on the mountains—greatcoat and all are gone." Not one word did he say about robbers; yet his broken sentences and forlorn appearance told plainly enough that he had fallen into the hands of highwaymen. After a little, he related the particulars of his having been robbed a few miles from Puebla. The brigands had an easy task, as save himself there was no foreigner in the coach. The passengers, one and all, were compelled to lie down with their faces to the earth, were stripped of everything valuable in the shape of money and clothing, and then allowed to proceed. In telling his story, the Scotchman mixed up with his discourse hearty and abundant curses against the Mexicans in general and the ladrones in particular, concluding with the remark that if he was once more fortunate enough to see his own native hills he would not be caught in outlandish parts again; but the most amusing feature of it was, the pride he appeared to take in his powers of divination—in the fact of his having told us, at Puebla, that he should be robbed, and the event turning out precisely as he had anticipated.

We passed some week or ten days at Jalapa, and pleasantly, too; for nothing can exceed the balminess and spring-like beauties of its climate, the exceeding richness of its endless variety of fruits, the delicious fragrance of its atmosphere, which is loaded with the perfume of innumerable flowers, or the picturesque views and romantic rides which abound in its vicinity. Pineapples, gathered from the stem ripe and of most luscious flavour, can be purchased for a trifle, and in this pure climate eaten without fear of consequences. Chirimoyas here arrive at their full perfection, bananas, such as I have never seen elsewhere, grow in most lavish profusion, while all the fruits of the tropics appear to be found in abundance. Often did I watch a party of Indian girls from the tierra caliente below, sitting upon the sidewalk opposite the Casa de Diligencias, selling, for a few coppers, plums of rare and delicious quality. Their loose dress seemed peculiarly adapted to the climate, and would of itself attract not a little attention from the foreigner; but their rich, bright olive complexions, their dark, mild eyes, and luxuriant hair, of glossy blackness and reaching nearly to the ground, formed their principal attractions. Upon their hair they bestow all their care and attention, and justly are they proud of it. Their mode of dressing this ornamental appendage is peculiarly their own. Two long braids, reaching nearly to the ground, fall from the back of the head, while two other braids, after circling the head twice, are fastened in front, with a rose or some other flower confined at the point where the ends meet. These braids are composed of two strands of hair and one of red cord or riband, neatly platted, lending an additional beauty to their otherwise picturesque appearance. Their dress is simple enough, consisting of a petticoat of some woollen stuff, without an under garment of any description; but in place of the latter they wear an oblong piece of cotton or linen cloth, elaborately ornamented, in many cases, with needlework, over their shoulders as a protection from the sun. Directly in the centre a hole is cut, large enough to admit the head—thus is this singular garment worn, and it certainly has a cool and comfortable appearance in a warm climate, if nothing more.

We were told that the girls lived at a village several leagues below Jalapa, a romantic situation upon the borders of a clear and swift stream, in which they bathe and wash their hair twice a day. The males are described as lazy, worthless, drunken fellows, living entirely upon the industry of the women; but the latter are invariably cleanly, frugal, laborious, and, singular enough for this country, virtuous. We intended paying their village a visit before we came away, for we heard many stories of its surpassing beauty of location; but some circumstance which I have now forgotten prevented us. A party of us, however, had a pleasant ride to another Indian town several leagues below Jalapa. It was during this excursion that I for the first time saw the coffee plant, the pineapple, the vanilla bean, and other products of the tropics, under cultivation, as also the weed from which the nauseous jalap, that medicine which has given this place a name, is extracted. The view of the city from several points below, as it stands boldly out on the mountain side at an elevation of more than four thousand feet above the level of the sea, is peculiarly picturesque. The towering Cofre de Peroté, rising high in air, affords a majestic background to the view, while still higher, and with its snow-capped summit apparently reaching the blue vault of heaven itself, the traveller catches an occasional view of Orizava as some opening in the trees allows the eye full scope to the southward.

On the 8th of May, after passing, as I have already mentioned, several days very pleasantly at Jalapa, Judge Ellis received intelligence from Vera Cruz that the vomito had left the Woodbury, and that everything was in readiness for her instant departure. The following day, therefore, saw us once more in the diligence and on our road homeward. While at Jalapa, I had several times noticed the arrival and departure of the *literas*, and had intended to take a seat, or rather a couch, in one of these easy vehicles; but as my passage had been paid in the diligence, and as the latter ran through in less time, I was compelled to give up all thought of being thus transported. The litera is a box some six or seven feet long by about four in width, with a top and covering somewhat resembling that of a common Jersey wagon. Within is a mattress of sufficient width to accommodate two passengers, with pillows and other comforts. The box is placed upon two long shafts or poles, which are lifted from the ground and securely fastened to the saddles of a pair of mules, one at either end of the litera. When everything is in readiness, the passenger has nothing to do but climb into his quarters, where he can sit, lie, sleep, read, or smoke, as may best please him. I certainly envied a gentleman whom I saw one morning, half lying upon his back in an easy posture, with a book in his hand and a cigar in his mouth. He seemed the very personification of comfort.

As we rattled through the principal street of Jalapa, and crossed a little stream, which dashes through the city, the eyes of all, but more particularly those of a group of washing-girls,* were drawn towards us; for the top and sides of the stage were ornamented with bird-cages, flower-pots, plants of different descriptions, fruits, of which we had laid in or on a goodly store, besides many usefuls and ornamentals which had been picked up and collected by the different members of our party. One gentleman in particular, of much taste in such matters, had purchased an assortment of tropical birds and plants, so that when we were in motion the diligence bore close resemblance to a travelling

---

* There are one or two establishments in Jalapa devoted entirely to the washing of clothes, at which numerous girls can be seen at all times working under the shelter of a roof, but in a building which has no sides. So white, and with such care do these girls get up linen, that it was told us they received custom even from Vera Cruz.

aviary set in the midst of a floating botanical garden. No wonder, then, that we attracted more than usual attention.

In half an hour we left the outskirts of the city—a city so celebrated for its delightful climate, its delicious fruits, and its pretty women—and began gradually to descend the mountains towards the tierra caliente. At the first place where we changed teams we met the stage from Vera Cruz. Among the passengers was Mr. Dorsey, just arrived from the United States with despatches for General Thompson, and on his way to the city of Mexico. Instead of one Yankee we now had two Mexican drivers for the diligence—instead of horses, the animals attached were a set of tolerably well-behaved mules. One of the drivers acted as postillion, riding upon a mule in the lead; the other sat upon the box, and appeared to have his hands full in so managing the wheel mules as to prevent an upset. The road, in many places, is extremely rough and uneven, and that we should meet with some serious accident appeared inevitable; but darkness came and we were yet safe, and as it was now impossible to see the dangers which beset our path, we gradually became more reconciled. In this way we passed Encero, Plan del Rio, with other small hamlets the names of which, if they have any, are forgotten. I recollect the crossing of the heavy bridge called, since the revolution, Puente Nacional, and of seeing the large village near it.* At a fonda by the roadside we obtained a very fair supper, and saw a very pretty girl—the circumstance that the chairs, which the

---

* Several of the Texan prisoners, who were released by Santa Anna in the June following, died of yellow fever, and were buried near this bridge. Among them were Doctor Whittaker and Lieutenant Seavy. Captain Holliday died of the same disease on his passage from Vera Cruz to Galveston

Mexican landlord had provided for the accommodation of his foreign customers, were so low that to sit in them while eating was extremely tiresome, is another souvenir I brought from this place.

We were now directly in the heart of the tierra caliente—amid the rank vegetation, the deadly malaria, the suffocating heat of the hot, tropical climates. Innumerable fireflies or bugs, of large size, and shedding a pale but brilliant light, were flitting about in the bushes by the roadside, and illuminating the dense masses of creeping vines with which the forests of the warm countries abound. At midnight, or a little after, we were travelling through the immense estate of Santa Anna, Manga de Clavo I think it is called. To this place he has always retired after his reverses, and here, it is said, all his plans for his own political advancement have been formed. About three o'clock in the morning we reached the village of Santa Fé, and while the driver was changing his animals we awakened two or three families in the hope of obtaining chocolate or some other refreshment. Nothing could we procure save a bottle of bad claret, and a draught of Catalan brandy which was worse. It is impossible to form an opinion, with anything like certainty, of the number of dogs that enjoyed the pleasure of barking at us during the ten minutes we passed at Santa Fé; but a rough calculation would set down at least ten to every door, and five to every yard.

As the sun rose, we were ploughing our way through a dreary region of deep sand, the land on either side of the road overrun with weeds and bushes of rankest growth. Flocks of screaming parrots and macaws were flying lazily over head, while birds of red, green, and richly-variegated plumage were crossing the road and fluttering among the bushes in every direction. After passing the rude huts of several negro families, who must here gain but a scanty subsistence, we at length emerged from this strange sandy region. A single turn of the road, and we were directly upon the beach of the Gulf of Mexico—we had left the hot and pestilential air of the sultry lands, and were inhaling the pure breeze from the ocean. Thus in one night had we passed entirely through the tierra caliente, and almost without seeing it. To be sure, we had beheld the rude bamboo or cane huts of the inhabitants, hardly one degree removed from the wigwam of the wildest Indian;* we had inhaled the indolent breezes which come loaded with the perfume of endless varieties of flowers; we had seen myriads of bright fireflies in all their midnight splendour—but we had not seen all that we had hoped to see in a region which, to use an Irish expression, is running over with parrots, bananas, pineapples, monkeys, and other tropical fruits.

* This may not be a fitting place, but it may be here mentioned that since the earlier part of this work was stereotyped the author has had several conversations with Mr. Gregg in relation to the Waco Indians, in which that gentleman has expressed his decided conviction that the pretended Wacoes were no other than a band of Cherokees, driven either from the main tribe in the United States for some misdemeanor, or a part of the band defeated in Eastern Texas at the time when the noted chief Bowles was killed. From the great knowledge Mr. G. has of the Southwestern Indians, the author is satisfied that he is correct. He describes the Wacoes, among whom he has travelled, as not being so far advanced in civilization as to warrant the belief that they are now living in the comfortable quarters described in the account of the village seen by the Santa Fé pioneers. The fact that they said they were Wacoes is no evidence, as lying is a prominent trait with all Indians. I might also add, in this note, that the name "Salezar" has not been rightly given in the earlier part of the narrative. Anxious to do that worthy all justice, I would here state that the true orthography is *Damasio Salazar.* He shall not say that I have robbed him of any fame by spelling his name wrong.

Mr. Gregg is shortly to publish a work upon the prairies and the Northern Mexican settlements, which, from his great experience and information, must throw a flood of light upon one of the dark corners of the earth.

From the point where we first struck the low, sandy beach, although it must have been five miles distant, we could plainly see the churches, houses, and even the walls which environ Vera Cruz. The drive along the water's edge was slow and tedious, for the wheels of the diligence sank deep, and the sun, although but an hour risen from his cool bed in the gulf, was pouring down a flood of such heat as is only to be felt upon this unprotected sandy shore. While yet a mile intervened between us and the city, we could see innumerable *sopilotes*, or Mexican buzzards, standing moodily and solemnly upon the walls, housetops, and different towers and steeples, their eyes turned watchfully downward, on the look-out for their accustomed food. They are the scavengers of the city, and are never molested. On reaching the gate, around which a crowd of soldiers were lounging, a short detention sufficed with the officer stationed there to grant us permission to enter. A large *conducta*, or escort guarding nearly a million of dollars in silver, was entering the city at the same time. A drive of some fifteen minutes, through the wide and well-built streets, brought us to the principal hotel of the place, where we were soon safely housed.

We were not long in learning that the much-dreaded black vomit was still raging in the city, although it had left the Woodbury. The stranger, as he looks through the comparatively clean and airy thoroughfares of Vera Cruz, and sees the wide waters of the Gulf of Mexico lying directly before him, is at a loss to account for the sickness which yearly carries to the grave its hundreds of victims. The low and damp region, through a part of which we had passed in the morning, is the section whence come the noxious miasmas that generate the vomito. The friends who had preceded us from Jalapa were fortunately all well when we reached Vera Cruz, although some of them had suffered from the effects of the climate.

Our stay in the infected city was short, the next morning seeing us all on board the cutter; but I cannot take my leave of Vera Cruz without expressing my warmest thanks to Mr. Hargous, the then acting American consul, as well as to the countrymen I met at his residence, for the many acts of kindness and attention I received at their hands. The liberality of the Americans of this place, as hundreds of my unfortunate comrades can testify, was ever active in alleviating their wants and sorrows.

Previous to the sailing of the Woodbury, a salute was fired by her commander, Captain Nones, in honour of Judge Ellis and of Mr. Hargous, as well as of the then chief of the Mexican navy, Commodore Marin, who was on board at the time. The salute was answered from the barque Ann Louisa, an American packet then in port under command of Captain Clifford. After Commodore Marin had left the Woodbury and reached his own vessel, the Libertad, another salute was fired by him, which was duly returned by the cutter. These ceremonies over, we got under way with a fair breeze, and before nightfall nothing could be seen of the low coast upon which stands the once rich and populous city of Vera Cruz, or the True Cross, or of the frowning Castle of San Juan de Ulua, which commands the harbour—the towering peak of Orizava, rising far in the distance, was the only point of Mexico visible.

It was on the 12th of May that the cutter Woodbury sailed from La Villa Rica de la Vera Cruz, as the Spaniards were wont to call this city in the proud days of her prosperity. To the commander of our vessel,

Captain Nones, as well as to Lieutenants Peters, Wilson, and Faunce, we were all under great obligations, and I cannot let the opportunity pass without an expression of thanks for their kindness. On the morning of the 18th of May, exactly one year from the date when I left it so full of expectation of a pleasant four months' excursion, the low coast which surrounds the mouths of the mighty Mississippi appeared in sight—we had reached the Balize.

And here, after begging pardon of my reader for sending him ashore at a point so desolate and dreary, I must take my leave. For one year we have journeyed together through scenes of varied nature. If his random recollections of travel have served to beguile an idle hour, to interest and amuse the reader who has accompanied him, the knowledge of it will more than compensate the author for his many dark days of privation and suffering upon the prairies, and the months of captivity he shared with his companions in Mexico.

THE END.

Milton Keynes UK
Ingram Content Group UK Ltd.
UKHW010237170224
437973UK00006B/660